THE
PAUL QUEST

THE RENEWED SEARCH FOR
THE JEW OF TARSUS

BEN WITHERINGTON III

InterVarsity Press
Downers Grove, Illinois, USA
Leicester, England

InterVarsity Press, USA
P.O. Box 1400, Downers Grove, IL 60515, USA
World Wide Web: www.ivpress.com
E-mail: mail@ivpress.com

Inter-Varsity Press, England
38 De Montfort Street, Leicester LE1 7GP, England

InterVarsity Press®, U.S.A., is the book-publishing division of InterVarsity Christian Fellowship/USA®, a student movement active on campus at hundreds of universities, colleges and schools of nursing in the United States of America, and a member movement of the International Fellowship of Evangelical Students. For information about local and regional activities, write Public Relations Dept., InterVarsity Christian Fellowship/USA, 6400 Schroeder Rd., P.O. Box 7895, Madison, WI 53707-7895.

Inter-Varsity Press, England, is the book-publishing division of the Universities and Colleges Christian Fellowship (formerly the Inter-Varsity Fellowship), a student movement linking Christian Unions in universities and colleges throughout the United Kingdom and the Republic of Ireland, and a member movement of the International Fellowship of Evangelical Students. For information about local and national activities write to UCCF, 38 De Montfort Street, Leicester LE1 7GP.

Scripture quotations, unless otherwise noted, are from the New Revised Standard Version of the Bible, copyright 1989 by the Division of Christian Education of the National Council of the Churches of Christ in the USA. Used by permission. All rights reserved.

Cover illustration: "Saint Paul," Duomo/Monreale/Italy

USA ISBN 0-8308-1503-1
UK ISBN 0-85111-772-4

Printed in the United States of America ∞

Library of Congress Cataloging-in-Publication Data

Witherington, Ben, 1951-
    The Paul quest: the renewed search for the Jew of Tarsus/Ben
Witherington III.
        p.   cm.
    Includes bibliographical references and index.
    ISBN 0-8308-1503-1 (alk. paper)
    1. Paul, the Apostle, Saint. I. Title.
BS2506.W56 1998
225.9'2—dc21
[B]
                                                                98-8647
                                                                    CIP

British Library Cataloguing in Publication Data

A catalogue record for this book is available from the British Library.

23	22	21	20	19	18	17	16	15	14	13	12	11	10	9	8	7	6	5	4	3	2	1
17	16	15	14	13	12	11	10	09	08	07	06	05	04	03	02	01	00	99	98			

*To Margaret Thrall, Morna Hooker
and Margaret Mitchell,
the three "M"s who indirectly have provided
the most encouragement and help
in my work on various aspects
of the subject matter of this book.*

Pentecost, 1998

Introduction _____ 9

Chapter 1/ ON CONSTRUCTING AN ANCIENT PERSONALITY _____ 18

Chapter 2/ THE TRINITY OF PAUL'S IDENTITY _____ 52

Chapter 3/ PAUL THE WRITER AND RHETOR _____ 89

Chapter 4/ PAUL THE PROPHET AND APOSTLE _____ 130

Chapter 5/ PAUL THE REALIST AND RADICAL _____ 174

Chapter 6/ PAUL THE ANTHROPOLOGIST AND ADVOCATE _____ 204

Chapter 7/ PAUL THE STORYTELLER AND EXEGETE _____ 230

Chapter 8/ PAUL THE ETHICIST AND THEOLOGIAN _____ 263

Conclusion/ A PORTRAIT OF PAUL _____ 299

Appendix/ TIMELY REMARKS ON THE LIFE OF PAUL _____ 304

Bibliography _____ 332
Index of Authors _____ 341
Index of Subjects _____ 345

INTRODUCTION

As if the quest for the historical Jesus were not enough to take one's breath away, hard on its heels comes the quest for the historical Paul. At first it might seem we would be on more obviously solid ground in this search, for all scholars are in agreement that we have at least six or seven undisputed letters from Paul's own hand, and perhaps more, whereas Jesus left no writings of his own. Yet as Leander Keck has reminded us, the "quest for the historical Paul has turned out to be nearly as complex, and almost as controversial, as the better known quest of the historical Jesus."[1]

On Questing for Paul

Like those who seek the historical Jesus, those who want to understand the historical Paul must decide what to make of a narrative about the man that is written by someone else (the Gospels in the case of Jesus, portions of Acts in the case of Paul). But interestingly, while we cannot do without the Gospels in reconstructing an image of the historical Jesus, many scholars are quite prepared to leave the Paul of Acts almost entirely out of the equation, or to affirm an image of the Paul found in the letters at the expense of the Paul of Acts.

We have four sources about Paul: (1) the Paul of the undisputed letters, (2) the Paul of the later canonical Paulines, if they are by a later hand, (3) the Paul of Acts and (4) the Paul of the later extracanonical sources, such as the Acts of Paul and Thecla. Comparing the portraits of Paul that emerge from these four sources of information would be a useful exercise. It is my judgment, however, that "major differences" among the Pauls found in these four sources have been considerably overblown. The extracanonical Paul proves to be considerably more ascetic in character than the canonical Paul of the other three sources, but in most other respects it seems to be the same Paul. As for the Paul of Acts versus the Paul of the letters, I have argued elsewhere that the former is on the whole quite compatible with the

---

[1]Leander Keck, "Review Essay," *Pro Ecclesia* 6, no. 3 (1996): 359.

Paul of the undisputed letters[2]—especially given that Acts focuses on Paul the missionary and his efforts in that role, not Paul the pastor of Christian churches, who is always to the fore in the letters (with the possible exception of Romans). It is not an accident that the one place in Acts where Paul sounds most like the Paul of the letters is his one speech in that entire book that is specifically addressed to his converts—the Miletus speech of Acts 20.

Since Paul himself provides few autobiographical remarks in the undisputed letters, we can hardly do without some help from Acts in any case. Because the Pauline letters are not by and large autobiographical in *subject matter*, it is a mistake to consider them an overwhelmingly more primary source for reconstructing a picture of the historical Paul than Acts. As with Acts, the letters must be critically probed if we are to get at the historical Paul, and we need to take their epistolary and rhetorical character and function fully into account when assessing these matters.

I believe that the Pastorals, whether they were written by Paul or by someone else, do not add a great deal to a picture of the historical Paul gleaned from the undisputed Paulines with some occasional help from Acts.[3] On the issue of Paul's feelings about being under arrest and facing the prospect of death, we already have Philippians, and as for Paul's concern for order in the churches and leadership structures we may turn to 1 Corinthians 11—14. About Paul's relationships with his coworkers Timothy and Titus we learn a few new things from the Pastorals, but again, nothing so novel that we could not have gathered most of it from the earlier Paulines with a little help from some traditions in Acts. Theologically, ethically and socially, the Pastorals do not offer the Paul quester much that is surprising or new. Nor, I would add, do they present us with a Paul that is at odds with the image of Paul found in the earlier Paulines.[4] This being

---

[2]See Ben Witherington III, *The Acts of the Apostles* (Grand Rapids, Mich.: Eerdmans, 1997), pp. 430-38.

[3]Luke may well have written the Pastorals for Paul right at the end of Paul's life, or perhaps afterward as a memoir, passing on information he had gathered from Paul. In light of this possibility, note that the Paul of Acts sometimes resonates with the Paul of the Pastoral Epistles. On the issue of the extended meaning of authorship in relationship to the Pastoral Epistles, see now even so conservative a commentator I. H. Marshall, "Prospects for the Pastoral Epistles," in *Doing Theology for the People of God: Studies in Honor of J. I. Packer*, ed. Donald Lewis and Alister McGrath (Downers Grove, Ill.: InterVarsity Press, 1996), pp. 137-55. On parallels between Luke's vocabulary and style and those of the Pastorals see S. G. Wilson, *Luke and the Pastoral Epistles* (London: S.P.C.K., 1979). It is no argument against this conclusion that the Pastorals do not reflect Luke's theology, as Luke was trying to formulate not his own thoughts but those the apostle had passed along to him, yet using his own grammar, syntax and choice of vocabulary.

[4]Despite the strident assertions of Neil Elliott, *Liberating Paul: The Justice of God and the Politics*

the case, I intend to focus on the less disputed material and use the other sources, if needed, for corroboration and as a check against a possible misreading of the undisputed Paulines. I intend to treat Colossians as very likely Pauline, and Ephesians as probably Pauline as well, but I will not be focusing primarily on them in this study.[5]

My study aims to expose the reader to some of the new approaches to Paul and his letters as they bear on a quest for the historical Paul, for the discussion today is in some essential respects very different from the discussion in the 1940s, 1950s and 1960s. The older discussions of the Hellenistic Paul versus the Judaistic Paul (compare and contrast A. D. Nock's *St. Paul* to W. D. Davies's *Paul and Rabbinic Judaism*) are still with us, but the discussions have taken on new directions with the rise of rhetorical studies of Paul's letters in the 1980s and 1990s and the work of E. P. Sanders and others influenced by his important works such as *Paul and Palestinian Judaism* and *Paul, the Law and the Jewish People*. The discussion of Paul's theology or thought world has also taken some interesting turns in response to the work of the SBL Pauline Theology Seminar in the 1980s and 1990s and to some individual seminal studies, particularly in the area of Paul's narrative thought world.

We may want to ask whether the whole question of the pursuit of the historical Paul, as if he were like a modern Western individual, is not improperly framed. I intend to pursue this question by examining social and cultural analysis of antiquity as it bears on Paul. The insights arising from such analysis do raise some major question marks about the whole way we construe ancient eastern Mediterranean persons and their relationships; for example, we should avoid the anachronistic enterprise of trying to *psycho*analyze Paul, as opposed to analyzing him as a product of his own social environment. Approaching Paul in a historical manner sheds interesting light on various key Pauline texts—for example, we realize that

---

of the Apostle (Maryknoll, N.Y.: Orbis, 1994), Keck's critique of Elliott is apt, especially in the analogy he draws between Elliott's approach and that of Marcion (Keck, "Review Essay," pp. 358-59).

[5]The form of Ephesians, a grand example of epideictic rhetoric following some stylistic traits of Asiatic Greek and rhetoric, explains some differences with the earlier Paulines. None of the earlier Paulines follow the conventions of epideictic or Asiatic rhetoric on such a large scale, though some instructive formal comparisons can be made between the form of the epideictic showpiece in 1 Corinthians 13 and what we find in Ephesians. Also, Ephesians seems to be meant for a larger audience than one congregation. Unlike most of Paul's letters it does not seek to deal with the particular problems of a local church. Rather its theme is of general interest to the Pauline churches as a whole. It should be added that the ecclesiological implications of Ephesians set a natural foundation for what we find being put into practice in the Pastorals.

Romans 7 probably is *not* Paul's autobiographical reflection about his struggles as a Christian, despite suggestions to the contrary by Luther and his successors in the West. So some of the newer studies of Paul's letters in their original social/rhetorical/cultural eastern Mediterranean environment bid fair to shed some fresh light on the quest for the historical Paul. It is a propitious moment to reflect on the gains of some of these new studies and newer approaches in Pauline studies.

The plan of this book can be described as follows. An introductory chapter surveys the cultural setting in which the historical Paul operated. This is continued at the other end of the book by an appendix that attempts to puzzle out the chronological details of his life. The second chapter deals with what Paul was by birth or new birth—the most important and ineradicable facts about him—a Jew, a Roman citizen, a Christian. Chapters three and four constitute a discussion of Paul in his major roles as prophet and apostle, rhetor and writer. Various aspects of how Paul *functioned* in his basic roles—realist and radical, anthropologist and advocate, storyteller and exegete—are taken up in the chapters that follow. Chapter eight focuses on Paul as a theologian and ethicist, and a conclusion assembles what I hope is a credible portrait of Paul.

Precisely because Paul never claimed to be the Christ or the Son of God, nor was he acclaimed by his disciples to be such, a study of him as a historical person must necessarily take a somewhat different shape from a study of the historical Jesus. There is both more and less that we can say about Paul as a person than is possible with Jesus. There is more because we have far more data about Paul than we have about Jesus. There is less because his claims, and the claims made about him, are far less imposing. Thus the present book spends less time delineating the discussions in the secondary literature than was the case in my earlier book *The Jesus Quest* (1995, rev. ed. 1997). This book is less a review of the all the relevant literature than a sampling of materials both secondary and primary that may help us gain a new, fresh and hopefully more historically accurate picture of Paul.

I hope that the study of the historical Paul will help us also, if indirectly, in our quest to understand and draw closer to the One about whom Paul continually spoke and wrote—the historical Jesus. For these two figures, the historical Jesus and the historical Paul, arguably had more to do with the shape of early Christianity, and indeed with Christianity since the first century, than any other two people.

Paul's letters are our earliest source for knowledge about Jesus and early Christianity. We learn from Paul of a heavy stress in early Christianity on the last week of Jesus' life—his Passover meal with the disciples, his betrayal, his death and resurrection—and this emphasis we find reinforced in the Gospels, which were written later. We learn from Paul that the earliest Aramaic-speaking Christians prayed *Maran atha*, "Come, O Lord." Thus we learn that it was not only Paul who had a strong faith in the second coming of Jesus.

Paul shows us that the heart of the gospel is the good news about Jesus Christ crucified, risen and coming again—an impression only further confirmed by the Gospels. There is thus an urgency to learning more about Paul. He is the one historical figure from whose hand we have documents about or involving Jesus from well before the fall of Jerusalem in A.D. 70. We owe our earliest knowledge of Jesus to him. If the historical Jesus matters to us, then, so must the historical Paul. The quest for the latter is in some senses the prerequisite for the quest for the former, for if we cannot trust Paul's witness, our prospects of getting at the historical Jesus are considerably dimmed.

It follows from all this that those who care about the Christian faith in its ancient or modern forms should care passionately about these two quests. If this book encourages even a few persons to reconsider the historical Paul and the Master he served in a new light, I will be content. I can promise that the quest will not be fruitless or boring, for Paul was and is controverted and controversial, just like the historical Jesus.

About "Lives of Paul"

This book is not an attempt to write a life of Paul; rather it is an examination of what sort of person Paul was. Such vitae do exist, and a variety of them do an admirable job of opening up various dimensions of the person and works of the enigmatic first-century apostle to the Gentiles.

For dealing with the social milieu and context in which Paul worked, few studies have equaled the classic one written just after the beginning of the twentieth century by Adolf Deissmann; its English version is titled *Paul: A Study in Social and Religious History* (New York: Harper, 1957). Deissmann realized that an understanding of social context, of Paul's world, often reveals the meaning of content in the New Testament, and that detailed study of inscriptional, archaeological, geographical and literary evidence is crucial to historical reconstruction. Deissmann opens his study by describing Paul as an

> Anatolian . . . a man of the ancients, a *homo novus*, rising from the mass of the insignificant many, heeded by no man of letters among his pagan contemporaries, yet destined to be a leading personality in the world's history; a *homo religiosus*, at once a classic of mysticism and a most practical man of affairs; a

prophet and dreamer, crucified to the world in Christ, yet forever memorable as a citizen of the world and traveller in it, and still moulding the world at the present time.[6]

It is important to clarify that Paul was *not* a "new man" in the sense of someone who rose up from poverty and deprivation to achieve fame and success. He did not come from the masses, and his Greek and rhetoric do not deserve to be thought of as plebeian. That Paul was not born into the patrician class or the Greco-Roman elite does not mean he cannot have come from another of the many social elites in the Greco-Roman world. Yet despite underestimating the apostle's social and literary level, Deissmann's study still bears close scrutiny today—and emulation for its close attention to detail of the social *realia* of Paul's world.[7]

A further study, tantalizingly brief but very helpful, appeared in 1938. Simply titled *St. Paul*, it was written by one of the greatest American scholars in any field of this century, A. D. Nock. Nock, in many ways like Deissmann, was as adept and at home in the Greek and Latin classics as in the literature of early Judaism and early Christianity. One can only wish there were more such scholars today in this age of overspecialization.

Consider the erudition and close study that went into Nock's comparison of Paul to that other great first-century Jewish writer from the Diaspora, Philo.

> For Philo, as for Paul, the Old Testament is the supreme revelation not only of God's will for every [one], but also of all the wisdom after which man was thereafter to strive. But Philo's interest in the Old Testament was principally in the Pentateuch. . . . He was mainly interested in the Law, which by implication contained all that man needed to know of himself and of God, and had very little interest in the possibility of the sudden establishment of a new order on earth. Further, while Philo quotes the Old Testament constantly as the ultimate authority, his style is not saturated with reminiscences of it, but is the normal philosophic Greek of the period. Philo retained the Law, which Paul rejected: but whereas Paul interpreted it with reference to what he held to be the novel facts of the situation, Philo . . . [related] the Law to general concepts and to

---

[6]Adolf Deissmann, *Paul: A Study in Social and Religious History*, trans. W. E. Wilson (New York: Harper, 1957), p. viii.

[7]He states his task as "to come back from the paper Paul of our western libraries, from the Germanised, dogmatised, modernised stilted Paul to the historic Paul, through the labyrinth of the 'Paulinism' of our New Testament theology. . . . Paul is essentially first and foremost a hero of religion. The theological element in him is secondary. . . . Christ means more to him than Christology, God more than the doctrine of God. He is far more a man of prayer, a witness, a confessor and a prophet, than a learned exegete and close thinking scholastic" (pp. 4, 6).

psychological and metaphysical abstractions. . . . Philo is a speculative thinker, Paul an authoritative teacher. Philo shows an intense interest in contemporary and earlier Greek philosophic thought, and follows pagan thinkers very freely when their doctrines were not wholly irreconcilable with Jewish tradition; Paul uses an occasional concept . . . but that is all, and the authority of human teachers is nothing to him. . . .

For Philo and his like the central issue turns on man as an individual, who by the aid of God and thanks to God's powers in the world and God's willingness to accept repentance, must strive so as to realize the full stature of which man was capable. This stature was the expression of the soul as a thing immortal. . . . Paul represents the older, un-Hellenized Jewish view which was preoccupied with the nation and not with the individual. It was the old hope of Israel, not the immortality of the soul. . . . The present universe was to Philo a revelation of God, to Paul at best indifferent. For Paul there would be a new heaven and a new earth, and the salvation of the elect individual was part of the salvation of the Elect as a whole. Paul says with passionate sincerity that he would be willing to lose his own salvation if only his people, the Jewish people, could at that price be saved [Rom 9:3]. This statement would have been entirely unintelligible to Philo.[8]

As usual, Nock's insights are penetrating, especially on this last point, the kind of person Paul was vis-à-vis what we would call "individualism." I will have more to say on this subject throughout this study. Nock's work reminds us that not all ancient persons were the same in personality, but even more important, ancient persons tended to be very different from modern ones in the way they derived their sense of identity.

Of the more modern "lives" of Paul, there are several that can be commended to one degree or another. The study of F. F. Bruce, *Paul: Apostle of the Heart Set Free*,[9] is still the best by a conservative scholar who is prepared to reckon with Paul's having a period of ministry after release from house arrest in Rome about A.D. 62. Though not really a life of Paul, C. K. Barrett's *Paul: An Introduction to His Thought*[10] is very useful for its clarity and combination of biographical and theological analysis. It distills a lifetime of study on Paul by one who has been called the greatest New Testament scholar in the English-speaking world in the twentieth century.

More recently three significant works have appeared, two by New

---

[8] A. D. Nock, *St. Paul* (London: Thornton Butterworth, 1938), pp. 237-41. "Man" here is used in the universal sense.

[9] F. F. Bruce, *Paul: Apostle of the Heart Set Free* (Grand Rapids, Mich.: Eerdmans, 1977).

[10] C. K. Barrett, *Paul: An Introduction to His Thought* (Louisville, Ky.: Westminster John Knox, 1994).

Testament scholars, one by an ancient historian, that merit mention. Jerome Murphy-O'Connor's *Paul: A Critical Life*[11] shows great learning and attention to historical detail that is not always characteristic of analysts of Paul's thought world. In my judgment, however, it is marred by eclecticism at several points. (1) The author has been too swayed by trends toward chronological revisionism spurred by Gerd Luedemann and others, especially when discussing the period of the 40s in Paul's life, and he places too many eggs in the Ephesian-imprisonment-theory basket.[12] (2) He is overly given to parsing up Paul's letters, including 1 Thessalonians and Philippians, without adequate justification.[13] (3) He places too much weight on Paul's time in Tarsus, despite the fact that the only evidence we have on this subject (Acts) says he did not grow up there. (4) Inexplicably, he wishes to argue that 2 Timothy is so different from the other Pastorals in style and substance that it can be said to be Pauline while the other two cannot be. I think he is right to argue for the Pauline *substance* of 2 Timothy, but the style and vocabulary it shares with the Pastorals bespeak a common author of all three. Despite these criticisms, Murphy-O'Connor's work deserves to be seen as the current benchmark by which other studies of the life of Paul should be evaluated. It is thorough in dealing with historical, chronological and rhetorical issues and gives a reasonable feel for Paul's thought world as well.[14]

The second of these studies, by a New Testament scholar and an associate, is Martin Hengel and Anne-Maria Schwemer's *Paul Between Antioch and Damascus*. This work, like Hengel's previous *The Pre-Christian Paul*,[15] is a gold mine of detailed information, attempting to set one period of Paul's life in its proper historical context. It is not of course a "life of Paul" in the broad sense because of the short period it deals with. One suspects that it would take at least three or four thousand closely argued pages for Hengel to deal with the "life of Paul." We may be thankful for 530 pages on the "hidden years"! Nonetheless, in this work we get a rather clear picture of

---

[11]Jerome Murphy-O'Connor, *Paul: A Critical Life* (Oxford: Oxford University Press, 1996).

[12]See the critique by Martin Hengel and Anne-Maria Schwemer in *Paul Between Damascus and Antioch* (Louisville, Ky.: Westminster John Knox, 1997), pp. 135-50.

[13]About such dismembering of Paul's letters Deissmann (*Paul*, p. 16) was to remark: "The extant letters of Paul have innocently had to suffer over again in the nineteenth [and I would add, even more in the twentieth] century a good part of the martyrdom of the historic Paul:- 'Thrice I was beaten by rods, once was I stoned, thrice have I suffered shipwreck.'"

[14]It is instructive to compare this work with J. Becker's *Paul: Apostle to the Gentiles* (Louisville, Ky.: Westminster, 1993), a work which certainly could be included in this survey of vitae. On the whole, however, while Becker may have a slight edge in the theological issues, Murphy-O'Connor's work is stronger on historical, social and rhetorical issues.

[15]Martin Hengel and R. Deines, *The Pre-Christian Paul* (Philadelphia: Trinity, 1991).

Hengel's views of the one he calls "the second founder of Christianity."[16]

Finally, A. N. Wilson's *Paul: The Mind of the Apostle*[17] should be mentioned. Wilson is not a New Testament scholar, but he is conversant with some of the literature. His strength is his broad knowledge of ancient history, a knowledge he brings to bear in telling ways. His first chapter on Nero and the setting of early Christianity is informative in several respects. But besides Wilson's lack of knowledge of the vast corpus of Pauline literature, the reader detects a distinct lack of sympathy for the views of Paul on various subjects (he is seen as a brilliant but tormented mystic and at one point is said to have a Nietzschean mind), which skews the evaluation. Perhaps somewhat surprisingly for an ancient historian, Wilson falls into the trap of evaluating Paul as if he were a modern person, to be judged by modern psychological and sociological criteria.

In fact, if there is one general complaint to be raised with most otherwise helpful and important studies,[18] it is precisely that they fail to treat Paul on his own terms as an ancient Mediterranean person. It is my intent in this study to go some way toward remedying such anachronism. This work intends to challenge the assumption of many moderns that "Paul as a human being was basically just like me." To the extent that each human being is a product of a particular environment, culture, language group, education, and social and religious upbringing, this assumption is manifestly false. Just how false it is in the case of Paul this study will attempt to expose.

---

[16]Hengel and Schwemer, *Paul Between Damascus and Antioch*, p. 309. This judgment is quite different from that of Paul as simply the founder of Christianity and so the perverter of the simple Jewish faith of Jesus.

[17]A. N. Wilson, *Paul: The Mind of the Apostle* (New York: Norton, 1997). See the strong critique by N. T. Wright, *What Saint Paul Really Said* (Grand Rapids, Mich.: Eerdmans, 1997).

[18]As the earlier quote from Nock shows, he was aware of this problem of treating Paul like a modern individualist.

CHAPTER 1

ON CONSTRUCTING AN ANCIENT PERSONALITY

Paul lived in a very different social environment from ours, and to the extent that environment conditions and shapes personality, he was very different from modern persons, especially modern Western persons. This chapter investigates various aspects of first-century Mediterranean culture that have a bearing on Paul's personality. For example, in antiquity people did not assume our current theories of personality development. Rather, it was believed that gender, generation and geography determine a person's identity, which is to say it is fixed at birth. Paul or anyone else who claimed to have become a different person as a result of some experience (such as conversion) would likely be seen as a deviant, liar or outcast. Furthermore, people did not strive to be individuals but rather derived their sense of identity from the group of which they were a part. Paul was Paul of Tarsus, or Paul the Pharisee, or Paul the servant of Jesus Christ. Yet very unlike many ancients, he gained his primary sense of identity not from his physical family but from his Christian family and his relationship with Christ. It was more a matter of whose he was than who he was, and even after his conversion he did not become an individualist but simply a different kind of dyadic personality.

Like most other ancients, Paul viewed the human body and its contribution to personality differently from the way we do. For Paul as both Pharisee and Christian, the body was an essential part of human personality and would be part of who Christians were in the world to come. In fact, the body was believed to be a mirror of the sort of person one was, so that you could judge a person by his or her appearance.

Finally, Paul lived in a culture that valued honor over life, and boasting rather than humility was seen as proper. It is interesting to see how Paul mirrors these values yet inverts them by boasting of shameful things (the cross) and considering someone else's honor (Christ's) more important than his own life. In the matter of reciprocity as well, Paul understands and uses the conventions but injects grace and real giving into a society always looking for recompense. Thus the Paul we see is to some degree a product of his time yet changing the paradigm of human personality and how a person should be evaluated. This deviance from the norm in a highly conformist society goes a long way to explain why Paul was such an outcast and invariably produced strong reactions from others.

SUPPOSE YOU WERE ASKED TO FILL OUT A MISSING PERSONS REPORT FOR SAUL OF Tarsus. What would you include in the report? What could you gather from the written sources available about him? Would you stress his ideas,[1] or would you concentrate on the facts about his life that are relatively secure and well known? Would you attempt to draw a composite sketch of his activities, his known associates and the places he was known to frequent? Would you focus on his background and early influences ("Saul: The Early Years"), to the extent that they can be deduced, or would you concentrate on the mature apostle and his adult undertakings? Would you concentrate on the evaluations of Paul by his friends, by his enemies, by the apostle himself? Would you try to explain why this apostle seems to spend a good deal of his time defending and explaining himself, even to his own converts?

Immediately when someone begins asking questions about how to discern the character of the historical Paul, a host of complex questions arise. Is the "real" Paul knowable, or must we settle for the public face of Paul as known through his letters and through Acts? Even if we content ourselves with examining the public face of Paul, will we be wise enough to realize that there is much more to the historical Paul than the sources reveal? Clearly, we must reconcile ourselves to the fact that we do not really have any sources on Paul from his cultured or not so cultured detractors. One can imagine the composite portrait that would have been drawn up by the Christian agitators in Galatia who were troubling Paul's Gentile converts and trying to get them to accept circumcision and the Mosaic law![2] Yet alas, we have no such portrait.

All we have are the apostle's own somewhat oblique remarks and those of one of his greatest admirers, Luke. Yet Paul as an apostle, and even when he was Saul the Pharisee, was clearly a controversial figure.[3] Rather than

---

[1]As has been done in S. Westerholm, *Preface to the Study of Paul* (Grand Rapids, Mich.: Eerdmans, 1997).

[2]I am unconvinced by the attempts of some scholars to portray James's letter as an anti-Pauline broadside, despite the long pedigree of such a suggestion dating back to Luther. I would suggest that the author in James 2:14-16, like Paul in his letters, is correcting a misunderstanding of the Pauline gospel or improper conclusions drawn from that gospel.

[3]This fact becomes a bit clearer in Paul's letters than it does in Acts, where Luke downplays some of the controversies of earlier generations.

putting a halo on the man, various pagans, Jews *and Christians* were prepared to tar and feather him, stone him, even perhaps put out a contract on his life (see 2 Cor 11:26—"danger from my own people [Jews], dangers from Gentiles, . . . dangers from false brothers and sisters"). Paul's résumé looked like a Most Wanted poster pinned up in a post office— always causing trouble or in trouble, frequently forced to be on the move, frequently whipped or stoned, run out of one town after another, not infrequently spending nights in a jail cell. What church or religious organization today would be prepared to hire such a person as a pastor, teacher, evangelist or missionary? Yet humanly speaking, it is fair to say that if this man had not done what he did, the Christian church would likely have not had the predominantly Gentile character it has had for these many centuries.

If a person's importance is measured not by likability but by his or her influence on the course of human history, then Saul of Tarsus deserves all the energy we can expend to get a clear fix on who he was, what made him tick and why he did the things he did.[4] We need to gain a clearer understanding of the man if we are to understand early Christianity and the course it took in the post-Pauline era.[5]

It must be freely granted at the outset that Paul is such a towering figure that like a great mountain, he has appeared differently to viewers depending on the point from which he has been viewed. The Jewish authorities in Jerusalem with whom he associated before his conversion saw Paul the Christian one way, the Jewish Christians in Jerusalem a somewhat different way, and Paul's own companions and converts still other ways. Yet in all cases he aroused passionate responses. Why was this? Did he simply live in a age full of short-tempered and mean-spirited persons? I wish to start our pilgrimage toward a clearer view of Paul by stressing that Paul really did live in a world that was very different from ours, especially different from the modern industrialized West. So we will begin our quest by examining how an ancient personality was constructed, since all persons are to a significant degree a product of their environment.[6]

---

[4]Of course Paul is not an object of faith, but he is an object of admiration and emulation, and this fact alone makes him important. Even today I would place him among the one hundred most influential persons in the Western world.

[5]For those who have seen Paul as something of a model and hero, a prototype of Luther, Calvin, Zwingli, Wesley, Asbury and the like, it is doubly important to understand "brother Paul."

[6]See the appendix of this book, "Timely Remarks on the Life of Paul," for a detailed chronological outline Paul's life.

PROFILING, FIRST-CENTURY STYLE

We live in an age of the psychologizing of all human thoughts, actions and personal characteristics. It is sometimes difficult to imagine what the world must have been like before Freud and Jung. Psychology has so affected the way we think about persons and cultural influences that even historians and biblical scholars who read works written by ancient persons come up with studies with titles like *The Mind of Paul*[7] or *Pagan and Christian in an Age of Anxiety.*[8] Even significant recent treatments of Paul that are aware of the perils of trying to psychoanalyze an ancient person still give way to doing so, in order to explain why Paul was as he was.[9]

In the age-old debate about which most determines human personality, nature or nurture, the former seems to have had the upper hand in analyses of Paul's personality and works, as is witnessed by the recent intriguing study by Gerd Theissen entitled *Psychological Aspects of Pauline Theology.*[10] The focus on "nature" has been especially obvious in studies indebted to the Lutheran reading of Romans 7. These studies suggested that this text unveils a profile of Paul's inner self, and some would even say the passage is a confession of a deeply troubled individual. Though there has been a sharp reaction to such a reading, even by a famous Lutheran New Testament scholar,[11] such readings continue unabated, based in large measure on the fundamental assumption that ancient persons thought, acted and existed much as we moderns do. This assumption deserves to be and has been vigorously challenged of late.

A fundamental protest to this whole approach to Paul and to ancient persons in general has come largely from scholars of social history, cultural anthropology and social-scientific theory. In fact, the sociological and anthropological study of the New Testament has been a major new window on the apostle to the Gentiles during the last two decades of the twentieth century. Modern sociological concepts (group and sect theory analysis, theories of status inconsistency) have been applied to produce landmark works such as the much-praised *First Urban Christians* by Wayne Meeks,

---

[7]An influential work by C. H. Dodd.

[8]By the classics scholar E. R. Dodds.

[9]See, e.g., two intriguing recent studies by Jewish scholars—Alan F. Segal, *Paul the Convert* (New Haven, Conn.: Yale University Press, 1990), and Daniel Boyarin, *A Radical Jew: Paul and the Politics of Identity* (Berkeley: University of California Press, 1994).

[10]Gerd Theissen, *Psychological Aspects of Pauline Theology* (Philadelphia: Fortress, 1987).

[11]Krister Stendahl, *Paul Among Jews and Gentiles* (Philadelphia: Fortress, 1976), which includes a reprint of his classic essay "Paul and the Introspective Consciousness of the West."

the equally lauded work of Theissen, and a statistical analysis of the growth of early Christianity and its social causes by Rodney Stark, *The Rise of Christianity*.[12] There has also been a whole body of work undertaken or engendered by E. A. Judge, a social historian of antiquity, and he has been followed by Bruce Winter and a host of others.[13] From the anthropological side of the equation, the seminal works of Mary Douglas have spurred scholars like Bruce Malina and Jerome Neyrey to consider the New Testament in general and the Pauline material in particular in the light of cultural concepts.[14] Malina's *The New Testament World: Insights from Cultural Anthropology* has become the textbook of choice for introducing students to this approach to the data.[15] Malina and Neyrey's *Portraits of Paul* is an essential resource for the subject matter of this chapter.[16]

A cautionary word is in order regarding such studies by cultural anthropologists and sociologists. To a very significant degree the concepts being used in these studies are modern, not ancient, and so there is a danger of anachronism if these concepts and theories are applied too heavy-handedly to the ancient data. For example, modern Mediterranean culture is not exactly identical to ancient Mediterranean culture. Ancient notions of honor and shame are not exactly identical to the ones held today in the eastern Mediterranean. This means that the focus must be on the historical data, and the theories must be used only as helpful tools for sifting the data. Always preference should be given to social-historical data over modern social theories.

---

[12]Wayne A. Meeks, *First Urban Christians* (New Haven, Conn.: Yale University Press, 1983); Gerd Theissen, *The Social Setting of Pauline Christianity* (Philadelphia: Fortress, 1982); Rodney Stark, *The Rise of Christianity* (Princeton, N.J.: Princeton University Press, 1996). Stark is a sociologist rather than a New Testament scholar. Another very interesting study is that of R. A. Atkins, *Egalitarian Community: Ethnography and Exegesis* (Tuscaloosa: University of Alabama Press, 1991), which applies group-grid analysis to Paul's communities to see what sort of communities they were. The best general introduction to this subject is still B. Holmberg's *Sociology and the New Testament* (Minneapolis: Fortress, 1990).

[13]See especially E. A. Judge, *The Social Pattern of Christian Groups in the First Century* (London: Tyndale, 1960), or his *Rank and Status in the World of the Caesar's and of St. Paul* (Christchurch, U.K.: University of Canterbury, 1982), and Bruce Winter, *Are Paul and Philo Among the Sophists?* (Cambridge: Cambridge University Press, 1996).

[14]Mary Douglas, *Purity and Danger: An Analysis of the Concepts of Pollution and Taboo* (Baltimore, Md.: Pelican, 1970).

[15]Bruce Malina, *The New Testament World: Insights from Cultural Anthropology* (Atlanta: John Knox, 1981; rev. ed., Louisville, Ky.: Westminster John Knox, 1993). See also Jerome Neyrey, *Paul in Other Words: A Cultural Reading of His Letters* (Louisville, Ky.: Westminister John Knox, 1990).

[16]Bruce Malina and Jerome Neyrey, *Portraits of Paul: An Archaeology of Ancient Personality* (Louisville, Ky.: Westminster John Knox, 1996).

Nevertheless, such studies have brought major gains. For example, we are reminded that nurture played a far larger role than we have ever imagined in the construction of ancient personality. Indeed, it has been argued that there was such a thing as ancient Mediterranean personality, which was very different from modern Western personality.[17] Even the way the human body and its relationship to the mind and the world were viewed was fundamentally different from the modern view.[18]

Given all this, it is not surprising to find that ancient attempts at biographies such as Plutarch's *Lives*, Josephus's *Life of Apion*, Tacitus's *Agricola* or even the Gospel of Mark seem very different from modern biographies.[19] Instead of a womb-to-tomb analysis of the development of a human personality, we often find little or no treatment of "early childhood influences." What we do find is a basic assumption that a person's character does not develop over time at all! Time simply *reveals* such character. We also often find the assumption that the subject is not what we would call a unique individual at all, but rather a mirror of the virtues and values, flaws and faults of some particular ancient group. What we might call stereotypes ancients would often see as character types or traits that explained both individuals and the groups they were a part of. "Cretans are always liars, vicious brutes, lazy gluttons," says Titus 1:12, but as this text also says, this is a quote from a famous Cretan!

The theme of much of this social-scientific, anthropological and historical analysis of our subject is the need to avoid anachronism in scrutinizing Paul and his thought. The message is conveyed that the past is much like a country that modern Westerners would find extremely foreign. Things were done very differently in that time and place, and if we were to travel back to that time, people would appear more like aliens than cousins to us. There is much to be learned from these sorts of studies, so let's sort out some of the data before we begin our analysis of Paul the Jew, the Roman citizen and the Christian.

ONE OF THE CROWD

Certain fundamental values of the ancient Greco-Roman culture held sway to one degree or another throughout the Mediterranean crescent during

---

[17]See especially ibid.

[18]See Dale B. Martin, *The Corinthian Body* (New Haven, Conn.: Yale University Press, 1995).

[19]See especially the important treatment of the Gospels as ancient biographies in Richard A. Burridge, *What Are the Gospels?* (Cambridge: Cambridge University Press, 1992).

New Testament times. This is not to deny that subcultures within the Roman Empire had some distinctive values and ways of critiquing the values of the larger dominant culture. This is especially true of Jewish and Christian subcultures, and groups like the Cynics offered their own cultural critiques. Nevertheless, it is fair to say that certain dominant assumptions affected and infected even all these subcultures to one degree or another.

Family Values of First-Century Persons

In the wake of modern movements like the Promise Keepers and popular radio programs like James Dobson's *Focus on the Family,* many Christians may be excused for thinking that they understand exactly what family values are all about, especially biblical family values. Family values have to do, we would say, with the nurturing of the nuclear family of father, mother and children. They have to do with parents' obligations to make sacrifices and assume their responsibilities as fathers and mothers. They have to do with putting the nuclear family first, after God, and ahead of one's career or other obligations. There have been some protests even in conservative circles against such a simplistic reading of the biblical evidence,[20] but missing from this whole discussion has been anything like a historical analysis of the ancient family structures and networks of the biblical world.

The most basic and fundamental remark that can be made about the ancient Greco-Roman world is that all its cultures and subcultures were highly patriarchal and all or almost all the literature written about these matters by the participants takes an androcentric, or male-centered, point of view. Furthermore, not surprisingly in view of the lack of literacy in many quarters of the ancient world, writing was largely a domain of the well-to-do or the well educated. The classical literature we read from the period is largely elitist fare, the view from above.

The world of Paul, and for that matter of Jesus, was indeed, to a greater extent than modern Western culture, a man's world, a male-dominated world. Traditional Near Eastern or even Far Eastern culture today is far closer to this sort of social structure than is Western society. And unless one is willing to presuppose that whatever exists in a given culture is right and a manifestation of biblical values, it is necessary to ask to what degree patriarchal culture represents the biblical vision of human society. As an illustration of how our own cultural presuppositions affect the way we

---

[20]See, e.g., Rodney Clapp, *Families at the Crossroads: Beyond Traditional and Modern Options* (Downers Grove, Ill.: InterVarsity Press, 1993).

read the biblical data, I offer two examples, one from the Old Testament, one from the New Testament.

The curse placed on woman because of her part in the original sin, according to Genesis 3:16, is not only that labor pains will be increased but also that her husband will take advantage of her desire for him and lord it over her or rule her. This is not seen as part of an original blessing or a God-ordained family structure, but rather a punishment for sinning![21] Yet this verse is frequently quoted as justification for the "creation order mandate" that man is the lord or ruler of woman. The text itself should lead us to ask when we see patriarchal family structures on page after page of the Bible, to what degree, if at all, such a structure is given divine imprimatur, or to what degree we see grace attempting to change such a structure. Is what we are looking at an effect of the Fall or of a creation mandate? Is it original blessing or original curse?[22]

The second example would be placed by many moderns in the category of egregious child neglect. I am referring to the famous story about Jesus in the temple in Luke 2:41-52. Here we have the holy family traveling off and leaving their twelve-year-old son in a bustling metropolis under no relative's care, but rather with strangers! In my country that would often lead to an immediate phone call to social services. Notice, however, what the text says. Mary and Joseph traveled for a day back toward Galilee assuming that Jesus was in the group of fellow travelers (v. 44). In all likelihood this is not an example of bad parenting but a clear pointer to a family situation we are not used to—an extended family. The family unit in Jesus' culture included far more than the nuclear family. It involved not only several generations of one family but relatives and cousins as well. Joseph and Mary were not the only persons expected to be caregivers and guardians for Jesus. So to even begin to assess what the Bible says about families, we need to understand the structure of ancient families, what their values were and how they worked.

Families in antiquity, like other social groups, were based on ancient kinship principles and operated with a group mentality. Individual persons

---

[21]The failure to recognize the context of curse in Genesis 3:14-19 is really quite startling. Genesis 3:16 is the only verse in this passage that could be construed as some sort of compensatory blessing; no compensation for the man and his "labor" pains is mentioned. Yet the LXX rendering of 3:16 makes the negative tone of this verse clearer.

[22]This question must be kept in mind especially when one is reading, for example, Colossians 3:18—4:1 or Ephesians 5:21—6:9. What stands out about these passages is not that they reflect the status quo, which they do, but the degree to which they attempt to change and Christianize such structures from within the Christian community.

derived their sense of identity in the main not from what distinguished them from the crowd but rather from what crowd they were a part of, where they lived, their gender and what values were upheld by their group. The group was clearly primary, the individual clearly secondary. From the New Testament we can readily see how this worked in families.

For a start, people do not have last names in the New Testament. Rather they are identified, for example, as "Simon bar Jonah" or "the sons of Zebedee." In these instances a person is identified by a patronymic (the name of their father). There was indeed a widespread assumption "like father, like son." Notice the discussion in John 8:39-42:

> They [the Jews] answered him, "Abraham is our father." Jesus said to them, "If you were Abraham's children, you would be doing what Abraham did, but now you are trying to kill me, a man who has told you the truth. . . . This is not what Abraham did. You are indeed doing what your father [the devil] does." They said to him, "We are not illegitimate children; we have one father, God himself." Jesus said to them, "If God were your Father, you would love me, for I came from God and now I am here."

It is not "personality" or any sort of laudable individuality for persons *not* to manifest the character of their parents. Rather, if their parents are good persons, it is deviance to be unlike them, and so such differentness is not at all commended. No wonder that in this environment we hear "I and the Father are one" as a statement of identity.

What identified persons was not how they were *different* from their parent or parents but indeed whose child they were. This collective or family mentality was all-pervasive in the first century, and it affected Jewish, Greek and Roman understandings of persons and the world. It was not just the emperor who had multiple names, various of which indicated who his important male ancestors were (e.g., Gaius Julius Caesar Octavianus Augustus = Emperor Augustus).

A Different Kinship

Obviously if "generation" or whose progeny you were was so crucial for identity, a person who had a notorious parent—or in a patriarchal culture, a person who had only a woman for a parent—had to operate with certain inherent ongoing liabilities. Consider the pejorative cast of Mark 6:2-3. Jesus' hometown folks ask, "'Where did this man get all this? . . . Is not this the carpenter, the son of Mary and brother of James . . . ?' And they took offense." The problem here is not just Jesus' rustic trade but that he did not have an illustrious, well-educated father, living or dead. Yet we also see in this story an inkling of a response to this whole way of judging people, for Jesus responds that prophets are not without honor "except in their own hometown, and among their own kin, and in their own house" (Mk 6:4). Notice the ever-narrowing circle of relationships—hometown, kin, one's own house. A person was assumed to belong to all three of these groups permanently, and if he was rejected by them or if he rejected them, then he was a deviant and an outcast. Anyone who tried to stand out from the crowd or from the family was normally going to be viewed in this manner. Individuality was not encouraged or seen as a good thing. I suggest that both Jesus and Paul were indeed seen as deviants by their peers, so that anything they did or said was considered immediately suspect.

Yet Jesus was able to put a positive interpretation on his distinctiveness by calling himself a prophet of God, just as Paul insists he is an apostle of God. It was allowed, and indeed to some degree expected, that God's messengers would be out of the ordinary (remember John the Baptist), even strange at times. They were not seen as normal or as necessarily reflecting the normal family values of their society.

But it was not just lifestyle but also teachings that caused Jesus and Paul not to be seen as normal first-century persons. Neither of them advocated all the accepted first-century family values, as we shall see, for both of them proposed that there was a different kinship, a belonging to the circle of Jesus' followers, which was to take priority always over one's obligations to physical family or kin.[23]

Paul repeatedly refers to his converts and Christian friends as his true brothers and sisters, but notice also how Jesus treats this matter in Mark 3:31-35. Jesus' family is standing outside a large gathering of his followers, seeking Jesus so they may take him home. They think he is not in his right mind (Mk 3:21), and so they have come out to get him. Upon hearing that his "nuclear" family is there and is asking for him, Jesus replies, "Who are my mother and my brothers?" And looking at those who sat around him, he said, "Here are my mother and my brothers! Whoever does the will of God is my brother and sister and mother" (Mk 3:33-35). This is the same Jesus who says that if a physical family is divided over its allegiance to him, it should indeed be divided (Mt 10:34-38). The physical family should not be loved more than one loves and follows Jesus himself. This is also the same Jesus who saw a viable place among his followers for single persons

---

[23]*Fictive kinship* is a familial relationship that exists between people that are not necessarily blood-related. They treat one another as brothers and sisters.

who remain single to serve God. Some would say that this teaching provides the justification for Jesus' own chosen lifestyle (see Mt 19:10-12 for his "scandalous" teaching on eunuchs).

Similarly, Paul says that being single or being married requires a gift or grace from God; neither is a natural state of being (1 Cor 7). He wished that his converts would be like him—single. Paul also said to engaged but unmarried virgins that it would be good if they did not go on into marriage (1 Cor 7:25-31). And like Jesus before him, Paul believed women could and should be his coworkers and traveling companions in the gospel (cf. Lk 8:1-3 to Phoebe in Rom 16; Euodia and Syntyche in Phil 4; Priscilla in 1 Cor 16:19).

The teachings of both Jesus and Paul include suggestions that went against the flow of dominant and normal assumptions about family and family values. We still see such assumptions in the church today when it is assumed that blood is and should be thicker than baptismal water, and when the definition of "a family church" is not a church that is one's primary family but a church that nurtures nuclear families as the major unit or building block of society, even Christian society. For both Jesus and Paul, fictive kinship rather than natural kinship is the primary identity unit, and radical individualism is nowhere to be found as a value in the teaching of either of these men.

As Jerome Neyrey and Bruce Malina have put it, even these crucial figures must be understood as collectivist or group-oriented persons, not as individualistic selves.[24] The groups they were a part of and helped to found and construct were not built using the usual building blocks of generation, gender and geography, however, but were founded on the basis of faith adherence or allegiance. According to Paul, "There is no longer Jew or Greek, slave or free, there is no longer male and female, but rather all are *one person* in Christ Jesus" (Gal 3:28, my translation). That is, boundary, status and identity determinants in Christ are neither ethnic/geographical nor social.[25]

---

[24]Malina and Neyrey, *Portraits of Paul*, p. 156.

[25]It needs to be noted, and will be covered in more detail later, that Paul does not say "no male *or* female" but rather "no male *and* female." He is commenting on the necessary coupling of the two sexes and so on a social relationship here, not on gender per se. As 1 Corinthians 7 makes evident, he does not think Christians are obligated to be fruitful and multiply. Paul rather believes that men remain men and women remain women in the body of Christ and that these distinctions are divinely intended. Creation is redeemed by the overcoming of ethnic and social divisions, but the sexual distinctions are fundamental and so not obliterated —Paul was no androgynist.

Marriage Rules

The same could not be said for first-century society as a whole, whether Jewish society or Greco-Roman society. In first-century Judaism, as in the Greco-Roman world, marriage was generally monogamous,[26] but there were strong taboos against what we would call intermarriage with other tribes or clans or ethnic or religious groups. There "was a marked preference for keeping daughters as close to the nuclear conjugal family as the prohibitions of incest permitted. . . . Cross-cousin marriage between the offspring of either parent's siblings was eagerly sought, marriage with cousins from the father's side of the family was always preferred. This option . . . is called Mediterranean endogamy."[27] It is fair to say that most Americans would look askance at the prospect of marrying their first or second cousin, but in fact this was the regular practice in the New Testament world, even among Jews, so long as the Mosaic law's specific prohibitions about incest were observed. There was a strong reason for this approach. Since marriage was often seen as essentially a property transaction involving dowries and inheritances, it was deemed critical to keep the property in the family. Marrying within one's own larger kin or clan group or extended family was expected, then, and in some cases required.

Marriage in antiquity looked very different from today's Western version. Elsewhere I have chronicled in some detail some of the Jewish and Greco-Roman world's rules and procedures surrounding marriage and divorce.[28] Reading the sources, it becomes clear that the norm in antiquity was arranged marriage, with the fathers of the couple performing the transaction as a sort of business deal. Daughters, as soon as they were nubile, and in some cases before they were nubile, were "contracted" in marriage. This could happen as early as ages eleven or twelve. What we would call romance or courtship was rare. Indeed the whole modern Western notion of romantic love as a feeling, and that feeling constitutes a basis for a permanent relationship, would have seemed rather strange to the ancients. In the New Testament, in fact, love is regularly commanded; it is presupposed to involve a decision of the will and to entail feelings, if at all, only secondarily.

---

[26]Polygamy did exist during the time of the patriarchs and later, but this was largely a thing of the past for common Jews in the first century A.D.

[27]Bruce Malina, *The New Testament World*, rev. ed. (Louisville, Ky.: Westminster John Knox, 1993), p. 121.

[28]See Ben Witherington III, *Women in the Ministry of Jesus* (Cambridge: Cambridge University Press, 1984), pp. 1-10 and notes, on women in Judaism; also Ben Witherington III, *Women in the Earliest Churches* (Cambridge: Cambridge University Press, 1988), pp. 5-23 and notes, on women in the Gentile world.

If a culture's family values are largely revealed in the way its marriages are contracted, we can conclude that families in antiquity served rather different purposes and often had different goals from families today.[29] Marriage was a patriarchal and economic issue, with the goal being to keep things "all in the family." We in the West apply open-market free-competition principles to the process of selecting marriage partners, without the strictures the ancients would normally apply. In our society a married couple is not required to fit into a broader kinship group. They can move away and make their own choices, and in fact they will be expected to become "independent" of their parents.[30] Independence would not be seen as a virtue in the ancient world of extended families and arranged marriages, nor would it be seen as a virtue in many non-Western societies today.

In the world of arranged marriages, the "affection we expect as a mark of the husband and wife relationship is normally a mark of the brother-sister and mother-son relationships."[31] Furthermore, in the Mediterranean world a family often included not only parents and children but also the father and mother of the firstborn son (now married with children) and any other unmarried children who were this son's siblings. If not under the same roof, the kin would still try to live in very close proximity so they could pool their efforts.[32]

In contrast to most modern families, ancient extended families, especially agrarian ones, were often not merely consuming units but producing ones, with all members working together to produce a crop or a product. Family members did not go out to look for jobs or pursue a career; they took up tasks or trades that the family needed done and was already

---

[29]It is also striking that things seen by modern Western society as making a marriage a marriage were not boundary markers in antiquity. For example, a ceremony performed by some official such as a clergy or justice of the peace, in some particular building such as a church, synagogue or mosque and requiring a state-provided license was not in antiquity the indicator that one had entered a married state. There were ceremonies in the presence of friends and family in both the Jewish and Greco-Roman world, but there were no ceremonies performed by clergy in religious buildings and with a certificate from the state. Marriage was very much an in-house family matter in antiquity. This is especially clear in the parable found in Matthew 25:1-12. After two fathers haggled over a dowry, the bridegroom would go to the house of the bride to collect her and her companions for a torchlight procession through the town, perhaps with an open-air ceremony and some dancing. The bridegroom or his father would provide a dinner in his home, after which the new husband and wife immediately consummated their relationship. See Witherington, *Women in the Ministry of Jesus*, pp. 41-44 and notes.

[30]See Malina, *New Testament World*, p. 124.

[31]Ibid., p. 122.

[32]Ibid.

doing. Like David the shepherd, Jesus the carpenter, Peter the fisherman and Paul the tentmaker, they carried on the family business.[33]

Source of Identity
Although many Westerners have a strong interest in their ancestry, our ties with more remote kin are far less formal and important than they were in the first-century biblical world. Ancestry had to do with economic, political, ethnic and religious realities, such that one's clan or kin defined the very essence of one's identity. Notice how Paul chooses to describe himself as a Jew—"of the people of Israel, of the tribe of Benjamin, a Hebrew born of Hebrews, as to the law, a Pharisee" (Phil 3:5). When he is challenged by adversaries, notice how he responds: "Are they Hebrews? So am I. Are they Israelites? So am I. Are they descendants of Abraham? So am I" (2 Cor 11:22). True, the larger context of the Philippians passage reveals that Paul now evaluates this heritage differently as a follower of Christ than he did as a Jew. Yet he still claims it ("so am I"), and he still uses it when necessary to identify himself. And in the 2 Corinthians passage, it is not what *distinguishes* Paul from his adversaries that he first remarks on, but rather what characteristics he assumes he may share with them.

Paul was indeed thinking like an ancient person for whom the group was the primary source of identity. The difference of course for Paul the Christian is that he is now a part of a new family (the family of Christ, or Christians) and serving a new master or lord. He is not ashamed of his past or his heritage; rather, the past is transvalued in light of the new family commitments he has made.

In the anthropological literature, the personality whose basic sense of identity comes from the group or groups of which a person is a part is called a *dyadic* personality. Such a person does not go around asking who he is but rather *whose* he is, or to whom he belongs. In other words, one's social network defines identity. Three of the fundamental building blocks of such a personality were, in the words of Malina and Neyrey, generation, gender and geography.[34] These of course overlapped and must be supplemented with factors such as wealth, education and religion; these latter factors, however, were secondary and depended on whose family one was born into, where one was born, and one's gender.

---

[33]More attention should be paid to the fact that Jesus seems to have deliberately recruited family units or significant portions thereof to be his disciples—for example, Peter and Andrew, the sons of Zebedee, and Mary, Martha and Lazarus.

[34]See the discussion in Malina and Neyrey, *Portraits of Paul,* pp. 153-74.

The importance of geography in antiquity needs to be stressed. Though we today may often have a strong sense of loyalty toward or pride in our birthplace or home state or region, we would hardly suggest that location necessarily determines what sort of persons we are. And I would not identify myself simply as Ben of Charlotte (N.C.), though I love my home state and city. Yet the ancients frequently did these very things. Saul was not merely Saul; he was Saul *of Tarsus*, a city with a considerable honor rating in antiquity. It was one of the two or three great university towns of Paul's age, and certainly the greatest metropolis of its region (see Acts 22:3). Contrast this with Jesus of Nazareth; Nazareth was a small, out-of-the-way village from which few would expect any important person to come (Jn 1:46). Geography mattered far more in antiquity than today in evaluating what sort of person someone was. Notice how Jesus responds to Nathanael's slighting remark about Nazareth, by speaking of Nathanael in more positive tribal identity terms: "Here is truly an Israelite in whom there is no deceit!" (Jn 1:47).

Geography mattered partly because most people and families, especially nonelite families, were far less cosmopolitan and mobile than we are today, and so their locale did indeed tend to shape not only their accent (see Lk 22:59) but also their customs, habits, behavior and thought patterns. Geography also mattered because many persons had a strong sense of sacred space. For Romans "all roads led to Rome," as it was their point of reference and identity marker. They did not call themselves Italians. The modern notion of nation-states was not present to color their thinking. It was mostly locale, tribe and gender that shaped their thinking and evaluation of a person's identity. For Jews, similarly, all roads led to Jerusalem, the holy city. In general, the farther one was removed from Jerusalem, the less likely it was that one could be considered a significant or important Israelite (see above on Jesus). Bethlehem was associated with the coming of Messiah not just because it was the city of David but also because it was near to the Holy City.

Geographic, tribal and ethnic designations quite naturally overlapped, with expectations about one carrying over to the other. For example, Luke's audience probably heard the story of Acts 8:26-40 against a background of assumptions about Ethiopians as the blackest of all peoples who lived on the southern edge of Empire and earth, and so were seen as boundary people with distinct customs and culture.[35] Pliny the Elder says in his

---

[35]See Ben Witherington III, *Acts of the Apostles* (Grand Rapids, Mich.: Eerdmans, 1997), pp. 290-301.

Natural History 2.80, 189,

> It is beyond question that the Ethiopians are burnt by the heat of the heavenly body near them [because they live at the edge of the earth and so nearer the sun], and are born with a scorched appearance, with curly beard and hair, and that in the opposite region of the world the races [northern Europeans, in particular Scandinavians and Germans] have white frosty skins, with yellow hair that hangs straight; while the latter are fierce owing to the rigidity of their climate but the former wise because of the mobility of theirs [the need to move around due to the heat].

Luke's point in including the story is to show fulfillment of the promise and prophecy that the gospel will go out to all peoples and to the ends of the earth.

So gender, generation and geography served as the major sources of identity and personality in antiquity. It was understood, of course, that there were exceptions to the rule. Deviants and outcasts existed. Some people were not considered true Romans or true Jews.

Deviants but Not Individualists

Paul, and Jesus before him, launched a process of deconstructing some of the culture's basic assumptions about human beings based on gender, generation and geography. Texts like Romans 2:28-29 and Mark 10:13 function in precisely this way. Both Jesus and Paul believed that radical change can happen to a person, overcoming stereotypes and stigmas of gender, generation and geography. A person can start over—indeed should start over (2 Cor 5:17; Gal 3:28)—but he or she must be prepared to be rejected by a world that would go on judging people on the basis of gender, generation and geography. The convert must be prepared to be despised and rejected as a deviant. To one degree or another, becoming part of a conversionist sect meant becoming an outcast. This was even more the case with Paul, who was an outcast even from some parts of his own Christian group. Consider the following remarks:

> What is also interesting about Paul is that there is precious little evidence in the Pauline letters about his ever being integrated into a Christian community of faith, and equally little or nothing about his going through a rite of passage when he became a Christian, though Acts provides us with a little information on both scores. That Paul does not talk about a faith community of which he was a part, but only about communities which he helped found, and likewise he does not speak of spiritual mentors or his instructors in the faith (unless Peter counts, . . .), but only about those he has mentored and the co-workers he has chosen or with whom he has done missionary work is striking. One gets

the strong sense of Paul not being socialized or at least not well socialized into existing Christian communities at the point of his conversion. To the contrary Paul says he immediately went to the mission field in Arabia. From Gal. 2, one does get the sense that later Paul was a part of the Christian community in Antioch, something Acts confirms, but even here Paul says very little about the community or his life in that community. He largely leaves the impression of being an isolated holy man. Sociologists would want to ask how much of Paul's independent spirit seems to have derived from a lack of thorough integration into a faith community after his conversion. How much of this isolation also contributed to his being seen as a maverick by various other Christians, perhaps especially by members of the Jerusalem church? These are questions worth pondering, and certainly one must say that Paul's independence of a "home" community suggests he could not be seen as a typical example of dyadic personality if by that term one means someone whose identity is almost completely defined for him or her by the community of which he or she is a part.[36]

Still, conversion did not make a person a radical individualist. It was not a matter of abandoning the group mentality and becoming a "lone ranger." To the contrary, conversion meant joining a new family or community that would supply essential aspects of a new identity.

Another crucial aspect to this change was that the change agent was seen to be a particular person, Jesus Christ, and personality in the group of his followers henceforth would be modeled on Christ himself. In some sense the followers of Jesus would be incorporated into a spiritual reality that involved direct union with Christ, so becoming his body. They would take Christ into their very beings, as the continued celebration of the Lord's Supper would stress. They would be in Christ, and Christ would be in them. Not only would the story of Christ be recapitulated in the life of believers, but in a sense they would participate in the continuation of Christ's story by being his body on the earth. A question like "Saul, Saul, why do you persecute *me*?" posed by the heavenly Christ to Saul the persecutor of *Christians* (Acts 9:4) makes sense in this context.

As noted above, Paul continued to identify himself in Jewish terms, and he continued to think of his personhood as formed by an essentially external source of influence. "For to me, living is Christ and dying is gain" (Phil 1:21). In other words, he retained a collectivist mentality. He still reflected what would be called dyadic personality. Even Paul's conversion experience was a matter not of introspective reflection that led to change, but rather an intrusion into Paul's life from an outside source that redefined his

---

[36]Ben Witherington III, *Grace in Galatia* (Edinburgh: T & T Clark, 1998), p. 111.

identity (Gal 1:15-16). A powerful experience, coming from an outside person, made clear to whom he belonged, who he now was, what community he was a part of and what he must do. After his conversion, then, Paul still manifested dyadic personality; he had not suddenly become a late-twentieth-century Westerner.

To sum up: In antiquity, belonging to a family, like belonging to a faith, was usually a matter of being born into a existing set of relationships. Even marriage continued to foster this arrangement, except of course when a daughter or son had to look beyond the immediate extended family for a mate. Even in such circumstances there would be an attempt to avoid marrying outside the larger kin group, especially if one's neighbors were not fellow Israelite monotheists (see the poignant tale about Jacob in Gen 28—30). Finally, conversion to a new family or body of believers in antiquity was in various essential ways different from what it is today, not least in that one was not merely joined to a new religion, one was joined to a new people.

BODY LANGUAGE

Human beings have always evaluated themselves at least in part on the basis of their bodies. In the past as now, it was assumed that one's appearance tells us something essential about what kind of person one is. In modern Western society, however, so much stress is placed on one's appearance that we find ourselves combating disorders like anorexia nervosa or bulimia, problems apparently unknown in antiquity. And in a culture where "image is everything," it is no wonder that televisions, computer screens and movies reign supreme.

But even without such modern devices as televisions and computers, the ancients were also very concerned about image. In antiquity there was both a science of the body and a careful study of how to read that body for information about character—a study known as physiognomics.[37]

D. B. Martin postulates, and in this I think he is essentially correct, that our own modern ways of thinking about the relationship of the body and the mind, or the body and the spirit/soul, have largely arisen out of Cartesian ways of thinking.[38] René Descartes distinguished pointedly

---

[37]I am indebted to Dale B. Martin for his book *The Corinthian Body* and to Malina and Neyrey for *Portraits of Paul* for pointing out the essential primary source data and paving the way in its analysis, though I will differ from their interpretations at key points.

[38]See the discussion in Martin, *Corinthian Body*, pp. 4-20.

between mind, the nonphysical realm and the supernatural on the one hand and body, material existence and the natural on the other. For Descartes the "I," or the sense of human identity, could be identified with the mind or soul: "I think, therefore I am."

In such a worldview the body can be neatly distinguished from the mind as simply a physical nature, a house of the soul. There is no essential ontological connection or relationship of substance between body and mind, or body and soul, or body and spirit. "On the one side were body, matter, nature, and the physical; on the other were soul or mind, nonmatter, the supernatural, and the spiritual or psychological."[39] Whatever we may think or say about this dichotomy, such a dichotomized approach has affected and continues to affect modern ways of thinking about human life and personality, and also about the way God works in a mechanistic natural universe (e.g., consider *Webster*'s definition of a miracle as something that violates or interrupts nature or known natural laws). To be sure, there has been some quite proper reaction to this mode of thinking in modern medical discussions of humans as psychosomatic wholes and in explorations of holistic medicine. But we still remain deeply influenced by the Cartesian model, and it prevents us from hearing ancient texts and ideas about the body and the human person as we should—for Cartesian ways of thinking would have been quite foreign to the ancients.

Martin suggests that the ancients saw the human body as hierarchically arranged, in a sense a microcosm of the hierarchically arranged society of the times. In fact, he says, "the hierarchical concept of the body . . . supports and maintains the power structure of Greco-Roman society."[40] Within the bodily hierarchy there were various dimensions or parts.

The Greeks and Romans did make a distinction between body and soul, but there was considerable discussion about the nature of "soul." Aristotle, like many others, assumed that the soul was a part of nature. From his point of view, nature included everything, from the mind or soul to what we would call biology and physics (cf. Aristotle's *On the Soul* 1.1. 402a). Aristotle quotes a number of other authors and philosophers on the nature of the soul. Democritus says it is fire and heat, Pythagoreans that it is identical with the particles of the air, Leucippus that it is constructed of highly mobile spherical atoms (1.2.404a). In other words, while the soul might not have form and might not be visible to the naked eye, it did have substance and so was a part of nature. Earth, air, fire and water were

---

[39]Ibid., p. 6.
[40]Ibid., p. xviii.

assumed to be the elements of which all nature was composed.

Plato, however, offered a dissenting voice. He argued that the soul is antithetical to the body, not just a "finer" kind of body. The realm of the soul is known only by thinking of the mind and is hidden from the human senses (*Phaedo* 66D; 79A; 82B). An impure soul, one too closely affected by or mingled with the body, may have difficulty escaping the body at death; it may sink into another body at death rather than ascend to the eternal realm (see *Timaeus*).

The important point, though, is that "for most ancient philosophers, to say something was incorporeal was *not* to say that it was immaterial."[41] The ancients were far more likely than we to believe that all things, including the soul or mind, fall under the category of nature, and probably in the category of some kind of substance. Matter and spirit were not seen as ontological opposites.

Furthermore, it was widely believed that the human body is a microcosm of the universe itself. Remember, it was assumed that the human body was made up of the same elements or materials as the universe itself—earth, air, fire and water (see, e.g., Hippocrates *The Nature of Humankind*). It was assumed that conditions in the macrocosm affect conditions in the microcosm. The same violent wind that uproots trees could also cause apoplexy if it occurred within an individual (Hippocrates *Breaths* 3, 13). The boundaries between individual and world became on this showing rather blurred, such that "the workings of the internal body are not just an imitation of the mechanics of the universe; rather they are part of it, constantly influenced by it."[42]

The state of the soul was believed to be affected by the condition of one's blood, and both were linked to the appearance of the body. Blood was thought to be either hot or cold, thick or thin, moist or dry, swift or slow, and these characteristics affected not only the physiology of the soul but also a person's behavior and appearance. If a person was hot-blooded, for example, he might be quick to be angry. The ancient physician Galen put it this way: "For if very much heat dominates, straightway there is bitter anger and madness and rashness" (*Ars Medica* 10). In this view "the faculties of the mind follow the mixtures of the body" (see *Ars Medica* 4.767-822).

From such reasoning we can easily see why ancient persons might believe that one's outward appearance mirrors one's soul. The modern clear boundary between the psychological and the physiological, the inner

---

[41]Ibid., p. 15.
[42]Ibid., p. 17.

and outer person, was by no means so clear-cut in antiquity. Indeed, the boundary was thought to be quite porous (if it existed at all), with influence going in both directions, from inner to outer and outer to inner.[43]

This sort of thinking supported and perhaps in part led to the basic assumption that "no man is an island entire of himself. Every man is a piece of the continent, a part of the main" (John Donne). The isolated individual did not really exist, because of the ongoing interchange between an individual's body and soul with the outside forces and world. The self was shaped by outside forces, material as well as social. People were thought to take in "spirit" *(pneuma)* when inhaling; they needed air for nourishment (Dio Chrysostom *Discourse* 12.30). "The outside air (which either is or contains pneuma) sustains the inner pneuma by inhalation. . . . The body is a refinery for processing, among other things, pneuma."[44] This inhaled *pneuma* (wind or spirit) was considered by Galen (*Hygiene* 1.4, 11) as the basic stuff from which came thought, rationality and sensation. It was also believed to be susceptible to pollution and corruption (as we speak of air being polluted).

Not only was there an interaction between the inner and outer person, the inner and outer world, but a hierarchical ordering was assumed to exist in the universe, in society and in the human body. God ruled the universe as the emperor ruled society and the mind or soul ruled the body. Plato explains succinctly that the human head is spherical because that is the shape of divinities and the head is the most divine part of the body, meant to rule the rest. In fact, Plato adds that the body is just a stand or vehicle for the head, to keep it from rolling around on the ground (*Timaeus* 44D)!

How does this background help us to understand Paul as a person and as a thinker? First, it helps us to understand how Paul could consider a body so necessary to full and proper human existence. The soul or spirit animates the body, and the body gives a vehicle to and expresses the soul. The idea of life without a body in the eternal state of affairs, or a disembodied state, was unappealing to Paul (see 2 Cor 5:1-9). It was seen as nakedness and incompleteness, to be remedied with a resurrection body at the Lord's return (1 Cor. 15).

Second, the permeability of the body and its dependence on its surrounding environment, including the human and social environment, helps us to understand why the body metaphor in 1 Corinthians 12 is not merely a metaphor. Paul believed that human beings really could be by

---

[43]See ibid., p. 20.
[44]Ibid., p. 22.

faith joined to other human beings in a unity of Spirit that produced a body of believers.[45] The alternative was to be merely a part of the body politic known as the Empire, or of some other body of believers. Being an isolated individual was not really an option unless one wanted to be a totally unnatural deviant, like some traveling Cynic philosophers who did not seek disciples.

The hierarchical arrangement of the individual's body is reflected in the body of Christ, but in this case it is Christ (not the emperor) who is the head, with all believers as valuable parts of the body. No one group or class of ordinary human members (such as males) is singled out to be the head of this body. Rather, all members are under the rule that comes from heaven in the person of Christ, and they are all citizens of a heavenly commonwealth (see Phil 3:20). In other words, while Paul uses the notion of the hierarchical body to talk about a hierarchy in Christian society (and over the universe), he does not, like some, use such thinking to justify a form of male-female hierarchy within the church.[46] While not denying the proper existence of hierarchies in self, society and the universe, he does not use this idea to justify some particular kind of sexual or ecclesial political agenda.[47] All are one in Christ and equal under his lordship. Paul was neither a radical individualist in the modern sense nor a radical egalitarian. He does not fit neatly into any of our usual modern pigeonholes, and we do well to try to avoid clichés in describing the personality of this apostle.

Judging by Appearances

We are used to the modern dictum that form follows function. In antiquity, however, just the opposite was assumed. Function was assumed to follow form, in both the animal and the human world. In other words, it was possible to tell what sort of person someone was by close analysis of their appearance and body characteristics. Sextus Empiricus stresses that "the body is a sort of outline sketch of the soul, as is shown by the science of physiognomics" (see *Outlines of Pyrrhonism* 1.79-91). Humans were being analyzed in a manner similar to animals, in terms of genus and species, the

---

[45]It would also be fruitful to consider the implications of this discussion for a text like Romans 8:18-27. Here Paul considers the future fate of the created order as intertwined with the fate of believers. Specifically he links renewal of the earth to the resurrection of believers. This is in part because Paul believed that the world as macrocosm and the human as microcosm were always interrelated and interactive.

[46]This statement will be developed in greater detail further on in this book.

[47]Here I would disagree with Dale B. Martin's major thesis.

latter being the general type involving characteristics shared by the whole group, and species involving subcategories under the genus heading, used to explain differences. Though the idea that humans are a kind of animal is familiar to us today, we need to understand that the ancients, at least as early as Aristotle (who described human beings as "rational animals"), drew from this concept a variety of different conclusions from those we might draw.[48] Nature rather than nurture was assumed to determine personality.

For example, Pseudo-Aristotle says in his treatise devoted to physiognomics that "these are the marks of the little-minded man. He is small limbed, small and round, dry with small eyes and a small face, like a Corinthian or a Leucadian" (*Physiognomics* 808a.30-33). This same author paints the brave man as having

> stiff hair, an erect carriage of body, bones, sides, and extremities of the body strong and large, broad and flat stomach; shoulder-blades broad and far apart . . . a strong neck but not very fleshy, a chest fleshy and broad, thick, flat calves of legs broad below; a bright eye, neither too wide open nor half closed; the skin on the body is inclined to be dry; the forehead is sharp, straight, not large, and lean, neither very smooth nor very wrinkled. (807a.31—807b.4)

I do not think it is an accident that in this sort of body-conscious and judging-by-appearances climate Paul says little or nothing about his appearance, except by way of apology (see Gal 4:12-20, and see what others say about his bodily presence in 2 Cor 10:10). It may also be significant that we have no description of Jesus' appearance in the Gospels either.

Pseudo-Aristotle considered some regions of the body more revealing than others: "The most favorable part for examination is the region around the eyes, forehead, head and face; secondly the region of the chest and shoulders, and lastly that of the legs and feet" (*Physiognomics* 814b.2-8). Cicero similarly remarked, "The eyes declare with exceeding clearness the innermost feelings of the heart, but also that which is called the countenance, which can be found in no living creature save humans, reveals the character [*mores*]" (*De Legibus* 1.26-27). Eyes were especially revealing of character; they were the windows of the soul. Aristotle says, "Shame resides in the eyes" (*Problems* 31.957b).

In view of this, texts like Galatians 4:12-20 must be reconsidered. If indeed Paul was suffering from an obvious and repulsive eye condition, this would immediately precondition his audience to see him as unreli-

---

[48]See Malina and Neyrey, *Portraits of Paul*, pp. 101-17.

able, perhaps cursed by God. After all, what was one to make of someone who claimed he had seen Jesus but had bad eyes, who claimed to be a healer but himself had an ongoing "thorn in the flesh"? Ancients were at least as likely to judge a book by its cover as moderns. Yet graciously and surprisingly the Galatians had received Paul as if he were an angel or even Christ himself.[49]

The study of physiognomics was not done in isolation from the assumptions about geography, generation and gender that I have already discussed; rather it was done in tandem with those assumptions. Thus discerning "personality" types was not just a matter of evaluating a person's body but also of noting the features they shared with the ethnic and geographical group into which they were born. For example, consider the stereotypical remarks of Polemo, who wrote in the first century A.D., "You will scarcely find keen insight and excellence in letters among the Egyptians; on the other hand keen insight is widespread among the Macedonians; and you will find among Phoenicians and Cilicians the pursuit of peace and pleasure; and finally you will be offended by Scythians, a treacherous and devious people" (*Physiognomics* 31.236). Xenophon draws on similar considerations to explain that tasks should be divided based on gender: "For God made the man's body and mind more capable of enduring cold and heat, and journeys and campaigns; and therefore imposed on him the outdoor tasks. To woman, since God has made her body less capable of such endurance, I take it that God has assigned the indoor tasks" (*Oeconomicus* 7.22-23, 29-30). This is not different from Philo's Jewish perspective that men should rule and inhabit the public and outdoor sphere (including all political or military activities) while women are by body and nature best be suited for and so should inhabit and order the indoor sphere (*Specialibus Legibus* 3.169).

Obviously, point of view was critical. No doubt the Scythians did not evaluate themselves as they were evaluated by various Greeks and Romans; no doubt many women did not evaluate themselves the way many men evaluated them. A good deal of physiognomics involved what can be called ethnocentrism, the assumption that one's own race or gender or locale defined the essence of what was desirable and normal.[50] Since

---

[49]The possible connection of this information in Galatians 4 with the story found in Acts 14:8-18 should not be lightly dismissed. Perhaps the Galatians, knowing their own cultural myth, were discounting the usual physiognomic rules lest they miss out on a blessing from the divine a second time around. See the discussion of the Acts 14 text and its drawing upon the story found in Ovid *Metamorphosis* 8.26-28 in Witherington, *Acts*, pp. 418-28.

[50]See Malina and Neyrey, *Portraits of Paul*, pp. 120-24.

ethnic groups had rather fixed locales in antiquity, ethnocentrism also involved a certain geocentrism, with one's own locale being the center of the universe, the vantage point from which to judge all other peoples and ethnic groups. Generally a strong sense of in-group belonging nurtured the belief that one's appearance, determined by generation, gender and geography, necessarily expressed and revealed one's character.

One was either a classic example of one's type or an exception to the prevailing rule, as could be deduced in part by how one looked. A male Roman without an aquiline or Roman nose might well have an uphill struggle in attempts to establish his public honor and advance up the *cursus honorum,* the social and political pecking order of Roman society. He might be seen as a "new man" rather than part of an "old" family and so of questionable parentage.

Analyzing Paul's Appearance

Let us return to the description of Paul from the apocryphal *Acts of Paul.* Even if this description of his appearance is not accurate, the exercise can serve as a helpful reminder of how ancients thought about matters of body and character. *The Acts of Paul* appears to have been written late in the second century A.D. by a presbyter in Asia Minor.[51] Tertullian says the author lost his ecclesial office for writing this document, apparently because it propagated a false view of Paul and the role of women in the church.[52]

Paul is described as a man of small stature, with a bald head and crooked legs, eyebrows meeting and a somewhat hooked nose, full of friendliness and having the appearance now of a human and now of an angel (*Acts of Paul* 3.2). This entire description may be an example of physiognomics in reverse. That is, this may be an attempt to draw a portrait of Paul based on character traits revealed in the extant Pauline letters. For example, Paul's name as we find it throughout his letters, Paulos, may well have suggested the comment about his small stature, since Paulos, or in Latin Paulus, can mean little or short. We do not know whether Paulos was a Roman name that Saul had always had as a Roman citizen[53] or whether it was a nickname he adopted once he became a missionary to Gentiles (see Acts 13—14). If it is the latter, the name might indeed provide a signal about his height.

Notice how carefully the author avoids saying anything about Paul's

---

[51]See F. F. Bruce, *Paul: Apostle of the Heart Set Free* (Grand Rapids, Mich.: Eerdmans, 1977), pp. 467-69, for an assessment of this tradition.
[52]See the discussion in E. Schneemelcher, *New Testament Apocrypha,* trans. R. M. Wilson (Louisville, Ky.: Westminster John Knox, 1992), 2:1214-16.
[53]Paul's name will be discussed in greater detail later in the book.

eyes, which is not surprising if Galatians 4 is telling us he had an eye disease. The author would want to convey Paul's positive character by dwelling on other aspects of his appearance if the eyes were a liability, especially in view of how they were seen as a window on the soul. It does appear that the author is familiar with the material in Galatians 4:12-20, given the way he ends his description by saying Paul had the face of an angel (Paul said the Galatians received him as an angel). It may also reflect knowledge of Galatians 1:8, where Paul compares his task of proclaiming to that of an angel from heaven.

As for the description of the nose, it must be remembered that a prominent and sometime hooked nose was considered a good Roman feature. Those in the Greco-Roman world who knew about Roman physiognomics would have been well aware of this fact. Consider Suetonius's description of Emperor Augustus (and compare it to what is said above about Paul): "He had clear bright eyes. . . . His eyebrows met. His ears were of moderate size, and his nose projected a little at the top and then bent slightly inward. His complexion was between dark and fair. He was short of stature . . . but this was concealed by the fine proportion and symmetry of his figure" (*Lives of the Caesars* 2.79.1-2). From this laudatory description of Augustus we can gather that our Christian author's description is meant to be complimentary, not derogatory, of the apostle Paul. Meeting eyebrows were considered a mark of beauty (Philostratus *Heroicus* 33.39), hooked noses a sign of nobility or royalty or perhaps magnanimity (cf. Plato *Republic* 5.474D; Pseudo-Aristotle *Physiognomics* 811a.36-38). As Abraham Malherbe has rightly stressed, the description of Paul is not unflattering; it can be properly compared with the description of the great Greco-Roman hero figure Heracles (Hercules) as short, dark and having a hooked nose (Clement of Alexandria *Protrepticus* 2; Plutarch *Antonius* 4.1).[54]

What then of the bald head and crooked legs but good state of body? Malina and Neyrey suggest in mentioning baldness the author is thinking of what is said about Paul in Acts 18:18 and 21:24, that he shaved his head to fulfill a religious vow.[55] This conclusion makes very good sense in view of the ascetical tone of *The Acts of Paul*.[56] As for the crooked legs yet good

---

[54]See Abraham Malherbe, "A Physical Description of Paul," *Harvard Theological Review* 79 (1986): 170-75.

[55]Malina and Neyrey, *Portraits of Paul*, p. 130.

[56]It is however true that baldness was seen as a liability for orators so far as one's ethos was concerned. If the author here means to depict baldness rather than a shaved head, perhaps he wishes to give some credibility to the description in 2 Corinthians 10:10 while yet saying that Paul was nonetheless a friendly and kind person, of angelic countenance despite some aspects of his appearance.

state of body, Philostratus describes a Celtic warrior as an admirable figure whose "legs were slightly bowed outward, which made it easy for him to stand firmly planted" (*Lives of the Sophists* 552). The point of this description, then, is to indicate a person who was stable, firm of foot, strong and therefore firm in conviction and values.

A person less well disposed toward Paul might well have read the physical signs of his body differently, especially concentrating on his eyes. Consider what Pseudo-Aristotle says about the low-spirited man: "His face is wrinkled, his eyes are dry and weak, but at the same time weakness of eye signifies two things, softness and effeminacy on the one hand, depression and lack of spirit on the other. He is stooping in figure and feeble in movements" (*Physiognomics* 808a.9-13).

This analysis of the description in the *Acts of Paul* serves to remind us that ancients evaluated appearance rather differently from the way we do today, and they drew different conclusions about personality from the signals a body was thought to reveal. Those who lived in the Greco-Roman world of Paul's day had certain key values, such as honor and shame, and since appearance was a public matter, as was honor, some appearances were definitely thought to be honorable and some thought to be shameful. Our author has sought to portray Paul as a good and honorable man. But what was honor in antiquity, and what does it mean to speak of Paul's world as an honor and shame culture? To this fundamental value of the ancient Mediterranean world we now turn.

THE HONOR CODE

Many modern Westerners find it hard to grasp why not only ancients but also many Near and Far Eastern persons today value "face" more highly than even life itself.[57] Why was public honor such an issue? What is it that conveyed shame in such a world, and why was it a matter to keep hidden? What does this tell us about how ancients viewed persons and personality?

First, we must remember that the world in which Paul lived was indeed a male-dominated world. Honor was bound up with male ideology and seen as in essence a value for males to uphold.[58] It was by and large only

---

[57] A useful place to start learning about first-century values is to read selectively in J. J. Pilch and Bruce Malina, eds., *Biblical Social Values and Their Meaning* (Peabody, Mass.: Hendrickson, 1993).

[58] Honor and public office in the first century is discussed more fully in another form in Ben Witherington III, *Conflict and Community in Corinth* (Grand Rapids, Mich.: Eerdmans, 1994), pp. 154-55.

males who could aspire to public offices (with the exception of some women priestesses) or be lawyers, rhetoricians, masters of the games or leaders of armies (royal women such as Cleopatra were clearly anomalies). Honor was fundamentally bound up with the public order and involved establishing one's public reputation by public deeds or "liturgies," acts of public service. So honor was closely linked to wealth and power and also to authority. The reward for honorable behavior—behavior that upheld the status quo—was public acclaim, which took the form of inscriptions on public columns, proclamations, celebrations or even a "triumph" (celebratory parade) if one was a conquering Roman hero.

In such a culture where the collectivist mentality was strong, people did not live to "do their own thing" and "be their own persons." They lived for the acclaim of others, which showed that they were important persons of honor and note. Humility in the Greco-Roman world was not really seen as a virtue or an honorable thing, especially in a man. Indeed, the very term we translate "to humble" in the New Testament would normally mean to have the mind of a slave or to act in slavelike fashion.

What a society gives honor or homage to tells us a great deal about that society's major values. And if a culture loses its sense of shame, it also loses its sense of honor, for these two concepts work in tandem. In Paul's world the quest for honor and praise was one of the most important forces binding society together and preserving the male-dominated status quo.[59] Note, however, that though the Greco-Roman world was a world of self-promoters seeking public recognition and honor, this was not because they wanted to stand out from the crowd but because above all else they wanted to be recognized by and so *be* one of the crowd, in particular the elite of society.

It was more than a little difficult to shame a person of high social status or considerable power or wealth. Shaming was normally what superiors did to inferiors to put them or keep them in their place. Though it may seem strange to us, because honor had such a public and also a male face, it had little to do with what a person did in private. In particular it had little to do with what men did with their private parts apart from conjugal relations with their spouse. In the Greco-Roman culture, extramarital male sexual involvements, particularly if they involved a prostitute or "companion," were not deemed shameful at all.

In some ways a similar view of public honor is manifested today among

---

[59]See the discussion in H. Moxnes, "Honor, Shame and the Outside World in Paul's Letter to the Romans," in *The Social World of Formative Christianity and Judaism*, ed. J. Neusner (Philadelphia: Fortress, 1988), pp. 207-18.

some notable public officials. They assume there is a double standard by which they may live: as long as they follow certain kinds of honor codes in public, they should not be troubled about their private business or sexual activities, which should involve an entirely different standard of evaluation and honor/shame ratings. Whatever may be said about this view, it is clearly not in accord with Judeo-Christian views about honor and shame.

A clear example of how different Paul's approach to honor and shame was from that of many of the pagans he evangelized can be seen in 1 Corinthians 5—7. Here Paul is concerned to restrict male privileges and activities in sexual relationships and to make clear that he and his master Jesus regard as shameful acts what pagans saw as perfectly acceptable. Paul, in other words, was setting out to redefine the zones of honor and shame in his culture, based on mores he learned in Judaism and from other early Jewish Christians. Paul was no baptizer of the status quo in these matters.[60]

If honor was primarily a male matter in antiquity, shame was primarily a female matter, or better said a matter for the so-called inferior members of society: women, children and slaves. Wives were supposed to uphold the honor of their husbands, in part by not causing any shame to the family (for example, by not having an extramarital affair or committing some other unfaithful act). Successfully avoiding shame led to public recognition of wives on grave inscriptions, where they are praised for having been a *univira*—married to one man and faithful to him throughout their life together.[61]

While we would see all of this as involving a double standard, one for men, one for women, in the highly stratified patriarchal world in which Paul lived it was believed that there were clearly defined roles for different members of society, roles in part determined by gender, and so there were different honor and shame codes. The idea of a double standard implies that all persons are the same and should all be measured in the same way. Most ancients did not believe all persons were created equal or were essentially the same. Indeed, most ancients believed that gender, geography and generation predetermined where one was in the pecking order of society and what codes of honor and shame should apply. In comparison to this, Galatians 3:28 and Paul's application of basic sexual mores to both male and female would have been seen as a radical teaching, redefining honor and shame codes and the ontological and social assumptions on which they were based.

---

[60]See chapter seven of this book for a discussion of Pauline ethics.

[61]W. Ziesel, "*Univira*: An Example of Continuity and Change in Roman Society," *Church History* 46 (1977): 19-32.

Though Malina and Neyrey have done a good job in indicating the general and differing effects of the honor and shame codes on women and men, it must be noted that during the Empire there was a trend of women rising in status and gaining more public face, for example by being patrons of important clubs or society. Roman law had changed and allowed women to have their own money and so obtain considerable wealth through their own business ventures. Wealth was the key to power, and power was obtained by patronage of others (the dispensing of funds, food and favors with strings attached).

Competition for Honor

Paul lived in an *agonistic* culture, in which every social interaction that took place outside one's family or circle of friends was perceived as a honor challenge. An honor challenge is an occasion to accrue honor from one's social equals or superiors by performing some deed or service. Gift-giving, invitations to dinner, buying and selling, and arranging marriages were all seen as means by which one could gain higher honor ratings for one's family. To invite someone to dinner was seen as an honor challenge, which unless one wished to be shamed had to be responded to in kind, or if one wanted to gain greater honor, with a superior invitation and dinner.[62] In fact not just athletic games but almost every public activity turned out to be some kind of competition for honor and praise.

Honor was in a limited supply, so the competition for it was stiff. Every honor challenge involved winners and losers. The term *agonistic* highlights the struggle aspect of this social system and the fact that there could be only one winner in any particular struggle. The loser's enmity toward the winner was an inevitable result, and a serious loss might set in motion a whole series of enmity conventions (slapping, spitting, defaming and the like).

In an honor and shame culture, caught up in honor challenges, reciprocity was the name of the game. It was a "you scratch my back and I'll scratch yours" world. An actual gift (given with no thought of return) was a rarity, and the concept of grace, or an undeserved benefit that came without strings attached, was virtually unknown. Everyone was seeking not merely to get what was coming to them but to rise in status and gain a larger share of the limited good known as honor. But in a highly stratified world where power and wealth were largely in the hands of the few, gaining honor and advancing up the ladder of society required help. There was no open or

---

[62]See Malina, *New Testament World*, pp. 32-40.

free-market approach to gaining status or honor. One needed *patronage*—a social arrangement that dominated relationships and shaped personality in Paul's world.

The Expense of Recompense

A wide variety of social relationships in antiquity required reciprocity—some between social equals and others between persons of differing social status.[63] Patronage was a relationship between a superior and an inferior. We should not be misled by the euphemisms about "friends" and "friendship" used to describe such relationships. Most involved a transferral of goods, services and funds from a social superior to a social inferior in exchange for honor, praise, loyalty, votes, influence and favors.[64]

There were three very good reasons why a person striving for greater honor might need patronage. First, the business and social world did not at all involve a level playing field or a free-market economy. In this highly stratified world, the privileged few had enormous advantages over the many in business and other public arenas. Only in athletics, entertainment or the military was a talented person more likely to rise to the top than others. Second, banks in antiquity were basically treasuries or storage vaults. Generally they did not loan money. If one needed business capital one had to find a willing patron. Third, there was not an adequate social safety net in the Greco-Roman world. Patronage was often necessary to simple survival.

How would a patronage relationship be established? Generally it was initiated by the party who needed something. He or she might give a gift to a wealthy person known to be a patron or do him a favor as a means of setting up the reciprocity cycle. Or a patron might do a favor to set up a new client relationship. Accepting a gift or favor placed the recipient in the inferior position in the relationship. If the initial recipient was not wealthy, what might be expected in return would be expressions of gratitude, praise, honor, votes and the like. These relationships were usually informal and outside the stipulations of normal law, and sometimes they involved illegal actions. In theory, a patronage relationship might appear to be voluntarily entered into, but social inferiors usually had no choice if they wished to survive economically and socially.[65]

---

[63]See Witherington, *Conflict and Community in Corinth,* pp. 414-20.

[64]On patronage and its relation to Paul see J. K. Chow, *Patronage and Power: A Study of Social Networks in Corinth* (Sheffield: JSOT, 1992).

[65]See J. H. Elliott, "Patronage and Clientism in Early Christian Society," *Forum* 3 (1987): 39-48.

It cannot be stressed too much that Paul did not live in a democratic world. Indeed as the Empire and its ideology grew during the first century, hopes of a return to the earlier Greek state of democracy or of even the reestablishment of the Roman Republic became increasingly remote. Society was becoming more autocratic, not less. More and more hierarchical structures were being established to encompass more and more aspects of Mediterranean culture—including religious life, with the spread of the emperor cult.[66] Patronage, then, was becoming more prevalent and necessary in this sort of world, as the elite accrued power and wealth at the expense of others. Benefits and gifts bound this world together and served the social end of maintaining the status quo or improving the position of the privileged. Patronage, in other words, was a prophylactic against theft or revolt.

People did sometimes refuse gifts or favors. For a social superior to do so was more common than the other way around, not least because in an agonistic honor and shame culture to refuse a gift was to shame the giver. Such a refusal might set up a cycle of negative reciprocity involving enmity conventions.[67] Enmity might lead to a train of verbal abuse, charges of immorality, slurs on one's social background, accusations of greed or shady dealings, and even physical attacks. Hades had no fury like a client or a "friend" scorned.[68] It should be clear from what has just been said that patronage was not just a matter of economic and social power but also involved honor and shame.

If we ask how Paul fit into this social situation, two things may be noted in response. Just as he was busy redefining the zones of honor and shame, so also he was busy redefining, but not abandoning, notions of patrons and clients. Paul in general sought to avoid patronage because of the entangling ongoing alliances it entailed. He needed to remain mobile to fulfill his missionary calling free of obligation to local patrons (see 1 Cor 9). He did on occasion portray himself as his convert's patron in spiritual matters (a "father" or even "mother" figure for his converts—see 1 Cor 4:14; Gal 4:19), but more usually Christ is seen as the master or patron to whom one must turn (see 1 Cor 3:21-23). Paul's theological and christological vision led him to reconfigure his vision of how human society, and in particular social networks in the church, ought to work. There was still shame and there was

---

[66]See R. P. Saller, *Personal Patronage Under the Empire* (Cambridge: Cambridge University Press, 1982).

[67]See P. Marshall, *Enmity in Corinth: Social Conventions in Paul's Relations with the Corinthians* (Tübingen: Mohr, 1987).

[68]See Witherington, *Conflict and Community in Corinth*, pp. 414-19.

still honor, but they had significant new meanings in Paul's thought world. There was still hierarchy, still patrons and clients, but these too were redefined. Human beings were still defined in and by their relationships, but now one particular relationship was the prime definer—one's relationship with Christ—and secondary to this was one's relationship with Christ's body.

CONCLUSIONS

This chapter has drawn from recent gains in Pauline studies based on sociological and cultural anthropology studies of the ancient world. These studies help provide a solid social context or matrix for understanding various Pauline remarks. This material can serve as a hedge against anachronism. In particular it serves as a caution against pursuing a quest for the historical Paul on the basis of Western and post-Enlightenment assumptions about individuals and human personality.

Yet understanding the social context of Paul's life is not a substitute for examining the direct evidence about that life itself. Sociological and cultural anthropology studies necessarily depend on broad generalizations about a culture and its character. There is a high level of abstraction in such studies, and inevitably some generalizations will not apply to a particular individual within a cultural group. While such studies help us see Paul as part of the social networks of his day, they do not adequately show how Paul acted as a change agent, a deviant, a person swimming against the current of culture.

This chapter, then, sets the stage for our discussion of Paul as a Jew, a Roman citizen and a Christian. While some stress has been placed on the difference between Paul's world and our own, various similarities have been noted as well. What is of prime importance for this study is that human persons and personality were viewed differently in antiquity from the way they are today, and great care must be taken to avoid anachronism in analyzing an ancient person like Paul.

While Paul was certainly a real historical individual, it would appear he was not an individualist in the modern sense of the term. In the main he reflects the sort of dyadic personality that predominated in the collectivist culture in which he lived. For him, as for others, the group one belonged to provided one's sense of identity. While Paul would have been viewed by many of his Jewish and Greco-Roman contemporaries as a deviant, this was not because he was a modern Western individual but because he wished to redefine the most essential community from which one derived identity. The family of faith, not the physical family, the body of Christ, not the body politic of the Roman Empire, was seen as the context in which true human identity should be understood.

Paul lived in a highly patriarchal and androcentric world where gender, generation and geography were usually the primary identity and status markers, with wealth, religious affiliation and other factors being secondary markers. Paul worked within this world but sought to reconfigure its visions of family and family values, its notions of honor and shame, patronage and reciprocity, male and female. Galatians 3:28, as we shall see, gives us an essential clue as to how he saw human society being reconfigured in Christ.

Paul also lived in a world where people judged others on the basis of appearance or appearances and viewed the human body as a microcosm of the world or universe itself. Body and soul/spirit, person and world were all part of one overarching nexus of reality; they interacted with each other and were not radically distinguished from one another. Paul, while placing no emphasis on his own appearance, was aware that others would and did do so, and so some of his rhetoric aimed to compensate for his weak physical presence. Yet he did agree that the body was essential to human personality. His vision of the permanent state of affairs when the kingdom comes involved embodied existence. These factors must be kept squarely in view as we begin to look at Paul's primary identity markers—his Jewishness, his Roman citizenship, his Christianity.

CHAPTER 2

THE TRINITY
OF PAUL'S
IDENTITY

Paul was a complex person whose identity included at least three major components—he was a Jew, he was a Roman citizen, and he was a Christian. He did not cease to be a Jew when he became a follower of Jesus. Indeed, he believed Jesus was the Jewish Messiah, and so after the Damascus Road encounter he saw himself as a messianic Jew. Yet he viewed his Jewish heritage very differently as a result of his conversion. In all likelihood his fellow Pharisees no longer saw him as a practicing Jew. Paul himself says he was prepared to place his notable Jewish credentials in the loss column in order to gain Christ. Interestingly, in the recent scholarly discussion of Paul it is the Jewish scholars who have stressed the radical nature of his break with various of early Judaism's major tenets, while various Christians have stressed the continuity between Paul and early Judaism.

Zeal is a key clue to understanding Paul's personality both before and after he became a follower of Christ. This in part explains the strong reactions to Paul, both positive and negative, all his life. Paul was not an early advocate of "moderation in all things," particularly when the subject was religious matters. Most moderns would view him as a religious fanatic and something of a braggart, though his boasting after his conversion was always about what God had and was doing in and through him. Philippians 3 suggests that Paul, neither while a Pharisee nor later as a Christian, evaluated himself as being in the position of the person described in Romans 7:14-25.

Perhaps nowhere was the radical break with the past clearer than in the way Paul dealt with the Mosaic law as law. In his view, he and the followers of Christ, while still instructed by the Hebrew Scriptures, were no longer under the law covenant but rather now under the law of Christ—a very different matter. While the Mosaic law was obsolescent, having fulfilled its purposes as law once Christ came, there were still commandments to be obeyed in the new covenant.

Paul was also a Roman citizen, and this social status opened various doors for him

throughout the Roman Empire, including some jail doors. It allowed him to fraternize with
and convert not only the down and out but also the up and in. Paul often had to step down
socially for the sake of reaching all kinds of persons for Christ. As a Roman citizen Paul had
a preferential position in relationship to Roman law and justice; he was more likely to have
access to privilege and protection while traveling Roman roads, if he wished to call upon it.
Yet Paul was apparently reluctant to speak about this matter; nowhere in his letters does he
refer directly to his citizenship. Perhaps in a status-conscious world he did not want the
reception of his gospel to stand or fall on the basis of his social status.

It is right to emphasis how much hinges on Paul's Damascus Road experience, including
not only his sense of being called to be an apostle to the Gentiles but also various other aspects
of his message, including his theology of grace and his changed view of the law. It is wrong
to place all the emphasis on Paul's conversion, however, as the Christian life he lived after
Damascus Road was full of the Spirit and spiritual gifts, full of growth in Christ and strain-
ing forward toward the goal of full conformity to Christ's image. Paul was both a zealous,
spirited man and a man of the Spirit, yet this did not exempt him from considerable suffer-
ing, humiliation, failure and disappointment. Like all other Christians, he lived between the
times, feeling the tension between "already" and "not yet" (inwardly being renewed,
outwardly wasting away), living on the basis of faith, hope and love, seeking to manifest the
fruit of the Spirit and model the character of Christ.

PAUL ON ANY SHOWING WAS A COMPLEX PERSON. NO ONE CAN READ HIS LETTERS
without coming away with the impression that this is a human being of
considerable depth and scope. Our task in this chapter is to explore three of
the major facets of who Paul was—a Jew, a Roman citizen, a Christian.[1]

PAUL THE JEW

Perhaps the one thing all commentators agree on about Paul is that he was
a Jew. What sort of Jew he was is of course another question, one that has
been heavily debated not only among Christians but also by Jews.[2] During
the twentieth century the pendulum swung back and forth between
viewing Paul as a Hellenized Diaspora Jew and viewing him as a rather
traditional ("Palestinian") Pharisaic Jew. There are of course opinions

---

[1]For a useful brief character sketch of Paul which stresses his friendships and social networks
as a reflection of his character see F. F. Bruce, *Paul: Apostle of the Heart Set Free* (Grand Rapids,
Mich.: Eerdmans, 1977), pp. 456-63.

[2]See for the Jewish discussion J. Klausner, *From Jesus to Paul* (London: Allen & Unwin, 1943);
C. G. Montefiore, *Judaism and St. Paul* (London: M. Goshen, 1914); H. J. Schoeps, *Paul: The
Theology of the Apostle in the Light of Jewish Religious History* (Philadelphia: Westminster Press,
1961); Alan F. Segal, *Paul the Convert* (New Haven, Conn.: Yale University Press, 1990); and
now Daniel Boyarin, *A Radical Jew: Paul and the Politics of Identity* (Berkeley: University of
California Press, 1994).

ranging between these extremes. Part of the issue under debate is how much change actually occurred in Paul's life when he became a follower of Jesus. Was he simply a messianic Jew, a Jew who believed his Messiah had come? Was he a Jewish Christian, with more emphasis placed on the discontinuity than on the continuity with the past?

The discussion of Paul as a Jew has been a touchy subject in scholarly circles in the last few decades. Perhaps one reason is that in the post-Holocaust age human consciousness has been raised about attempts to exterminate Jews and Jewishness. Possibly by way of compensation, New Testament scholars have stressed the Jewishness of the two central figures of Christianity—Jesus and Paul. It is surely not an accident that a good deal of the voluminous literature emphasizing the Jewishness of Jesus and Paul and the character of their Jewish environment has come from Germany. And almost without exception the real landmark works, whether we think of W. D. Davies's *Paul and Rabbinic Judaism* or Martin Hengel's epoch-making two-volume work *Judaism and Hellenism* or E. P. Sanders's *Paul and Palestinian Judaism,* have been written by persons of Protestant Christian background who have been greatly exercised about Christian stereotypes about Jews and early Judaism.

What is relatively new in the quest for the historical Paul is the degree to which Jewish scholars have entered into the discussion at various levels. For instance, Jacob Neusner's numerous works on early Judaism and Pharisaism have made it quite impossible to think of one monolithic entity "early Judaism"; rather, we must think of many Judaisms, or forms of Judaism, and it becomes difficult to say what might count as messianic views that are beyond the pale of early Judaism.[3] In an earlier era a few Jewish scholars such as Samuel Sandmel made attempts to reclaim "brother Paul" as a Jew, but now we have a Jewish scholar, Alan F. Segal, frankly stating that Paul was indeed a convert to a form of religion that in various crucial regards was not just another form of early Judaism but rather an apostasy from it. And what are we to make of the work of Jewish scholar Daniel Boyarin, who wishes to say that Paul is a radical critic of early Judaism, a radical Jew, but nonetheless a Jew, yet he is seen as

> the fountainhead . . . of western universalism. In his authentic passion to find a place for the gentiles in the Torah's scheme of things and the brilliance of the radically dualist and allegorical hermeneutic he developed to accomplish this purpose, Paul had (almost against his will) sown the seeds for a Christian

---

[3]On this subject especially see Jacob Neusner, ed., *The Social World of Formative Christianity and Judaism* (Philadelphia: Fortress, 1988).

discourse that would completely deprive Jewish ethnic, cultural specificity of any positive value and indeed turn it into a "curse" in the eyes of gentile Christians.[4]

Oddly enough, then, a number of Jewish scholars want to emphasize the radicality of Paul's critique of Judaism, while some of the Protestant scholars want to stress his continuity with early Judaism.[5]

Obviously the real flashpoint of all such discussions is Paul's view of the law, and here I believe that on the whole Segal and Boyarin have the better of the argument, for it is difficult to successfully avoid the conclusion that in Galatians and elsewhere Paul is arguing for the obsolescence of the Mosaic covenant and the law contained in it, or at least the end of the boundary-defining aspects of the law and covenant, the aspects that separated Jews from other ancient religious people.[6] In Paul's eyes, the law of Moses is no longer a *normative* regulator or boundary definer for the lives of Christians, including Jewish Christians like himself. Boyarin is right that if we judge Paul by what he says about the proper way of living religiously (orthopraxy), he does indeed sound like a radical critic of Judaism, advocating a new, more universal approach to religious life.

The quest for Paul the Jew, however, must begin with Paul's own statements about his identity, because these statements provide us with direct evidence from the person who is the subject of our exploration.[7] Paul's Jewish heritage cannot simply be ignored or dismissed as a key to understanding his identity. Here is a person who, long after his "conversion," still reckons time by the dates of the major Jewish festivals (1 Cor 16:8) and when pressed is quite ready and able to offer a mock boast about his honor rating as a Jew (2 Cor 11:22; Phil 3:4-6). Significantly, in 2 Corinthians 11:22 Paul does not say "so *was* I" about being a Hebrew, an Israelite and a descendant of Abraham, but rather "so *am* I." In short, he still claims his

---

[4]Boyarin, *A Radical Jew*, p. 229.

[5]Ongoing revelations from Qumran and more generally the burgeoning corpus of early Jewish documents available to scholars have fueled this discussion. We know a good deal more about various forms of early Judaism today than was true even two or three decades ago. George F. Moore's classic work from the early part of this century, *Judaism in the First Centuries of the Christian Era* (Cambridge, Mass.: Harvard University Press, 1927), looks sadly out of date compared to the work of Neusner, Sanders, J. Collins and others who have had the luxury of dealing with a good deal more primary source material and better texts of some of the long-standing sources.

[6]See the discussion in Ben Witherington III, *Grace in Galatia* (Edinburgh: T & T Clark, 1998), pp. 341-56.

[7]In this study I will try to place an adequate emphasis on interpreting the main relevant New Testament texts. It is a mistake to get so bogged down in secondary scholarly literature that we never actually discuss primary material of direct relevance in the quest for the historical Paul.

Jewish heritage. Yet it is clear that he is able to sit lightly with significant aspects of his Jewish heritage, so that while he can identify with or "become as" non-Christian Jews, he can also identify with Gentiles, and so apparently sees himself as neither merely one or the other (1 Cor 9:20-23). Paul's Jewishness is then but one partial yet essential clue for understanding who he was. It follows from this that we must give his Jewish autobiographical remarks very careful scrutiny.

First, it cannot be stressed enough that the Paul we know from the letters talks about his Jewish heritage mainly when provoked. The remarks of Galatians 1:13-14 are found in a polemical context; 2 Corinthians 11:22 is an utterance offered in the middle of a honor challenge (and response) situation;[8] and in Philippians 3:4-6 Paul is attempting to forestall potential honor comparisons by other Jewish Christians (the circumcision party) who may have made much of their Jewish pedigree. The contentious rhetorical situation affects the way the material is discussed in the first two cases and may affect the third example as well.[9]

Galatians 1:13-14

It is my view that Galatians is a polemical deliberative argument meant to prevent Paul's overwhelmingly Gentile converts in Galatia from having themselves circumcised and taking up obedience to the Mosaic law. This letter also seeks to get Paul's audience to follow positive examples and avoid negative ones.[10] Among the negative examples to be avoided is Paul's pre-Christian behavior, summarized in Galatians 1:13-14. Perhaps the most important reason to begin our discussion with this polemical text is that it appears to be a part of the earliest extant letter we have from Paul's hand.[11]

Of supreme importance in this text is the contrast between "formerly" and "now," which involves a contrast between "Judaism" and "the assembly of God."[12] Galatians 1:13-14 is the only example of the use of the term *Ioudaismos* in the New Testament, but we do find it in the Jewish literature of this period (2 Macc 2:21; 8:1; 14:38; 4 Macc 4:26). In each case the term as used by Jews focuses not on geography (were this the focus, the translation "Judeanism" might be apt) but on the religious and social component. Paul is indicating that he was a part of one particular social community pursu-

---

[8]The first-century concept of honor was discussed earlier in this book.

[9]Paul and rhetoric will be discussed later in this book.

[10]See the discussion in Witherington, *Grace in Galatia*, pp. 25-35.

[11]See ibid., pp. 8-13.

[12]See G. Lyons, *Pauline Autobiography: Toward a New Understanding* (Atlanta: Scholars Press, 1985), pp. 150-58.

ing a particular way of life and belief, a way of life that led him to persecute a splinter group that he saw as an aberration from "Judaism." Now,
however, he is in the community and following the way of life of those he
once persecuted. Here Judaism is being contrasted with a life in accord
with the gospel, within the assembly or church of God.

Of course Paul continues to view himself ethnically as a Jew, and so he
can speak of his kin according to the flesh as "my people" (Gal 1:14; 2:15),
but his point is very clearly that he has made a break with that community.
His identity is no longer chiefly formed by it. I would also argue, without
going into a long discourse at this point about Paul's view of the law,[13] that
this apostle no longer sees himself as obligated to observe the Mosaic law,
for the time has come when God's people should go beyond the supervi-
sion of the "pedagogue" known as the Mosaic law and become part of the
new covenant community established through the person and work of
Christ and following the law of Christ (Gal 4 and 6).[14]

In short, Paul's approach to these matters is sectarian, and thus he
differed from various Jewish Christians in Jerusalem who are some of his
dialogue partners mentioned in Galatians 1—2. In Paul's view, Jew and
Gentile united in Christ are the assembly of God. Christians are not merely
in continuity with the assembly of God. This new creation, this new assembly, is distinguishable from Judaism.

The heritage of Israel, however, is by no means being renounced. In Paul's
view, it is being claimed and fulfilled by Jews and Gentiles united in Christ.
The promises of God to Abraham are fulfilled in Christ. The continuity
between the Christian assembly of God and the Old Testament people of God
is theological, not ecclesiological. They both claim the same sacred Scriptures.
In fact, in a later letter Paul goes so far as to say (in Rom 9—11) that non-
Christian Jews have been temporarily broken off from the people of God, with
the hope that they may be regrafted in on the basis of grace and faith in Jesus
Christ. This approach must not be called anti-Semitism, given that Paul was a
Jew and believed that God had not cast off his first chosen people forever, but
it is not inappropriate to call it a radical critique of Judaism.

Paul's statement that Christians know well about his "former" way of life
in Judaism clearly implies that he does not feel it necessary to follow that
way of life any longer. It is understandable that a Jewish scholar like Segal
would conclude that Paul, who he accepts was genuinely converted to
following Christ, had thereby committed apostasy from Judaism. It is also

---

[13]A more lengthy discussion of Paul and the law occurs later in the book.
[14]See the discussion of Paul's view of the law in Witherington, *Grace in Galatia*, pp. 341-55.

one of the significant findings of Segal's work that the two-ways (Gentiles saved through faith in Christ, Jews through the Torah) model of salvation proposed by Krister Stendahl, Lloyd Gaston, John Gager and others as an interpretation of Paul's thought is not warranted by the Pauline evidence itself.[15] Paul's critique of Judaism seems to have been more thoroughgoing than that.

Notice that Paul also is quite willing to say that he had advanced further than most of his peers in Judaism. He uses the term *anastrophen* to describe his former life. This term certainly refers more to orthopraxy than it does to orthodoxy, but then early Judaism was much more of a way of living religiously than a set of doctrines to be believed. (Of course there were certain fundamental convictions about God and the law and about Jews that undergirded such a way of life.)

In Galatians 1:13 Paul stresses that he persecuted the assembly of God severely. At that point he would not have recognized it as the assembly of God. He clearly must have believed the Jewish Christians he persecuted to be beyond the pale, apostate Jews who were heading in the opposite direction from himself as he advanced in Judaism. The key factor linking both Paul's advancement and his persecution was *zeal*, in particular zeal for the law and Jewish traditions.[16] Note that only after the fact, after his conversion, does Paul indicate that he was ashamed of persecuting Christians (1 Cor 15:9; Gal 1:13, 23; Phil 3:6). There is no hint that Paul had an uneasy conscience about persecuting while he did it. At the time he likely saw this activity as clear evidence of his positive zeal for the true faith and way of life, perhaps standing in the line of Elijah as he treated the prophets of Baal, or more proximately the Maccabees.

The Greek in Galatians 1:13 refers to more than just vigorous dialogue or debate. There is little reason to doubt that Paul carried out physical attacks on early Christians, perhaps much like those he later endured himself later (see Gal 6:12; 2 Cor 11:24). It is possible that N. T. Wright is correct that Paul before his conversion was a part of the extreme faction of Pharisaism that sought to follow the examples of Elijah, Phineas and the Maccabees.[17] He may well have been willing to own a motto later attributed to Barry

---

[15]See Segal, *Paul the Convert*, pp. 117-25.

[16]This historical explanation for Paul's persecuting behavior is much to be preferred to the unfortunate psychologizing of the matter by Jerome Murphy-O'Connor (*Paul: A Critical Life* [Oxford: Oxford University Press, 1996], pp. 64-65), who posits that Paul redirected anger against Christians that should have been directed toward God due to the loss of his wife or family, perhaps in an earthquake in Jerusalem. Of this, Acts and Paul's letters say absolutely nothing!

[17]See N. T. Wright, "Paul, Arabia and Elijah," *Journal of Biblical Literature* 115 (1996): 683-92.

Goldwater—"Extremism in pursuit of virtue is no vice."

I would agree with both Wright and T. L. Donaldson[18] that Paul's zeal is a key clue to understanding the man both before and after his conversion. Our modern distaste for violence propagated in the name of God or religion must not put us off from analyzing this factor closely. Paul came to Christian faith in the midst of a career as a persecutor who believed there was a fundamental contradiction between being a Torah-true Jew and being a Jewish follower of the crucified Jew Jesus. Donaldson argues cogently that for Paul the law and belief in salvation through faith in the crucified Jesus were two opposing and contradictory means of defining the boundaries of the people of God. This conviction he held both before and after his conversion; he simply changed sides on this issue. "The incompatibility of Christ and Torah [as the factor defining the nature, limits, and shape of a religious community] was the constant element in the syllogism that on the one side of the conversion led to the persecution of the church, and on the other resulted in fierce resistance to the Judaizers."[19]

Paul refers to his Pharisaic Jewish heritage as something he largely gave up when he became a Christian, or to put it as he does in Philippians, he reckoned it in the loss column in order that he might gain Christ. He did not see this Pharisaic heritage as a bad thing but as something no longer apropos, something obsolete now that Christ had come.

Apart from Paul's stringent adherence to and zeal for the law (perhaps especially for its distinctive practices), his belief in resurrection, his commitment to advancing in a Pharisaic lifestyle, and his commitment to and belief in the Hebrew Scriptures and their prophetic character, it is not at all clear what more we can deduce about his Pharisaic background, because we know little about pre-70 A.D. Pharisaism from other sources.[20] Hengel does argue persuasively that Pharisees were centered or based in Jerusalem and certainly not in the Diaspora. In view of Philippians 3:5, then, we must assume that Paul's formative Jewish years were spent in the Holy Land, and in particular mainly in Jerusalem.[21] This conclusion is

---

[18]See his important essay "Zealot and Convert: The Origin of Paul's Christ-Torah Antithesis," *Catholic Biblical Quarterly* 51 (1989): 655-82.

[19]Ibid., p. 656.

[20]See A. J. Saldarini, *Pharisee, Scribes and Sadducees in Palestinian Society* (Wilmington, Del.: Glazier, 1988).

[21]See Martin Hengel and Anne-Maria Schwemer, *Paul Between Damascus and Antioch* (Louisville, Ky.: Westminster John Knox, 1997), pp. 7-10, against Murphy-O'Connor, *Paul*, pp. 56-60. See D. Daube, "Rabbinic Methods of Interpretation and Hellenistic Rhetoric," *Hebrew Union College Annual* 22 (1949): 239-62, for the influence on Hillel of Alexandrian rhetorical education.

based on what Paul himself says, but it becomes virtually certain when we add the remarks found in Acts 22:3, 23:6 and 26:5, especially if it is true that Paul's father was also a Pharisee. This means that one must not make too much of the connection with Tarsus. Judaism in general was Hellenized in Paul's day, even in Palestine. Paul could well have gotten the rudiments of a good Greco-Roman as well as Jewish education right in Jerusalem.

Paul remained a zealous person after his conversion, but now that zeal was transmuted into a vigorous spreading of the message that earlier he had tried to stop; it was transformed by a commitment to following the nonviolent suffering example of Christ rather than the example of earlier Jewish zealots.[22] Most moderns, even most modern Western Christians, would have been taken aback by Paul. Certainly before his conversion, and probably after it as well, we would see him as a fanatic. We would likely prefer an enthusiastic person winning friends and influencing people through reciprocity and patronage to a fanatic going around trying to convert everyone, even those adamantly opposed to Jesus. We would also likely see Paul as too driven, single-minded and single-purposed—a person without a life apart from his ministerial work. Yet Paul was no anomaly in his day. He stood in a long and proud tradition of Jewish zealots, and he was by no means the only Christian who carried that zeal over from his Jewish to his Christian life.

2 Corinthians 11:22

Here we have in ever-narrowing specificity a description of a particular kind of Jew. "Hebrew" refers to the language and perhaps also the essential ethnic identity of a person. "Israelite" has to do with one's spiritual or religious allegiance. "Seed of Abraham" refers to one's ancestry and genealogical heritage. Note that this description suggests that Paul's primary source of Jewish identity was gained *while he was in Palestine*. He would not claim he was a Hebrew of Hebrews if in fact he had grown up in the Diaspora and did not know the sacred language. Of course it is not impossible that his parents were simply not very Hellenized Jews who lived in Tarsus and taught him the sacred language there, but all other things being equal, it is more likely that Paul is suggesting that he, apparently like the "bogus" apostles, had grown up in the sacred central context

---

[22]If Paul did not see a fundamental antithesis in what was appropriate since Christ had come as opposed to the ethic of the Mosaic covenant, it is hard to understand why after his conversion he did not become like those referred to in Acts 21:20, zealous for the law *and* believers in Christ, or like the Pharisaic Judaizers themselves (see Acts 15:5).

of Judaism—Palestine. They could not gain any rhetorical advantage over him by claiming they were true Palestinian Jews while he was just a Hellenized Diaspora Jew.

Paul's boasting here reminds us that he lived in a culture where such trotting out of one's pedigree or tooting of one's own horn was deemed not only acceptable but advisable. To be sure, Paul is boasting here somewhat tongue in cheek. He says he is playing the fool (2 Cor 11:21). He is boasting in fact to shame his opponents and to put his converts back in their place and in rightful relationship with Paul. In fact Paul is following the proper ancient conventions for what was called inoffensive self-praise; thereby he is mocking false, pompous, exaggerated eloquence and rhetorical self-praise.

Cicero provides the rules for this form of boasting if one wants to persuade and impress one's audience:

> We shall win goodwill for ourselves if we refer to our own acts and services without arrogance, if we weaken the effect of charges that have been brought or of some suspicion of less than honorable dealing that has been cast on us, if we dilate on the misfortunes that have come to us or the difficulties that we still face, and if we use prayers and entreaties with a humble and submissive spirit. (*De Inventione* 1.16.22)

A close examination of 2 Corinthians 10—12 will reveal that Paul is following all of these suggestions in this portion of the letter. Paul used contemporary conventions of boasting in order to persuade his converts to do or be something. Yet he used them in surprising ways, to deflate and defuse the pompous examples and remarks of his opponents while presenting himself as a figure inspiring deep feelings of pathos. In all of this Paul is not being simply an ancient Jew but participating in the Greco-Roman conventions of his age and using them to his advantage. Boasting was still appropriate, but one ought in the main to boast in the work of Christ in one's life, one's assembly and one's world.

Philippians 3:3-10

Here Paul says directly that one ought to boast in Christ, as in 1 Corinthians 1:31, quoting Jeremiah 9:23, he says that one should boast in the Lord. Galatians 6:14 suggests that a Christian should boast only in something that the world would see as shameful—the cross of Christ. This passage is clearly full of intentional irony (like 2 Corinthians 11:22), deliberate inoffensive boasting meant to shame the opposition. Paul first boasts of his Jewish pedigree and then turns around and says he now counts it as refuse or dung, not because it is not a good heritage but because of its small value in comparison to the surpassing worth of having and knowing Christ. Notice that here Paul goes beyond what we saw in 2 Corinthians 11:22. There Paul simply said "so am I," but here he says "I more so," outdoing his potential rivals. This is a typical honor-challenge approach where one tries to put one's self a cut above a rival.[23] If Paul's opponents could boast of circumcision, he could claim he was circumcised on the day required by the Old Testament. He was a Jew among Jews by birth and a Hebrew among Hebrews, speaking the native tongue (see Acts 6:11). Furthermore, as a Benjaminite he was named after the most illustrious member of that tribe—King Saul. The tribe of Benjamin was noted as the one that remained faithful to Judah. And in terms of the sort of righteousness one could gain through obedience to the law, Paul says he was blameless or faultless. This is not to be confused with a claim to being perfect. It means Paul could not have been charged with any violations of the Mosaic law or been accused of wrongdoing by a Jew.

Now of course Paul is saying all of this from the perspective of his Pharisaic past. This is how he would have evaluated himself while a Pharisee. He saw himself as devout and faithful and upright. So we have no basis at all to think that Paul was plagued by guilt feelings or self-doubt while a Jew and that this was what drove him to consider Christ and finally convert.[24] This all too prevalent, all too modern psychological approach to Paul fails to reckon with the clear statements Paul makes in Philippians 3. Paul's conversion involved a revelation and a miracle. There is no evidence of some tortured spiritual turmoil that led to this conversion. "We do not have in this text a portrait of a man at war with himself, crucified between the sky of God's expectation and the earth of his own paltry performance. Paul is not in this scene a poor soul standing with a grade of ninety-nine before a God who counts one hundred as the lowest passing grade."[25] It was Krister Stendahl who perhaps first drew our attention to the fact that we ought not to read Paul as an early example of "the introspective conscience of the West."[26]

---

[23]See chapter one.

[24]We will deal with Romans 7:14-25 in due course. It is sufficient here to say here that in light of Phillipians 3 this text cannot be taken as a description of how Paul felt about himself prior to his conversion.

[25]F. Craddock, *Philippians* (Atlanta: John Knox Press, 1985), p. 59.

[26]Krister Stendahl's enormously influential though now dated essay on this matter can be found in his *Paul Among Jews and Gentiles* (Philadelphia: Fortress, 1976). One wonders if Stendahl, a Scandinavian Lutheran, himself went through such a struggle before he reached his groundbreaking insight.

Stendahl knew that the whole history of that sort of interpretation of Paul went ultimately back to two figures who were enormously influential in church history—Augustine and that latter-day Augustinian Martin Luther. It must be remembered that Augustine did have an tremendous inner struggle on his way to becoming a Christian. No one can read his *Confessions* and not feel the agony and eventual ecstasy. And Luther went through an Augustinian-type gut-wrenching struggle on the way to becoming an exponent of justification by grace through faith. Interestingly, unlike Augustine's, Luther's struggle came after he already believed in Christ as his Lord and Savior, indeed after he was already the most religiously scrupulous and spiritually sensitive of monks. Both Augustine and Luther read Romans 7 and saw themselves in this narrative, and the rest, as they say, is history. The history of the interpretation of this text has never been the same, particularly since Luther. It was natural for these two towering figures to conclude that Paul himself had been their prototype in inner struggle. Yet in fact in Paul's clear and direct autobiographical remarks in his letters and in the indirect remarks in Acts, nothing of the kind is suggested. Perhaps it is time to stop reading Paul through the eyes of Augustine and Luther.

To sum up, we may say the following about these three autobiographical texts: (1) Paul is happy to still claim to be a Jew after his conversion. (2) He did not renounce this heritage as something wicked or worthless when he became a Christian. (3) Indeed he seems somewhat proud of his performance as a Pharisaic Jew in keeping the law, with the exception of his persecuting actions against Christians, for which he did later come to have regret and remorse (cf. 1 Cor 15:9; Gal 1:13, 23; see 1 Tim 1:13). (4) Yet it is clear that something has eclipsed or surpassed the influence and importance of that heritage in his present life, lifestyle and self-evaluation. This new something in fact has so surpassed that heritage that Paul is prepared to regard it as worthless in comparison to the supreme value of knowing Christ and obtaining salvation through him. This helps us to understand our next text.

1 Corinthians 9:19-23

Paul is portraying himself in 1 Corinthians 9:19-23 as a person who accommodates his style of living, eating and dressing—not his theological or ethical principles—in order by various means to win both Jews and Gentiles to Christ.[27] Yet of course this would be the rub for either a Jew or

---

[27]See D. A. Carson, "Pauline Inconsistency: Reflections on 1 Cor 9:1-23," *Churchman* 100 (1986): 6-45.

a true Judaizer, since Judaism involved at its very heart a way of living, eating and dressing religiously. It is important that we be struck by the oddity of hearing a Jew like Paul say he could "become a Jew to the Jew," apparently without any sense of incongruity or reneging on his conviction that Christians are not under any obligation to place themselves under the Mosaic law. Here is the clearest evidence that Paul feels no compulsion to be Jewish in the sense that he did before his conversion. He takes up Jewish orthopraxy as an evangelistic strategy, not out of habit or as a concession to those who think such things essential. And he is quite clear in verse 20 that this should not be interpreted to mean that he himself is still under the Mosaic law. Keeping the Mosaic law in fact could be seen as a matter of adiaphora, something that doesn't ultimately matter or count in the larger salvific scheme, since the new creation has already arrived (Gal 6:15). Again, here Segal's conclusion about Paul is fully warranted from a Jewish point of view. Segal argues that Paul would have indeed been seen as a bad or apostate Jew, if keeping the Mosaic law was considered essential to being a true Jew.

But perhaps there is another way to view Paul's Jewishness. Perhaps we may say that Paul was an apocalyptic and messianic Jew, a Jew who truly believed that the new creation had come because the Messiah had come, and new occasions taught new duties. This new creation had eclipsed the need for the specific form of God's law intended to guard and guide God's people until Messiah should come. Paul is perfectly happy to command obedience to instructions of the Lord's or of his own (see 1 Cor 7),[28] but he would prefer to persuade. He is perfectly happy to speak about the new law of Christ, meant for the new covenant situation, which incorporates the heart of the obsolete Mosaic law, albeit transfigured and transmitted through the example and teaching of Christ. Like a good Pharisee, Paul still believes in a day of reckoning, a future final judgment and final vindication after a final resurrection at least of those in Christ (1 Cor 15). He still believes in the importance of good works and of working out one's salvation with fear and trembling. He still believes the good news that the promises and salvation of God are for the Jew first and also the Gentile (Rom 1:16). He still celebrates a meal that he refers to as involving Passover or a Passover lamb.

Yet Christ has transformed all of this for Paul. Christ is the One who will bring in the day of judgment and provide vindication. He will be the One

---

[28] Against Murphy-O'Connor's *Paul: A Critical Life*, pp. 206-8, who sees Paul as essentially avoiding imperatives on principle.

sitting on the judgment seat (2 Cor 5:10). The future resurrection will not happen until Christ returns. The Lord's Supper focuses on Christ as Passover, not on the exodus/Sinai events. The law that Paul urges is founded on Christ as the norm and the norm-giver, Christ as the example and the lesson and the instructor. If this is Judaism, it is certainly not like the Judaism Paul says he left behind.

Paul and the Law

Obviously the ultimate litmus test and the major indicator of the type or degree of Jewishness of Paul must be his views on the law. I have treated this matter thoroughly elsewhere; here I simply summarize a few of the major pieces of evidence and the conclusions to be drawn from them.[29]

First, Paul sees the Mosaic law as part of Scripture and so God's Word. Indeed, so closely are they identified that he can use the term *nomos* simply to mean Scripture rather than the law in particular (Rom 3:19; 7:1; 1 Cor 14:21). He is even quite happy to cite portions of the so-called ceremonial law to make a point for his Christian converts that he thinks God wants them to understand (1 Cor 9:8-9). There is then no evidence that Paul makes a distinction between the moral and the ritual law as being a viable source of truth to speak to Christians. He uses it all. The more important concern is to explain why he uses it as he does.

Thus, second, Paul views and uses the Hebrew Scriptures, including the law, the way he does because of certain central convictions. (1) His readers are those upon whom the ends of the ages have come, meaning the time of the fulfillment of all Scripture is at hand. (2) His hearers are God's eschatological people for whom the promises of God are yea and amen in Christ. (3) Having received Christ, they have in him the hermeneutical key to understanding God's plan and Word.[30] (4) One must read the Old Testament in light of where God's people now are in the progression of salvation history: they are beyond the era when God's people were living

---

[29]See the excursus in Witherington, *Grace in Galatia*, pp. 341-55. The literature on the subject is quite extensive but some of the more helpful works are J. D. G. Dunn, ed., *Paul and the Mosaic Law* (Tübingen: Mohr, 1996), especially the detailed bibliography, pp. 335-41; Frank Thielman, *Paul and the Law* (Downers Grove, Ill.: InterVarsity Press, 1994); E. P. Sanders, *Paul, the Law and the Jewish People* (Minneapolis: Fortress, 1983); H. Räisänen, *Paul and the Law* (Tübingen: Mohr, 1983); H. Hübner, *Law in Paul's Thought* (Edinburgh: T & T Clark, 1984); J. D. G. Dunn, *Jesus, Paul and the Law* (Louisville, Ky.: Westminster John Knox, 1990); S. Westerholm, *Israel's Law and the Church's Faith: Paul and His Recent Interpreters* (Grand Rapids, Mich.: Eerdmans, 1988).

[30]On this point see Richard B. Hays, *Echoes of Scripture in the Letters of Paul* (New Haven, Conn.: Yale University Press, 1989).

under the Mosaic covenant and were bound to observe the Mosaic law. They are now living in Christ and according to his law.

Obviously, if one doesn't subscribe to Paul's Christology, one is not going to agree with his christological (the law points to and is about Jesus Christ), eschatological (we are now in the age of fulfillment, when old things have passed or are passing away) and even ecclesiological (the law is part of the church's book, the church being Jew and Gentile united in Christ) understanding of the law. Paul's views on the law are complex, bound up with his views on God, salvation, anthropology and human relations.

Much fervor and furor have been expended over the interpretation of Paul's views of the law, and the debate shows no signs of abating.[31] It is safe to say that the old views of Paul's assessment of the law are definitely on the wane in the era after Sanders's landmark *Paul and Palestinian Judaism* and his subsequent volumes. Under the old construction, highly influenced by Luther, Paul is either opposing legalism, the inevitable way fallen human beings handle the law, or opposing the works-righteousness that the law inculcates—or both. That is, Paul is opposing a way of using the law or an attitude about salvation and right standing with God as a result of attempting to keep the law. The problem with these views is that they do not take seriously Paul's narrative thought world, and there is also a tendency to misread the sense of Paul's calling of the law a slave guardian, or *paidagōgos*, in Galatians 3:23—4:7.

The failure to recognize the narrative character of Paul's thought and the role the law plays in it, as well as the failure to understand the implications of covenant theology and what Paul means when he speaks of a new covenant and a new creation, is a serious one. Paul asserts repeatedly in Galatians, by a variety of means and metaphors (see especially Gal 4), that the law had an important but *temporary* role to play as covenant law, providing stipulations, strictures, promises and curses, in the ongoing story of God's people. Asking why Paul takes this view of the law pushes us back to two facts. (1) Before and after conversion he saw faithfulness to the law as being at loggerheads with belief in a crucified Messiah, especially one who authorized a law-free mission to Gentiles. (2) His own conversion came about as a matter of pure grace. As a result of this conversion his view of Christ changed, and this necessitated a paradigm shift in his thinking

---

[31]See the interesting collection of essays from a variety of viewpoints in Dunn, *Jesus, Paul, and the Law*. Some of the more influential discussions on the subject are Sanders, *Paul, the Law and the Jewish People*; Räisänen, *Paul and the Law*; Hübner, *Law in Paul's Thought*; and Thielman, *Paul and the Law*.

about the law and its role in the life of God's people. The law, while a good thing, must now be seen as playing a covenantal role only until the maturity of God's people, until they came of age and no longer needed to be confined by a guardian or pedagogue. Just as a child, once coming of age, is no longer obliged to obey a guardian, so God's people are no longer under the constrictions and constraints of the Mosaic law.

What is the problem, in Paul's view, if the Mosaic law is used as the necessary modus vivendi for the Christian life? Unfortunately, the law's effect, though not its original purpose, is to imprison those who are under it in a form of slavery, as if being watched by a slave guardian (Gal 3:23—4:7). Indeed, following the law is to submit oneself not merely to a fading glory but to a ministry that leads to condemnation and death rather than to justification and life (2 Cor 3). Furthermore, since God intended for the law to be a temporary expedient until he sent his Son, to go back and submit to the Mosaic covenant now is not only anachronistic but tantamount to denying the efficacy and benefits of Christ's work on the cross, including the sending of the Spirit.

The law is incapable of giving what Christ and the Spirit can give. The law is not a bad thing, but it cannot empower someone to do the good. Paul is opposed to the *mandatory* observance of the law for either Jewish or Gentile Christians (see Gal 2:11-14 and Paul's reaction to Peter and Barnabas's withdrawal from mixed fellowship). Paul knows that for Jewish Christians to choose to be consistently Torah-true means the Christian community will be divided between clean and unclean, between sinner and holy one, between first- and second-class citizens. This is at odds with the reason Christ came in the first place (see Gal 3:28). If fellowship is defined by the law, then having fellowship requires law observance by all parties. So Paul is convinced that Christ came not to renew existing Jewish or Gentile religion but to get beyond both and form "a more perfect union" between all peoples, classes and genders. This is what Paul calls a new creation.[32]

---

[32]For another form of this argument see Witherington, *Grace in Galatia,* pp. 341-55. On the point of Paul's "universalism," Boyarin, *A Radical Jew,* pp. 136-45, is quite perceptive. What he does not see, however, is that we can't simply contrast Paul's universalism with Judaism's particularism. Paul believes in a form of universalistic particularism, if we may coin an apparent oxymoron. That is, Paul believes that salvation is in principle available for all but only by grace and through faith in Jesus Christ. I fail to see how this position is different in principle from the particularism of arguing that all may be saved or be included among God's people by submitting to the Mosaic law. Even the law has a place for Gentiles, or *goyim,* in the kingdom if they will but keep the law. Thus in the end this debate is not about universalism versus particularism but rather between two forms of particularism that have the potential to include all.

There is a difference in Paul's mind between being under the law covenant and listening to all parts of the Hebrew Scriptures as God's Word. Paul's covenantal theology allows him to affirm that the law tells the truth about human nature, human need, God and the need for relationship between God and humankind. But Paul does *not* believe that God has made only one covenant or contractual agreement, in various administrations or renewed forms, with humankind throughout all of history. Galatians 4:24 makes this quite clear, for there Paul speaks of "covenants" (plural).

When a potentate of the ancient Near East drew up a new covenant (contractual arrangement) with some subordinate kingdom or person, it was normal practice to reuse certain statutes from previous agreements or covenants. The subordinate party then would keep these stipulations not because they were once in the previous treaty or covenant but because they were now in the new one. Thus while Paul is quite capable of saying that Christians are obligated to *fulfill,* or allow to be fulfilled, various of Old Testament commandments, this is not because Christians are still under the Mosaic law. It is because these commandments are also now found in the law of Christ, the new law by which Christians must live.

Paul says that the whole of the (Mosaic) law and its essential requirements are summed up in a single commandment—love neighbor as self—which Christians are still to fulfill (Gal 5:14; cf. Eph 5:33). While clearly Paul is talking about the old Mosaic law, his point is that the essence of that law is found and summed up in the new covenant and should be taken to heart and obeyed *for that reason.* New treaties often summed up and affirmed portions of old ones without thereby binding the person to all the stipulations or codicils of the old treaty. Frank Thielman says that the essential requirements of the Mosaic law are fulfilled in the life of Christians "not because they continue to be obligated to it but because, by the power of the Spirit in their lives, their conduct coincidentally displays the behavior that the Mosaic law prescribes. . . . Paul is claiming that believers have no need of the Mosaic law because by their Spirit-inspired conduct they already fulfill its requirements."[33]

There is also the matter of consciously following the pattern or norm of Christ—both his life and teaching, the latter of which Paul calls the law of Christ. So not only do believers have a subjective power working to conform them to God's ways and the likeness of Christ—the person and presence of the Spirit—but they also have an objective model and standard to which conformity is expected, the law of Christ. The new covenant does

---

[33]Thielman, *Paul and the Law,* p. 140.

include objective imperatives. Paul is no antinomian, and he is not attacking legalism, even in Galatians. Paul's answer to the question "How then should Christians live?" is not either "Submit to and keep the Mosaic law," or even "Adopt Christ's interpretation of the law and then follow it" (as if the law of Christ were the Mosaic law intensified or in a new guise), but rather "Follow and be refashioned by the law of Christ while walking in the Spirit."[34]

A careful evaluation of Paul's view of the law shows that Paul was a sectarian person. He has taken his heritage with him into his new religious community—indeed he has said it belongs particularly or especially to them—but he has modulated that heritage into a different key because of his experience and understanding of Christ.[35] Previously he had looked at all of life through the lens of the law, but now he sees it all through the eyes of Christ.[36] And from this vantage point Paul can only say, as he does so powerfully in 2 Corinthians 3, that the old glory, the old covenant, the old ministry, the old law has had its day, and a new and surpassing glory has arrived and must be embraced.[37] In the end it is perhaps better to call Paul a Jewish Christian than a messianic Jew. The emphasis must be placed on the new thing Paul had become.

PAUL THE ROMAN CITIZEN

At first it might seem an exercise in futility to talk about Paul as a Roman citizen, since nowhere in his letters does he directly mention that he has this status. Nevertheless, there are a variety of good reasons to consider him in this light. First, of course, Acts says at various points that Paul was a Roman citizen. In Acts 16:37 an announcement of this citizenship extricates Paul from a sticky situation. Acts 22:25-28 recounts a similar announcement with similar effect, and here we also learn that he was *born* a Roman citizen. Acts also tells us that Paul appealed to the emperor, going over the head of the local procurator in Judea, something that only a

---

[34]See the fuller discussion in Witherington, *Grace in Galatia*, pp. 341-55 and the critique of other views there, particularly the views of Hübner, Sanders and Dunn.

[35]A sect is an offshoot of or schism from a larger religious group that takes and transforms elements of the parent religion in its own community. There is generally no continuity of community between the parent group and the offshoot. The two have largely if not entirely different members. A cult is a newly founded religious group, not an offshoot from an existing group.

[36]See Ben Witherington III, *Paul's Narrative Thought World* (Louisville, Ky.: Westminster John Knox, 1994).

[37]See the exegesis of this text in Ben Witherington III, *Jesus, Paul and the End of the World* (Downers Grove, Ill.: InterVarsity Press, 1990), pp. 109-12.

Roman citizen could have managed successfully (Acts 25:10-12). Finally, the lenient treatment of Paul recorded in Acts 28:16 strongly suggests that he is a person of considerable status; such respect and courtesy were normally given to Roman citizens. A later church tradition holds that Paul was executed by the Roman authorities not by crucifixion but by behead-ing—the normal procedure for executing a Roman citizen.

Yet some have argued that the Paul of Acts is not in fact the Paul of the letters. J. C. Lentz, after devoting an entire study to Luke's portrait of Paul as a high-status individual and a Roman citizen, concludes, "By the end of Acts, the Paul who has been described is, frankly, too good to be true."[38] C. K. Barrett says that in Acts we have the "legendary" Paul, not quite the Paul of the undisputed Pauline letters and not quite the Paul of the Pastorals but fairly closely related to both.[39]

What can we discern about the social status of Paul from his undisputed letters? First, we are clearly dealing with a person of considerable education and knowledge, and not just of Jewish matters. The writer has some knowl-edge of Greek philosophy (particularly popular Stoicism), and he reflects a considerable grasp of Greco-Roman rhetoric.[40] Furthermore, as E. A. Judge has pointed out, Paul's attitudes about manual labor and patronage (e.g., 1 Cor 9; 2 Cor 11:7) reveal a higher-status person deliberately stepping down the social ladder to identify with his converts and to be all things to all persons in order to win some.[41] Paul in general does not insist on his rights, but this shows that he presupposes that he *has* rights. In fact, nothing in Luke's portrait of Paul as a man of virtue and consequence, a rhetor and a person of social status, fails to comport with the hints we find in Paul's undisputed letters.

In terms of general historical probabilities, we do know of examples of Jews from before the middle of the first century A.D. (after which citizen-ship seems to have become more widespread) who were Roman citizens.[42]

---

[38]J. C. Lentz, *Luke's Portrait of Paul* (Cambridge: Cambridge University Press, 1993), p. 171.

[39]C. K. Barrett, *Paul: An Introduction to His Thought* (Louisville, Ky.: Westminster John Knox, 1994), p. 161.

[40]This latter point will be discussed later in this book. On Paul's knowledge of Greek thought see A. Malherbe, *Paul and the Popular Philosophers* (Minneapolis: Fortress, 1989) and a variety of the essays in D. Balch, Everett Ferguson and Wayne A. Meeks, eds., *Greeks, Romans and Christians* (Minneapolis: Fortress, 1990).

[41]E. A. Judge, "Paul's Boasting in Relation to Contemporary Professional Practice," *Australian Biblical Review* 16 (1968): 37-50, and his "Saint Paul and Classical Society," *Jahrbuch für Antike und Christentum* 15 (1972): 19-36, and "The Social Identity of the First Christians," *Journal of Religious History* 11 (1980): 201-17.

[42]See G. H. R. Horsley, *New Documents Illustrating Early Christianity*, vol. 4 (North Ride, N.S.W.: Ancient History Document Research Centre, 1979), no. 311; and Brian Rapske, *Paul in Roman Custody* (Grand Rapids, Mich.: Eerdmans, 1994), pp. 89-90.

Also, it was perfectly possible for a person to hold more than one citizenship at a time, so we cannot dismiss the possibility of Paul's Roman citizenship simply because he was a citizen of Tarsus (Acts 21:39).[43] It may be that Paul's family provided a great service to the Romans, perhaps by making tents for the Roman army (Antony's?), and as a result were granted citizenship.

Still, it is appropriate to ask why in Acts and on the prima facie evidence of the Pauline letters, Paul seems reticent to claim his Roman citizenship, at least until backed into a corner. Clearly Paul's Jewishness was a more primary factor in his identity than his Roman citizenship. As a Jew—even a high-status Jew—in a Greco-Roman world, Paul surely experienced considerable status inconsistency, and it may have been out of his great loyalty to his Jewish heritage, and later to his Christian faith, that he downplayed or even had ambivalent feelings about his Roman citizenship. After all, as he says in Philippians 3:20, the Christian's real *politeuma* is in heaven. Whether this term means citizenship or commonwealth or constituting authority, Paul had loyalties that transcended whatever earthly status he might have had by birth or by social status and privilege. Paul did not recognize the emperor and his decrees as the ultimate authority in his life; Jesus Christ was his Lord. Paul believed that the institutions or "forms" of this world were passing away in light of the eschatological situation already inaugurated in Christ (1 Cor 7:29-31).

Taken together, these factors make it understandable why Paul might have chosen to use his Roman citizenship only opportunistically, particularly in order to advance the gospel or, as in the drama played out in Acts 22—28, to get himself to the locale where he wanted to go next to spread the Word.

It is unlikely that Paul would have been pleased if someone became a Christian adherent because of having heard the gospel from Paul the high-status Roman citizen and seeking to follow a teacher of high social status. Paul wanted the claims of the gospel to stand on their own merits. No offense but the cross itself, no inducement but its compellingly persuasive message.[44]

In Paul's day, proving one's citizenship if called upon to do so could be a challenge. The small wooden diptych containing the certificate of citizenship was portable, but as Jerome Murphy-O'Connor points out, this item

---

[43]See Rapske, *Paul in Roman Custody,* pp. 71-112; Hengel and Schwemer, *Paul Between Damascus and Antioch,* p. 160.

[44]See the more detailed discussion in Ben Witherington III, *Acts of the Apostles* (Grand Rapids, Mich.: Eerdmans, 1997), pp. 679-84.

was too precious and too easily lost for carrying far from home. Furthermore, if the certificate's authenticity was disputed, the original witnesses who signed it had to be produced—something an itinerant missionary like Paul could not do.[45]

Thus it is indeed likely that Paul was a Roman citizen, but clearly this fact did not dominate his life or sense of identity. It was a resource he would draw on *in extremis*, or in order to advance the gospel, but he did not boast about it or flaunt it. Paul desired to boast only in Christ and his cross.

If, as is likely, Paul was a Roman citizen, he had a tripart name, composed of his given name (*praenomen*), the name of the founding member of his gens or tribe (*nomen*) and the particular family name (*cognomen*). An example of such a name is Gaius Julius Caesar. When a foreigner or a slave gained citizenship, he would retain his own name as the *cognomen* but would add the *praenomen* and *nomen* of the Roman who obtained citizenship for him. It is noteworthy that neither in Acts nor in Paul's letters do we find recorded Paul's threefold Roman name, nor do we find any significant evidence that Paul had skill with Latin (this was apparently not required of Roman citizens in his day).

Paulos is the Greek equivalent of the Latin Paulus. The latter is attested as both a *praenomen* (though rarely) and a *cognomen* (quite frequently—e.g., Sergius Paulus in Acts 13:8). This makes it likely that Paulos, if it is not a nickname, is in fact Paul's *cognomen,* his family name. The way the name is introduced ("who is also called . . ." cf. *Corpus Inscriptionem Latinae* 10.3377)[46] for the first time in Acts 13:8-9 may suggest it was indeed a nickname meaning "the small one."[47] Significantly, the change of names in Acts comes not at the point of Saul's Damascus Road encounter but when he begins to do missionary work in the Greco-Roman world, specifically when he begins to approach a man named Sergius Paulus! This may suggest an initial missionary strategy, attempting to identify with one's audience by assuming a Greek name. In any case, there was a very good reason for Paul not to go around the Greco-Roman world calling himself Saulos. In Greek *saulos* was used for someone who walked in a sexually suggestive manner like a prostitute![48]

---

[45]Murphy-O'Connor, *Paul: A Critical Life,* pp. 40-41.

[46]On this point see G. A. Harrer, "Saul Who Is Also Called Paul," *Harvard Theological Review* 33 (1940): 19-23.

[47]See the earlier discussion.

[48]See T. J. Leary, "Paul's Improper Name," *New Testament Studies* 38 (1992): 467-69, and C. J. Hemer, "The Name of Paul," *Tyndale Bulletin* 36 (1986): 179-83.

Paul's Roman citizenship would have provided him with advantages that would have assisted his work as a traveling evangelist. Besides having Roman justice on his side, he would have an instant entrée to any city in the Empire, especially Roman colony cities like Corinth or Philippi. Given his social status, he would command respect, especially whenever he announced his citizenship. He would have ready access to Roman roads and could have traveled with parties of other Roman citizens or even with Roman soldiers on a mission if need be. His positive interaction with the praetorian guard while under house arrest (see Phil 1) was no doubt in part because they were not disposed to ignore or despise a Roman citizen.

Though Paul's Roman citizenship is an important factor for understanding his life and identity—especially how he finally got to Rome and what he experienced there[49]—it is less crucial than either his Jewishness or his Christian faith.

PAUL THE CHRISTIAN

Discussion of Paul as a Christian has all too often focused just on his conversion, ignoring the rest of his Christian life. Yet when we meet Paul in his letters, even in his earliest letters, he has already been a Christian for at least fifteen years. Paul's letters do not reflect the musings of a neophyte Christian; the author speaks to us as a mature Christian person, a seasoned veteran. Even when speaking about his conversion and call, Paul is speaking with the benefit of hindsight—and in a highly selective and rhetorical manner. So though we begin with his conversion and call, we do well to keep in mind that Paul's recountings of this event are ad hoc and deliberately selective; they do not constitute a recent eyewitness account. It is rather like listening to what John Wesley said in the 1750s about the experience at Aldersgate in the late 1730s. Time and reflection have no doubt affected the perspective.

U-Turn on Damascus Road

Galatians 1:15-16 is part of Paul's *narratio* in this deliberative piece of rhetoric. Its function is to record salient facts that have bearing on the issues at hand. Various aspects of his conversion would have had no direct relevance to his discussions with the Galatians and so are omitted. So this is not Paul's personal testimony in anything like a full form. It is a highly selective and carefully couched presentation on a subject that the Galatians have

---

[49]See the earlier discussion.

already heard something about (Gal 1:13). Furthermore, the function of these autobiographical remarks is to substantiate a particular claim not so much about Paul and his Christian origins as about the nature and origins of his gospel and his apostleship to preach it. And Paul is presenting himself as a paradigm of the gospel he preaches to the Galatian Gentiles. "The formulation of Paul's autobiographical remarks in terms of 'formerly-now' and '[hu]man-God' serves the paradigmatic function of contrasting Paul's conversion from Judaism to Christianity with the Galatians' inverted conversion, which is really nothing other than a desertion of 'the one who called [them] in the grace of Christ' (1.6) and a surrender of Christian freedom for the slavery of law."[50]

Verse 12 offers two specific denials. Paul did not receive his gospel from human beings, nor was he taught it; it came through a revelation of Jesus Christ. Thus the issue is the source and nature of his gospel and the means and timing of its reception (at the beginning of his Christian life). There is debate as to whether we should take this last clause ("revelation of Jesus Christ") to refer to a revelation of which Christ is the content or a revelation that comes from or through Christ. Given the rest of Galatians 1, Paul is not denying that he ever received any information about Jesus from human beings. But here it appears, in light of Galatians 1:16, that Paul is speaking of a revelation that came from or through his encounter with Christ on the Damascus Road. The most reasonable suggestion is that this revelation entailed an indication not just of who Jesus was but also of the message that God wanted Paul to convey—the law-free gospel of redemption through faith in the crucified Christ proclaimed to the Gentiles. Paul admits that this message is not the kind of thing human beings could come up with on their own. It was revealed to him through a making known of the hidden, a "revelation." *Apokalypsis* refers to a revelation of a hidden secret about God's plan for human redemption.

Paul describes his experience in prophetic terms. In particular we hear an echo here of Jeremiah 1:5: "Before I formed you in the womb I knew you, and before you were born I consecrated you; I appointed you a prophet *to the nations*." Isaiah 49:1-6 may also be alluded to here. Paul then refers to his being called by grace. The point that God has had his hand on Paul since even before his birth, and all along had in mind for him to be God's spokesman to the Gentile nations. Paul's current occupation and vocation as apostle to the Gentiles was not a result of his careful career planning. Indeed it was against the flow of and quite apart from his pre-Christian

---

[50]Lyons, *Pauline Autobiography,* p. 171.

behavior, especially his persecuting activities. Paul's way of putting things here reveals a focus not on the personal salvific consequences of his encounter with Christ but rather on the basis of his ministry and message. The description is task-centered, not focused on conversion's effects on Paul as a person.

As Malina and Neyrey point out, Paul has framed this discussion carefully to fend off criticisms that he was guilty of chameleonlike behavior.[51] He does not wish to be seen as an opportunist or a fickle person. Ancients did not much believe in the idea of personality change or development. Or at least they did not see such change—a conversion, for example—as a good thing; it was rather the mark of a deviant, unreliable person who was not being true to type.[52] Thus Paul here presents his change in a rhetorically effective manner, making clear that it came about through an action of God.[53]

But it will not do to see this event simply as a prophetic call. Verse 16 speaks of a revelation of the Son either to or in Paul, probably the latter in light of Galatians 2:20 and 4:6. The coupling of "revelation" with "in me" suggests that Paul had an apocalyptic vision that changed the character and course of his life, his very identity.

Paul is *not* talking about having "made a decision for Christ" or having voluntarily changed the course of his life. He is saying that before he was born, *God* decided that Paul would be his witness to the Gentiles.

Compare Paul's words here to 1 Corinthians 9:1, where he speaks of having seen the risen Lord. If asked about the nature of this revelation, Paul probably would have rejected modern distinctions between objective and subjective. It was objective in that it was from God and did not come from fantasizing, dreaming or wish projection. It was subjective in that the revelation came to, and indeed even *in,* Paul. It was deeply personal and transforming. Its purpose was so that Paul might preach Christ among the nations. Thus there was a call that came with the conversion, not later. The verb *preach* is in the present tense, but the verbs *set apart* and *called* are in aorist, or past, tense.

---

[51]Malina and Neyrey, *Portraits of Paul,* p. 40.

[52]See the earlier discussion.

[53]See, e.g., Malina and Neyrey, *Portraits of Paul,* p. 39, which stresses that Greco-Roman culture valued stability and "constancy of character. Hence 'change' of character was neither expected nor praiseworthy. Normally adult persons were portrayed as living out the manner of life that had always characterized them." The virtuous Stoic philosopher was one who "surmises nothing, repents of nothing, is never wrong, and never changes his opinion" (Cicero *Pro Murena* 61).

What do we know about "conversions" from one religion to another in antiquity? *Conversion* is not a word that applies only to early Christianity and early Judaism.[54] Yet most conversionist groups or sects of the first century A.D. did not involve traditional Greco-Roman religions but Eastern religions, such as the cult of Isis, in addition to Judaism and Christianity. The ideological distance Paul traveled from one form of early Judaism to an offshoot of Judaism was considerably less than the distance involved in a conversion from worshiping Yahweh to worshiping Baal, or from worshiping the traditional Roman gods to worshiping Isis. In view of the general belief about the generally static, unchanging character of a person, it is not surprising that even among Judean Christians there might have been skepticism about Paul's conversion (Gal 1:19-20).

How does what we know about a pagan person's conversion and initiation into Judaism compare with Paul's description of his own conversion? As Alan F. Segal has pointed out, conversion to Judaism was almost always a gradual process culminating in circumcision and full conformity to the law.[55] The existence of "God-fearers"[56] supports this conclusion. God-fearers were in a sort of liminal state, neither pure pagan nor full convert. Of a different order is Josephus's description of his being initiated into various different parties or sects within Judaism (*Life* 7-12). Initiation and conversion were not one and the same. In the case of the God-fearer, conversion led to initiation. In the case of Josephus, we can hardly speak of conversion at all. As for Paul, Acts 9 strongly indicates that conversion *preceded* initiation into the community through baptism and Paul's acceptance by Ananias and the Christians in Damascus.

There is evidence that Jews knew about and even in some cases, however rarely, sought conversions to their faith. Matthew 23:15 bears witness to this phenomenon, as do Josephus's discussion of the royal house of Adiabene (*Antiquities of the Jews* 20.2.3-4) and perhaps some of the Qumran data. My point is that Saul of Tarsus would have know what a conversion was and what it meant for his life. It meant he would be viewed at best as a renegade and at worst an apostate crossing the boundaries of Judaism and heading in the wrong direction—and indeed texts like 2 Corinthians 11:24 suggest that this is how he was viewed by his Jewish peers in the Diaspora synagogues.

---

[54]See the classic study by A. D. Nock, *Conversion* (Oxford: Oxford University Press, 1933).

[55]Alan F. Segal, "The Cost of Proselytism and Conversion," *SBL 1988 Seminar Papers*, ed. D. J. Lull (Atlanta: Scholars Press, 1988), p. 341.

[56]That there was such a category of Gentile synagogue adherents is now demonstrable from the inscriptions. See the discussion in Witherington, *Acts*, pp. 341-44.

Equally important was the social dimension of conversion in antiquity. It was not a purely private matter between oneself and the deity. Conversion was into a community.[57] Paul's experience on the Damascus Road eventually led him to join the group he calls the assembly of God. As Galatians 1:13-16 shows, he saw this community as an entity distinguishable from Judaism. Paul found himself part of a new family whose members he called brothers and sisters. Yet if indeed Paul almost immediately went off into Arabia for missionary work and was never really integrated into the Jerusalem church afterward, it is easy to see why many Jerusalem Christians would have viewed him as a maverick or a deviant, not properly embedded in a Christian community.

This is one of the startling things about Paul. He was seen as strange and questionable not merely by fellow Jews but also by a number of fellow Jewish Christians! It is important to stress that he was a sectarian person whose sense of Christian identity came largely from his own conversion experience and his own outreach work and the communities and coworkers those efforts generated, not from some preexisting community of which he became a long-time member. In this sense the term "dyadic personality" does not fully describe the kind of person Paul was.[58]

A careful sociological analysis of what happened to Saul on the Damascus Road would have to conclude that he underwent a thorough resocialization. His symbolic universe was not just altered, it was turned upside down. Those he formerly considered insiders were out, and those considered outsiders were found to be in the people of God! In Paul's new worldview, the Jewish rite of passage was not fundamental for marking out Christians or those who were truly in the assembly of God. Notice too that Paul focuses clearly on the spiritual experience that changes human lives (see Gal 3:2-8), and he was willing to sit lightly with the Christian initiation rite (1 Cor 1:13-17). For him conversion, not initiation, was the truly crucial issue.

Especially in the wake of the work of Krister Stendahl,[59] it has become common to strongly suggest that what happened to Paul on the Damascus Road was *only* a prophetic call, not a conversion from Judaism to something else. I suggest that Stendahl is right in what he affirms but wrong in what he tries to deny. Though there was great diversity in early

---

[57]See R. Kanter, *Commitment and Community* (Cambridge, Mass.: Harvard University Press, 1972), pp. 61-74.

[58]On this term see the earlier discussion.

[59]See his *Paul Among Jews and Gentiles.*

Judaism, the Qumranites, Samaritans, Sadducees and Pharisees were not prepared to say what Paul says—that the Mosaic covenant has been now eclipsed, indeed has become a glorious anachronism (2 Cor 3; see Gal 4). Nor were any of these groups willing to say that full converts to their party would not have to be circumcised and keep the law. Paul, the former zealous Pharisee, could have never said "neither circumcision nor uncircumcision is anything" (Gal 6:15) had there not been a radical change in his worldview and symbolic universe. This change is quite properly called a conversion.

Probably the reason Stendahl overlooked this fact is that in our text he did not find the traditional language about repentance, forgiveness or being saved in our text, and so he concluded it is not about conversion. But the rhetorical function of this material is to explain the divine origin of Paul's gospel. Paul says nothing here about being saved or forgiven or repenting *not* because he does not believe such a thing has happened to him, just as it did to his Gentile converts (whom he wants to persuade to follow his example), but because in this passage he is making a different point. Paul is presenting himself as a paradigm of how God's miraculous grace works and leads to a life of proclaiming and living by the message of grace.

As Seyoon Kim has argued strongly and repeatedly, many key elements of Paul's gospel, including the idea of salvation offered freely apart from observance of the Mosaic law, go back to his own conversion experience and the revelation he received on that occasion.[60] Paul's gospel of grace was bound up with his experience of grace and grounded in the content of God's revelation of his Son in Paul. After this revelation, but clearly before he wrote Galatians or even visited the Galatians, he worked out the implications of this good news for his beliefs about God, Messiah, law, salvation and the identity of God's people.

As noted above, some discussions of Paul as a Christian unfortunately begin and end with a discussion of his conversion.[61] Much more can and should be said. Several key aspects of Paul's Christian life reflect who he was: (1) his life in the Spirit and spiritual gifts, (2) his future hope, for himself and for others, as part of his eschatology, and (3) his overarching concern for love and concord in the community of God.[62]

---

[60]See Seyoon Kim, *The Origin of Paul's Gospel* (Grand Rapids, Mich.: Eerdmans, 1981), and more recently his "The Mystery of Rom 11:25-26," a lecture given at the August 1996 Society for New Testament Studies meeting in Strasbourg.

[61]For a fresh set of discussions of the ongoing impact of the Damascus Road experience on Paul and his gospel see Richard N. Longenecker, ed., *The Road from Damascus: The Impact of Paul's Conversion on His Life, Thought and Ministry* (Grand Rapids, Mich.: Eerdmans, 1997).

[62]We will discuss Paul's thought or theology in a subsequent chapter.

THE SPIRIT AND FLESH OF THE APOSTLE

Apart from the seminal work of Gordon Fee, in the last two decades surprisingly few detailed English-language works have meaningfully discussed Paul's own life in the Spirit.[63] This is in part because Paul himself seems reticent to talk about such things; he is not a modern Western individual bent on revealing his innermost thoughts. Ancients in fact went out of their way to avoid discussing experiences that would distinguish them from the crowd. In the collectivist mindset, such discussions would seem antisocial.

Not surprisingly, then, when Paul actually does boast about his personal experiences (spiritual and otherwise), the boasting is clearly ironic or tongue in cheek. Second Corinthians 12:1-10, for example, follows a passage (2 Cor 11) in which Paul has "boasted" about his weaknesses, trials and tribulations, parodying common boasting about one's great deeds. Paul begins chapter 12 by speaking of visions and revelations. He is really claiming to have had such experiences once in a while, which makes him in various respects like John of Patmos; and he is writing to a highly "charismatic" audience who would be eager to hear about such experiences. Paul knows the emotional impact of such claims on them, and so here he raises their expectations but in the end just teases and shames them.[64]

In verses 2-4 Paul says he had a vision that was a source of revelation to him (in other words, he not only saw but also heard and learned), but coyly he says he is not permitted to convey the content of this revelation! It is possible that his opponents who were "bewitching" the Corinthians were claiming such experiences as well and that he is mainly trying to deflate their boasting. Paul puts the description of this experience in the third person, however, because he is following the rules of inoffensive self-praise.[65]

We are told that this experience happened some fourteen years prior to the writing of this letter—in other words, around A.D. 40-44, which probably places it during Paul's "hidden" years in Syria and Cilicia.[66] It is possible that precisely because Paul was not a modern individualist, the Corinthians were shocked to hear Paul recount this story, just as they may have been shocked to hear what Paul says about tongues and prophecy in 1 Corinthians 14 (see below). Some commentators have suggested that since

---

[63]See Gordon D. Fee, *God's Empowering Presence* (Peabody, Mass.: Hendrickson, 1994).

[64]See Witherington, *Conflict and Community*, pp. 459-65.

[65]See the earlier discussion.

[66]On Pauline chronology see appendix. On the so-called hidden years see Hengel and Schwemer, *Paul Between Damascus and Antioch*.

Paul mentions only an experience of fourteen years prior, such experiences must have been quite rare for him. On the other hand, Paul may mention this one because to him it was especially notable and outstanding. Andrew Lincoln notes that the plural in 2 Corinthians 12:1 suggests that initially Paul thought about relating more than one such vision or revelation.[67]

Recalling this event, Paul says twice that he does not know whether he was in or out of the body when he was "caught up." The language suggests an overpowering experience that overwhelmed him, rather than a state he deliberately worked his way into through spiritual exercises or ascetical practices. Paul says also that he got as far as the third heaven, which he calls paradise, a term from the Genesis story about Eden (cf. Lk 23:43; Rev 2:7). He is probably not suggesting that there are any levels above the third heaven, for if he shared such a notion with his audience, this would not be an unsurpassable mock boast. Paul's point is that he got all the way to the third heaven and this was no planned trip. Perhaps, unlike the Corinthians, he was not seeking such adventures in the Spirit.

Paul says in verse 4 that he heard unutterable words, but he clarifies by explaining that he was simply not permitted (by God? by the Spirit?) to repeat what he heard. The Corinthians might well understand this in terms of their knowledge of mystery religions, where secrets were revealed only to special initiates. The point of mentioning the experience without disclosing the message is to make clear that God thought Paul was a special person. In short, the Corinthians had badly underestimated him. Yet Paul also does not want them to overestimate him just because he has had an "excess" of revelations (see v. 6).[68]

This impression that Paul was a visionary is clearly confirmed in Acts (see, e.g., not only the account of his conversion in Acts 9 but also Acts 16:6-10; 23:11). Consider in addition the various texts where he indicates that he both knows and teaches mysteries and has special revelatory knowledge (cf. 1 Cor. 2:1, 10, 16; 4:1; 15:51).

As a deflation device, God gave Paul a "stake" (a sharp wooden object) in the flesh, lest he give way to the wrong sort of boasting. This "stake" or "thorn" had the effect of bringing Paul right down to earth. Despite repeated prayer, God chose not to remove this stake from Paul's flesh; likely it is a reference to a physical condition.[69] What we may have here is

---

[67]See Andrew Lincoln, "Paul the Visionary," *New Testament Studies* 25 (1979): 204-20.

[68]Another term which supports the theory that Paul does not suggest here that such experiences were rare for him.

[69]On Paul's infirmities see an earlier discussion.

a visionary with a sight problem (see Gal 4:11-15)! Second Corinthians 10:10 makes it clear that Paul's condition involved something visible and obvious to an outsider that led people to conclude that he was weak or sickly. Furthermore, as 2 Corinthians 12:12 goes on to say, when he was with the Corinthians miracles happened. Paul may have been a healer who himself was not entirely well!

Yet this same context (2 Cor 11:21-24) shows that Paul did not let this condition or other misfortunes slow him down. In fact, Paul's weaknesses showed that power and revelation came from God and not from the apostle. Indeed God's power comes to full expression or completion through and in the midst of human weakness. It is interesting that Paul says in 2 Corinthians 12:9 that this divine power made its home in him. This likely draws on the image of the shekinah glory descending on the temple and its holy of holies.

Paul may have patterned this account on the experience of Christ, as has been suggested by J. W. McCant.[70] Christ faced a cross, Paul a stake or thorn. Christ prayed three times for his suffering to pass; so did Paul. Jesus prayed that God's will, not his, be done, while Paul received an assurance that God's grace would be sufficient so he could endure the stake. Both the cross and the stake had to be faced and actually endured. Since Jesus was a suffering Messiah, it is no wonder that his agent was a suffering apostle.

As noted briefly above, Paul did indeed perform miracles, though he does not boast of such things but mentions them only in passing. Besides the reference to signs, wonders and mighty works in 2 Corinthians 12:12, Romans 15:18-19 is important because it closely associates powerful works with the power of the Spirit working through Paul. This impression of Paul as a miracle worker or *thaumaturge* is confirmed by various texts in Acts (see, e.g., Acts 13:11; 14:10; 16:18; 19:11; 28:3-6).

First Corinthians 14 tells us that Paul both prophesied and spoke in tongues. The former is simply implied (see, e.g., vv. 37-39—prophets should recognize his prophetic utterances as God's word—and cf. 1 Cor 13:1-2, where his remarks should probably be taken as autobiographical),[71] but the latter is specifically stated. Indeed, in an attempt to deflate the overly charismatic and chaotic Corinthians, Paul says, "I thank God that I speak in tongues more than all of you" (14:18)—not, mind you, more than *any* of the Corinthians, but more than *all* of them! Nevertheless, it is quite

---

[70]See his "Paul's Thorn of Rejected Apostleship," *New Testament Studies* 34 (1988): 550-72.

[71]See C. A. Holladay, "1 Corinthians 13: Paul as Apostolic Paradigm," in *Greeks, Romans and Christians*, ed. D. Balch, Everett Ferguson and Wayne A. Meeks (Minneapolis: Fortress, 1990), pp. 80-98.

clear that Paul affirms the gifts of prophecy and tongues (cf. 1 Cor 11 on the former, and on both 1 Cor 14:39) both in his own life and in the lives of other Christians.[72]

Close scrutiny of texts like 1 Corinthians 14:2 and 14:14 strongly suggests that Paul saw glossolalia as a prayer language, something prompted by the Spirit in the believer and uttered to God. The human spirit is involved in this kind of praying, but not the human mind. This leads us to Romans 8:15, to which we must compare 8:26. In the former verse we have the coordinate efforts of the human spirit and the Holy Spirit prompting the prayer "Abba! Father!" Notice how this differs from Galatians 4:6, where it is said that it is the Spirit who cries "Abba! Father!" This is of course an intelligible utterance or prayer, but in Romans 8:26 Paul seems to refer to glossolalia: the Spirit helps the believer at a loss for words and intercedes through the believer with inarticulate groanings or speech.[73] Such utterance does have meaning, though it is not immediately intelligible to the human speaker. God knows the mind of the Spirit and what the Spirit is saying through the believer. The Spirit intercedes for the saints according to God's will (v. 27). That is, while believers may not know exactly how to conform their prayer to God's will, the Spirit indeed does and will do so, so that believers may pray effectively.[74] For our purposes what is important about this material is that Paul is speaking from experience. The first-person plurals (when *we* cry with *our* spirit, the Spirit helps *us* . . . for *we* do not know how to pray) must be taken quite seriously.

Paul was not only a spirited man, as any reading of his more polemical letters will attest, but also a man of the Spirit. This must not be downplayed, nor should his life in the Spirit be anachronistically contrasted with his skills as a profound and rational thinker. Paul manifests both life in the Spirit and the life of the mind, and in fact we see a marriage of the two in passages like Romans 8. Paul might have said that the only persons really in their right minds are those who are filled with and inspired by the Spirit to think God's thoughts after God has revealed them.

Taken together, the data show that despite Paul's reticence to talk directly about his personal spiritual experiences,[75] he was in fact much more like his Corinthian converts than many modern commentators would like to think. He is not being facetious in 1 Corinthians 1:4-7 when he

---

[72]See Witherington, *Conflict and Community*, pp. 276-80.

[73]See the discussion in Fee, *God's Empowering Presence*, p. 583.

[74]See the discussion in ibid., p. 586, and J. D. G. Dunn, *Romans 1-8* (Waco, Tex.: Word, 1988), pp. 479-80.

[75]See Hengel and Schwemer, *Paul Between Damascus and Antioch*, pp. 1-10.

thanks God for the Corinthians' spiritual gifts. He was indeed a man of the Spirit, a "charismatic" individual not just in the secular sense of that term. His Christian life was punctuated and enriched with notable spiritual and ecstatic experiences.

GOING ON IN GRACE TO COMPLETION

This is not to say that Paul was unfamiliar with the notion of progressive sanctification in the Christian life, nor is it to say that Paul saw himself as already spiritually complete or totally perfect. Philippians 2:12-13 reads in part, "Work out your own salvation with fear and trembling; for it is God who is working in your midst, and the willing and the doing are according to his pleasure" (my translation). *Your* here is in the plural. This is an exhortation for Christians to collectively work out the salvation they share with fear and trembling. Paul is not exhorting each individual to pursue his or her private salvation in this matter. In this very chapter Paul has spoken about being self-forgetful and not regarding one's own interests (Phil 2:3-4).[76] His call is to work out the shared eschatological gift of salvation within and by the community of faith. Verse 13 makes evident that not only salvation but also the energy and the will to work out this salvation come from God. God's ongoing work in the body of Christ, which includes individual Christians, is indeed a part of progressive sanctification.

Lest we think Paul speaks only about his converts, in Philippians 3:10-13 he expresses his own determination to "know Christ and the power of his resurrection and the sharing of his sufferings, sharing the very likeness of his death, if somehow I might attain to the resurrection from the dead. Not that I have already obtained this or am already complete [or perfect], but I press on . . ." (my translation). Salvation for Paul has several tenses. He speaks of having been saved, being saved and going on to be saved.[77] Paul makes clear that he himself does not yet fully know Christ, nor has he fully experienced the power of his resurrection. In 3:10-11 resurrection is not a present spiritual experience but a future condition, being raised from the dead. Only at that point does Paul expect to be complete or perfect as a Christian person. He says in verse 12 that he has not yet attained the goal of perfection, which amounts to full Christlikeness in the resurrection body as in the spirit. Progressive sanctification and dynamic spiritual experi-

---

[76]See Ben Witherington III, *Friendship and Finances in Philippi* (Valley Forge, Penn.: Trinity Press International, 1994), pp. 71-72.

[77]See Witherington, *Paul's Narrative Thought World*, pp. 245-49.

ences can take us only so far in this life. Outwardly we are wasting away while inwardly we are being renewed day by day (2 Cor 4:16-17). However "charismatic" one may be, one must still live by and move on faith, looking forward to the day of resurrection when completion finally comes.

For Paul, life apart from a body is not seen as a full human life. Salvation is not seen as complete without the ultimate resurrection of the body.[78] This also means that we must take seriously "if possible I might reach . . ." in verse 11. Paul's view is that even those who have preached Christ could in the end be disqualified if they do not remain in Christ and obey him to the end (1 Cor 9:27). Even apostles must live by faith and are not eternally secure until they are securely in eternity or have obtained the resurrection. Until such time, one must work out one's salvation with fear and trembling.

Paul's ethical enjoinders have purpose and meaning because in the life of the believer there is an eschatological tension between already being saved and not yet being entirely saved. We not only may but *must* work out our salvation in conjunction with the body of Christ, with awe and respect for what is happening and must happen in their midst. The grace-induced and grace-empowered obedience of Christians does indeed have something to do with the final outcome. Paul calls his converts to, and models for them, the athletic spiritual discipline and moral effort of pressing toward the goal of final salvation, of fully knowing Christ, of obtaining the resurrection from the dead.[79]

Even with all of our straining, resurrection still comes as a gift from God, not something we achieve, though there is a sense in which Paul can speak of a heavenly prize for faithfulness to the end (Phil 3:14). A discussion of spiritual gifts, experiences and process in the life of the apostle, and of Christians in general, is incomplete unless one also speaks about the fruit of the Spirit. The Spirit not merely gives experiences or gifts but also shapes character.

It is a striking fact that many of the undisputed Pauline letters are exhortations to concord and unity within the body of Christ. We see this sort of deliberative argument in 1 Corinthians, Philippians and even Galatians. A part of Paul's overall strategy to produce harmony between himself and his converts, and within the congregations he is addressing, involves an attempt to model and commend the fruit of the Spirit.

---

[78]See Witherington, *Jesus, Paul and the End,* pp. 184-90.
[79]See the discussion in chapter one.

THE GOOD FRUIT

Galatians 5:22-26 is part of a larger discussion in which verses 22-23 stand in direct contrast to what has just been said about the deeds of the flesh, deeds prompted by sinful inclinations and leanings. It is possible to compare the fruit list here with ancient virtue lists,[80] but many of the main virtues Paul lists do not appear in such lists, and some of them, such as humility, would not have been seen as virtues by most ancient pagans. Lists of traits or habits seen as desirable for contributing members of Greco-Roman society look in many ways different from Paul's lists. Only some Jewish lists (such as 1QS 4.5) comment on love as Paul does. The first six virtues he lists are found elsewhere in the New Testament, mainly in the Pauline letters (2 Cor 6:6; 1 Tim 4:12; 6:11; 2 Tim 2:22; 2 Pet 1:5-7), while the last three are what might be called characteristic Greek or even Stoic virtues.

It is quite tempting to see Paul's sketch of fruit, as has been suggested for a part of 1 Corinthians 13, as a sketch of Christ's own character and characteristic teaching on the subject (see Gal 5:14).[81] While drawing on the best of the pagan virtues, Paul is largely trying to create a distinctive Christian ethos for the community of his converts.

He speaks of *fruit* singular, not "fruits." This suggests the unity and unifying nature of these qualities, as opposed to the division and discord produced by works of the flesh. The singular also suggests that all these qualities should be manifest in any Christian's life. The term *fruit* also suggests that we are not talking about natural virtues or personal attainments but character traits wrought in the believer's life by the work of the Spirit. Believers must work out these qualities in their social interactions, but the Spirit is their source.

Love is the signature Christian quality to which Paul refers here, as in 1 Corinthians 13. Romans 5:5 makes abundantly clear he is not talking about natural human feelings but rather about love poured into the hearts of believers by the Spirit. The noun *agapē* is not found in classical Greek writings, nor for that matter in Josephus, yet it dominates the New Testament discussion of personal relationships. Paul sees love as the means and the goal affecting all else, so he can talk about faith working through love (Gal 5:6), or about serving each other through love (5:13), or loving neighbor as self (5:14). The similarity between 5:13-14 and what we find in 6:2 should not be

---

[80]See Witherington, *Grace in Galatia*, pp. 389-405.

[81]See the discussion by J. D. G. Dunn, *The Epistle to the Galatians* (Peabody, Mass.: Hendrickson, 1993), p. 310.

overlooked. The law of Christ has to do with what Christ taught and modeled—love—and loving, self-sacrificial acts. There is no law against the fruit of the Spirit; indeed such fruit reflects the higher law of Christ.

The reader of Paul's letters is soon impressed with the way he modeled this fruit, especially love. The evidence of loving service for the gospel and for his converts at great personal cost is writ large in these documents (see 2 Cor 11:23-29). Like Francis Asbury when, after he himself had ridden a circuit of over one thousand miles, said to his circuit riders, "I am not wont to say 'go' but rather 'come,' " Paul set the example of Christlike loving service and then bid his converts "imitate me, as I Christ" (1 Cor 11:1, my translation).

In our culture, to say "imitate me" seems hubristic, but it would be a mistake to read Paul this way.[82] One of the major pedagogical tools of ancient teachers was modeling, especially for beginning or immature learners. Quintilian stresses the importance of modeling and indicates how he used it successfully (see *Institutio Oratoria* 10.2.1-28). This tool of course works best in a society where there is considerable respect for authority, for one's elders, for those in the know. Furthermore, 1 Corinthians 11:1 makes evident that Paul appeals for imitation only to the extent and in the way that he models Christ, the great paradigm. Were Paul an individualist, this appeal could be seen as hubris. But he sees himself as one who is in Christ, as one who is but a servant or messenger of Christ, who is embedded in the body of Christ, who is what he is by the grace of God (which is to say, because of what someone else has done to and for and in him).[83]

When Paul speaks of imitating Christ, he makes clear that his own pattern for identity and sense of identity come from another—Christ. Paul models himself on the narrative pattern of Christ's life of self-sacrificial giving, as the Christ hymn in Philippians 2 shows. There Paul calls his converts to have the same mind as Christ, but it is clear that he has already

---

[82]E. Castelli, *Imitating Paul* (Louisville, Ky.: Westminster John Knox, 1991), makes the mistake of reading this appeal to imitation as a power move on Paul's part, not recognizing the pedagogical context. See Witherington, *Conflict and Community,* pp. 144-46.

[83]Modern Western commentators, especially in the wake of William James's comments about the varieties of subjective religious experiences, have often made the mistake of taking the abundance of spirit language in Paul's writings as reflecting his subjective experiences or inner life. It needs to be understood however that Paul does not say much about his spirit, but rather dwells on the Holy Spirit. Paul's anthropology is complex, but it does not include the idea that the Holy Spirit is an inherent part of his being or personality. The Holy Spirit is seen by Paul as an objective reality that came into his life at the point of conversion and is the presence of God, the ultimate Other, in his life. Paul sees himself as a captive domain caught up by and filled with the life of God. From Paul's point of view this is not so much a case of the intersection of theology (human thoughts about God) and biography as it is the intersection of God's divine work on earth and the life of Paul.

heeded this exhortation personally (see 1 Cor 2:16). He has no interest in manifesting his own distinctive mind or imposing it on others. He wishes to embody and model the mind of Christ.

At times imitating Christ means being conformed to the pattern of Christ's death while one tries to serve Christ (2 Cor 10—13). At other times imitation is Paul's conscious effort to act and live humbly, deliberately stepping down the ladder of social status so he may relate to and help all, even slaves. Imitation of Christ then is for Paul both an event that happens and a choice, both being conformed to Christ's image (see 2 Cor 4:10) and choosing to conform to it. Imitation involves both the indicative and the imperative of the Christian life, and imitation does not fully become image until the believer is made fully christoform at the resurrection. Imitation also implies a clear distinction between Paul and the One he seeks to imitate. Paul should not be accused of having a messiah complex.[84]

CONCLUSIONS

The trinity of Paul's identity involves his Jewishness, his Roman citizenship and his Christianity. A variety of influences went into making him who he was. Both by choice and by accident of birth, he had a foot in more than one sector of the ancient world. He cannot be understood on the basis of any one of these factors. Even when we put the three together, much must go unexplained. Paul's letters are not like the *Confessions* of St. Augustine. They only occasionally include biographical remarks, and those remarks are never there simply to satisfy readers' curiosity. Paul, like most ancient persons, did not go around talking about his unique inner self. While he was an individual, he was not a modern individualist. He spoke of who he was in relationship to significant communities to which he belonged (Jewish and Christian ones), or of *whose* he was as a follower and servant and imitator of Jesus Christ.

It appears that of the three major identity factors, the least influential was his Roman citizenship. The matter is barely hinted at in his extant letters. Certainly more important is Paul's Jewish background, much of which he brought with him, though in transformed and transfigured shape, into his Christian life. Yet when Paul himself compares his illustrious Jewish past with his Christian present, he is prepared to place all of his former life in the loss column in comparison with the surpassing value of knowing Christ and being in him. Paul can in fact speak of his "former" life

---

[84]See Witherington, *Conflict and Community,* pp. 145-46.

in Judaism (Gal 1) in comparison with his present life, about which he says, "For me to live is Christ" (Phil 1:21, my translation).

The evidence suggests that Paul was a sectarian person. He had broken away from the community that mothered him and was helping to found a distinct one, though it was related in various ways to its forebear. Paul's sense of identity is like that of other dyadic persons. He derived his self-understanding from whom and what group he was embedded in. He stresses that his identity and lifework has been given him by another: God in Christ. In fact he says God had an identity and a calling in mind for him from before the time he was born (Gal 1).

We should then not be surprised, as some commentators still are, that we

> do not learn anything [in his letters] about his origin from Tarsus and his family, his twofold Roman and Tarsian citizenship, his Jewish (and his official tripartite Roman) name, the great significance of Antioch, and indeed of Syria and Cilicia generally over many years, for his biography, his mission in the interior of Asia Minor, the foundation and fate of the community of Rome, and the reasons for the acute danger to his life.[85]

This is not because Paul was shy or simply wanted to leave the past behind; it is largely because he was an ancient person. Yet there is an irony in all of this: for few persons has there ever been a closer link between theology and biography, belief and life, experience and exhortation, than for Paul. Not only did he teach about Christ, he lived a cruciform life. Not only did he talk about the Spirit, he was a man of the Spirit.

If Rudolf Bultmann was right that Paul's essential exhortation to his converts was "become what you already are," it is fair to say that Paul was busy hearing and heeding this same exhortation.[86] He was prepared to live in and walk by the Spirit. He was prepared to imitate and model Christ. We have no evidence from his letters of Paul's having what we would call an identity crisis. He is very sure of who he is and ought to be in Christ.

Yet a great deal of indirect evidence beyond Paul's semiautobiographical remarks is quite revealing about the apostle. Examining Paul in terms of his activities and actions, his tasks and toils, will advance the quest for the historical Paul. Thus we turn now to a consideration of Paul the writer and rhetor.

---

[85]Hengel and Schwemer, *Paul Between Damascus and and Antioch*, p. 16.
[86]See Rudolf Bultmann, *Theology of the New Testament*, 2 vols. (New York: Scribner, 1951, 1955).

CHAPTER 3

PAUL THE WRITER
AND RHETOR

In Paul's world only about two of every ten people could read. Thus he was a letter writer in a largely oral and aural culture; this bespeaks not only his own level of education but also that of at least some of his audience. Letters served for Paul as surrogates for face-to-face communication and were in essence oral documents, meant to be orally performed, not merely visibly read. It would appear that some of his converts were highly educated enough to appreciate his efforts at literarily powerful letters.

Paul was a multilingual person, knowing at least Greek, Aramaic and Hebrew, and presumably, since he was a Roman citizen, at least a bit of Latin. His education seems to have been considerable. It would have been primarily Jewish in character, yet the Jerusalem in which Paul was educated was a Hellenized place, and evidence suggests that he could have obtained some training in Greek philosophy and a good deal more in rhetoric there.

In his oral culture, not only the content but also the form of one's knowledge and self-expression was considered very important. Oratorical skills were the keys to advancement in a largely oral culture, and Paul tells us he was advancing in Judaism beyond many of his compatriots before he encountered Christ on the Damascus Road.

Yet whatever their oral skills, even the literate often found it helpful and even necessary to use scribes to compose their letters. It appears that Paul's scribes were always fellow Christians, and in some cases (e.g., 1 Thess) his prominent coworkers. Scribes understood letters to be very personal forms of communication, so that it was crucial that the author's, not the scribe's, personality come through. This required either dictation or the use of scribes who knew the author well. Paul sometimes dictated and occasionally relied on a coworker to compose. This may help to explain some but not all of the anomalies of the later Pauline epistles. It was the regular practice of scribes to make two copies of a letter and retain one; this may have later facilitated the rapid collection of Paul's letters and their distribution as a collection.

Paul had an elaborate social network through which he communicated with others. Letters were only a part of his communication strategy, which also included face-to-face visits, the visits of coworkers, the sending of messengers, and news passed along orally by traveling

Christians. Paul was considerably more long-winded than most ancient letter writers, even Cicero, and his letters contain far more religious content than those of most of his contemporaries. He was a creative person; though he used the usual skeletal structure of ancient letters, he made the form his own by modifying and adding to standard epistolary elements. His letters were true surrogates for oral communication, for he made them exercises in rhetoric— the ancient art of persuasion—within an epistolary framework.

Paul's letters essentially contain his acts of persuasion, his arguments attempting to convict, convince and convert his audience to his point of view on various matters. He mainly uses deliberative rhetoric, the rhetoric of the Greek assembly, to address his converts. This was the rhetoric of advice and consent, addressing what a group's future course of action or reflection ought to be, and it lets us know that Paul treats his converts as responsible adults who must make their own decisions. Though he was certainly prepared to command, he preferred to persuade. Like most ancient rhetoricians, Paul offered group communications, but his were uniquely intended to fit into and be an integral part of acts of Christian worship.

Far from being merely formal communications, Paul's letters and his rhetoric show how deeply he cared about his converts. He took considerable care in crafting his letters, partly because his oral performance was sometimes deficient, perhaps due to his thorn in the flesh. Paul's letters show that he knew how to appeal to the whole person, both the mind and the emotions, both the spirit and the will, and he was not afraid to use the whole arsenal of rhetorical devices to make his point and persuade. He was, in short, a well-educated, literate and skilled communicator. His decision to step down socially and practice the tentmaking trade should not fool us into thinking Paul was a working-class person. This was a missionary and survival strategy, not a full indication of his social location and inclinations.

AS STRANGE AS IT MAY SEEM, THOUGH LUKE DEVOTES NEARLY HALF OF HIS HISTORY of early Christianity to the apostle to the Gentiles, he says nothing whatsoever about Paul's being a letter writer! Yet Paul himself offers us no other kind of documents. Thus as we analyze what we can learn about Paul as a writer, we must rely exclusively on the Pauline corpus itself. Fortunately, when we discuss Paul as a rhetor or rhetorician, one who practiced the ancient art of persuasion, we have evidence from both Paul and Acts to help us. Paul's literacy and his skills with rhetoric and letter writing provide significant clues to the kind of person he was. He was by no means an ordinary first-century man.

THE EDUCATIONAL AND SOCIAL MILIEU OF THE EARLIEST CHRISTIANS

Scholars are showing a renewed interest in literacy and education in the ancient world. In part this interest reflects the past two decades' emphasis on social history in New Testament studies. Literacy and literary ability are seen as significant clues to the social level of this or that person or group. The work of classicists, ancient historians and literary scholars is finally being given due notice by some New Testament scholars. For example, the older studies of ancient education by H. I. Marrou and M. L. Clarke are now regularly being cited by New Testament scholars.[1] A variety of people such as W. Harris, A. D. Booth and H. C. Youtie highlight the value of literacy studies.[2]

Classics scholars have set the stage and agenda for the rhetorical study of the New Testament itself. This infusion of new data from other disciplines has been especially welcome and helpful in Pauline studies. Indeed, some scholars now say that the historical Paul cannot be adequately understood or evaluated without due attention to his literacy, literary abilities and his rhetorical skills.

To what degree were early Christians educated and literate? *Educated* and *literate* are not synonymous. Some early Jews had learned aurally a good deal about their faith and a variety of other subjects, yet they could not write, much less write in the lingua franca of the Empire—Greek. Some of them employed scribes or amaneuenses, or as we would call them, secretaries, to perform their writing tasks. We know from texts like Romans 16:22 that Paul used the services of such secretaries, and to judge by this verse, he used those who were already Christians. Yet texts like Galatians 6:11 show that Paul could not only read but also write in Greek, and that like many others, even when he used a secretary he himself would sign the document and write a concluding postscript. So we have clear evidence that the apostle was literate in Greek, and surely (in view of Phil 3:5) in Hebrew and probably also in Aramaic (see 1 Cor 16:22).[3] Furthermore, he writes to his converts, which means he expects that at least the one who delivers the letter for him can read, but presumably also some of the remote audience would have been literate in Greek. There was no point in writing a postscript in his own hand if they could not at least recognize that hand, and if at least some of them could not read and appreciate the postscript.

---

[1]See Henri I. Marrou, *A History of Education in Antiquity* (New York: Sheed & Ward, 1956) and M. L. Clarke, *Higher Education in the Ancient World* (Albuquerque: University of New Mexico, 1971).
[2]See William V. Harris, *Ancient Literacy* (Cambridge, Mass.: Harvard University Press, 1989), A. D. Booth, "Elementary and Secondary Education in the Roman Empire," *Florilegium* 1 (1979): 1-14; Jan Nicolaas Sevenster, *Do You Know Greek? How Much Greek Could the First Jewish Christians Have Known?* trans. J. de Bruin (Leiden: Brill, 1968); H. C. Youtie, "*Agrammatos:* An Aspect of Greek Society in Egypt," *Havard Studies in Classical Philology* 75 (1971): 161-76, and "*Upographeus:* The Social Impact of Illiteracy in Graeco-Roman Egypt," *Zeitschrift für Papyrologie und Epigraphik* 17 (1975): 201-21.
[3]See the earlier discussion of the meaning of these verses.

Yet determining the education and literacy level of the earliest Christians is difficult, and in any case the question is complex. As Harry Gamble has aptly put it,

> The question of literacy in early Christianity is complicated by the fact that Christianity developed and spread in multi-cultural and multi-lingual settings and thus incorporated from the start a diversity that forbids the generalizations that are possible for more culturally and linguistically homogeneous groups. A Christian in first-century Palestine might have been thoroughly literate in Aramaic, largely literate in Hebrew, semiliterate in Greek, and illiterate in Latin.[4]

There was probably not a large Christian reading and writing public in the first century A.D. All major literacy studies of the Greco-Roman world of the Empire basically come to estimates of *at most* between 10 and 20 percent of the entire population; the latter figure is an absolute upper limit.[5] In some places literacy would have been even less. It is true that Jews of the time seem to have been distinctively concerned about the education, at least the religious education, of their children.[6] Yet that fact does not help us much with Paul's audience, who were apparently overwhelmingly Gentiles and apparently did not grow up with the benefits of Jewish pedagogy that Paul himself probably enjoyed.

Likely more important was the high value early Christians placed on Scripture and on learning of and about it. Because of Scripture, literacy could never be a matter of indifference to the earliest Christians. Furthermore, a certain authority would accrue to someone who could not merely read but also powerfully interpret the Jewish sacred books. Literacy as a criterion for Christian leadership in the early church is a factor too seldom considered.[7] Whatever else one may wish to say about the Pastoral Epistles, they surely rightly suggest that Paul wrote to his coworkers from time to time. Unless such coworkers were well off enough to afford a scribe, this likely suggests that they were literate and could read and reply to such letters.

Literacy studies are in part based on the correct conclusion that literacy is a function of education. Any sort of higher education, beyond the mere learning of ciphers and rudimentary writing skills for business or personal

---

[4]Harry Gamble, *Books and Readers in the Early Church* (New Haven, Conn.: Yale University Press, 1995), p. 3.

[5]E.g., Harris, *Ancient Literacy* pp. 130-45. His final conclusion about literacy in the western part of the Empire is particularly sobering—no higher than 5-10 percent at any point during the Empire (p. 272).

[6]See Gamble, *Books and Readers,* p. 7.

[7]Ibid., p. 9.

matters, was by and large for the elite in Paul's world. Paul's letters were certainly not bestsellers, and we may be sure the majority of Paul's audience was not from the elite of society (see 1 Cor 1:26).

Yet in an oral and aural culture, a culture geared to learning more by ear than by eye, this may not have been as crucial a matter as we might think. As we will see, early Christian literary documents were intended to be read aloud in the assemblies (Col 4:16); in fact, nearly all ancient reading was done aloud (see Acts 8:30). Letters were seen as surrogates for oral conversation, as vehicles for carrying on such conversation. The living or spoken Word was primary; the written word was secondary and often no more than a record of the oral.[8] In our age of millions of books, e-mail, Internet chat rooms and the like, it is hard for us to grasp that visible text was not primary in antiquity. Text was largely a tool of oral culture. This is why the study of rhetoric in and of Paul's letters is crucial. Paul wrote his words so that they might be *heard* as persuasive, not merely seen to be persuasive.

A recent important sociological study on earliest Christianity points out that if "the early church was like all other cult movements for which good data exist, it was not a proletarian movement but was based on the more privileged classes."[9] I would not agree that early Christianity was *based* in privileged classes, but I support E. A. Judge's conclusion that early Christianity was led and largely supported by an elite minority who were of the higher social strata:

> If the common assertion that Christian groups were constituted from the lower orders of society is meant to imply that they did not draw upon the upper orders of the Roman ranking system, the observation is correct, and pointless. In the eastern Mediterranean it was self-evident that members of the Roman aristocracy would not belong to a local cult association. . . . [Nevertheless,] far

---

[8]Consider Papias, bishop of Hierapolis in the early second century, who is quoted by Eusebius (*Hist. Eccl.* 3.39.3-4) as saying that he always inquired primarily about what the apostles had said rather than what they had written, "for I did not suppose that things from books would benefit me so much as things from a living and abiding voice."

[9]Rodney Stark, *The Rise of Christianity* (Princeton, N.J.: Princeton University Press, 1996), p. 33. This conclusion however is based on crosscultural and crosstemporal evidence. It is also based on a distinction between cult (the founding of a new faith) and sect (a schism within an existing religious group or body) which I am not sure is apt when discussing ancient Christianity. It appears to me that Christianity began as a sect of Judaism, not as a cult. Stark eventually concludes that Jesus was the leader of a sect movement within Judaism, but he claims that at Easter something happened to turn the movement into a cult (p. 44). To be sure however, Christianity was seen by pagans as a cult movement within the larger Greco-Roman world. Contrast Stark to the older views of Adolf Deissmann, *Paul: A Study in Social and Religious History,* trans. W. E. Wilson (New York: Harper, 1957), pp. 6-10, about the proletarian or plebian character of early Christianity.

from being a socially depressed group, . . . the Christians were dominated by a socially pretentious section of the population of big cities. Beyond that they seem to have drawn on a broad constituency, probably representing the household dependents of leading members. . . . But the dependent members of city households were by no means the most debased section of society. If lacking freedom, they still enjoyed security, and a moderate prosperity. The peasantry and persons in slavery on the land were the most underprivileged classes. Christianity left them largely untouched.[10]

The point is not that the majority of early Christians were among the social elite but that there was a cross-section of society in the church, and that leaders seem to have been largely drawn from those more nearly able to be called elite—partly because they could provide the venue for the house church meetings. So Paul not only engaged in an urban ministry that put him in contact with the more well-educated and literate in the first place (concentrating on major cities like Ephesus, Philippi and Corinth, which were along major routes) but also deliberately presented his message in a way that attracted a cross-section of society, including the literate. Indeed, it attracted enough of the literate population to make letter writing a viable means of regularly nurturing distant converts in the faith. Both Paul the author and at least some of his audience were educated, literate and capable of reading and appreciating a good letter and responding to it (see 1 Cor 7:1).

Paul's Education

Paul was both a Roman citizen and a Pharisee. The former placed him in the elite category of Greco-Roman society already, the latter potentially among the elite in Jewish society. In particular his being a Pharisee meant, quite apart from the confirmation we get from Acts, that Paul likely cut his educational teeth in Jerusalem.[11] Yet the confirmation from Acts is not

---

[10]E. A. Judge, *The Social Pattern of Christian Groups in the First Century* (London: Tyndale, 1960), pp. 52, 60. A good test case is Paul's converts in Corinth. What we learn from 1 Corinthians, especially 16:15 and 16:19, is that there were households where Christians met which were sufficiently large for between forty and fifty people to meet there. We learn from 1 Corinthians 7:21-23 that there were domestic slaves among the converts. First Corinthians 16:2 and 2 Corinthians 8—9 strongly indicate that there was disposable income among the converts. There is furthermore the important case of Erastus in Romans 16:23. As I have argued elsewhere (see Ben Witherington III, *Conflict and Community in Corinth* [Grand Rapids, Mich.: Eerdmans, 1994], pp. 32-35), it is highly likely that this is the same person about whom there is an inscription in the pavement in Corinth, mentioning that he had performed a public service in order to obtain the office of aedile.

[11]See Martin Hengel and R. Deines, *The Pre-Christian Paul* (Valley Forge, Penn.: Trinity Press International, 1991), pp. 27-30.

unimportant, especially if, as many scholars would still say, Luke may have known about these matters from the apostle himself. Luke tells us that Paul received his essential education not in Tarsus but in Jerusalem—"I am a Jew, born in Tarsus in Cilicia, but brought up in this city at the feet of Gamaliel, educated strictly according to our ancestral law" (Acts 22:3).[12]

Self-evidently, this means that Paul learned to read and write, not just in Greek but also in the sacred language Hebrew, and likely also Aramaic. Some of Paul's language training and literacy may have been obtained at home, but without doubt these skills were honed in his schooling outside the home. Through the offices of Herod the Great, Jerusalem had become a cosmopolitan and in some respects almost Hellenistic city, complete with hippodrome and Greek theater. It must have been extremely attractive to many Greek-speaking Jews from the Diaspora, such as Paul's parents.[13] Tellingly, of the inscriptions from the period in Jerusalem, 33 percent are in Greek and another 7 percent are bilingual.[14] Jerusalem was the great pilgrimage site for all Jews from all over the Mediterranean Crescent (cf. Acts 2), so that some of the great Jewish thinkers and educators visited or moved to this city.

For both pagan and Jewish boys, formal education began at about six years of age.[15] (Girls generally did not receive formal education outside the home in the first century.) The importance of such an early start and thorough grounding in Jewish traditions was impressed on the Jews in Palestine and elsewhere, not least because they feared simply being amalgamated into the syncretistic Greco-Roman culture. Philo is not merely being rhetorically apt when he says, "All people are eager to preserve their own customs and laws, and the Jewish nation above all others; for looking upon theirs as oracles directly given to them by God himself, and having been instructed in this doctrine from their earliest infancy they bear in their souls the images of the commandments" (*Legatio ad Gaium* 210; cf. Josephus *Against Apion* 2.178). Second Timothy 3:15 speaks of Timothy's having been trained in the sacred writings from childhood.

Thus the conclusion of Murphy-O'Connor is fully warranted that in the home and also in school Paul would have been thoroughly grounded in the

---

[12]Here the insights of W. C. Van Unnik, "Tarsus or Jerusalem: The City of Paul's Youth," in *Sparsa Collecta I* (Leiden: Brill, 1973), pp. 259-320, especially pp. 301-5.

[13]See Hengel and Deines, *Pre-Christian Paul*, pp. 54-60.

[14]Ibid., pp. 55, 136 n. 258.

[15]See Marrou, *A History of Education in Antiquity*, pp. 194-200.

Scriptures, perhaps in the Septuagint first and then the Hebrew Scriptures.[16] Detailed study of Paul's Old Testament citations supports the conclusions that he regularly consulted and followed the Greek Old Testament but that he seems to have known the Hebrew text as well.[17] While still at home Paul would have also learned from his parents to speak, read and write Greek. There is evidence that elite Jewish children learned to read not only Torah but also some of the Greek classics such as Homer (*m. Yadayim* 4.6). Secondary studies would start forthwith when a youth had learned to read and write, at least as early as eleven or twelve.

So far as we know, there was no rabbinate or ordination of rabbis before A.D. 70, and Paul's training should not be envisioned as just like that of today's seminary or theological college students. Clearly he became learned in the Hebrew Scriptures and, as he himself suggests, in the traditions of his ancestors (Gal 1:14—though it is not completely certain that this means more than just the Scriptures). Unfortunately, we know almost nothing about his teacher Gamaliel I, apart from what Acts says, because rabbinic traditions regarding Gamaliel I are much later and reflect later agendas.[18] Acts 5:33-39 suggests that Gamaliel was not among the zealots—which is to say that Saul may not at the time have learned enough from his teacher. The Pharisaic movement does not in any case appear to have been unified. Though not rabbis, teachers such as Gamaliel were among those Paul would categorize as sages or wise men (*sophoi*—1 Cor 1:20), and without doubt Paul learned much about the Word from them.

Paul seems to have soaked up the eschatological as well as the theocratic and political teaching of the Pharisees.[19] While much later Paul is still agonizing over the future fate of his ethnic kinspeople and is prepared to talk about "all Israel" being saved (Rom 9—11, especially 11:26-27), he says hardly a word about the future of the temple or the land. Surely in his Pharisaic days he would have learned much about Torah, temple and territory, but just as his conversion radically changed his view of Torah and its function, it must have also changed his views about temple and territory.

---

[16]Jerome Murphy-O'Connor, *Paul: A Critical Life* (Oxford: Oxford University Press, 1996), p. 47.

[17]See D.-A. Kopf, *Die Schrift als Zeuge des Evangeliums: Untersuchungen zur Verwendung und zum Verstandnis der Schrift bei Paulus* (Tübingen: Mohr, 1986). His knowledge of the Hebrew text is not completely clear, because in some cases he likely relied on a Greek OT text other than the LXX.

[18]But see J. Neusner, *Rabbinic Traditions About Pharisees Before 70*, 3 vols. (Leiden: Brill, 1971), 1:341-76.

[19]See Hengel and Deines, *Pre-Christian Paul*, pp. 51-55.

Saul the persecutor of Christians surely must have had quite specific convictions about the sanctity of the temple and the Jews' right to their own territory. These notions may well have been instilled in him in Jerusalem, though perhaps not all of them came from Gamaliel, especially if Paul became familiar, as is likely, with Maccabean lore. Apparently there was also a dualistic and quietistic tendency among some early Pharisees, coupled with a certain fatalism that considered Rome's domination to be punishment for Israel's sins and therefore not to be resisted by violence. Rather one must concentrate on living in the Jewish way and pursuing ritual purity in hopes that God would recognize this repentance and come to cleanse the land. Saul did not subscribe to this view, which may have characterized the Hillelites as opposed to the more radical Shammaites.

Paul would surely have learned methods of debating or persuading, such as arguing from current experience to scriptural proof in midrashic fashion (see 1 Cor 9:7-14), or using what could be called pesher or even allegory to make a point (Gal 4:21-31). Such creative handling of the Hebrew Scriptures should not all be put down to the inventiveness or idiosyncrasies of Paul himself. At least a good measure of it came from his education.

It is believable that Saul the persecutor, who was earnest about strictly preserving the boundaries of early Judaism, was also Saul the propagator of the true faith as he saw it. This would have provided considerable impetus for Saul to become conversant and literate in Greek, including rhetoric, and to gain some knowledge of Greek literature and philosophy so that he could communicate well with Diaspora Jews coming to Jerusalem. Hengel puts it this way:

> It is natural to suppose that the young Paul was at home in this environment of Pharisaic Hellenists; he studied Torah in the school on the temple mount and at the same time improved his Jewish-Greek education, since as a Greek speaking *talmid hakham* he must have felt it important to instruct Jews who came to Jerusalem from the Diaspora in the true—Pharisaic—understanding of the Law.[20]

Perhaps it seems odd to think of a Jew such as Paul learning Greco-Roman rhetoric in Jerusalem, but during this period Nicolaus of Damascus instructed Herod in rhetoric;[21] moreover, Josephus remarks that he, a Jew

---

[20]Ibid., pp. 57-58.

[21]See the discussion in Martin Hengel, *The Hellenization of Judaea in the First Century After Christ* (Philadelphia: Trinity, 1989), pp. 35-40. A useful parallel between very Jewish content and highly rhetorical form can be found in 4 Maccabees. There are also some interesting content

among the elite like Paul, and like Paul a Pharisee well conversant with the Jerusalem scene, knew that Herod Agrippa I and his descendants also received a thorough Greek education, as had Josephus to a lesser degree (*Life* 359).[22]

Great monarchs aspired to have great libraries, and Herod the Great pursued this goal with the help of Nicolaus. Herod would have needed a fairly large Greek library in order to compose the historical chronicles he undertook during his reign. The leading modern expert on these matters, Ben Z. Wacholder, concludes that in addition to the royal family and its circle, "certainly the leading Pharisees studied Greek."[23] We may also point to the figure of the rhetor Tertullus (Acts 24:1-2), enlisted by the high priest to persuade the Romans to hand Paul over.[24] There are other small hints of a degree of Hellenization in Jerusalem even well before the time of Paul. For example, the grandson of Jesus ben Sira, who translated his grandfather's work into Greek in the second century B.C., would have acquired his knowledge of Greek in Jerusalem before he moved to Egypt. And someone in Jerusalem was likely responsible for the Greek translation of 1 Maccabees, a document Saul/Paul must have been well familiar with in view of his persecuting activities and commitment to Maccabean-style zeal.[25]

As Murphy-O'Connor has rightly stressed, "Oratorical skills were the key to advancement in an essentially verbal culture. The acquisition of such skills fell into three parts . . . the theory of discourse which included letter writing, . . . the study of the speeches of the great masters of rhetoric, . . . the writing of practice speeches."[26] Paul had the motive, the means and the opportunity to obtain these skills, even in Jerusalem, and he is likely to have done so before he even took up formal training outside the home. As we shall see, his letters bear witness that he used these skills, both epistolary and rhetorical, to great advantage.

---

parallels between this document and Paul's letters. See Martin Hengel and Anne-Maria Schwemer, *Paul Between Damascus and Antioch* (Louisville, Ky.: Westminster John Knox, 1997), pp. 191-96.

[22]I agree with A. D. Nock, *St. Paul* (London: Thornton Butterworth, 1938), p. 235, that we should not classify Paul's Greek with that of the popular letters (contra Deissmann), but neither does it rank with the highest levels of literary Greek. It lies somewhere between those extremes.

[23]Ben Z. Wacholder, *Nicolaus of Damascus* (Berkeley: University of California Press, 1962), p. 48; see pp. 33-40.

[24]See the discussion of this person in Ben Witherington III, *Acts of the Apostles* (Grand Rapids, Mich.: Eerdmans, 1997), pp. 704-5; and Hengel and Deines, *Pre-Christian Paul*, p. 59.

[25]See Hengel, *Hellenization*, pp. 23-25.

[26]Murphy-O'Connor, *Paul: A Critical Life*, p. 50.

PAUL THE LETTER WRITER

Letter Writing in Antiquity

In a time long before the development of printing presses, typewriters and computers, letter writing was an arduous task and, if one did it very much, a somewhat expensive one. One needed a writing implement, ink and, of course, something to write on. Cicero, writing in about 54 B.C., sums up the situation: "For this letter I shall use a good pen, a well-mixed ink, and ivory polished paper too, for you write that you could hardly read my last letter . . . [because] it is always my practice to use whatever pen I find in my hand as if it were a good one" (*Letter to Quintus* 2.15.1). Throughout antiquity the reed was the pen of choice (the bird's feather appears to have been first used in the seventh century A.D.),[27] papyrus made from reeds of the Nile Delta was the paper, and carbon deposit or soot put into a water solution served as ink.

After obtaining these physical objects, one needed to prepare them. Since there was no ready-made lined paper, one needed a lead disk to lightly line the paper and a straight ruler of sorts to keep the lining even. Other requirements were a reed sharpener—an abrasive stone—and a knife to cut the end of the reed if necessary to start a new point (see, e.g., *Greek Anthology* 6.63-65). None of this came cheaply, especially not the papyrus.[28]

Pliny the Elder describes the process of making papyrus. (1) The papyrus reed is split with a needle into very thin and wide strips; the center portion of the reed is the best and most durable part. (2) These strips are laid on a board moistened with Nile water; sometimes a sort of flour glue might be added to the water. (3) The ends of the papyrus strips are trimmed. (4) The strips are laid horizontally and vertically and "woven" together. (5) The papyrus is put in presses and dried in the sun. (6) Finally the individual pieces might be sown together, never more than twenty sheets in any one roll (*Natural History* 13.74-77). Yet this was not all. Before using papyrus for

---

[27]I am indebted to the fine study by Jerome Murphy-O'Connor, *Paul the Letter-Writer: His World, His Options, His Skill* (Collegeville, Minn.: Glazier, 1995), pp. 2-3.

[28]This is why papyri were often reused, or in desperation one might even use a potsherd or a clay tablet as had been common in the ancient Near East. It is highly unlikely that Paul or any of his contemporaries ever got to the point of regularly using the products of animal hides— namely, parchment or vellum (but cf. 2 Tim 4:13). Such products were even more expensive than papyri and came to the fore only when the codex or book began to be more prevalent than the roll. Martial *Epig* 14.184 is familiar with the parchment codex of many folded skins, but this format was only for the wealthy. The earliest manuscript we have of the Pauline corpus is P[46], the Chester Beatty Papyrus from around A.D. 220. Yet even it, though in codex form, is composed of 52 papyrus sheets folded once.

writing, the writer needed to smooth the paper out with a shell or a piece of ivory (see the quote from Cicero above), taking care not to give the paper too fine a sheen or gloss, as then it would not take the ink very well.

It is not surprising, in view of all that was involved in gathering equipment and preparing to write, that persons who did a lot of writing relied heavily on secretaries, who were skilled in all parts of the process except the making of the paper. Careful study has been done on the use of secretaries for letter writing, and the results are interesting.[29] Since writing materials were expensive, Greek texts were written in what was called *scriptio continua*, without division between words, without punctuation or accents, and without paragraphing.[30] Under these circumstances, and in view of the great length of Paul's letters compared to most ancient letters (cf. below), it would have been crucial that Paul not only use a good secretary with a fair hand but also make sure that the person who delivered the document could actually read it and probably "deliver" it orally. Simply handing a letter to the recipients, leaving them to puzzle out what Paul said and meant, would not have been sufficient. Paul would surely have preferred that one of his coworkers who knew his mind and meaning take a letter, read it to the congregation and answer questions, though doubtless this was not always possible (cf. Col 4:7, 16—"when this letter has been read among you . . .").

Then as now, secretaries had varying degrees of skill, and various skills were required of them. The ancients believed that letters ought to portray the personality of the writer, and to a lesser degree of the recipients.[31] That is, the secretary had to be skilled enough to know the personality, and if possible the writing style, of the author, but also to know what would communicate well with a particular audience. Furthermore, since the letter would be read aloud, clear attention had to be paid to its oral and aural features. If "the well-delivered and persuasive speech [was] the most characteristic feature of civilized life . . . linguistic skill focused on oral speech; the written word was secondary, derived from primary rhetoric."[32] This meant that the rules for certain types of speeches were adapted for use in corresponding types of letters. Not surprisingly, handbooks for secretaries on letter writing gave attention to rhetorical matters and topics, and already in Demetrius's *On Style* (first century B.C.) letter writing is treated

---

[29]See especially E. R. Richards, *The Secretary in the Letters of Paul* (Tübingen: Mohr, 1991).
[30]See Gamble, *Books and Readers*, pp. 48-54.
[31]See the discussion of Theon and Nicolaus's remarks by S. K. Stowers, *Letter Writing in Greco-Roman Antiquity* (Philadelphia: Westminster John Knox, 1986), pp. 32-33.
[32]Ibid., p. 34.

with the issues and definitions of rhetoricians clearly in view.[33] In short, a good secretary would have to know the mind of his employer, how to write, the proper form for a letter, and also rhetoric and its conventions.

It appears that already in the first century B.C. a form of Greek shorthand had been developed, which was in due course taken over by the Romans.[34] This important skill, called *tachygraphy* (fast writing), was not a skill possessed by all secretaries. A collection of Greek stenographic symbols from the early second century A.D. (*PMur* 164) has been found in Palestine. *Papyrus Oxyrhynchus* 724 tells of a man who took his slave to a secretary to learn "the signs" for shorthand. E. R. Richards's conclusion is surely warranted that already in the first century there was a flourishing practice of using Greek shorthand.[35] It is possible, then, that Paul's secretaries took dictation, but we cannot be sure.

Richards has also shown that normally secretaries did not have license to compose letters on their own for their employer or master, except perhaps a formal acknowledgment of the receipt of something or submission of a simple request.[36] So the all-too-ready suggestion of epistolary pseude-pigrapha for some of the later Paulines is problematic. The people of Paul's day would have been concerned about the moral problem of deception, even if occasionally it happened that some wrote in the name and style of another. Producing epistolary pseudepigrapha was quite different from a secretary's occasionally composing documents in his master's or employer's name. The initiator in the latter case would often let the recipient know how the document had been written (see Cicero *Letter to Friends* 8.1.1). Thus the burden of proof must lie with those who argue that some of the later Paulines are not ultimately by Paul. Strong evidence of differences in both style and substance must be produced before such a conclusion can be warranted.

Yet what about the case where the secretary was in fact a trusted coworker? Was there such a thing as epistolary coauthorship? To judge from Cicero *Letters to Atticus* 11.5.1, such a thing was apparently rare. Yet it was equally rare for the opening line of a letter to formally mention the name of someone who had nothing really to do with the document. In short, "the naming of another person in the address was anything but a meaningless convention."[37] Neither was it pro forma to say "we" even if one meant "I" in a letter. This means that in Pauline letters where more than

---

[33]Ibid.

[34]Murphy-O'Connor, *Paul the Letter Writer*, pp. 10-11.

[35]Richards, *The Secretary*, p. 39.

[36]Ibid., p. 111.

[37]Murphy-O'Connor, *Paul the Letter Writer*, p. 18.

one person is mentioned in the address *and* the first-person plural *we* is used to refer to the senders of the letter, we should probably assume that collaborators were involved in composing the letter. For example, 1 and 2 Thessalonians are from Paul, Silvanus and Timothy.

But while *we* is prominent in 1 and 2 Thessalonians, 1 Corinthians begins with a greeting from Paul and "our brother Sosthenes," yet *I* is the dominant pronoun throughout. So Sosthenes may be mentioned as the scribe who wrote the letter, or as a person familiar to the Corinthians who had read and agreed with the letter, yet here we should probably not think of coauthorship. Similarly, in 2 Corinthians Timothy is mentioned in the address, as are "all the members of God's family who are with me" in Galatians (Gal 1:2), but the pronouns that follow do not suggest that multiple authors were involved in the writing.[38] If we are concerned to look for the characteristic Pauline style or diction, we would probably do best to focus on letters where Paul seems to be the sole author, though he may have had help from a secretary.

Evidence from Cicero (*Letter to Friends* 9.26.1) suggests that it was a normal practice for a secretary to make two copies of a letter, one of which was retained by the sender. This has led to Richards's plausible suggestion that collecting Paul's letters was far less difficult than we might assume. It was a matter of simply finding or having the author's copies of the various letters all in one place or in one person's possession.[39] In view of ancient practice, this suggestion should not be lightly dismissed, but we have no firm evidence that this was the case. Perhaps the allusion to knowledge of "all" the Pauline corpus in 2 Peter 3:15-16 suggests that already in the first century there was such a master collection, and it may be that that collection itself had been copied and circulated.

How were letters sent? There was no regular postal service before the time of Augustus, that is before about the turn of the era, and this service was used only for official business. Private persons had always to make their own arrangements. Wealthy or elite persons might well arrange a regular courier who was reliable (Cicero *Quintus* 3.1.8), but this seems to have been rare. Cicero says of a letter he has just written, "I am thinking of giving it to the first person I meet tomorrow" (*Atticus* 2.12.4). Paul seems to have relied on the social network he built up of coworkers, converts and fellow Christian travelers. It was a regular practice in antiquity to commend the letter bearer to the recipients in some way, and this practice

---

[38]See ibid., pp. 33-34.
[39]Richards, *The Secretary*, p. 165 n. 169.

seems to be reflected in Romans 16:1-2 and Colossians 4:7-9.[40] Paul did not likely entrust his letters to just anyone.

Paul and His Letters

Paul in his epistolary context. Available evidence from the first century suggests that apart from an inveterate long-winded letter writer like Cicero, Paul had few peers and no superiors in the writing of lengthy epistles. His most personal of all letters, the one written mainly to Philemon, is longer than most ancient personal letters. Paul's short letters were long by ancient standards. Indeed, Cicero's letters generally pale in comparison to Paul's in terms of both length and strength. Even Paul's opponents begrudgingly recognized that "his letters are weighty and strong" (2 Cor 10:10), and his friends struggled with these letters, saying "there are some things in them hard to understand, which the ignorant and unstable twist to their own destruction" (2 Pet 3:16).[41] The great English cleric and poet John Donne was later to remark that whenever he opened one of Paul's letters he found thunder, indeed a thunder that resounded throughout the earth.

How very distinctive Paul's letters must have appeared, given the ordinary epistolary fare. Consider the following first-century letter written only shortly before Paul wrote 1 Corinthians:

> Mystarion to his own Stoetis:
> Greetings.
> I have sent you my Blastus to get forked sticks for my olive gardens.
> See that he does not loiter, for you know I need him every hour.
> Farewell.

This uninspiring little document (written September 13, A.D. 50) is quite characteristic of ancient letters. They were mostly business and very little pleasure. Cicero's and Paul's epistles are the exceptions, not the rule.

Yet some ancient letters do express passion and personal interest. The following is a letter from an irate wife to her wandering husband, begging him to return:

> Isaias to her brother Hepaestion greeting.
> If you are well and other things are going right, it would accord with the

---

[40]See ibid., pp. 70-71.

[41]For what it is worth, G. Murray and other classicists have spoken of Paul's vigorous and distinct prose style and have even called him one of the great figures of Greek literature, "a classic of Hellenism." Cf. G. Murray, *Four Stages of Greek Religion* (New York: Putnam, 1912), p. 146; F. F. Bruce, *Paul: Apostle of the Heart Set Free* (Grand Rapids, Mich.: Eerdmans, 1977), p. 15.

prayer which I make continually to the gods. (I myself and the child and all the household are in good health and think of you always.)[42] When I received your letter from Horus, in which you announce you are in detention in the Serapeum at Memphis . . . I thanked the gods, but I am disgusted that you have not come home, when all the others that have been secluded there have come. After having piloted myself and your child through such bad times and been driven to every extremity owing to the price of corn, I thought that now at least, with you at home, I should enjoy some respite, but you have not even thought of coming home nor given any regard to our circumstances, remembering how I was in need of everything while you were still here, not to mention this long lapse of time and these critical days during which you send us nothing. As moreover, Horus, who delivered the letter, has brought news of your having been released, I am thoroughly displeased. Notwithstanding as your mother also is annoyed, for her sake as well as for mine please return to the city, if nothing more pressing holds you back! You will do me a favor by taking care of your bodily health. Goodbye. (*P. London* 42)[43]

Clearly, Paul was not the only person of his day who sometimes expressed anger in his letters.

In the 1950s through the 1970s a great deal of useful literary and form-critical analysis of Paul's letters was undertaken, but not much fruitful comparison of Paul's letters with those of other writers of his era. In part this was because fewer and fewer New Testament scholars were receiving the kind of classical education that had been required in the nineteenth and early twentieth centuries—learning of classical languages, study of the Greek and Latin classics, the training in ancient rhetoric. However, in the more recent quest for the historical Paul and the social context of his proclamation and letters, scholars have been paying renewed attention to ancient educational and letter-writing practices, the classics and other ancient sources. Harry Gamble, Jerome Murphy-O'Connor, E. R. Richards and others have done invaluable work in these areas.

Paul's epistolary style. Not just in order to understand Paul, but in view of the fact that as many as twenty of the twenty-seven documents of the New Testament contain or are letters, it behooves us to consider how these sorts of documents worked and communicated in the hands of Paul and other early Christians. First, letters in antiquity were, at least before Cicero went public, intended as private communications, much as they are today. They

---

[42]This line was added as an afterthought, perhaps to tone done the hostile overtones of what follows. See Murphy-O'Connor, *Paul the Letter Writer*, p. 56 n. 1.

[43]See C. K. Barrett, *The New Testament Background: Selected Documents*, rev. ed. (San Francisco: Harper & Row, 1987), pp. 28-29.

were generally not for public consumption and certainly not for publication. I suspect Paul would be astounded that these intense and personal communications he sent to his converts in Asia Minor, Greece and elsewhere are now circulating to millions, being printed over and over again. Second, letters were seen as poor surrogates for face-to-face communication. This is clearly Paul's own feeling on the matter (see Rom 15:14-33; 1 Cor 4:14-21; Gal 4:12-20; 1 Thess 2:17—3:13).

From about four centuries before until four centuries after Christ, letters had a rather stereotyped format or structure usually involving the following elements: (1) the name of the writer, (2) the name of the addressee, (3) the initial greeting, (4) the health wish or prayer, (5) the body of the letter and (6) conclusion, usually with final greetings. Especially in business letters, the style was usually simple and directly to the point, though personal letters could be more expansive and interesting.

To these bare bones of epistolary structure Paul adds considerable flesh. Basically Paul's letters contain the following features:

1. opening, sender, addressee
2. initial greeting
3. thanksgiving or blessing
4. body, complete with introductory formula, the body proper, eschatological or doxological conclusion, sometimes a travelogue
5. paraenesis or ethical remarks
6. closing greetings
7. writing process and signature
8. closing benedictions

Each of these sections can find some precedent in other ancient letters, but Paul tailors these elements again and again to suit his purposes. For example, the opening will often give a clue as to the message Paul will convey, or will prepare for that message. Thus in Philemon, Paul reminds the slave owner that Paul himself is in chains for Christ. Slaves, especially runaway ones when caught, would have such chains. In other words, Paul is identifying with the plight of Onesimus from the outset, aiming to persuade Philemon that he should treat Onesimus as he treats Paul.[44]

---

[44]See C. Roetzel, *The Letters of Paul: Conversations in Context*, 3rd ed. (Louisville, Ky.: Westminster John Knox, 1991). This work is the best brief, readable summary of the gains from the 1950s to the 1970s of the literary critical study of Paul's letters. It has rightly become the standard textbook for students beginning to study this material. It can be compared to S. K. Stowers, *Letter Writing in Greco-Roman Antiquity* (Philadelphia: Westminster Press, 1986), which focuses more on recent gains from comparisons to letter writing in antiquity and social scientific studies of such data.

Paul also customizes the greeting. The standard Greek greeting was *chairein*, from the same root as *charis*, which we translate as grace. The standard Jewish greeting was *shalom*, or peace. Paul combines the two standard greetings in order to greet both the Gentiles and the Jews in his audience.[45]

In a pagan letter a health wish or prayer often seems simply perfunctory, but Paul turns this portion of the letter into a major opportunity for prayer. Here especially we find a preview of coming attractions. Paul prays about the issues he will later address in the letter. For example, in 1 Corinthians 1:4-9 he gives thanks for the spiritual gifts and knowledge of the Corinthians, two issues he will deal with at length in chapters 1—4 and 12—14.

It is equally telling when Paul omits a standard feature of the ancient letter. Among the congregational letters, Galatians is the only one without a thanksgiving or blessing section. This is likely because Paul is so upset with the Galatians that he can think of nothing to be thankful about! In Thessalonians, by contrast, the thanksgiving section seems to go on and on. The situation dictates the use of the form.

As a particularly clear example of how a thanksgiving section can provide a preview, consider Romans 1:8-17, where Paul expresses (1) his desire to come to Rome (see Rom 15:22-25), (2) his wish to impart to the Romans some spiritual gift to strengthen them, namely a useful summary of some of the essence of his gospel (Rom 1:18 to the end of Rom 8), (3) his conviction that salvation is for the Jew first but also for the Gentile (Rom 9—11) and (4) his confidence in the basis of this salvation, the faithful one, Christ, whose gift must be accepted by faith and lived out faithfully (Rom 12—15).

These are ad hoc documents, written for specific situations. Paul seems to have customized his letters in either of two major ways. Letters that aim basically to solve problems (e.g., 1 Corinthians) devote much space to the body and ethical sections. Other letters are more progress-oriented, including only a few corrective exhortations; Philippians is a good example. The epistolary elements are tailored to suit the circumstances. The progress-oriented letter include more praise and thanksgiving, the problem-solving letters more instruction and correction.

The body of the letter is of course where we find the bulk of the content. Since the content varies according to the situation being addressed, there is

---

[45]It is perhaps a sign that his audience is mostly Gentile that he always says "peace" second rather than first in his greeting.

more diversity here than elsewhere in these documents. There are certain regular ways that Paul will signal he is beginning the body of a document:

- an appeal or a request—"I appeal to you, brothers and sisters . . ." (1 Cor 1:10)
- a disclosure remark—"I want you to know . . ." (Rom 1:13; 2 Cor 1:8; Phil 1:12; 1 Thess 2:1)
- an expression of amazement—"I am astonished that . . ." (Gal 1:6)
- a remark about hearing—"I have heard of your faith . . ." (Eph 1:15)

Eschatological remarks regularly crop up either at the end of the body of the letter or the end of a major section (Rom 8:31-39; 1 Cor 4:6-13; Gal 6:7-10). Travel plans also tend to be mentioned at the end of the body or the end of a particular argument (cf. Rom 15:14-33; 2 Cor 12:14—13:13; Gal 4:12-20).

It has been frequently said that in the next major section of the letter, the paraenetic or ethical section, Paul is more conventional and tends to draw more on traditions than elsewhere. There is a real measure of truth in this observation; in fact, it is in the ethical portions of his letters that Paul alludes to or cites the teaching of Jesus (Rom 14; 1 Cor 7), the Old Testament (see Gal 6) or Christian traditions (Col 3:18—4:1). Yet his ethical remarks are not confined to this section, and in a problem-solving letter like 1 Corinthians we find ethical enjoinders throughout the body. Sometimes too Paul takes a particular ethical topic and gives it more extended treatment, as in Romans 13 (relations with governing authorities) or 1 Corinthians 7 (marriage and singleness).

In his closing remarks Paul seems least bound to Greco-Roman epistolary conventions. He uses not just the standard closing greeting or greetings but also benedictions or doxologies (Rom 16:27; Phil 4:20).

Clearly Paul modified the standard epistolary elements and used them creatively, yet his writing approach was not entirely original. In various places he specifies that he is drawing on traditional confessional material (1 Cor 11:23-26; 15:3-11); some of his ethical catalogs reflect a definite indebtedness to earlier Jewish, Christian and even Greco-Roman material (e.g., Gal 5:19-26), particularly in his virtue and vice lists (cf. Rom 1:29-31; 13:13; 1 Cor 5:10; 6:9-10; 2 Cor 6:6-7, 14; Phil 4:8; Col 3:18-25) and hymnic material (Phil 2:6-11; Col 1:15-20). His autobiographical remarks tend to have an ethical thrust, encouraging emulation or occasionally shaming the audience into proper behavior (cf. 2 Cor. 11—12; Gal 1:17—2:14; Phil 1:12-15; 1 Thess 2:1-12).

Paul's letters stand out from many of his day not only for their length but also because they are group communications, and as such are often closer to official pronouncements than private correspondence. Because he expects his letters to be read aloud in the congregation (Col 4:16), Paul writes only what he wants all those present to hear. Doubtless he conveyed more private messages through the bearer of the letter. Paul's letters were but a part of a total communication effort that involved (1) personal visits and face-to-face discussions, (2) the sending of oral messages by Christian courier and (3) the sending of letters, presumably with oral messages as well. Furthermore, since many of Paul's letters are parts of ongoing conversations, listening to them is rather like hearing one half of a phone conversation. One needs to reconstruct the other half to make complete sense of what has been said.

Colin Morris has made a humorous attempt to reconstruct some of the letters Paul received.[46] Consider the following imaginary reconstruction of a letter sent to Paul from Thessalonica by someone who heard his preaching about the eschaton and was converted (cf. 1 Thess 4—5; 2 Thess 2):

> My dear Paul,
>   The followers of Jesus in this city are in receipt of your letter which was read out in church a month ago and which appears to confirm a widely held view here that our Lord will be returning in glory at any moment to take believers such as my humble self back with him to heaven. Being a hard-headed businessman I took your words with utmost seriousness. To prepare myself and my family for the Day of the Lord, I sold my business at a knock-down price and gave the proceeds to the poor—and that let me add was a tidy sum, but I assume I won't need cash in heaven! So here I am with my bags packed, my property disposed of and myself, my wife, and my children taking it in shifts to scan the skies for something unusual to appear. In fact, every time I hear a trumpet, I nearly jump out of my skin! And what has happened? Nothing.
>   I can't help feeling that I've been made to look an utter fool in the eyes of my friends and business acquaintances. They all think I've gone stark, raving mad. Meanwhile, the man who bought my business, far from suffering the catastrophe reserved for the wicked, is making a handsome profit and living in my house, which is one of the finest in the city. . . .
>   Would you kindly tell me what I do next? The tax people are pestering me for last year's assessment, and I haven't a lead shekel to pay them with. Being a man of God you are probably unaware that disposing of one's assets in the interests of a religion which is not recognized by the state does not qualify one for retrospective tax exemption. So, I'm in a pretty pickle, let me tell you! I feel most strongly that the financial implications of the Second Coming should have been given more serious consideration by the apostles. . . .

---

[46]Colin Morris, *Epistles to the Apostle: Tarsus Please Forward* (Nashville: Abingdon, 1974), pp. 13-16.

I am in a most embarrassing situation, what with a nagging wife and three children who have gotten completely out of hand because they prefer earthly pranks to what they imagine will be heavenly boredom. . . . It is one thing to suffer for the faith; quite another to be made to look ridiculous. However I do not intend to move from this spot until Jesus comes to collect me. Meanwhile it would be quite dishonest of me not to express grave concern at the most unbusinesslike way in which this whole matter is being dealt with. I await an eager reply, otherwise I shall be forced to turn the whole matter over to my lawyers.

Paphlos

(There follows a letter from Paphlos's lawyer telling Paul he has exactly thirty days to make good on his promise of heaven or face litigation in Thessalonica!)

Another distinctive attribute of Paul's letters is they seem to have been geared to become part of an act of worship. For example, notice how some of them end. In 1 Corinthians 16:20 (cf. 2 Cor 13:12), Paul tells his converts to greet one another in the assembly with a holy kiss—a gesture appropriate between Christian friends or family, especially in a household setting, that in our era has become the handshake in a moment of fellowship and greeting during the service. Or again, notice how Paul tends to begin his letters with a prayer and end with a benediction (cf. 1 Cor 1:4-9; 16:23). Imagine being present at the worship service at which 1 Corinthians was first read! It must have been a long service, and apparently would have involved a fellowship meal and the Lord's Supper as well (1 Cor 11).

Paul was concerned about the issue of miscommunication or the suggestion that a letter delivered was not really from him. Signing and postscripting one's own letters as marks of authentication was a very regular practice in antiquity, and Paul was insistent on doing this (Gal 6:11; 2 Thess 3:17). Here the question arises of the particular relationship of Paul to his secretaries and coauthors. Did Paul dictate word for word to his scribe? Did he give the gist but leave the detailed formulation of the material to the secretary? Did he instruct a trusted literate Christian friend such as Timothy or Luke to write in his name without indicating specific content?

It is possible that Paul did all of these things, depending on the situation. We have reasonably clear evidence both from the personal signature remarks (see above) and from the reference to a scribe (Rom 16:22) that Paul regularly used secretaries. It is also reasonable to think of 1 and 2 Thessalonians as involving joint authorship. One would suspect that the degree of dictation by the apostle depended on how trusted and experienced a Christian friend he was relying on when a given letter was written.

For what it is worth, however, among the capital or basically undisputed

Paulines (Romans, 1 and 2 Corinthians, Galatians, Philippians, 1 Thessalonians, Philemon) there is a remarkable degree of stylistic similarity, involving not just vocabulary but also grammar and syntax. Furthermore, there are indications of writer's distress: sentences broken off in midstream. For example, 1 Corinthians 9:15c reads literally, "For it would be better for me to die [than] . . . No one will deprive me of my boast." This and other examples of anacoluthon (incomplete sentences) surely suggest that Paul was dictating these letters and that the scribe at various points simply could not keep up.

For these reasons and others, most scholars have rightly not doubted that we have the mind of Paul in these letters. Even in the case of coauthored documents, we must assume that Paul agreed with what was said, especially given that in 2 Thessalonians 3:17 Paul puts his own signature and imprimatur on the document.

The perils of the later Paulines. Yet because of the relative homogeneity of style and thought of the capital Paulines, many scholars have raised serious questions about the source of other letters ascribed to Paul. Some have doubted 2 Thessalonians, but not on grounds of style or vocabulary. More have doubted Colossians, and even more Ephesians. Perhaps a majority of scholars today doubt the authenticity of the Pastoral Epistles. An adequate treatment of the issue would have to consider each of these documents individually. In general, however, knowing what we know about Paul's use of secretaries, difference in style and vocabulary should not be taken as clear proof of difference in authorship.

For example, it is perfectly plausible that Paul used Tychicus to write Colossians (4:7), a person to whom Paul had perhaps given unusual leeway to write in his own manner, since he was more directly related to the Colossians and their church than Paul. Paul may have read over what was written, agreed with it and wrote the closing greeting in his own hand (4:18). Perhaps Paul and Tychicus discussed the content of the letter beforehand or as the document was being composed. This hypothesis would account for various of the usually noted differences between this document and the earlier Paulines.[47]

To take another example, why does Ephesians manifest such a verbose, Asiatic style of Greek, unlike much of the Pauline corpus? Two interesting factors may have been at work. First, this document is, if a letter at all, a

---

[47]Notice that there appears to have been a regular method for the scribe or another party to identify himself near the end of the document: e.g., *Oxy. Pap.* 1067, "I also Alexander, your father, salute you much," should be compared to Romans 16:22.

circular letter, not one addressing a particular congregation about particular issues. It can even be said to be more of a homily than a letter. Second, the document is an excellent example of epideictic rhetoric, the flowery rhetoric of praise and blame, focusing on the praise of the church, or better said, of God's work of creating one new people of God out of Jews and Gentiles.

This document is different in character from other Pauline documents. We cannot simply because of its style and rhetorical form exclude the possibility that it came from Paul. As with Colossians, concepts and content must be the deciding factor. Is there content in Ephesians or Colossians that is not merely un-Pauline, in the sense that we do not find it in the undisputed letters, but quite clearly non- or even anti-Pauline? This would be a clear sign that these documents did not originate in any way with Paul, unless we are prepared to suggest that Paul changed his mind on major issues during his ministry. From my viewpoint, differences in purpose, function, secretaries and rhetorical character can quite readily explain the differences between the earlier Paulines and these documents.[48]

The Pastoral Epistles are another matter. While some have tried to argue for the authenticity of one of these documents and not the other two,[49] this must be a hard sell, since there is so much continuity of style and vocabulary among the Pastoral Epistles, as well as some notable differences from the undisputed Paulines. The earlier Paulines never say "It is a faithful saying . . ." but this phrase crops up regularly in the Pastorals (1 Tim 1:15; 4:9-10; 2 Tim 2:11-13; Tit 3:3-8). Such factors have led even some conservative scholars to conclude that the Pastorals must have been written in the post-Pauline era by someone other than Paul, perhaps using a few Pauline traditions and seeking to apply his insights to new situations.[50] Yet there are

---

[48]Here is not the place to argue at length for Pauline authorship of Ephesians. I am aware that some will see this emphasis on realized eschatology as a sign pointing to non-Pauline authorship, but frankly one would expect the focus in epideictic rhetoric to be what is true in the present and not what will be true in the future, as would be the case with deliberative rhetoric. The notion of the headship of Christ in this document is clearly more developed than in the earlier Paulines, but it is to some extent foreshadowed in 1 Corinthians 11:3. The cosmic role of Christ is also clearly alluded to in 1 Corinthians 8:6. The case against Pauline authorship cannot be lightly dismissed, but most of those who stress it have not sufficiently taken into account the rhetorical character of this document. See, e.g., J. Christiaan Beker, *Heirs of Paul* (Minneapolis: Fortress, 1991).

[49]See most recently Murphy-O'Connor, *Paul: A Critical Life*, pp. 356-59.

[50]David G. Meade, *Pseudonymity and Canon* (Grand Rapids, Mich.: Eerdmans, 1986), but see the critique of E. Earle Ellis, "Pastoral Letters," in *Dictionary of Paul and His Letters*, ed. Gerald F. Hawthorne, Ralph P. Martin and Daniel G. Reid (Downers Grove, Ill.; InterVarsity Press, 1993), pp. 658-66. Another way of configuring the whole issue of authorship of the Pastorals is found in I. H. Marshall, "Prospects for the Pastoral Epistles," in *Doing Theology for the People of God: Studies in Honor of J. I. Packer*, ed. Donald Lewis and Alister McGrath (Downers Grove, Ill.: InterVarsity Press, 1996), pp. 137-55.

several real problems with this line of thinking, and one mitigating factor needs to be considered.

First, if the Pastoral Epistles were written at the very end of Paul's life, when he was actually in Mamertine prison, perhaps as late as A.D. 67-68, he likely lacked the resources and tools (see above) to write letters personally, and probably he would not have had one of his trusted Christian scribes with him all the time. At most they may have been allowed to visit once in a while. Possibly the Pastorals are the only Pauline documents that did not involve some form of reasonably close dictation. It is plausible that someone like Luke, allowed to visit and attend Paul (see 2 Tim 4:11), actually wrote these documents in his own style and on Paul's behalf, based on things Paul said to him shortly before he was executed. (The similarities in style, vocabulary and syntax between Luke—Acts and the Pastorals require an adequate explanation.[51]) The writing may have even been carried out after Paul's death.

It makes sense that at the end of his life Paul would make some remarks about church order and organization, to smooth the way for postapostolic leadership in his churches. It also makes sense that he would try to strengthen his right and left hands, Timothy and Titus, and prepare them for the burdens and decisions they would face without him.

There is no good reason to doubt the plausibility of such a scenario, unless of course one can demonstrate that these letters contain not merely *non*-Pauline but *un*-Pauline material. Has such a compelling demonstration been given thus far? I for one am not yet convinced by the arguments for inauthenticity, and it is notable that many New Testament scholars who had spent years on these letters were not convinced either (cf. the commentaries by J. N. D. Kelly, C. Spicq, Joachim Jeremias, George Knight, and on 2 Timothy especially, Luke Timothy Johnson).

Perhaps these documents came from a later Paulinist and not Paul. Yet there are several problems with this hypothesis. First, if these documents are by a later disciple of Paul, would he really write personal letters like these to convey his message for a later age? Why not a tract or circular letter like Ephesians, or even a homily like Hebrews? Would a real admirer of Paul include bogus traveling plans and personal remarks like we those we find in 2 Timothy 4:9-15, 19-21, knowing full well that the apostle would not be going to these places or dealing with these things? The problem of deception should not be dodged, and it is to Murphy-O'Connor's credit that he faces it by arguing for the authenticity of 2 Timothy. Yet this leaves

---

[51]On this see S. G. Wilson, *Luke and the Pastoral Epistles* (London: SPCK., 1979).

hanging the question of why 1 Timothy and Titus are so similar in style to 2 Timothy.

Furthermore, we do have early extracanonical evidence that Paul was released from house arrest and did travel again as he had planned. First Clement 5:1-7 is probably written in the late first century A.D., apparently in Rome, by someone who knows the traditions of the Roman church. It reads in part: "He was exiled, he was stoned, he was a herald both in the east and in the west. . . . He taught righteousness throughout the whole world, and having reached the limit of the west [presumably Spain] he bore testimony before the rulers, and so departed from the world." Both the *Acts of Peter* and the Muratorian Canon from the second century also contain some form of this tradition.

It is quite unbelievable that Paul the letter writer, if indeed released from house arrest in Rome in 62, would never again write to his converts and never again be concerned about the churches he had already founded, even if he still planned to head west to Spain. It is even more unbelievable that he would have left Timothy and Titus in the lurch if he had had an opportunity to encourage them shortly before he died.

The suggestion of pseudepigraphy in the case of the Pastorals, whatever merits it may have in regard to other religious documents of this period like the *Letter of Aristeas*, creates more problems than it solves. From the very first verse, each of these documents claims to go back to Paul in some form. Disputing this ascription requires solid evidence. This is why E. E. Ellis is right to conclude,

> The role of the secretary and the use of preformed traditions in the composition of the Pastorals cut the ground from under the pseudepigraphal hypothesis with its mistaken nineteenth-century assumptions about the nature of authorship. They require the critical student to give primary weight to the opening ascriptions in the letters and to the external historical evidence, both of which solidly support Pauline authorship.[52]

Significantly, these letters add little to what we know of Paul's theology or his general ethics. They are personal in character and not the kinds of pronouncements we would expect from an imitator of the earlier Paulines. They do not in fact look like the earlier Paulines! Yet there is nothing un-Pauline or anti-Pauline in them, nothing Paul might not have said as his life came to a close. In this circumstance, the positive evidence that they go back to Paul in some form outweighs the negative evidence. Nevertheless,

---

[52]Ellis, "Pastoral Letters," p. 661.

due to the weight of scholarly opinion, none of the significant conclusions of this study about the historical Paul are based on the Pastoral Epistles.

Conclusions: Paul and His Letters

What then do we learn about Paul himself from his letter writing? First, we gain a clear picture of someone who cares deeply about his converts. Not just the joyful passages but also the angry ones make clear how much he loved them. We find a man prepared to go to considerable trouble to nurture relationships with people who are a good distance away. There is a poignancy to Paul's letters, for they reflect his great desire for community, to be one with his converts and have good fellowship with them. Paul is no loner; he is far more like a parent who misses his faraway children. We cannot assume that Paul was much like a modern individualist. His chief desire was for communion and community, not just with his God but also with his people—Christians and, as Romans 9—11 makes evident, also Jews. In his letters he reflects the collectivist mentality again and again. His social networks are crucial to him personally but also in carrying out the shared task of spreading the good news.

Honest readers of his letters must also recognize Paul as an authority figure, however troubling that side of his personality may be to postmodern folk. In letters like Galatians and 1 Corinthians, when he is nearly driven to distraction by his converts' misadventures, it is quite clear that he is prepared to take charge and command. Paul the apostle comes through loud and clear in passages like 1 Corinthians 4:14—5:13. Paul was not an advocate of congregational church polity. He reflects the hierarchical bent of his society. The difference is that Paul's hierarchy is ultimately theocratic. Christ is the head of the body, and Paul is simply his servant and agent on earth. It is possible that this theocratic approach was a carryover from Paul's days as a zealous Pharisee.

Paul's letters also reveal that by ancient standards he was a very well-educated and articulate person. He would surely have been among the top 5 percent of his society in literacy and education (see Acts 26:24). Obviously he was primarily learned in the Hebrew Scriptures, but there are hints of considerable wider learning as well (e.g., 1 Cor. 15:32-33). We will learn more of this shortly when we reflect on Paul the rhetor. Texts like 1 Corinthians 9 and Philippians 3 hint that Paul was a person of considerable social status, stepping down to win others for Christ.

The letters suggest that Paul attracted an important minority of people who had a similar status, people like Erastus, Stephanus, Phoebe, Priscilla and Aquila, who could be key players in the advancement of the gospel.

House churches were required for a religious group that had no priests, no temples, no sacrifices and no means of support from cities or emperors.

Paul's letters bear clear witness not only to his commitment to the conversion of households (1 Cor 1:16) but also to his urban missionary strategy. Paul went to venues like Corinth, Ephesus, Philippi and Psidian Antioch where his Jewishness and his Roman citizenship could provide him with open doors and where his trade of tentmaking could support him so he could offer the gospel freely and without need of patronage. We have no letters from Paul's hands to noncity dwellers. Paul knew that the cities and the Roman roads that linked them were the keys to reaching the Mediterranean Crescent quickly for Christ.

Finally, we learn from these letters that Paul had a profound relationship with God in Christ. Among the characteristics that most distinguish his letters from other ancient ones is the amount of religious and spiritual content and the fact that it is never perfunctory in character. To many ancients Paul must have seemed a great holy man, philosopher, sage or prophet. Ironically, the answer to the questions "Where is the one who is wise? Where is the scribe? Where is the debater of this age?" (1 Cor 1:20) is in fact right before our eyes and those of Paul's converts. Paul himself was trained as a scribe, learned in the Scriptures and Greek wisdom, always a pundit. Surely he was scarcely ever dull or uninteresting. Every page of his letters shines with his zeal and earnestness—along with his formidable powers of persuasion.

PAUL THE RHETOR

The Rhetorical Climate and Character of Paul's World

In an oral culture, the ability to speak well is always important, and the ability to persuade is required of any public figure. In Paul's day, rhetoric, though it might degenerate into the art of speaking well, was in essence the art of persuasion. So important was this ability that rhetoric was a fundamental staple of ancient education. "For the great majority of students, higher education meant taking lessons from the rhetor, learning the art of eloquence from him."[53] This education would begin ideally as soon as a young person had finished learning the rudiments of grammar, or as we would say, when he finished grammar school. Rhetors were everywhere in the Roman Empire. There was no need to travel to a major university town to find one. If Eretria, a small city on a Greek island in the Aegean (*Sylloge*

---

[53]Marrou, *A History of Education,* p. 194.

Inscriptionum Graecarum 714), could have one, a cosmopolitan, Hellenized city like Herod's Jerusalem surely had several.

Powers of persuasion and eloquence, always highly admired in the Greco-Roman world, were especially important for the underdogs if they wished to obtain what they wanted from their rulers. Likely there was considerable desire and pressure for upwardly mobile young Jewish males in Jerusalem to gain rhetorical skills. The importance of these skills would certainly have not been lost on anyone who was a Roman citizen and desired to take advantage of what that meant in the Roman Empire, or on a Pharisee who was zealous to see others become Torah-true. Perhaps rhetorical skills would have been particularly prized by Diaspora Jews living or staying in Jerusalem. By the time Paul was being educated, rhetoric had become the primary discipline of Roman higher education.[54] There is thus an a priori likelihood that Saul dedicated a considerable portion of his educational years to learning rhetoric. If this was the case, what did he learn?

There were three primary kinds of rhetoric, each tooled for a particular setting. Judicial, or forensic, rhetoric was for use in the law courts; deliberative rhetoric was meant to be used in the assembly; and epideictic rhetoric was meant to be used in funeral oratory or public speeches lauding some event or person, or in oratory contests in the marketplace or the arena. Public speaking had become a major spectator sport, drawing crowds in all these venues.

With the demise of democracy and the more significant tasks of the public assembly (see, e.g., Acts 19:35-38: the dismissal of the crowd with reference to the proconsuls and the courts), and with the rise of empire, the rhetoric of display, of pomp and circumstance, and of entertainment came to the fore. And it is not surprise that in an agonistic culture such as the Greco-Roman world of Paul's day,[55] lawyers were kept quite busy throughout the Empire (see 1 Cor 6). The main venues for deliberative rhetoric in Paul's day were the royal court (among ambassadors, those interceding with a patron and those seeking votes) and voluntary religious associations, where people had to be persuaded to join and then to believe and behave in a specific fashion. The cities with a *demos* or assembly would also have another venue for such rhetoric, although these assemblies did not have the democratic character of the ancient Greek ones.

Paul was capable of using all the forms of rhetoric, but he preferred

---

[54]See S. Bonner, *Education in Ancient Rome* (Berkeley: University of California Press, 1977).
[55]See the earlier discussion.

deliberative rhetoric. Now that public democratic societies had become mere perfunctory tools of the elite, he saw the *ekklēsia*, the assembly of believers, as the ultimate place of freedom, where it was appropriate to use discourse, dialogue and debate to encourage people to believe and live as they ought.[56]

Forensic rhetoric was the rhetoric of attack and defense. Its focus was the past, since one was normally taken to court for something that had already been said or done. Deliberative rhetoric was the rhetoric of advice and consent, and its focus was the future, for an *ekklēsia* would always be debating appropriate policy for the future. This rhetoric concentrated on issues of advantage or harm. Epideictic rhetoric was the rhetoric of praise or blame, and its focus was the present, for it sought simply to produce admiration or revulsion, mirth or anger, joy or sorrow in a crowd, moving them without prompting them to do more than appreciate and applaud. It was often pure entertainment.

Over the course of time, speakers learned more and less effective ways of arranging a speech. The standard forms from the time of Aristotle through the time of Paul and beyond entailed the following: The speaker would attend to his own ethos or character, with an attempt to make the audience favorably disposed toward himself and so his topic. Then the rhetor would focus on *logos*, the actual acts of persuasion, through argumentation and insinuation. Finally the speech would turn to pathos, the emotional appeal meant to arouse the deeper passions and so move the audience to convict or exonerate, act or refrain from acting, applaud or boo.[57]

Just as there were certain regular parts of an ancient letter, a speech was made up of certain requisite elements:

- *exordium*—the beginning of the speech, meant to make the audience well disposed and open to what followed
- *narratio*—explaining the nature of the disputed matter, or of facts that needed to be taken into account as a basis of the argument
- *propositio*—where the essential proposition of the speaker and perhaps also of the opponent were laid out
- *probatio*—the essential arguments of the speech
- *refutatio*—often included in the *probatio*, where the opponent's arguments were dismantled, disproved or at least disparaged

---

[56]On all of this see Witherington, *Conflict and Community*, pp. 40-50.

[57]Anyone who wishes to get the sense of what rhetoric was all about should read either Aristotle's *Rhetoric* for the earlier Greek side of things or Quintilian's *Institutio Oratio* for an able first-century compendium of both the Greek tradition and its adaptation by the Romans for use in Latin.

• *peroratio*—recapitulating the main points of the *probatio* and making the final emotional appeal to the audience

A whole array of rhetorical devices and tropes could be trotted out to enhance or embellish any of these portions of a speech. In addition, any good rhetorical handbook, such as Quintilian's, would spend considerable time addressing voice, including tone and volume, gestures, appearances and the like. The art of persuasion involved more than just eloquence; it involved the whole impact of a speaker on his audience. It was not uncommon for a rhetor to use a variety of kinds of rhetoric to persuade in a given speech. The end justified the variety of means.

In many ways rhetors were the ancient equivalent of preachers or evangelists, and this is yet another reason Paul would want to be adept at rhetoric, especially after his conversion to Christianity—"so that I might by all means win some for Christ" (see 1 Cor 9:22). Duane A. Litfin sums up the significance of rhetoric in Paul's day:

> Rhetoric played both a powerful and pervasive role in first century Greco-Roman society. It was a commodity of which the vast majority of the population were either producers, or much more likely consumers, and not seldom avid consumers. . . . Oratory became more prevalent than ever. In both the Roman and the Greek setting the frequency with which speakers rose to address audiences, for whatever reasons, seemed to be on the rise during the first century. The quality of oratory may have declined but the quantity had not.[58]

Paul's Rhetorical Letters

In some ways it is not surprising that the recent rebirth of rhetorical analysis of Paul's letters has taken some scholars by surprise.[59] The twentieth century witnessed a demise of classical studies, both in public (state-funded) schools and to a lesser extent in private schools, and in universities as well. By and large, most New Testament scholars, particularly in the second half of the twentieth century, have not studied the Greek and Latin classics, and rhetoric is for them a *terra incognita*. It was not always so.

In the United States, for example, as late as the end of the nineteenth century rhetoric was among the three or four major subjects taught at major universities. The famous war veteran and hero of the battle of Gettysburg Joshua Chamberlain was prior to his enlistment a professor of rhetoric and

---

[58]Duane A. Litfin, *St. Paul's Theology of Proclamation: 1 Corinthians 1-4 and Greco-Roman Rhetoric* (Cambridge: Cambridge University Press, 1994), p. 132.

[59]For a brief helpful survey on the history of rhetoric see ibid., pp. 1-134.

metaphysics (or "natural and revealed religion"), and he was no isolated phenomenon.

Reading some of the early church fathers' commentaries on Paul's letters, such as John Chrysostom's commentary on Galatians, one becomes aware that those who lived in a rhetorical environment recognized Paul's letters for what they were—rhetorical speeches within an epistolary framework and with some epistolary features. After all, a letter was a surrogate for oral speech, and a good letter would seek to model as many of the best and most persuasive features of speech as possible.

In fact, the rhetorical forms of Paul's letters are more revealing of his concerns and content than are the epistolary forms and elements. The structures themselves are more dependent on rhetorical forms than on epistolary forms, especially beyond and between the prescript and the postscript.

The renewal of the study of Paul's rhetoric may in large measure be ascribed to two important developments in the late 1970s and early 1980s. First H. D. Betz's landmark commentary on Paul's letter to the Galatians appeared, and then the work of G. A. Kennedy on rhetoric in the New Testament, following his other key studies on ancient Greco-Roman rhetoric.[60] The doctoral students of these two scholars then began to carry forward the discussion. Today many others have joined the dialogue, to the point that rhetorical criticism has become a major growth area in New Testament studies. Since the modern discussion really began with Betz's analysis of Galatians, we will begin there as well.

Galatians is one of the most obviously rhetorical of all Paul's letters. It includes the usual epistolary framework at the beginning and the end (1:1-5; 6:11-18), but for the most part it is pure speech material. Unlike most of Paul's other letters, Galatians has no thanksgiving section, no greetings to particular persons, no health wish, no mention of present or future travel plans. Any educated ancient person would surely have seen Galatians 1:6—6:10, being composed of mostly arguments and narrative that supports them, as a rhetorical tour de force—"full of sound and fury." But what sort of rhetoric is it? There are three major possibilities: (1) it is forensic in character (so Betz), (2) it is a mixture of forensic and deliberative rhetoric,[61] or (3) it is an example of deliberative rhetoric, but of a polemical sort (so Kennedy).[62]

---

[60]H. D. Betz, *Galatians: A Commentary on Paul's Letter to the Churches in Galatia* (Philadelphia: Fortress, 1979); George A. Kennedy, *New Testament Interpretation Through Rhetorical Criticism* (Chapel Hill: University of North Carolina Press, 1984).

[61]So Richard N. Longenecker, *Galatians* (Waco, Tex.: Word, 1990), pp. c-cxix.

[62]J. D. Hester, "The Rhetorical Structure of Galatians 1:11-14," *Journal of Biblical Literature* 103 (1984): 223-33, seems to be all alone in arguing that Galatians is epideictic rhetoric.

In analyzing a speech or rhetorical letter, one needs to remember that there is a difference between the emotional tone of a letter and its argumentative substance. All three major forms of rhetoric can be polemical in tone. This does not make them apologetic in character. Close inspection reveals that all of the arguments in Galatians have one aim—to convince the Galatians to take a particular course of action in the near future as they deliberate whether to get themselves circumcised and submit to the Mosaic law. As Kennedy says, the issue is "not whether Paul had been right in what he had said or done, but what they themselves were going to believe and to do."[63] Even Galatians 1—2 is not an example of apologetic or forensic rhetoric, the rhetoric of attack or defense. Paul's remarks about the gospel and his autobiography do not function to defend his apostolic office or message. The issue is not Paul's past but the Galatians' future. Paul's past is brought up to help the audience see how they should and should not behave—following his good example since his conversion, avoiding his pre-Christian example.

There are other very good reasons that a forensic analysis of Galatians won't work. First, forensic rhetoric has no place for exhortations such as we find in Galatians 5:1—6:10. Exhortations belong to the deliberative form of rhetoric, the attempt to persuade or dissuade about a future course of action.

Second, Paul calls upon his audience to imitate his behavior (4:12), something quite appropriate in a deliberative speech but not in a forensic one.

Third, the essence of the major arguments in Galatians is that the Galatians are foolish to listen to the agitators and wise to heed Paul. Paul argues, in effect, that if the Galatians submit to the law they will be harming themselves and losing the advantages they already have in Christ by faith. Arguments about harm or advantage are deliberative arguments.

Fourth, the function of the *narratio* in Galatians 1—2 is precisely what Aristotle says a deliberative *narratio* ought to do—speak of things past "in order that being reminded of them, the hearers may take better counsel about the future" (*Rhetoric* 3.16.11). Quintilian says it is most appropriate in a deliberative *narratio* to "begin with a reference either to ourselves or to our opponent" (*Institutio Oratoria* 3.8.8-10), which is what we find in Galatians 1—2. It is true that the tone here is somewhat polemical and even defensive. This is because Paul must establish his ethos or character at the beginning so the audience will be ready to receive the arguments that follow.

Notice too that Paul says this is a discourse for the assemblies in Galatia

---

[63]Kennedy, *New Testament*, p. 146.

(1:2), another pointer that it is a deliberative act of persuasion. The following outline shows the structure of Galatians and the deliberative discourse it contains.[64]

Epistolary Opening (1:1-2)
Epistolary Greeting (1:3-4)
Doxological Conclusion to Epistolary Section (1:5)
Exordium: Two Gospels? (1:6-10)
Narratio: The Origin and Character of the Gospel of Grace (1:11—2:14; 1:11-12 is transitional)
    1. The Gospel of Grace (1:11-12)
    2. A Narrative of Surprising Developments: Jerusalem, Antioch and Beyond (1:13—2:14)
Propositio: By the Faithfulness of Christ, Not by Works of the Law (2:15-21)
Probatio
    Argument One: The Faith of Abraham and the Foolishness of the Galatians (3:1-18)
        1. The Appeal to Spiritual Experience (3:1-5)
        2. The Appeal to Scripture (3:6-14)
        3. The Appeal to Legal Covenants (3:15-18)
    Argument Two: The Goal of the Guardian, the Function of the Faithful One (3:19—4:7)
        1. Why the Law Was Added (3:19-22)
        2. The Guardian's Goal (3:23-29)
        3. The Heirs Apparent (4:1-7)
    Argument Three: Shared Experience (4:8-20)
        1. Déjà Vu (4:8-11)
        2. Paul's Labor Pains (4:12-20)
    Argument Four: The Allegory of Antipathy (4:21—5:1)[65]
    Argument Five: The Unkindest Cut of All (5:2-15)
        1. Testimony from the Top (5:2-6)
        2. What Cuts and What Counts (5:7-12)
        3. Freedom's Service, Love's Law (5:13-15)
    Argument Six: Antisocial Behavior and Eschatological Fruit (5:16-26)
        1. Foiling the Fulfillment of the Flesh (5:16-21)

---

[64]For more along these lines see Ben Witherington III, *Grace in Galatia* (Edinburgh: T & T Clark, 1998), pp. 25-35.

[65]It is possible to see this portion of the discourse as a *refutatio* if in fact Paul is countering arguments of the agitators about Jerusalem and the Sinai covenant and Abraham, but this is not certain.

2. The Spirit's Fruit (5:22-26)
Argument Seven: Bearable Burdens and the Yoke of Christ (6:1-10)
    1. The Law of Christ (6:1-5)
    2. Doing Good to Teachers and Others (6:6-10)
Epistolary Authentication Formula (6:11)
Peroratio (6:12-17)

Galatians is not the only example of deliberative rhetoric in the Pauline corpus. Another fine example, a little shorter in length, is the deliberative argument for concord and harmony found in Philippians.[66] Whereas Galatians seeks to head off harm and enhance advantage for Paul's converts, Philippians aims in classic fashion (by appeal to multiple examples) to produce harmony, unity and oneness of mind among believers in Philippi.[67] Here is a brief outline of this rhetorical piece.

Epistolary Prescript (1:1-2)
Epistolary Thanksgiving/*Exordium* (1:3-11)
Propositio (1:27-30)
Probatio (2:1—4.3)
Peroratio (4:4-20)
Epistolary Greetings and Closing (4:21-23)

This letter focuses largely on positive and negative examples for the audience to follow or shun: (1) Paul (1:12-14, 18b-30) versus the rival preachers (1:15-18a), (2) Christ (2:5-11) and Timothy and Epaphroditus (2:19-30) versus this crooked generation (2:15), (3) Paul (3:5-17, 20-21) versus the Judaizers (3:2-6, 18-19), (4) the negative examples of Euodia and Syntyche (4:2-3). The concluding *peroratio* includes a statement of the quali-

---

[66]In passing it is important to remark that there is no basis for the theory that Philippians is a combination of several Pauline letters. First, there is no textual evidence to support such a conjecture. Second, this conjecture is based on a complete failure to see the unifying rhetorical structure of the whole document; it presents a series of arguments from examples meant to invoke unity. It was always important to produce both negative and positive examples for the audience to learn from. Philippians 3:2–21. is not a piece of another letter. Rather, it provides the essential negative counterpart to the positive examples of Christ, Paul and the Pauline coworkers already presented in Philippians 1—2. It is followed by a further example of discordant behavior in Philippians 4:2-7. Against Murphy-O'Connor, *Paul: A Critical Life*, pp. 211-13, see Ben Witherington III, *Friendship and Finances in Philippi* (Valley Forge, Penn.: Trinity Press International, 1994), pp. 11-14.

[67]For a helpful brief analysis of Philippians as deliberative rhetoric see D. F. Watson, "A Rhetorical Analysis of Philippians and Its Implications for the Unity Question," *Novum Testamentum* 39 (1988): 57-87.

ties or virtues one looks for in such examples (4:8-9).

Elsewhere I have provided a lengthy discussion of how 1 Corinthians is, as a whole, another excellent example of deliberative rhetoric,[68] but this "speech" is almost four times as long Philippians, and interesting or entertaining digressions were necessary for any long speech (see Quintilian *Institutio Oratoria* 3.7.1-4). Digressions would often take the form of a different kind of rhetoric, such as we find in 1 Corinthians 13—an excellent and poetic example of epideictic rhetoric in praise of love. On the macrorhetorical level 1 Corinthians is deliberative in form and function, but in the digression in 1 Corinthians 13 we have microrhetoric of an epideictic sort. Yet even 1 Corinthians 13 serves the larger deliberative purposes of the letter by showing the more excellent way by which the Corinthians should exercise their gifts from God. Interestingly, deliberative rhetoric in ancient arguments for social concord often appealed to love (Aristotle *Nicomachean Ethics* 8.1.4).

Many commentators have noted the especially eloquent and elevated style of this section of 1 Corinthians, but prior to the rhetorical analysis of the letter there was no adequate explanation for the fact that this material has a different form from other parts of the letter. First Corinthians 13 functions as an emotional appeal, attempting to win the audience's heart after many arguments directed at their minds. Epideictic rhetoric was especially useful for such purposes and provided an opportunity to display one's skill and culture, something the Corinthians clearly sought in their teachers.[69]

Second Corinthians can be taken as another example of Pauline macrorhetoric. This letter has sometimes been thought to be a combination of several Pauline letters. Usually the division is thought to come between chapters 1—9 and chapters 10—13. But there are problems with this assessment. First, 2 Corinthians 8—9 constitutes a different sort of material and rhetoric from what comes before and after it. Second, 2 Corinthians 6:14—

---

[68]Witherington, *Conflict and Community*, pp. 39-41, where I largely follow the excellent study of M. Mitchell, *Paul and the Rhetoric of Reconciliation* (Tübingen: Mohr, 1991). See, however, the useful critique by S. M. Pogoloff, *Logos and Sophia: The Rhetorical Situation of 1 Corinthians* (Atlanta: Scholars Press, 1992).

[69]See Witherington, *Conflict and Community*, pp. 264-73, and also C. A. Holladay, "1 Corinthians 13: Paul as Apostolic Paradigm," in *Greeks, Romans and Christians*, ed. D. Balch, Everett Ferguson and Wayne A. Meeks (Minneapolis: Fortress, 1990), pp. 80-98. His argument shows that we must take the first-person singular seriously in this chapter. Paul indeed presents himself as an example, but as part of the praise of love, not of himself. Notice how the change in rhetorical mode is signaled directly at the beginning of this piece when Paul says "and now I will show [or display] a more excellent way." Epideictic rhetoric is the rhetoric of show or display.

7:1 seems to be of a different order or ilk as well. So if we are going to start partitioning this document, good arguments could be made that it actually includes fragments of at least four letters, not just two.

In fact, however, none of this speculation has any textual evidence to support it, and an adequate rhetorical analysis allowing for significant digressions in a lengthy rhetorical piece can explain the letter's structure. In my view, 2 Corinthians is essentially a lengthy piece of forensic rhetoric with two significant deliberative digressions (6:14—7:1 and 8—9), digressions that still serve Paul's larger forensic purposes.[70]

Again, forensic rhetoric is the rhetoric of attack and defense, and nowhere is such rhetoric as plainly evident in the Pauline corpus than in 2 Corinthians 10—13. Here Paul pulls out all the stops, using irony, sarcasm, mock boasting, a fool's discourse and a host of other rhetorical devices to persuade his converts that he is indeed an innocent and honorable man, unlike his opponents. Understanding the rhetorical function of this material is the key to understanding its character. For example, as a deflation device, meant to prick a hole in the balloon of the opponents' grandiose claims about themselves, in 2 Corinthians 11:30-33 Paul presents himself as a great ancient warrior going in reverse. In antiquity a Roman soldier who was first up a wall and into a conquered city would win a special award called a wall crown. Paul says he will boast of being first *down* the wall, in a basket, escaping his foes.[71] Paul makes himself the butt of his joke in order to disarm the audience and make them see the foibles of the false teachers. It is a subtle way of attacking the opponents indirectly, using a kind of argument, *insinuatio,* appropriate to the situation.[72] The overall structure of 2 Corinthians can be outlined as follows.

Epistolary Prescript (1:1-2)
Epistolary Thanksgiving/*Exordium* (1:3-7)
Narratio (1:8—2:14, with further thanksgiving and transitional elements in 2:15-16)
Propositio (2:17, stating the basic fact under dispute)
Probatio and Refutatio (3:1—13:4)
    1. Paul's characterization of his ministry and his rhetorical approach (3:1—6:13)

---

[70]See Witherington, *Conflict and Community,* pp. 355-65.
[71]See ibid., pp. 458-59.
[72]The situation was that the Corinthians were favorably impressed with the "bogus apostles," and so Paul must resort to indirect means, sarcasm and irony to disengage them from such an attitude.

2. A deliberative digression (6:14—7:1) in which Paul puts the audience on the defensive by attacking their attendance at feasts in pagan temples (cf. 1 Cor 8—10)

3. Paul's defense of the severe letter (7:2-16)

4. A deliberative argument for the collection (8—9)

5. A comparison of Paul and his rivals in Corinth, the false apostles, with a strong emotional appeal (10:1—13:4)

Peroratio (13:5-10)

Epistolary Greetings and Closing Remarks (13:11-13)

Second Corinthians shows Paul's great flexibility in using rhetoric, but note that he does not violate any rhetorical conventions in doing so. Digressions were a quite proper part of rhetorical strategy, especially in long speeches. The essential forensic character of the document is shown at the beginning in the long defensive *narratio*, in the further defense of the severe letter, in the attack on the continued Corinthian practice of attending idol feasts, and of course in chapters 10—13. The other portions of the letter serve these larger forensic purposes and arguments.

How does rhetorical analysis help us understand Paul's letters and the apostle himself? For one thing, careful attention to the *propositio* and the *peroratio* in a given document provides direct clues to Paul's purposes. What is the essential proposition he will defend or advance? Of what is he trying to convince his audience? It is easy to get lost in Paul's arguments unless we know the thread that ties them together. The *propositio* and *peroratio* help us see the function and purpose of the whole, where the arguments are meant to lead us.

Also, understanding rhetoric helps us to know when Paul is being serious and when sarcastic, when ironic and when irenic. Tone is of course difficult to judge in a written document, but things become easier when, for example, one picks up the rhetorical signals that the writer is engaging in inoffensive self-praise, or *insinuatio*.

Furthermore, we discover that Paul's letters in fact are arranged quite carefully according to the patterns of ancient speeches. They were meant to be delivered orally, not just delivered by hand to the audience. The arguments that make up the bulk of the letters are carefully arranged and often build to a climax, as in 1 Corinthians 15 (the quintessence of the logical Pauline tour de force) or 2 Corinthians 10—13 (a powerful emotional appeal that has real pathos). Surely few in Paul's audience could hear the incredible list of his trials and not be moved (2 Cor 11:23-29).

Paul was an excellent preacher and persuader, so excellent that despite the hindrances of his "thorn in the flesh" he could convert many. He knew that the heart as well as the mind had to be won if the day was to be won. Rhetoric provided him with a powerful tool for "preaching for a verdict" or persuading with success. Many modern preachers would do well to study ancient rhetoric carefully, perhaps by reading through Quintilian's handbook and comparing what he says to what we find in Paul's letters. Paul's writing shows a splendid grasp of how one can persuade people to be, do and think things they have not been, done or thought before.

But how does rhetoric help us understand the apostle himself and what sort of person he was? First, it reminds us that we are dealing with a well-educated, articulate person. Paul was no rustic backwoods preacher rattling off whatever exhortations came to mind. To the contrary, these letters reflect significant learning, skill, organization and preparation. No wonder even Paul's opponents begrudgingly admitted his letters were powerful and weighty.

Second, Paul's use of rhetoric reminds us that he was concerned to reach his audience where he found them, which meant he had to use strategies that would work with a largely Gentile audience. He wanted his proclamation and persuasion to be a word on target, not merely a shot in the dark. So Paul used all available ancient tools of persuasion to achieve his ends, being careful not to violate basic ethical commitments and his commitment to truth. Paul was a man of his time, and he was a successful evangelist in part because he knew what would and wouldn't work with the audiences he addressed in the Greco-Roman world. He also knew enough about Mediterranean temperament to know that all the logic in the world without pathos would not likely appeal, much less persuade. As Pascal once said, "The heart has reasons that reason knows not of." Paul sought to appeal to the whole person, so that by all means he might win some. To win some in a rhetorically saturated environment, one's speech needed to be winsome. It must not be forgotten that *paideia*—culture, and particularly eloquence—was one of the great Greco-Roman cultural values.

Rhetorical analysis tells us that Paul was very much at home in the Gentile world. Though a Jew, he would not have seemed a stranger to Gentiles. He could speak their language, and he was prepared to fellowship with and even live with them, at great cost to his Jewish heritage and friendships, and indeed to his Jewish Christian friendships, as Galatians shows. It is clear that Gentiles were willing to listen to and be persuaded by such a person. Yet it may be that Paul had to spend many years in the Gentile world honing these rhetorical skills before he could find success in

Galatia, Philippi, Corinth and elsewhere. This may be why the ten or more hidden years in Syria and Cilicia, before Paul's time with Barnabas in Antioch, still remain largely hidden.[73]

Paul's use of rhetoric reminds us that he desired to be a part of a larger world than many of his Jewish Christian contemporaries who were dragged kicking and screaming into a cosmopolitan church. It reminds us that Paul valued a good deal of Greco-Roman culture.

Paul believed in sifting culture, not merely criticizing it. His faith was not world-negating but world-transforming. His model was not the Amish-style enclave but an aggressive approach aiming to take every thought captive for Christ. We would do well to ponder this approach in an age when anathemas rather than engagement, critique and persuasion seem to be the usual conservative Christian approach to the larger society.

Last, Paul's use of rhetoric or persuasion reminds us of his commitment to freedom, the value of democracy touted in the old Greek assemblies. Christian assemblies in homes could be replicas of that old assembly if they were places of discourse, dialogue, debate and persuasion. To be sure, Paul could and would command if driven to it, but he would far rather win an audience's compliance in matters theological, ethical and social. "For freedom Christ has set us free" is his stirring cry in Galatians 5:1. As a collectivist, Paul longed for a community that voluntarily lived in harmony, served one another in love and freely shared Christ with the world. If love is the chiefest of Christian virtues, and love can never be compelled or coerced, then a community of freely interacting like-minded and like-hearted persons is the intended end product.

Rhetorical analysis, then, reveals Paul drawing on a great Greco-Roman heritage and working toward a great Christian community, a cosmopolitan family that would embody the best of both Jewish and Gentile worlds. Such a vision of the kingdom come on earth is still "a consummation devoutly to be wished."

CONCLUSION: REEXAMINING THE ASSUMPTIONS

As we conclude our quest for Paul the letter writer and rhetor, we must focus in on one objection to this whole line of approach. Going back to Adolf Deissmann in the early part of the twentieth century, the objection goes something like this: Paul was by no means a member of the social elite

---

[73]Pauline chronology will be discussed later. On the hidden years see Hengel and Schwemer, *Paul Between Damascus and Antioch.*

in the Greco-Roman world. His sometimes awkward Greek and various elements of his lifestyle, especially his trade of tentmaking, locate him several social rungs below the Ciceros of the ancient world. As Deissmann saw it, Paul shared the social level of most of his converts, which is to say at best the artisan or lower class.[74] Paul's reminder in 1 Corinthians 1:26 describes not only the predominant character of his audience but also himself. Most of them were likely freedmen and freedwomen, slaves and the like.

There are a variety of problems with this assessment. Paul was a multicultural person, and while it is true that the Greco-Roman elite considered working with one's hands demeaning, first-century Jews did not share this view, nor did Greco-Roman artisans.[75] The assessment of E. A. Judge and other social historians appears more accurate: Paul deliberately stepped down the social ladder in order to reach as wide an audience for the gospel as possible. Such downward mobility sometimes led Paul to take up his trade. In 1 Corinthians 9 he admits that he deserves to be remunerated for his work of sharing the gospel, but he chose not to accept offers of money from various Corinthians because it would have enmeshed him in the social networks of patrons and clients. Paul did not wish to become anyone's client, because he *did* wish to be everyone's apostle and spiritual parent.

Ronald Hock has suggested that Paul's tentmaking was right at the heart of what Paul was about, and in fact it consumed most of his time.[76] This suggestion goes too far, as a careful evaluation of texts like 2 Corinthians 11:23-25 shows. Paul spent most of his time evangelizing and traveling, not making tents. Yet when he was in a city like Corinth, Ephesus or Thessalonica for an extended period, he may well have regularly practiced his trade.[77] There would have been considerable inducement to do so; for example, the Isthmian Games were held in Corinth, and surely many tourists who came for the games would have looked for a tent to rent or purchase. This provided Paul with a golden opportunity to reach all sorts of people.

Most important, the attitude Paul expresses about his tentmaking in 1 Corinthians 9 does not reflect an artisan's point of view. He says he made a conscious decision to forgo patronage. Artisans had no such options. Paul's

---

[74]See Adolf Deissmann, *Paul: A Study of Social and Religious History* (New York: Harper & Brothers, 1957). This study appeared in English originally in 1911.

[75]See R. MacMullen, *Roman Social Relations 50 B.C. to A.D. 284* (New Haven, Conn.: Yale University Press, 1974), pp. 73-83.

[76]See R. Hock, *The Social Context of Paul's Ministry* (Philadelphia: Fortress, 1980), pp. 67-77.

[77]Acts 18 suggests that Paul practiced his trade only in Corinth, but 1 Thessalonians 2, when compared to 1 Corinthians 9, suggests Paul practiced his trade in various places.

letters reveal that he was not reluctant to accept financial aid from his converts so long as it was seen as part of a partnership in the gospel, not a form of patronage (see Phil 4:10-13). We must assume, then, that Paul had specific reasons for taking up the trade he practiced for a while in Corinth.[78] He was not simply carrying on with his trade as he did always and everywhere. To the contrary, he made tents in Corinth to avoid patronage and to have ready access to people who would frequent the market during the Isthmian Games. It was part of his strategy of being all things to all persons so that he might by all means reach some. Paul the apostle made use of Paul the tentmaker's skills when it was useful or necessary for the sake of the gospel.

Some Cynic philosophers were known to frequent workshops, and so even when Paul did practice his trade, it would not necessarily have sent the signal that he was a person of low social status. In this regard Martin Hengel makes reference to a man named Isaac, a linen merchant from Tarsus who was an elder in the Jewish community in Jaffa. He was, in short, a relatively high-status person in his own community, yet like Paul he was not reluctant to practice a trade—indeed, his work is proudly mentioned on his tombstone![79] But also like Paul, Isaac had lived in more than one social world, and while he may have had high status in the microcosmic Jewish community in Tarsus and in the Holy Land, elsewhere he would have been seen as a Jew and an artisan, which in the anti-Semitic environment of the Roman Empire would have represented two strikes against him.

The Jewish apostle to the Gentiles had to work in that larger Greco-Roman environment, and thus in spite of his learning and his freedom to choose, he had to prove himself in each new place he went. He must have regularly experienced considerable status inconsistency, and 2 Corinthians 11:23-24 shows that he often was treated in ways unbecoming of someone of his social status and education. Yet Paul did not spend much time worrying about what the world thought of him, for he was utterly convinced of what God thought of him and had done in him—making him an agent and a prophet of the good news.

---

[78]It would appear likely from 1 Thessalonians 2:5-10 that Paul also practiced his trade in Thessalonica so as not to be a burden and perhaps so as not to appear like a money-grubbing orator or Sophist. That Paul was mainly a wordsmith meant that, when he first came to a town, many in the Greco-Roman world would see him as suspect, especially if he immediately accepted patronage or lavish gifts for his oratory. His rhetoric would have been compromised and the gospel would have been viewed as just another subject speakers discoursed on to entertain or educate and so to earn one's crust of bread.

[79]See Hengel and Schwemer, *Paul Between Damascus and Antioch*, pp. 160-61.

CHAPTER 4

PAUL THE PROPHET AND APOSTLE

This chapter examines Paul in two of his roles of power—prophet and apostle. While the latter role has been the subject of intense scholarly scrutiny, the former has been largely neglected. In early Christianity both prophets and apostles were Spirit-inspired, Spirit-led figures. Both prophets and apostles appear in lists of early church functionaries. Paul identifies himself frequently as an apostle but only rarely, and mostly indirectly, as a prophet.

Prophesying in early Christianity does not seem to have been the same as teaching, preaching, exegeting or applying sacred texts. It was instead a matter of offering spontaneous utterances from God, speaking as God's mouthpiece. Often, but not always, these utterances had a predictive or forward-looking component. Paul himself spoke about the future, not merely on the basis of common Christian tradition but also on the basis of "mysteries" or words of revelation given to him by God. Examples appear in some of what he says about resurrection in 1 Corinthians 15 and his words about Israel in parts of Romans 9—11.

Paul should not be considered a false prophet, as he did not predict the certain return of Christ during the first century A.D. He spoke rather of the possible imminence of Christ's return. Paul believed that the eschatological age had been launched by the Christ event, which meant that Paul himself lived between the eschatological "already" and the eschatological "not yet." The certainty of the "not yet" led him to express a variety of hopes about the future. His prophetic language about the future is sometimes metaphorical, yet the metaphors were meant to point to a coming historical reality, not merely an eternal truth about the nature of the divine-human encounter.

As a Pharisee and a Jewish Christian, Paul would not have thought of resurrection in a purely metaphorical sense, or even as just the form of the afterlife in heaven. Resurrection for Paul has to do with being raised out of the realm of the dead and given a body like Christ's. The resurrection of believers will be triggered by the return of Christ and followed by the final judgment, the conquering of the last enemy, death, and the establishment of God's full kingdom on earth as in heaven. Though this does not entail the end of the space-time continuum, Paul the prophet certain saw it as entailing the end of human history as we know it, in particular the end of human misery and wickedness.

Paul's discussion is couched in the terms of and meant to be seen as a counterclaim to the imperial eschatology and propaganda of his day. The combination of prophecy and the work of the Spirit in and through his life made Paul a powerful figure, one who quite readily might be welcomed as a messenger of God (Gal 4:14).

For Paul, being an apostle of Christ meant being Christ's agent, envoy or ambassador. He had been given a specific commission and authorized by the Master to do specific things. His authority was derived, not inherent.

Paul's apostolic status was disputed in the early church. Some apparently thought that Christ authorized as his agents only those who had been his traveling companions and whom he had sent forth while he was still on earth—or at least whom had been sent forth by the Twelve and perhaps also James. Paul admits in 1 Corinthians 15 that his means of becoming an apostle was irregular, but he believed the outcome of the process was the same.

Paul's need to swim against the current of opinion may explain why he was vocal and combative about his apostolic status. Evaluating Paul involved great controversy in his day as it does now. Doubts about him likely arose partly because in antiquity there was little belief in the possibility of radical change in human personality.

Paul had disputes with most other major leaders in the early church. He steadfastly maintained that his authority did not derive from below: he was not merely an agent of a particular church commissioned to a limited missionary task. The letter to Philemon provides an excellent example of how Paul exercised his apostolic authority among his converts, preferring rhetoric, even of the arm-twisting variety, to simple commands. This letter also reveals that he enabled and relied on local leaders and his coworkers to carry out various tasks and exercise authority in his absence. Paul did not feel that he had to hold all the reins of power in his own hands. He was an empowerer of the disfranchised, including the poor and women, though his vision of the power structure was to some extent hierarchical, with apostles at the top. Yet these apostles must model themselves on the ultimate servant leader, Christ, which meant they were at the bottom of the pyramid, lifting everyone else up and enabling them.

IT WAS ONCE ASKED ABOUT ISRAEL'S FIRST KING, "IS SAUL ALSO AMONG THE prophets?" (1 Sam 10:12-13). If we ask the same about Saul of Tarsus, the answer must be the same—yes, for like his forebear he was a prophet, and apparently an ecstatic one as well. Yet Paul was also an apostle. In this chapter we look closely at Paul in his roles of power, particular prophet and apostle, and see what this tells us about Paul as an ancient person. These roles, along with his ministry as a teacher, placed him at the top of the power hierarchy in the early church (see the hierarchial list in 1 Cor 12:28).

PAUL THE ESCHATOLOGICAL PROPHET

Power was conveyed in many ways in antiquity, but one of the most powerful persons in any of the cultures of the Mediterranean world was the prophet or the messenger of God. Power and authorization that came directly from God or the gods was deemed the most valuable and valid of all powers; for this reason most ancient rulers claimed such powers or filled their court with such persons. The famous story of how Josephus avoided execution by prophesying, as it turned out correctly, Vespasian's rise to the emperor's throne reveals the great respect even people of the west had for the prophecies of eastern and perhaps especially Jewish seers. Paul's converts likewise would have been impressed with whatever prophetic gifts Paul may have had. This may have been one reason the Galatians received him with great joy: they saw him as a messenger of God (Gal 4:14).

I have already discussed Paul as a man of the Spirit, and all that I said there about his being a seer, a person who had apocalyptic visions, must stand as background for the first portion of this chapter.[1] Texts like 1 Corinthians 3:6-16 show that Paul believed that God was still revealing his will to the world through persons in whom the Holy Spirit dwelled (v. 10). This revelation included the making known of things hidden and of mysteries having to do with God's plan to save humankind. This Paul calls wisdom. There is clearly an overlap between the concepts of seer and of sage here, as there was in the cases of Daniel, Ben Sira and Jesus.[2]

Perhaps even more revealing is what Paul says about himself in 1 Corinthians 13:2—"And if I have prophetic powers, and understand all mysteries and all knowledge, and if I have all faith, so as to remove mountains, but do not have love, I am nothing." Here *if* with the present-tense verb probably connotes not a purely hypothetical possibility but a real condition.[3] Paul has prophetic powers and understands mysteries and matters of spiritual knowledge—but then he had already told his converts about spiritual knowledge earlier in 1 Corinthians 3. We must take seriously what Paul says about himself in 1 Corinthians 14:6-19, especially verse 6—"How will I benefit you unless I speak to you in some revelation or knowledge or prophecy or teaching?" These are not terms picked at

---

[1]See the earlier discussion on Paul as a seer of visions.

[2]On this overlap and on Paul as a sage, see Ben Witherington III, *Jesus the Sage: The Pilgrimage of Wisdom* (Minneapolis: Fortress, 1994), chapters 1-3, 8.

[3]See C. A. Holladay, "1 Corinthians 13: Paul as Apostolic Paradigm," in *Greeks, Romans and Christians*, ed. D. Balch, Everett Ferguson and Wayne A. Meeks (Minneapolis: Fortress, 1990), pp. 80-98.

random; they reflect Paul's view of some of what he had communicated to the Corinthians in the past.

Definitions and Distinctions

To judge from recent scholarly work, there has been a revival of interest in Paul as a prophetic figure. Earlier in the twentieth century Paul's apostleship was much debated, but precious little was said about Paul as a prophet. When there was some discussion about Paul as a prophet, he was mainly compared to prophets connected with various forms of Hellenistic religion, especially mystery religion,[4] though Christian prophecy was directed to and intended for the edification of whole congregations and was not merely a response to an inquiry by a private individual.[5] A full-length monograph on the subject of Paul as a prophet by K. O. Sandnes[6] now confirms that Paul's understanding of prophecy and prophets owes far more to the Jewish tradition than to the Greco-Roman tradition. There have also been other significant treatments of the subject within larger studies of prophecy in the New Testament era.[7] E. Earle Ellis and others following him have insisted that Paul's way of handling the Old Testament shows him to be a prophetic figure.[8] In an influential study on prophecy in the Corinthian church, Wayne Grudem argues that there was overlap in terminology and that "the New Testament can sometimes view apostles as 'prophets.' "[9] Unfortunately, in some of these studies the term *prophet* becomes a catchall label for diverse activities and aspects of Paul's ministry.

Scholars have long noted that Paul speaks of his conversion and call in Galatians 1 in prophetic terms. Martin Hengel sums up the opinions of many when he says,

> For Paul the eschatological "apostolic" sending by God or Christ is orientated

---

[4]E.g., H. Leisgang, *Die vorchirstlichen Anschauungen und lehren vom pneuma under der mystisch-intuitiven Erekenntnis* (Leipzig: Teubner, 1919); R. Reitzenstein, *Die hellenistichen Mysterienreligionen: Nach ihren Grundgedanken und Wirkungen* (Leipzig: Teubner, 1927).

[5]See E. Boring, "Prophecy, Early Christian," in *Anchor Bible Dictionary*, ed. D. N. Freedman (New York: Doubleday, 1992), 5:498.

[6]K. O. Sandnes, *Paul: One of the Prophets?* (Tübingen: Mohr, 1991).

[7]See especially D. E. Aune, *Prophecy in Early Christianity* (Grand Rapids, Mich.: Eerdmans, 1983), pp. 195-262; and see the survey of literature by C. A. Evans, "Prophet, Paul as," in *Dictionary of Paul and His Letters*, ed. Gerald F. Hawthorne, Ralph P. Martin and Daniel G. Reid (Downers Grove, Ill.: InterVarsity Press, 1993), pp. 763-65.

[8]E. Earle Ellis, *Prophecy and Hermeneutic in Early Christianity* (Grand Rapids, Mich.: Eerdmans, 1978).

[9]W. Grudem, *The Gift of Prophecy in 1 Corinthians* (Lanham, Penn.: University Press of America, 1982), p. 53.

on the sending of the prophets of the Old Covenant, indeed it surpasses these. Now the sending relates to the eschatological final salvation and therefore to decision. . . . In other words, with the Christ event and Paul's present apostolic ministry the prophetic promise is being fulfilled. For Paul, who like Jeremiah remained unmarried, entering into this service for the sake of this salvation is from the beginning like a compulsion which he cannot avoid without putting his existence at risk.[10]

The discussion among scholars raises a whole series of questions about Paul. On the one hand, since he so rarely identified himself as a prophet (but see 1 Cor 14), it could be argued that he simply used Old Testament prophetic language to characterize his call to be an apostle, which is a rather different role from that of a prophet. Grudem, for instance, has rightly pointed out that while Paul suggests that the words of the Corinthian prophets are expected to be weighed (1 Cor 14:29) and says prophets should prophesy in proportion to their faith (Rom 12:6), he expects his own words to be seen as having the same authority as the words of Jesus or of the Hebrew Scriptures![11]

So it is not enough to note that both prophets and apostles are Spirit-inspired authority figures who speak for the Lord. The same could be said of Jewish sages or teachers, as a careful reading of Sirach would show. Furthermore, when Paul does use a formula such as "the Lord says," he is not offering fresh revelations but quoting or interpreting the Jesus tradition (see 1 Cor 7:10-12; 11:23; and probably 1 Thess 4:15). In Paul's letters we generally do *not* find him using the first-person singular to speak as the mouthpiece of God or the risen Christ.[12] Paul does frequently allude to the prophetic Scriptures in describing the condition of his converts or of himself;[13] yet this is also the case of the sage who wrote the Wisdom of Solomon, but it does not make the author a prophet. Unlike an oracular prophet, though, Paul is quite prepared to speak on his own authority as an authorized agent of Jesus Christ and expect that to carry its own weight (see 1 Cor 7:12).[14]

Grudem has argued that Paul has authority like that of the Old

---

[10]Martin Hengel and Anne-Maria Schwemer, *Paul Between Damascus and Antioch* (Louisville, Ky.: Westminster John Knox, 1997), p. 95.

[11]Grudem, *The Gift*, pp. 48-49.

[12]A quotation of an OT prophetic "I" word, identified as such, probably should not count as a prophetic "I" word from Paul. See for example Romans 14:9, which is prefaced by "as it is written" to make clear it is a quotation of an older sacred tradition, not the spontaneous creation of a new one.

[13]But see Evans, "Prophet," p. 763.

[14]See the second half of this chapter.

Testament prophets whose word was not to be questioned.[15] This is true enough, but it seems to be a matter of analogy. How do we know that apostles in the early church were not viewed as having equivalent or even greater authority than the Old Testament prophets? In other words, Paul's authority doesn't necessarily prove that he was a prophetic figure. Unlike most of the Israelite prophets, Paul saw his task as being not primarily to confront Israel with its sin but to convert the pagans. Jonah cannot be taken as Paul's forerunner in this sense, but a case could be made that the prophecies found in Isaiah 40—55 significantly influenced Paul's understanding of his own call. Indeed, it could be urged that he saw himself as the servant referred to in those texts, or at least a servant modeled on Christ whom he saw reflected in those texts (see, e.g., Phil 1:1, and cf. Phil 2:1-11).

Identifying Old and New Testament prophets and prophecy too closely runs into another problem. Prophecy in early Christianity seems to have had a liturgical setting—it happened in Christian worship services as part of what was expected to be communicated there (see 1 Cor 14; cf. Acts 11:27-30). The political setting and nature of much Old Testament prophecy is missing from Paul's letters.

Against the suggestion that the early church simply identified or amalgamated the roles and functions of apostles and prophets, they are *both* listed in Paul's lists of Spirit-led leaders, which suggests that he assumes his audience would understand the distinction between the two roles (see Rom 12:6; 1 Cor 12:10, 29; Eph 4:11). These same lists suggest a distinction between a prophet and a teacher, or a prophet and an evangelist.[16] Generally, then, there is far too much methodological confusion among scholars regarding how we evaluate the prophetic material in Paul and Paul as a prophetic figure.

The work of David Aune, however, has set us on the path toward more rigorous analysis of these issues. Aune has shown that greater methodological precision is necessary in evaluating early Christian prophets and prophetic speech. The following points help clarify the nature and function of New Testament prophets and prophecy.

• Christian prophets, to judge from texts like 1 Corinthians 14, Acts 11:27-30 and Acts 21:10-11, spoke intelligible, fresh messages that were spontaneously granted to them by God by means of the Holy Spirit.

• On occasion God might reveal truths or ideas to these prophetic figures in visions or dreams, and Paul claims to have occasionally had such

---

[15]See Grudem, *The Gift*, pp. 48-49.
[16]See Aune, *Prophecy*, pp. 203-11.

visions and dreams (see 2 Cor 12:1-10). Again, this is not simply identical:
to evangelizing Gentiles or speaking in synagogues.

• Prophets in the Old Testament, while they can be said to be like prose-
cutors of the covenant lawsuit Yahweh brought against his people, are not
by and large exegetes or scribes.[17] They deliver a late, pertinent word from
God to his people.

In view of this last point, it is not clear that "charismatic" contemporizing or interpreting of Old Testament texts at Qumran or by various New
Testament figures should be seen as a prophetic activity. Other persons
filled with the Spirit—teachers, scribes or sages—are more likely candidates to have carried out such activities.[18]

Thus prophets were apparently distinguishable in function from
apostles, scribes, teachers and evangelists, even if there was occasional
overlap between their roles and functions. The goal of the study of the
prophetic material in Paul's letters should be to discern what is *distinctively
prophetic* about Paul's activities.[19] One thing that can be said with some
assurance is that prophetic figures in the New Testament era, like Old
Testament and intertestamental prophets, continued to offer oracles about
the future. So we do well to closely examine some of the things Paul had to
say about the future, evaluating not only what he thought was yet to
transpire but also what this tells us about Paul himself.

Paul's Language of Prediction

Perhaps the first question that needs to be raised about Paul and predictive

---

[17]Note that Jeremiah is not portrayed as being a scribe but rather as having one—Baruch. See
the discussion in Michael Fishbane, *Biblical Interpretation in Ancient Israel* (Oxford: Oxford
University Press, 1985), pp. 15-100, which stresses that prophets by and large don't work with
texts but do recapitulate and expound on the present significance of Israel's traditions.

[18]Aune's remarks in *Prophecy,* pp. 204, 205, are telling: "Paul names a great many individuals
in his letters, *but none of them are designated prophets.* Prophecy for Paul is a divinely bestowed
gift, and the prophets who exercise that gift appear to do so only within the framework of
services of worship. . . . The prophet was unique among early Christian leaders in that,
unlike other functionaries, he claimed no personal part in the communication which he
conveyed. Prophets acted as leaders in many early Christian communities because they
were regarded by themselves and others as inspired spokesmen for the ultimate authority
God. . . . There is no evidence that prophets occupied a prophetic 'office,' nor is there
evidence that they possessed personal or professional qualification or talents other than the
ability to prophesy."

[19]There are hints in both 1 Thessalonians 5:20 and 1 Corinthians 14 that Paul took a different
view of Christian prophecy than did his converts. Some converts came close to ignoring or
despising Christian prophecy. Others showed unbounded enthusiasm for it. Part of the
danger in Corinth seems to have been that the partially socialized converts there continued
to view prophecy according to the familiar pagan models.

prophecy is whether he should be counted among the false prophets. In particular, did Paul believe or predict, as many twentieth-century scholars have said, that Christ would return within his own lifetime? This widespread opinion may be traced to the great influence of Albert Schweitzer's work; it was his view that "from his first letter to his last Paul's thought is always uniformly dominated by the expectation of an immediate return of Jesus, of the judgment, and the Messianic glory."[20] Since I have addressed this question at length in another book, here I simply summarize the evidence that undergirds my conclusion.[21]

Texts like 1 Thessalonians 4:13—5:11, 1 Corinthians 7:29-31 and Romans 13:11-14 make evident that Paul believed he was living in the eschatological age and considered it possible that the Lord might return during his lifetime. Yet is there is any evidence that Paul believed Jesus must or would necessarily return *imminently?*

Before dealing with the texts themselves, we need to consider a proposal about Paul's eschatological language that keeps surfacing due to the work of N. T. Wright.[22] This proposal actually was first made prominent through the work of G. B. Caird,[23] who influenced a host of his doctoral students including Wright, Marcus Borg and L. D. Hurst. The proposal goes like this: Paul uses eschatological language metaphorically, not literally. He is not talking about a literal meeting of Jesus in the sky or a literal end of the world. His eschatological language actually indicates the imminence of various historical crises that faced early Judaism. In short, this is language about the end of a particular world, a particular culture, not the end of the space-time continuum.

On the surface, this proposal could explain, for instance, how some Thessalonians might have actually believed that the Day of the Lord had already come, perhaps due to a crisis that involved considerable suffering for their faith (2 Thess 2:1-2). It could also make sense of a good deal of Mark 13, seen as events leading up to the destruction of Jerusalem in A.D. 70, not events leading up to the end of the world. I have even heard it argued, though certainly not by Wright, that Christ *did* return in A.D. 70

---

[20]Albert Schweitzer, *The Mysticism of Paul the Apostle,* trans. W. Montgomery (New York: Holt and Company, 1931), p. 52.

[21]See Ben Witherington III, *Jesus, Paul and the End of the World* (Downers Grove, Ill.: InterVarsity Press, 1992).

[22]See most recently N. T. Wright, *What Saint Paul Really Said* (Grand Rapids, Mich.: Eerdmans, 1997).

[23]See G. B. Caird, *New Testament Theology* (Oxford: Oxford University Press, 1994); and *The Language and Imagery of the Bible,* 2nd ed. (Grand Rapids, Mich.: Eerdmans, 1997).

(though invisibly), bringing an end to Jerusalem-centered Jewish culture.

In response it needs to be noted, first, Paul does use metaphors to talk about things eschatological. The question is, what reality is being described by his poetic language? Is it an event that came about in the first century or a more remote one? No one is disputing the use of figurative language in eschatological passages ("the moon will turn to blood" and the like).

Second, Paul also does see some eschatological events as having already transpired. No one who calls the resurrection of Jesus the firstfruits of the harvest sees that event as an isolated anomaly in the midst of otherwise noneschatological history. To the contrary, Paul believes this event set the eschatological age in motion. It would then not be surprising if he believed that several other eschatological events had happened or were happening in his lifetime, including judgment on some who were opposing the gospel and persecuting Christians (see, e.g., 1 Thess. 2:14-16).

Furthermore, when Paul speaks about the end, he is probably not talking about the end of the space-time continuum. It does not follow from this, though, that he is talking only about the end of some particular historical period or culture.

The problems with the Caird-Wright proposal, which would by and large reduce eschatology to events of the first century A.D., are considerable. In the first place, though the events described as birth pangs of the end in Mark 13 did certainly involve historical events and processes, some of which did happen in the first century, not all the events the Gospel writers and Paul discuss are of that ilk. The second coming of Christ, the resurrection of the righteous, the banishment of death, the new heaven and new earth are of a whole different order from "wars and rumors of wars" or the appearance of pseudomessianic figures.

The events that bring in the end involve direct divine intervention and an interruption of the normal processes of this world. Resurrection is not like putting toast in a toaster, where what goes down must come back up. Resurrection comes by the work of God in Christ, not by the natural processes of history, and this death-defying event has clearly not yet happened in history. Nor on any fair reading of 1 Corinthians 15 can resurrection be said to be a process of spiritual transformation during this life or a metaphorical way of describing the afterlife. Paul clearly links the future resurrection of those in Christ with the past resurrection of Jesus, which took place on earth, and he sees them as being of the same order and nature. As a first-century Pharisee, Paul is unlikely to have ever thought in terms of a nonmaterial resurrection in any case.

But Paul also closely links believers' future resurrection with the return of Christ. The latter triggers the former. To use the form of Paul's own syllo-gistic logic (see 1 Cor 15:12-19), if the dead have not yet been raised, Christ has not yet returned. Paul closely links the "not yet" of the future resurrec-tion of believers with the "already" of Christ's resurrection and also with the return of Christ.

It is true that 1 Corinthians 15 does not envision the annihilation of the space-time continuum, for life will continue on the earth after Christ returns and the dead are raised. Yet this passage does envision the end and goal of all human history as we know it, not merely the end of a particular culture or historical age. In Paul's view it will not be business as usual when the Lord returns. Things will not carry on as they had before all over the world. Resurrection, and linked with it the renewal of the earth (see Rom 8), are what Paul has in mind for the future of humanity.

More recently Wright seems to have clarified his views, for in *What Saint Paul Really Said* he seems to suggest that while "resurrection of the dead ones" should probably be taken literally, "coming on the clouds" should not. But what are the operative criteria for deciding which eschatological statements should be taken literally and which should not?

Thus while the Caird-Wright proposal highlights some truths about Paul's eschatological language, it also has some significant problems. But perhaps these will be overcome in Wright's forthcoming major work on Paul and early Christianity.

I suspect that at least part of the motive behind this reading of Paul's eschatology is to exonerate Paul from the supposed flaw of guessing wrong about the timing of the eschatological end. But Paul needs no such exoner-ation, since he did not predict the certain return of Christ within a genera-tion or so. He spoke only of the possible imminence of the end.

This last point requires some demonstration. Some texts thought to prove Paul's conviction that Jesus' return was near or at hand on closer inspection prove no such thing. Take Philippians 4:5—"the Lord is near." We need to ask, near in space or near in time? Failure to hear the echo of Psalm 145:18-19 here has caused a misunderstanding. Note that Philippians 4:6 goes on to add, "Do not worry about anything, but in prayer and supplication with thanksgiving let your requests be made known to God." The psalm says, "The LORD is near to all who call on him" (Ps 145:18). In fact, God's nearness to the supplicant is a regular theme in the Psalms (cf. Ps 118:5-9 and Ps 151 in the LXX). So given the context in Philippians 4 and the exhortations we find there, which echo themes in Psalms, it is likely that here Paul is not making predictions or promises about the temporal nearness of Christ's return. This conclusion is supported by the fact that elsewhere when *engys* is used to speak of temporal nearness, it refers to a thing or event, not a person.[24]

Four points about Romans 13:11-14:

1. *Engys* is used here to describe the coming of a time or event called "the day" (vv. 12, 13), not the coming of a person. It seems plausible that "the day" refers to the same matter as "salvation" (v. 11), which is said to be "nearer" (*engyterion*) than when we believed. Whatever else one may say, it is clear that "salvation" in this text is not seen as having already transpired.

2. Converts are exhorted to *now* wake up and live as in the day (vv. 11, 14). In short, there is no more waiting for eschatological ethics. The time to act with knowledge of the dawn of the eschatological age is known by the Romans to have come.

3. The waking/sleeping and darkness/light metaphors echo what Paul wrote earlier in 1 Thessalonians 4:13—5:10 about the return of Christ, which in turn echoes the Jesus tradition on these matters.

4. The statement "salvation is nearer to us now than when we became believers" must not be made innocuous. Clearly Paul conjures with the *possible imminence* of Christ's return and yet clearly does not succumb to date-setting.

Nevertheless, one must preserve the already/not yet tension, for the larger context of Romans 13:11-14 makes suspect the suggestion that Paul means Christ's return must be near. Remember, these verses are preceded by a discussion of the ongoing conversion of the full number of the Gentiles, after which "all Israel will be saved" (Rom 11), and followed by Paul's plans to go to Rome and visit the west beyond (Rom 15). The function of Romans 13:11-14 is to remind the Romans not to start looking up in the sky but that they are already in the eschatological age, and that there are no more crucial eschatological or salvific events that must happen before the Lord comes.[25] The focus here is on "the night is already far spent" and on behavior appropriate to the current, eschatological age[26]— which leads us to another similar text in 1 Corinthians 7.

First Corinthians 7 confronts us with a crucial matter of grammar. Note first, however, that Paul says that the form of the world is already passing away (v. 31) and also speaks of a distress that is present, not imminent (v.

---

[24]See Ben Witherington III, *Friendship and Finances in Philippi* (Valley Forge, Penn.: Trinity Press International, 1994), pp. 112-13.

[25]See ibid., pp. 32-33.

[26]See Joseph A. Fitzmyer, *Romans* (New York: Doubleday, 1993), p. 683. The eschaton is in progress, between Christ's resurrection and his parousia. Hence every step that Christians take brings them closer to "the day of the Lord."

26). Because this distress is already happening, believers should not seek to change their status just now. This takes us to verse 29—"I mean . . . the appointed time *synestalmenos estin.*" Should the first of these two words be translated "short" or "shortened"? It is a participle, not an adjective, and should surely be translated "shortened." Something or someone has shortened the time, and because of this Christians are to live differently from others, recognizing that the form of the world is already passing away. So we cannot conclude that Paul says here, "The time is short." Rather he says, "The time left has been shortened," presumably by the Christ event. As in Romans 13:11-14, Paul is talking about the present time and the things already transpiring as he looks forward to the conclusion of history. Christians are already in the distressful times; the form of the world is already passing away. These are signs that salvation is nearer now than it ever was before, for Christ has already come and set eschatological events in motion. At most what we have here is a reminder of the possible imminence of the end, not a prediction or promise that "the time is short."

Finally, let us consider 1 Thessalonians 4:15—"For this we declare to you, . . . that we who are alive, who are left until the coming of the Lord, will by no means precede those who have died." This is followed immediately by a description of the return of Christ. Surely here, it has been argued, it is clear that Paul expected that he would live to see the return of Christ. But there are at least three major problems with this conclusion.

1. Paul immediately goes on to stress that the day of the Lord will come like a thief in the night (5:2), which is to say it will come *at an unexpected time.* This sense is conveyed both by the term *thief* and by the term *night.* Paul's point is that Christians should be prepared whenever the Lord comes. Though they may be surprised by the event's timing, they should not be surprised by the fact that it happens. They are people of the day and of the light, and so they are not in the dark like others about the reality that this event will happen.

2. Paul continues, " . . . so that whether we are awake or asleep [when he comes] we may live with him" (5:10). Clearly, then, he entertains either possibility for himself and his converts. They may live to see the day, or they may die before the Lord returns.

3. When Paul wanted to speak of those Christians who would be alive when the Lord returns, precisely because he did not know the timing of either his own death or the return of Christ, he had no choice but to place himself in the category of the living in 1 Thessalonians 4:15. He could not say "we who will have died before the Lord returns," unless he knew for sure that his death would precede Christ's coming. In fact, Paul had no

ᴺᴼ revelation or certain conviction about the timing of either event.

Thus while 1 Thessalonians 4:15 and other such texts suggest that Paul reckoned with the live possibility that the Lord might return in his lifetime, they certainly do not warrant the conclusion of Schweitzer.[27] We have no clear evidence to support the conclusion that Paul was a mistaken prophet whose teaching on eschatology may be considered generally suspect because he was wrong on the timing. Possible and necessary imminence are two different things. We would do well to remember this fact.

Paul as Apocalyptic Seer

What does Paul's lack of calculations about the timing of the end tell us about his character as a prophet and the heart of his theology? Consider the words of J. C. Beker:

> Paul's Christian hope is a matter of prophecy, not a matter of prediction. The incalculability of this hope is for Paul one of its essential marks. . . . Whereas the apocalyptic composition often concentrates on a timetable of events or on a program for the sake of calculating apocalyptic events, Paul stresses to the contrary the incalculability of the end . . . the unexpected, the sudden, the surprising character of the final theophany (1 Thess. 5:2-10). Moreover, the incalculable character of the end motivates Paul to restrain severely his use of apocalyptic language and imagery. . . . Thus the delay of the parousia is not a theological concern for Paul. It is not an embarrassment for him; it does not compel him to shift the center of his attention from apocalyptic imminence to a form of "realized eschatology," that is, to a conviction of the full presence of the kingdom of God in our present history.[28]

There is much wisdom in these words, but we do well to remember that apocalyptic thinking and literature by no means always include calculations about the end; indeed, often they do not.[29] Thus it is not necessary to conclude that Paul was *not* an apocalyptic prophet (like John of Patmos) *just because* he did not offer calculations.

Paul's letters are not rich with apocalyptic images. Is he, then, more like Amos than like Daniel? Despite the sparseness of his apocalyptic imagery, the apocalyptic dimension of his thought and picture language should not be dismissed. His admission to having visions and revelations would seem to be the one really telling piece of evidence that he sometimes functioned as an apocalyptic seer (2 Cor 12). But what makes this whole matter devil-

---

[27]Witherington, *Friendship and Finances*, pp. 24-25.

[28]J. Christiaan Beker, *Paul's Apocalyptic Gospel: The Coming Triumph of God* (Philadelphia: Fortress, 1982), pp. 48-49.

[29]See on this J. J. Collins, *The Apocalyptic Imagination* (New York: Crossroad, 1984).

ishly difficult is that Paul lived at a time following the confluence of three great Jewish traditions—prophecy, apocalyptic and wisdom. Sages could use prophetic ideas in their aphorisms. Prophets could use apocalyptic images. Seers could speak like sages, and apparently apostles could speak like all of the above. Thus Paul's occasional use of apocalyptic language may in the end tell us little or nothing about Paul as a prophet, but his admission to having revelations and visions does indicate that he acted as a prophet from time to time (see 1 Cor 14:6).

The Day of the Lord
At this juncture we could spend considerable time looking at the positive things Paul says, apparently as a prophet, about various future events such as the character of the return of Christ and the judgment and redemption it will entail, the future resurrection and the final coming of God's dominion on earth. There is little or no dispute among scholars that Paul believed in such future realities. I have, however, addressed these issues at length elsewhere,[30] so here we will focus only on the return and the resurrection.

Paul's discussion of the return of Christ and the resurrection owes a good deal not just to Old Testament prophetic traditions or general Jewish or Christian traditions, but also to the "eschatological" language that was used in his day to speak of the accomplishments of the emperor and the nature of the times in which Empire dwellers lived. The way Paul presents future realities suggests that he is not simply conveying revelations verbatim but discoursing in a mode that his mostly Gentile converts would understand and identify with. Thus we must distinguish between a received revelation or "mystery" and the *literary form* in which the prophet chooses to convey his revelations. Revelation is the basis of prophecy (a spoken word from God), but it is not identical with prophecy. Revelation is also the basis of teaching nuanced so as to be a word on target.

That Christ would return Paul had no doubt, and that this event would prove to be the catalyst for a whole series of other remarkable events he indicates in various ways. It may be that Paul was the first person to use *parousia* to refer to the return of Christ. Certainly he was one of the chief New Testament users of the term: out of twenty-four appearances of the word, fourteen are in the Pauline corpus. *Parousia* is not a technical term for the second coming; it simply means "arrival" or "presence." Applying this

---

[30]See Witherington, *Jesus, Paul and the End,* and also the relevant passages from 1 Corinthians in Ben Witherington III, *Conflict and Community in Corinth* (Grand Rapids, Mich.: Eerdmans, 1994).

term to Christ's return, however, changes its normal connotation. Only in three letters does Paul use this term of Christ's return—1 Thessalonians repeatedly (2:19; 3:13; 4:15; 5:23), 2 Thessalonians (2:1, 8-9) and 1 Corinthians (15:23). In all three letters the apostle feels it necessary to correct his audience's misunderstandings about matters of eschatology.

Despite the best efforts of scholars, no developmental schema can be detected in Paul's thinking about Christ's return.[31] Even as late as Philippians 1:6 and 3:20 Paul can still speak of "the day of Jesus Christ" and of eagerly awaiting his return from heaven. So far as we can tell, Paul never gave up on this keen expectation during his lifetime.

First Thessalonians 2:19, the earliest use of the term *parousia*, depicts a celebration involving a great deal of joy. There is no hint here that the believer will undergo any kind of judgment. Paul speaks of his converts as the crown in which he will boast when the Lord arrives. It seems quite probable that he draws here on a standard, familiar image of the arrival of a dignitary or royal figure to visit a city. F. F. Bruce puts it well: "When Christians spoke of the parousia of their Lord, they probably thought of the pomp and circumstance attending those imperial visits as parodies of the true glory to be revealed on the day of Christ."[32]

Support for this idea may come from a close scrutiny of 1 Thessalonians 3:13, Paul's second reference to the parousia: the Lord will arrive with all his "holy ones" (my translation). This is likely an allusion to the coming of Yahweh with his angels (Zech 14:5 LXX), which suggests the presenting of believers on the day of judgment for God's final review, in the hope that they will be seen as blameless and holy.[33] Yet the image of a ruler and his entourage coming to town to hold court would surely be conjured up in the minds of a largely Gentile audience of Thessalonians. In any case, this text tells us that the Lord Christ will not come alone. His retinue, presumably angels, will be coming with him, and we may expect judgment to ensue thereafter.

First Thessalonians 4:13-18 is meant to encourage the Thessalonians, assuring them that the Christian dead are at no disadvantage just because they died before the parousia of Christ. This text has several dimensions. First, we learn that Paul connects the parousia with both the resurrection of believers and the meeting of Christ in the air. The latter two events are

---

[31]See W. Baird, "Pauline Eschatology in Hermeneutic Perspective," *New Testament Studies* 17 (1970-1971): 314-27.

[32]F. F. Bruce, *1 and 2 Thessalonians* (Waco, Tex.: Word, 1982), p. 57.

[33]See Tremper Longman and Daniel G. Reid, *God Is a Warrior* (Grand Rapids, Mich.: Zondervan, 1995), pp. 171-75.

clearly triggered by the former one, and we should notice that there is no connotation of judgment. Verses 14-16 indicates that God will bring forth the dead when Christ comes, in particular the dead in Christ. Then we learn that what accompanies the parousia is a loud command, the voice of the archangel and the trumpet call of God. A specific kind of public event is in view here. When a king went to visit a city, his herald would go before to the city walls to proclaim his coming with a trumpet blast and a spoken announcement. It might even have entailed a cry of command for the gates to be opened up so the monarch could enter the city (see the entrance liturgy in Ps 24:7-10).

The use of *apantēsin* in 1 Thessalonians 4:17 further supports the notion that Paul is drawing on this secular picture. Cicero, describing Julius Caesar's tour through Italy in 49 B.C., says, "Just imagine what *apantēseis* he is receiving from the towns, what honors are paid to him" (*Atticus* 8.16.2; cf. 16.11.6). This word refers to the action of the greeting committee, going out beyond the city walls to welcome the king and then ushering him back into the city. "These analogies (especially in association with the term *parousia*) suggest the possibility that the Lord is pictured here as escorted the remainder of his journey to earth by his people—both those newly raised from the dead and those who have remained alive."[34] So the living believers are the reception committee. They go forth into the clouds,[35] meet the Lord at his arrival and then return to earth, where Christ will reign (see 1 Cor 15). The Thessalonians, knowing very well the language and imagery of parousia, would know that after meeting the arriving lord outside a city, the greeting committee would welcome him into the city from which they had come. This leads us to consider 2 Thessalonians 2:1, 8-9.[36]

Second Thessalonians 2 presents us with a tale of two parousias, one of Christ (vv. 1, 8) and one of the man of lawlessness (v. 9). The former is a royal and divine one, while the latter is but a poor imitation. The man of lawlessness will come into God's temple, like a pagan god into a pagan temple, proclaiming himself to be a god. By contrast, Jesus is said to come like the prince of the house of David mentioned in Isaiah 11:4 (LXX), who comes "to smite the earth with the rod of his mouth" and destroy the wicked one "with the breath of his lips."

Second Thessalonians 2:8 uses the term *epiphaneia*. Like *parousia*, this is a

---

[34]Bruce, *1 and 2 Thessalonians*, p. 103.

[35]Like the clouds of dust created by the king's entourage?

[36]If 2 Thessalonians proves to be non-Pauline, the main conclusions of this section about Paul's use of appropriate and timely language for his Gentile converts would still stand.

cultic and royal term used to describe the appearance of a divinized emperor or the visible appearing of a god (cf., e.g., the coin struck for Hadrian with the inscription "epiphany of Augustus").[37] This language is not accidental; it is possible that Paul has in mind Antiochus Epiphanes, who desecrated the temple in Jerusalem, as a sort of antitype of the man of lawlessness, or even Gaius Caligula, who attempted to do so in order to assert his claims to divinity in A.D. 40 (Philo *Legatio ad Gaium* 203-346; Josephus *Antiquities of the Jews* 18.261-301).

For our purposes, what is most important about this text is that 2 Thessalonians 2:1 says believers will be gathered to the Lord when he comes—the same idea found in 1 Thessalonians 4:17. He will save them, but at the same time he will judge the man of lawlessness. Christ's coming, like a king's coming to a city to hold court, will involve both redemption and judgment, exoneration and execution, praise and blame, fellowship and finality.

It would be wrong to conclude that Paul envisioned "that day" as simply joy and good news for Christians. First Corinthians 3:13 makes clear there will be a testing of believers' works, and some will escape only as through fire (cf. 1 Cor 5:5). The One sitting on the judgment seat is "the Lord Jesus" (2 Cor 5:10), but this does not rule out recompense, either good or ill, for what the Christian has done in the body. Accordingly, moral preparedness is necessary for that day (1 Cor 1:8), and moral living will give Paul a reason for boasting about his converts on the day of judgment (2 Cor. 1:14). Yet they are not left to achieve moral maturity on their own, for Paul also promises that God will carry to completion his work in the believers until "the day of Jesus Christ" (Phil 1:6).

The good news is that the Day of the Lord is the Day of the Lord Jesus. But believers will surely not want to be shamed by him on that day. Paul's prayer in Philippians 1:10 is not an idle one—he wishes for his converts to be found blameless or faultless on that day (see Phil 2:15). "The life of faith does not free the Christian from the life of obedience."[38]

To sum up:
- Paul affirmed the return of Christ consistently throughout his ministry, from early days when he wrote 1 Thessalonians to later days when he wrote Philippians.
- This return is the trigger for a series of other events that will involve

---

[37]See Adolf Deissmann, *Light from the Ancient East* (Grand Rapids, Mich.: Baker, 1978), p. 373; and W. M. Ramsay, "The Manifest God," *Expository Times* 10 (1899): 208.
[38]Ralph P. Martin, *2 Corinthians* (Waco, Tex.: Word, 1986), p. 114.

both redemption and judgment, including a judgment of the works of the believer.

- These events will transpire on earth, which is not surprising since the "Day of the Lord" imagery Paul draws on also depicts judgment by God on earth.
- The Lord on the judgment seat will be none other than the Lord Jesus Christ.

This is indeed the kind of material we would expect a prophet or an apocalyptic seer to focus on, but once again note the lack of prophetic oracular form and the adaptation of material to suit a Gentile audience. Clearly Paul's words on this subject do not constitute a verbatim transcript of a supernatural revelation. Could his words fall into the category of eschatological teaching rather than prophecy?

The Resurrection

Our consideration of the much-beloved and much-belabored subject of the resurrection will focus not on the resurrection of Christ but on that of his followers. As a Pharisee, Paul would certainly have believed in the resurrection, at least the resurrection of the righteous at the Day of the Lord (see Acts 23:6-8). Yet his beliefs had changed since his Pharisaic days, for as a Christian he affirmed something no Pharisee did: the isolated resurrection of Messiah in the midst of history, which still is to be connected to the resurrection of believers as first and latter fruits of the same crop.

What Paul believes about Christ causes him to alter the eschatological framework he inherited from his Pharisaic days. While resurrection was to become after A.D. 70 a sort of litmus test of a true Jew (see *m. Sanhedrin* 10.1; *b.t. Sanhedrin* 90b; *2 Apocalypse of Baruch* 50.1-4), already in Paul's mind belief in the resurrection is a test of a true Christian.

As J. C. Beker has noted, the attempt to remove ontological and historical referents from Paul's view of resurrection fails to do justice to the apostle's teaching.[39] When Paul speaks of resurrection he does not mean only some present spiritual transformation in the lives of human beings. In fact, Paul believed in both the spiritual revivification of persons in this life *and* the resurrection of persons from the dead when Christ returns. Not only so, but texts like Romans 8:18-25 suggest that Paul linked the future resurrection of believers to the actual environmental renewal of the earth itself.

Furthermore, Paul the zealous Pharisee surely knew of the Maccabean

---

[39]J. Christiaan Beker, *Paul the Apostle* (Philadelphia: Fortress, 1980), p. 152.

ideas about resurrection as a vindication, rescue and reward for the right-eous (1 Macc 7). It is not surprising that we find this basically positive connotation of resurrection for Christians in texts like Romans 1:4 and 1 Corinthians 15. Notice also how in 1 Thessalonians 1:10 Christ's own resur-rection is connected to the delivering of believers from God's future wrath. Christ's resurrection is the proper grounds not only for believing that Christians will be raised but also for believing they will be vindicated (1 Thess 4:14-16).

Significantly—and here again Paul's Pharisaic background may come into play—Paul does not talk about the resurrection of any and all persons but specifically of the raising of the dead in Christ (1 Thess 4:16). This is not simply attributable to Paul's background. He seems to have believed that resurrection involves being finally conformed to the image of Christ. Being a reward, it will happen only to "those in Christ" (cf. below). *Imitatio Christi* entails even resurrection like Christ's. If one has not participated in the process of being conformed to Christ's image in this life (Rom 8:29), one cannot expect to receive the final installment of such conformation in the next life. In fact, the resurrection of both Christ (see Rom 1:3-4) and believ-ers entails entering into a new phase of sonship that involves not only a deathless state but also the possession of unique glorious power.[40]

In 1 Corinthians 6:14 it becomes abundantly clear that *resurrection involves a body*. Paul is making a point here about present ethics, but ethics includes bodily conduct here and now because the body has a place in the eschatological future of the believer. A purely spiritual resurrection is out of the question, and in any case it is not at all clear that Paul, being an ancient person, would have seen "spirit" as nonmaterial. It is far more likely that he saw it as simply a different sort of stuff.[41]

A. J. M. Wedderburn is certainly correct in reminding us that " 'resur-rection' would mean, especially to Hellenistic readers, something physical, earthy, which only gradually came to be spiritualized as groups of Christians . . . sought to reconcile their Hellenistic or gnostic aversion to the body with the ineluctable presence of the idea of resurrection in . . . Christian tradition."[42] To many Gentiles, resurrection likely suggested the standing up of corpses; this notion is perhaps what produced the scoffing and quick dismissal of Paul in Acts 17:31-32. Paul must explain to his

---

[40]See G. Vos, *The Pauline Eschatology* (Grand Rapids, Mich.: Eerdmans, 1972), pp. 155-56.
[41]See the earlier discussion.
[42]A. J. M. Wedderburn, "The Problem of the Denial of the Resurrection in 1 Corinthians XV," *Novum Testamentum* 23 (1981): 236.

largely Gentile converts what is entailed by resurrection of believers without losing them along the way.

While Paul is able to cite and rely on church traditions about Christ's death and resurrection and his subsequent appearances to various persons, including Paul himself—traditions he had already conveyed to the Corinthians before (1 Cor 15:1-8)—it is not at all clear that he is relying on preexistent Christian traditions for what he says in 1 Corinthians 15 from verse 9 on. Indeed, given the tour-de-force character of this argument, in which Paul uses every rhetorical weapon in his arsenal (logical syllogism, analogy, implications of a common existing practice, unacceptable things implied if one rejects resurrection), it becomes clear that he is sailing in rather uncharted waters, at least as far as his audience is concerned. Apparently he had to combat what can only be called Roman imperial eschatology and substitute for it a viable form of Christian eschatology.

Roman imperial eschatology was the increasingly popular notion that the emperor was a god, and that since the time of Augustus the new age had dawned, bringing the fulfillment of divine prophecy and the divine plan for humankind. The new age had a savior figure, the emperor, who was son of the gods—indeed was himself a god—and whose epiphany in various cities throughout the Empire brought peace, prosperity and other blessings. There was to be a celebration of this new age and its savior wherever the imperial games were held throughout the Empire, including at Isthmia near Corinth. A thriving emperor cult already existed in Corinth in Paul's day.[43]

Paul would have to compete with this notion of realized eschatology when he spoke of future eschatology, in particular the resurrection of the dead. Yet his words do not amount to a revolutionary program against the Empire, for it is only the returning Christ who accomplishes the reversal and transformation he is describing.[44] So Paul uses the present imperial eschatology as a foil for his own "already/not yet" schema. The political implications of 1 Corinthians 15:23-28 would not likely have been lost on all of Paul's audience. If one lives in the light of Christian future eschatology, all loyalties to any sort of human realized eschatology become pointless. The emperor has no divine clothes and certainly cannot dispense lasting divine benefits as Christ can. In critiquing other eschatologies, then, Paul is careful to put in their place a clear future hope for his Corinthians.

---

[43]See my discussion of all this and the inscriptional evidence in Witherington, *Conflict and Community*, pp. 295-98.
[44]See the later discussion on Paul the politician and revolutionary.

The key phrase for our purposes is found in 1 Corinthians 15:12—
"resurrection from out of the dead ones" is what the text literally speaks of.
This does not mean merely resurrection from the grave or from death, but
from out of the realm where the dead dwell. This makes very good sense if
Paul is discussing the raising of believers from the realm of dead persons
in general.

Notice that Paul does not here speak of resurrection *of* the body one
previously had. Resurrection for Paul clearly involves embodied existence
(see vv. 35-49), but the old body is not necessarily involved. Perhaps he is
cognizant that a major stumbling blocks for the Corinthians regarding
resurrection would be that their normal association of a body with mortal-
ity, decay and corruption, so the combination of body and immortality
would seem very strange. This may be the reason Paul stresses that flesh
and blood in their present condition cannot inherit God's kingdom (vv. 50-
54). The perishable must put on the imperishable.

Thus it would seem that we must carefully examine the elements of both
continuity and discontinuity between this body and the one to come in
Paul's scheme of things. The elements of continuity are (1) the same person
(2) in a body (3) that has life. The elements of discontinuity are as follows:

sown	raised
perishable	imperishable
in dishonor	in glory
in weakness	in power
natural body	spiritual body[45]

So for Paul resurrection entails a body, but he envisions a replacement body
for the dead and a transformed one for the living. This body, as he makes
clear, manifests very different qualities from the flesh and blood the
Corinthians currently have.

Paul's vision of the future, though involving a transformed condition
called resurrection, definitely entails life on earth. The final future of believers seems not to be "away from the body and at home with the Lord," an
interim condition that Paul identifies with "nakedness" until the Lord
returns (2 Cor 5:1-10). Paul's preference is to live until the resurrection and
be further clothed with the resurrection body, rather than having to first go
through a condition without the body, however blessed that temporary state
might be (Phil 1:21-26; cf. 3:11, 20-21). Our humble bodies will be trans-

---

[45]See Witherington, *Jesus, Paul and the End,* pp. 195-201.

formed into the likeness of Christ's glorious one at his return (Phil 3:21).[46]

Clearly Paul the prophet has very specific ideas and hopes about the future. His is not, or at least not primarily, a vision of "pie in the sky by and by." He looks forward to a new earth and new earthlings, not merely a new heaven. He is quite clear that the Pharisaic vision of the resurrection of the righteous is essentially right. Resurrection is something that happens to persons on earth, not in heaven. This condition will be triggered by the return of Christ. It will be followed by the judgment of believers, and then finally, as the early Christians long prayed, the kingdom of God will come on earth as in heaven.

Oracular Writings

The content of Paul's eschatological writing is precisely what we might expect an early Christian prophet to focus on. Yet little or none of this Pauline material about the future comes to us in the form of a prophetic oracle, nor does it appear to be a mere recitation of a revelation. Let us then look a bit more closely for material in Paul's letters that takes a prophetic or apocalyptic form.

The term *mystērion* in an introductory clause may be taken as a signal that what follows is a quoted oracle. For example, in 1 Corinthians 15:51 we have "Listen, I will tell you a mystery! 'We will not all die, but we will all be changed, in a moment in the twinkling of an eye, at the last trumpet. For the trumpet will sound, and the dead will be raised imperishable, and we will be changed'" (my quotation marks around the oracular material). There follows an explanation of this oracle, backed up by a supporting quotation from the Old Testament. Unlike 1 Corinthians 15:3-7, this information would come as news to Paul's converts. It is a "late word from God," a revelation of a mystery that would otherwise not be known.

Another example is found in Romans 11:25. Again introductory remarks about a mystery are followed by the quotation of an oracle: "I want you to understand this mystery:[47] 'a hardening has come upon a part of Israel, until the full number of the Gentiles has come in, and in like manner all Israel will be saved'" (my translation). Once again this is backed up with two quotations from the Hebrew Scriptures (in this case Is 40:13 and Job 35:7).[48]

It says something about Paul's view of prophecy and how he expects it

---

[46]See Witherington, *Friendship and Finances*, pp. 102-3.

[47]It is interesting that this term is also used to introduce pagan oracles. See Aune, *Prophecy*, p. 251.

[48]See ibid., p. 333.

to be received that he feels it necessary to back up revelations with explanations and quotations from the Scriptures. It comports with 1 Thessalonians 5:19-21, where he urges his converts not to quench the Spirit or despise prophecy, yet to test it and hold fast only to that part of it which is true and good.

An important conclusion from form-critical study of prophecy, whether Jewish, Christian or pagan, is that oracles were typically given in poetic form.[49] So to identify prophetic oracles in the Pauline corpus we should seek poetic forms. Another feature is direct speech by God, such that the prophet simply serves as an instrument through which God speaks. We do find one example of this in 2 Corinthians 12:9, where Paul speaks coyly about a revelatory experience he once had without actually revealing its content, except to say at the end, "But he said to me: 'My grace is sufficient for you, for my power is made perfect in weakness.'"[50] Furthermore, in 2 Corinthians 13:3 Paul stresses that Christ is speaking in, or better *through*, him.

Another example of material that likely meets the formal requirements of an oracle is 1 Thessalonians 4:15-17, with its introductory formula "For this we declare to you by the word of the Lord . . ." followed by the content of the oracle, describing how the living and the dead in Christ will go forth to meet the returning Christ in the air.

Sometimes Paul refers to times when he prophesied or predicted something when he was with his converts, and once he offers a fresh prediction in a letter. The former includes 1 Thessalonians 3:4, "For when we were with you we predicted, 'We are about to suffer persecution,'" and 1 Thessalonians 4:2-6, ending with "'no one should transgress and wrong his brother in this matter, because the Lord is an avenger in all these things,' as we predicted and testified to you" (my translations). The fresh prediction occurs in Galatians 5:21: "I predict for you now, just as I predicted formerly, that 'those who do such things shall not inherit the dominion of God'" (my translation).[51] Direct commands from God in Christ are also sometimes conveyed by Paul (see, e.g., 2 Thess 3:6, 10, 12).

One further form found in Paul's letters may have originated when he or another Christian prophet was speaking oracularly—that is, the christo-

---

[49] Here one may compare Aune, *Prophecy*, pp. 335-42, to most any of the form critical surveys of Old Testament prophetic material, e.g., C. Westermann, *Prophetic Oracles of Salvation in the Old Testament* (Louisville, Ky.: Westminster John Knox, 1991), and the study of pagan prophecy in D. Potter, *Prophets and Emperors* (Cambridge, Mass.: Harvard University Press, 1994).

[50] This is part of a rebuke by Paul of the Corinthians' overeagerness for things revelatory. See Witherington, *Conflict and Community*, pp. 442-64.

[51] See the discussion by Aune, *Prophecy*, pp. 258-59.

logical hymn fragments, particularly Philippians 2:6-11 and Colossians 1:15-20. Certainly this material has distinct formal and poetic features, and there is precedent both within and outside of the Old Testament for prophets' singing their messages. There may even be a hint of this singing by Paul's namesake, King Saul (cf. 1 Sam 10:9-12—16:16; 2 Chron 25:1; 1 QH 11:3-4). And it would be surprising, given Paul's references to psalms, hymns and spiritual songs (Eph 5:19-20; Col 3:16), if we found no traces of such forms in the letters.

Discussions of christological hymns in the New Testament generally neglect to note that the likely candidates to have originated such forms are the Christian prophets. This is so for two reasons: (1) the poetic form of the utterances points us in this direction; (2) the profound message of the hymns, like some of the mysteries Paul refers to (see, e.g., Eph 5:32), would appear to be likely contents of revelation, as such high Christology might not have naturally occurred to some of the earliest Jewish followers of Jesus. If this conjecture has merit, then we have a further category of material within Paul's letters that provides evidence that he was himself a prophet, or at least given to repeating Christian prophetic utterances.

The author of the book of Acts seems to have believed Paul was a prophet. In Acts very little is said about Paul's being an apostle (but see Acts 14:4, 14), but Paul is rather clearly identified as a prophet (Acts 13:1) and then portrayed as one in Acts 13:9-11. He receives revelations in Acts 16:6-10, 23:11 and 27:23-25. This provides something of an independent confirmation of Paul's prophetic status, since it appears that the author does not know Paul's letters, or at least the capital Paulines,[52] and says nothing about Paul as a letter writer.

Conclusions: Paul as a Prophet

Paul was by no means reluctant to speak with assurance about the future and indeed even offered formal predictions that are occasionally quoted in his letters. This is not unexpected, since in the Greco-Roman world one went to an oracle, whether at Delphi or elsewhere, or to a prophet to get answers to questions about one's future.[53] Paul would have been recognized as a prophet because he answered the sorts of questions we find him answering in texts like 1 Thessalonians 4—5 or 1 Corinthians 15. It was not

---

[52]See Ben Witherington III, *Acts of the Apostles* (Grand Rapids, Mich.: Eerdmans, 1997), pp. 51-64.

[53]See the discussion on prophecy in the Greco-Roman world in Witherington, *Conflict and Community*, pp. 276-82.

absolutely necessary for him to say "thus saith the Lord" and then speak as the voice of God to be recognized as a prophet in a largely Gentile context, yet he does regularly preface his oracles with an introductory formula about a mystery or a word from the Lord.

Paul was an eschatological prophet in both the character and the content of his prophecy. He believed that the eschatological age had already dawned through the death and especially the resurrection of Jesus, and that as a result the form of the old world is passing away and the new creation is already partly in evidence. Paul believed that the future is indeed as bright as God's promises, and what is promised is the sure return of the Lord Jesus, the resurrection of believers, the final judgment and the coming of the kingdom of God on earth. Paul's words about the future, while they did involve similes and metaphors like the "thief in the night" motif, were not meant to be taken as mere vague hints about what was to come.

For Paul, who had been a Pharisee, the resurrection, and in particular the resurrection body, was no mere metaphor, nor merely a description of a spiritual state. He expected something just as dramatic to happen to believers and their bodies as had already happened to their Lord on Easter. The linking of Christ's resurrection with that of believers makes clear that Paul has something quite concrete in mind.

Paul was an apocalyptic prophet, in that on occasion he used apocalyptic images to describe the future (2 Thess 2). He was an apocalyptic prophet also in the belief that he was conveying mysteries hidden from normal view. We should not divorce what we know about Paul as a man of the Spirit,[54] who on occasion was taken up by a vision into heaven and received revelations, from what we learn about him as a prophet. Paul was also an apocalyptic prophet in that he believed that it would take nothing less than direct divine intervention to finally and forever change the world and humankind into what they ought to be. No visit from an emperor can bring the state of blessedness human beings need. Yet Paul was not all future promises and no present delivery. Believers were exhorted to become what they already were beginning to be. Not just talk but power is already available through the Holy Spirit.

The combination of prophecy and the work of the Spirit made Paul a powerful figure to reckon with. He could deliver more than just spiritual words: he was a conduit for spiritual *works* as well. He was in some respects like the charismatic performance prophets of old, such as Elijah and Daniel. The reaction to Paul as the true Hermes, the true messenger of God,

---

[54]See the earlier discussion of oracles and prophecy.

depicted in Acts 14:8-18 was surely not atypical. If indeed he came with powerful words and miraculous deeds to a Greco-Roman world starved for both, it is not surprising that he was often welcomed with open arms. It is also not surprising that authority figures and power brokers in the synagogue, in the secular assembly and even within the church saw him as a threat. Charismatic leaders always rattle the cage of institutional leaders, especially when they claim to answer solely or almost solely to God.

We can glean several insights from examining the forms of prophetic speech in Paul's letters:

• The majority of the content of Paul's letters is not oracular, but there is enough evidence to suggest that he did regularly offer such oracles.

• It is possible but uncertain that some of the hymn fragments in the letters reflect prophetic activity.

• Where mysteries or oracles are cited, there is a repeated emphasis on prediction. It would appear that prophecy cannot be simply equated with preaching the good news, which as texts like 1 Corinthians 15:3-8 suggest was based largely on received tradition, not instantaneous oracles.

• Paul often teaches *on the basis* of both received traditions and revelations about the future, but most of this material is now no longer in the form of prophecy but rather has been made serviceable for teaching and persuading Gentiles. It has the form of discourse, not poetry. A distinction can and should be made among a revelation, the conveying of a revelation in a prophecy and teaching on the basis of a revelation.

• There is very little encouragement for the suggestion that "charismatic" interpretation of the Hebrew Scriptures should be seen as a prophetic activity, unless those texts where Paul creatively cites an Old Testament text to back up a revelation count.

The description of the effect of prophecy in 1 Corinthians 14:3 as something that builds up, encourages and consoles, and later in 14:24 as something that reproves and calls to account, suggests a strong ethical content to some prophecy—not surprising since the major audience for Christian prophecy was the body of Christ, along with the occasional outsider who came and observed their worship.

Paul has little to say about the office of prophet. He seems strangely reluctant to use the term *prophētēs* as a way of characterizing who he is and his role in his churches. This contrasts dramatically with his use of the term *apostle*. Yet this reluctance is understandable when we recognize that New Testament prophets did not have the same status, standing or unquestioned authority as did some Old Testament prophets. In fact, Paul repeatedly suggests that the utterances of Christian prophets needed to be weighed, for in the enthusiasm of the moment of revelation, their prophecy might exceed the proportion of their faith and understanding. Thus on the one hand Paul has to encourage even "charismatic" Corinthians to seek to prophesy, and on the other hand he has to urge the Thessalonians not to despise prophecy or quench the Spirit. It seems that the prophet did not have the highest honor rating in Paul's communities. Yet Paul clearly rated prophets as very important to the early church, placing them behind only apostles in his lists of church roles and functionaries.

Again, there is no reason to blend together the roles of prophet and apostle; in fact, there are good reasons to distinguish the two, as Paul regularly does. Clearly in Paul's view an apostle has greater authority and a wider scope of responsibilities and ministry. When Paul characterizes his conversion and call to ministry, he does draw on accounts of the calls of some of the great Old Testament prophets such as Jeremiah, and he applies the language of the Servant Songs to himself. Yet it is hard to tell whether he is just using biblical language to characterize his call to be an apostle or whether he sees himself as called to be a prophet at the same time as an apostle.

PAUL THE APOSTLE AND SERVANT OF CHRIST

The origins of the term *apostolos* in its more specific Christian sense are shrouded in mystery. The term is rare in early Greek literature outside the New Testament, and where it does occur it refers generally to an envoy or message bearer (see Herodotus 1.21; Plato *Epinomis* 7.346a).

Origen, an early church father who certainly knew Greek well enough to understand its nuances, says, "Everyone who is sent by someone is an apostle of the one who sent him" (*Commentary on John* 32.17). This definition emphasizes the root meaning of the term, coming as it does from the verb *apostellō,* "to send out." Such a person is not self-directed but in the employ of or acting for another. It is possible that Paul's concept of himself as a servant is a subset of his concept of himself as an apostle, for both comport with the notion that likely underlies the concept of *apostolos*—the Jewish concept of the *shaliah*. A *shaliah* was an official agent given a specific commission, authority and power by the one who sent him. The Mishnah stresses that "a man's agent is as himself" (see especially *m. Berakot* 5.5; *m. Me`ila* 6.1-4), and it was expected that he be treated as the sender would be if the latter had come in person. The "*shaliah's* relationship with the sender is primary, the content of the commission secondary."[55] How much to stress

---

[55]P. W. Barnett, "Apostle," in *Dictionary of Paul and His Letters*, p. 45.

this Jewish concept of agency when we are seeking to understand Paul as an apostle has been debated by C. K. Barrett, H. D. Betz, Karl Rengstorf, Paul W. Barnett and others.[56]

Such discussion and debates over terminology, are not unimportant, for terminology may be part of the problem in the early church's debates over whether Paul was an apostle and if so, what sort. It is quite clear from texts like 1 Corinthians 9:2 ("if I am not an apostle to others, at least I am to you") that there was such a debate. Luke, ever one to downplay the heavy polemics of most of the earliest in-house battles in the church, reflects very little of the controversy over Paul's apostleship and in fact chooses not to use the term of Paul at all in Acts, except in Acts 14:4, 14, where the term seems to have the more general sense of an envoy sent by a church (in this case Antioch).[57] Paul also uses the term in this more general sense at 2 Corinthians 8:23, where he speaks of the "messengers of the churches" involved with the collection for the Jerusalem church.

In Acts 1:21-26 Luke reflects what may well have been the original concept of the term: an apostle is someone who traveled with Jesus during his ministry and was a witness to his resurrection. Herein lay a major problem for Paul, for he had not traveled with the historical Jesus. He was not among the Twelve. His claim then to be an authentic apostle hinged on his claim that he had seen the risen Lord and been commissioned by him (1 Cor 9:1; cf. Gal 1). Apparently such claims were not enough for some of Paul's detractors in the Jerusalem church, whom he calls "false brothers" (Gal 2:4) and who may have been the ones who called him "an abortion of an apostle" (1 Cor 15:8, my translation). The noun *ektrōma* means one brought forth from the womb in undue season, prematurely, and therefore either a miscarriage or an abortion. The idea might have been that Paul's claims were inappropriate either because he did not see the risen Lord before the ascension (cf. Acts 1 and the story of Paul's conversion in Acts 9) or, more likely, because Paul was rushed into apostleship prematurely. One moment he was persecuting Christians, and seemingly the next he was wishing to fellowship with them and proclaim Christ. It seemed to many unnatural and too good to be true (see Gal 1:22-23). No wonder Paul felt

---

[56]See H. D. Betz, "Apostle," in *Anchor Bible Dictionary*, ed. D. N. Freedman (New York: Doubleday, 1992), 1:309-11; C. K. Barrett, *The Signs of an Apostle* (Philadelphia: Fortress, 1972); Karl Rengstorf, "apostolos," in *Theological Dictionary of the New Testament*, ed. G. Kittel and G. Friedrich (Grand Rapids, Mich.: Eerdmans, 1964), 1:407-47; Barnett, "Apostle," pp. 45-50.

[57]See Witherington, *Acts*, pp. 419-20. There is even some textual doubt as to whether the term is used at all, even in 14:14.

compelled to go to Jerusalem and lay his gospel for the Gentiles before the pillar apostles, lest he be running in vain (Gal 2:2).

The Controversial Apostle

The various gaps in the story of Paul's conversion and its sequel and the differing concepts of apostle that apparently floated around in the early church have led to endless debates about the historical Paul. Did only Paul and his converts consider him a true apostle? This would seem to be unlikely in view of both Galatians 2:9-10 and Acts 15. Furthermore, to judge from 1 Corinthians 15:7, it appears that a distinction was made early on between the Twelve and all the apostles, with the latter being a larger group. Paul would never have been seen as one of the twelve original envoys of Jesus, but he could have been viewed as a member of the wider circle of apostles, and I suggest this is how the pillars came to view Paul.

Still, there were some in the Jerusalem church, the so-called Judaizers, who never accepted Paul's apostolic authenticity or his gospel and, to judge from Galatians, made it their mission to go around resocializing his converts into a far more Jewish form of Christian faith, requiring circumcision and the duty to keep the entire Mosaic law (see Gal 3—4).[58] But to judge from 2 Corinthians 10—13, this was not the only trouble Paul had. Others came to Paul's churches in Corinth claiming to be superior apostles with more ability to perform spiritual pyrotechnics, more claims to visions and miracles, so that Paul was forced into an honor challenge, a spitting contest, to see which apostle had the most power and rhetorical skill.[59]

The challenging of Paul's authority and authenticity as an apostle is the context in which we must read texts like 1 Corinthians 9:1-3, where Paul vehemently insists he has indeed seen the risen Lord. This context also explains why Paul keeps insisting he has been commissioned by no mere church but by Jesus Christ himself (see Rom 1:5; 1 Cor 1:1; 2 Cor 1:1; Gal 1:1). Finally, it explains Paul's stress on being a "called" apostle or an apostle "by the will of God," phrases he particularly uses with audiences that do not know him well but have heard the rumors and disputes about him (see Rom 1:1; Col 1:1) or with congregations that had come to doubt his status and standing (Gal 1:1). The opening of a Pauline letter reads very differently when Paul is addressing a group where his apostleship is not in doubt or under fire (Phil 1:1).

---

[58]See the discussion of these difficult issues in Ben Witherington III, *Grace in Galatia* (Edinburgh: T & T Clark, 1998), pp. 21-25, 197-205.

[59]See Witherington, *Conflict and Community*, pp. 217-73.

The previous paragraphs highlight the debate that swirled around Paul's apostleship in the early church. This makes clear that the early church was not a purely harmonious entity and that there were marked disputes even among the church's great early leaders. At the eye of the hurricane was Paul, partly because of his background as a persecutor, partly because of the extraordinary means by which he became a Christian and an apostle, partly because of his focus in ministry on Gentiles, and partly because of the message he was proclaiming to those Gentiles—salvation by grace through faith in Christ crucified and risen, without obligation to the Mosaic law.

Paul is still at the center of controversy today when Jews and Christians talk, as is especially clear in two major books written by Jewish scholars about Paul—one that sees Paul as an "apostate Jew" and one that insists on the term "radical Jew," though in the end there is little difference between these terms.[60] While Alan F. Segal does not dispute that Paul really was a convert, he does dispute whether Paul is still entitled to be called a Jew or at least a true Jew, since he became a Christian. Daniel Boyarin, on the other hand, says Paul is a radical Jew but nonetheless still a Jew. Perhaps this issue comes down to how radical a view of the Mosaic law one thinks Paul had. Not many Jews then or now would be prepared to recognize Paul as a true Jew if he argued for the obsolescence of the Mosaic law, or at least that it was no longer binding on God's people. And as Galatians makes clear, he did argue such a case, and this is why the Judaizers so vehemently opposed his apostleship and his gospel. Paul was no more acceptable to Jews and the more Jewish of Christians (Jewish in conviction of a Christian's ongoing obligation to the Mosaic law) in his day than now.

As noted already, however, in antiquity the very idea that a person could undergo a radical change of worldview, lifestyle and character was very much doubted and even denied by many (see Gal 1:23-24 and the sense of wonderment), whereas in Western cultures today the concept of conversion or radical change is widely accepted.[61] This is why understanding Paul as an apostle requires that we consider Christianity as a social movement of antiquity.

Christianity as a Social Movement

A major twentieth-century thesis about the sociology of early Christianity

---

[60]See Alan F. Segal, *Paul the Convert: The Apostolate and Apostasy of Saul the Pharisee* (New Haven, Conn.: Yale University Press, 1990); and Daniel Boyarin, *Paul and the Politics of Identity* (Berkeley: University of California Press, 1994).

[61]See the earlier discussion.

has been that the movement developed from a charismatic and functional approach to leadership to a system of offices and titles, thus becoming increasingly institutionalized. It is often said that this sort of change is to be expected when a millenarian sect becomes an established "church." Sometimes it is also assumed that early Christianity developed from an egalitarian, charismatic origin to a rather patriarchal and hierarchical society. Yet Ulrich Brockhaus has rightly pointed out that elements of institutional office (e.g., permanence of position, titles, legitimation, authority, right to compensation) were already issues in Paul's earliest churches, as especially 1 and 2 Corinthians bear witness. Brockhaus concludes that a strong distinction between charismatic and official functions in the Pauline churches is neither historically possible nor completely justified.[62] Thus there are problems with the established sociological arguments, yet it is undeniable that there was growth and development of various forms of recognized leadership. One such form was apostleship.[63]

Given that *apostolos* means "a sent-out one," someone commissioned to do something,[64] the question is, commissioned by whom, and to what end? Paul believed his commission came directly from the risen Lord Jesus, with the end that Jesus' name be carried to the Gentile nations. In Paul's view, then, the essential qualification for apostleship was not proximity to the Jerusalem church, or having been a member of the Twelve, or even having personally known the historical Jesus. Paul puts the matter succinctly in two places. In 1 Corinthians 9:1-2 he asks rhetorically: "Am I not free? Am I not an apostle? Have I not seen Jesus our Lord? Are you not my work in the Lord? If I am not an apostle to others, at least I am to you; for you are the seal of my apostleship." This may be supplemented by 1 Corinthians 15:8-9: "Last of all, as to one untimely born, he appeared also to me. For I am the least of the apostles, unfit to be called an apostle, because I persecuted the church of God." In both these texts Paul makes a close connection between seeing the risen Lord and being an apostle.

There are some other interesting implications of 1 Corinthians 9:1-2. Notice that for Paul the validation that he is an apostle is the existence of real converts from his evangelizing. Paul is not above using the "you can't

---

[62]See Ulrich Brockhaus, *Charisma und Amt: Die paulinische Charismenlehre aus dem Hintergrund der fruhchristlichen Gemeindefunktion* (Wuppertal: Theologischer Verlag R. Brockhaus, 1972), pp. 237-47.

[63]On all this see Witherington, *Conflict and Community*, pp. 453-57.

[64]It is interesting that the word *apostolos* could mean "passport" in a secular context. See Adolf Deissmann, *Paul: A Study of Social and Religious History* (New York: Harper & Brothers, 1957), p. 231.

quibble with results" argument. Notice also that he connects apostolicity with being free—free to evangelize and to work as he feels the Lord is leading, free from encumbering alliances, free from local patronage that would tie him down. This same text bears witness, however, to the fact that some in the church did not accept that Paul was an apostle.[65]

First Corinthians 15:8-9 shows that Paul is aware he is an apostle by God's grace and not by merit. Indeed, he knows that normal criteria would have disqualified him from being an apostle, since he persecuted the church. These two texts remind us that Paul's claims to apostolicity were controversial, even among some of his converts!

Simply a list of those Paul had difficulties with is a veritable who's who of early Christianity. First, of course, there is Peter (Gal 2:11-14), and behind him perhaps James as well, since James sent emissaries to investigate what Paul and Barnabas were up to in Antioch (Gal 2:12). There was the fallout with Barnabas (Acts 15:36-40; Gal 2:13), not only over Judaizing issues but also over John Mark, who himself apparently couldn't take large doses of Paul's company (Acts 13:13). Paul's real in-house adversaries were Judaizers in Galatia, false apostles in Corinth, rival preachers in Rome, "dogs" in Galatia—and the list could go on. There were many controversies between Paul and his fellow Jews, alluded to in 2 Corinthians 11:24 and more fully on display in Acts. Finally, he also had controversies with his converts.[66] The Corinthians immediately come to mind, but even the dearly beloved Philippians were not immune (see Phil 4:2-3).

Any portrait of Paul must take seriously those whom he left in his wake and those to whom he felt he had to give repeated wake-up calls. An accurate portrait must also take seriously that various other early Christians did not accept, or had serious doubts about, Paul's apostolic status. Indeed, according to C. K. Barrett, 2 Corinthians 11:26 may suggest that there was a contract out on his life—a contract taken out by other Christians![67]

Yet Paul was also greatly loved by many of his converts. Even his most polemical letter, Galatians, contains the remark "You . . . welcomed me as

---

[65]Is it because of the controversy in the early church over Paul being an apostle that Luke mentions Paul's apostolic office only in connection with the first missionary journey undertaken by both Paul and Barnabas under the auspices of the church in Antioch (see Acts 14:4, 14)? One could very well conclude that Luke calls Paul an apostle only with a small *a*, one sent out by a local church rather than directly by Christ. Paul speaks of such figures in 2 Corinthians 8:23. On this mystery see Witherington, *Acts*, pp. 430-38.

[66]To this we might even add controversies with his own coworkers!

[67]See C. K. Barrett, *Paul: An Introduction to His Thought* (Louisville, Ky.: Westminster John Knox, 1994), pp. 22-54.

an angel of God, as Christ Jesus" (Gal 4:14), and a loving relationship clearly existed between Paul and at least most of the Philippians.

What do we make of a person who was both greatly loved and greatly hated? What sort of person arouses such passions? Surely it is a gifted and passionate person, a person who has "charisma" in both the normal modern sense of that word and its more technical sociological sense.[68]

That Paul had charisma few in the church doubted. He conveyed an impression of inherent power and authority, power he claimed worked through him but was ultimately from the Lord. Obviously the essential ingredient in any sort of charismatic leadership is *presence*. One must be with people to make such an impression on them. If one is absent for a considerable period, the sense of one's presence, power and authority wanes or disappears.

A. J. Blasi's helpful study on the sociological phenomenon of charisma also points out that while recognition, like presence, is necessary for charisma to work, it is not sufficient. What is most crucial is the identity of the authority figure and the trust his audience places in his character. The audience must admire, and to some extent be able to identify with, the authority figure, or else his authority will be rejected.[69]

What happened after Paul first left Corinth, and when he wrote the letter we know as 1 Corinthians? First, there is no evidence that he left any of his immediate surrogates or coworkers behind in Corinth. His presence, authority and views thus were not carried on by an authorized secondary figure. Apparently during Paul's time away from Corinth, some doubters in the congregation, and perhaps even detractors who had arrived on the scene, encouraged a reconstruction of Paul's image, insisting that he did not live up to the image of a proper charismatic leader, a pneumatic apostle, a wise rhetor. Paul's charisma, ethos and character were questioned, and thus his authority could not work as it ought to have. Thus he needed to rebuild the trust factor, reconstruct his ethos[70] and strengthen the relation-

---

[68]Much work in Pauline studies has been done on Paul's opponents through reading between the lines of Paul's own letters. A good example of how far such a reading can go is shown by D. Georgi's major study *The Opponents of Paul in Second Corinthians* (Philadelphia: Fortress, 1986). See the useful critique of the mirror-reading technique (assuming that Paul's opponents held the exact opposite views of what Paul advocates and reconstructing their whole theology by means of such an approach) by J. L. Sumney, *Identifying Paul's Opponents: The Question of Method in 2 Corinthians* (Sheffield: JSOT, 1990). One certainly cannot lump all Paul's opponents into the same category. They were not all Judaizers, for example.

[69]See A. J. Blasi, *Making Charisma: The Social Construction of Paul's Public Image* (New Brunswick, N.J.: Transaction, 1991), pp. 10-30.

[70]See the earlier discussion of this rhetorical term.

ship with his converts that was strained, because he knew that rhetoric, wisdom and prophecy are normally received only when there is rapport. If the character of the speaker is accepted, the door is open for persuading, giving advice, leading, even commanding.

Yet it would be a mistake to see Paul's apostolic authority as some form of achieved authority. Though he repeatedly appeals to results as proof or evidence of his apostolicity (cf. 1 Cor 9:1-2 to 2 Cor 12:12), this is a matter of local verification, not legitimation. Paul's autobiographical remarks, from Galatians to the end of the Pauline corpus, make plain that he saw his authority as grounded in and derived from his relationship with Christ. His audiences might accept or reject him, but this did not affect his ultimate authorization or legitimacy. If rejected, he simply went on to the next city where he could attempt again to establish a relationship with potential converts by exercising the gifts and powers Christ had granted him.

If it is not true that Paul's apostleship exemplifies achieved authority, an authority derived and legitimated from below,[71] then it is also not true that Paul's communities were constructed on purely egalitarian or democratic principles, however voluntary the participation or compliance of the converts may have been. Paul would have liked to work always on the basis of persuasion and voluntary compliance, but he was not above arm-twisting, strong-arm tactics, even commanding. As an ancient person, Paul saw his relationship to his converts as in many ways like that of a parent to a child (see, e.g., 1 Cor 4:14-15; Gal 4:19-20). The more immature the child, the more commands and direct action may be necessary (see 1 Cor 5:4-5). If the convert is a bit more spiritually mature, simple arm-twisting may suffice. A sample case can help show how Paul exercises his apostolic authority.

A Case Study of Apostolic Persuasion

Consider the letter to Philemon, in which Paul appeals to his convert Philemon to deal with his runaway slave Onesimus in a particular fashion. First, Paul creates a sense of pathos in the audience by stressing his chains for Christ (v. 1). Then he calls Philemon his dear friend and coworker (v. 2). He reminds Philemon of his great love and generosity toward all the believers and that he, Paul, has personally been encouraged by Philemon's love and generosity (vv. 4-7). Thus far he has built up considerable rapport with

---

[71]Pace R. A. Atkins, *Egalitarian Community: Ethnography and Exegesis* (Tuscaloosa: University of Alabama Press, 1991), pp. 134-44. Basically Atkins misreads 1 Corinthians 12 as an antihierarchical argument when in fact it is an antifactionalizing argument. Note that there is still a head on this "body."

his audience.

Next Paul says that while he is bold enough to command Philemon to do the right thing, he would far rather appeal to him to do so on the basis of love (vv. 8-9). This two-edged sword reminds Philemon who is really in charge, but at the same time shows confidence in and puts pressure on Philemon to show his magnanimity and do what Paul wants him to do. In other words, Paul is laying down a clear honor challenge. If Philemon does not respond appropriately, he will be shamed not just in the eyes of Paul but also in the eyes of the church that meets in his house. Notice that this is not a private letter but is addressed to Philemon, his household *and* the church that meets in that house. When this letter was read aloud in the house-church meeting, all eyes of the congregation were surely on Philemon to see how he would respond. This is a not very subtle form of pressure.

Paul then starts the violins playing in the background by reminding Philemon that he (Paul) is an old man, a prisoner, who shouldn't have to worry about the fate of someone he has come to recognize as his own child—Onesimus. Paul claims to have recently become Onesimus's father (v. 10).[72]

Notice that only about halfway through this little letter does Paul bring up the sore subject that he wants to address with Philemon. Such a delay in mentioning the main bone of contention is a rhetorically adept move.

Immediately Paul tries to lighten the mood by making a play on words, lest Philemon become startled, defensive or angry. Onesimus was a common slave name in Asia Minor, and it means "useful." In verse 11 Paul says in effect that "old Useful," while he did not live up to his name when he was with Philemon, now with Paul has become Onesimus indeed, truly useful both to the apostle and to Philemon.

Paul then makes a show of doing what the law requires—sending the slave back to his master (v. 12). Just to punctuate again how much he cares about this matter—and to pull on his audience's heart-strings—he calls Onesimus "my own heart." In other words, if Philemon keeps Onesimus, he will be plucking Paul's heart right out of his body!

Then in verse 13, bringing in the old reciprocity argument, Paul says he wanted to keep Onesimus with him so he might be of service *in lieu of*

---

[72]Here the concept of adoptive parenthood—an extremely prevalent practice in the Greco-Roman world usually undertaken to place a child in an higher-status or more financially stable family—comes into play. Paul is saying that in effect Onesimus has already changed hands through God's work, and that Philemon should simply accept and validate this change.

Philemon during his house arrest. In other words—what have you done for me lately?

By verse 14 Paul once again, not so subtly, lets his readers know who is in charge here. Paul could have acted unilaterally and simply kept Onesimus with him, but his *preference* was to do nothing without Philemon's consent. In this way, says Paul, Philemon can himself have an opportunity to achieve more honor in the community—"that your good deed might be voluntary and not something forced." Paul then suggests that God intended things this way so that Philemon could have Onesimus back, only now as a brother, not merely a slave.

Verse 16 is crucial because it speaks of Onesimus as becoming, both in the flesh and in the Lord, Philemon's brother. This should likely be taken to mean that Paul is expecting Philemon to formally manumit Onesimus and so give him the new higher social status of being an actual person, while at the same time treating him as his spiritual brother. One wonders how difficult this was for Philemon to swallow. It would be one thing to accept Onesimus back without punishment, a punishment the owner had every legal right to exact. It would be another to relinquish the runaway straightaway after Philemon had recovered his "property." It would be still another to treat his former slave as a Christian brother. Paul was indeed asking a lot. This was a true test of Philemon's sanctification level.

The coup de grace comes in verses 17-22. First Paul says, in effect, "Do not merely welcome him, but welcome him as you would me! Treat him as you would me, your apostle and spiritual patron."[73] Notice the preceding "if" clause—"*if* you [still] consider me your partner . . ." In other words, Philemon's status as a Pauline partner is on the line. Paul puts the matter in a rhetorically effective way, not "if you wish to be considered *my* partner" but rather "if you consider me yours." In other words, Paul places Philemon in the superior position as the local Christian leader, the one who must make this decision, the one who is in charge of this situation. This only puts more pressure on him to do the right thing; otherwise the members of his house church will say, "I guess he didn't consider Paul his partner anymore."

In verse 18 Paul turns to damages. He says he will gladly repay if anything is owed. Of course the time that Onesimus was not present to work in Philemon's household is involved here. "Charge it to my account," Paul is saying, "and here is my I.O.U." (v. 19), as he writes his signature. Yet then he continues, "Now that I look closely at the ledger and the balance

---

[73]See R. W. Wall, *Colossians and Philemon* (Downers Grove, Ill.: InterVarsity Press, 1993), p. 214.

sheet, I could say something"; then, as if reconsidering, "I say nothing about your owing me even your [spiritual] self" (or life)! With great rhetorical effectiveness, Paul is working the reciprocity conventions and engaging in emotional arm-twisting.[74] He manages to mention the unmentionable. But then, Paul the master rhetor knew the *peroratio* was the place for such emotional pressure, and he has reached that summing up at least as early as verses 19-21.[75]

Paul then says, as if he were recording a transfer in the ledger, "I from you, benefit in the Lord" (my translation). *Onaimēn* is a variant from the same stem as the name Onesimus, so we have another play on words here as Paul pulls out all the rhetorical stops. But in addition *onaimēn* is in the second aorist optative—"let me have benefit" (beginning now). Though not quite a command, it is a strong request that reinforces what has come before. In this same verse Paul returns to his opening theme that Philemon is a refresher of the hearts of the saints (v. 7), only now Paul himself will become the test case to show whether this is so.

The force of verse 21 should not be missed. Paul says he is persuaded of Philemon's *obedience (hypakoē)*. Paul really is in charge here. Indeed, he can even presume to say, "I know you will do even more than I ask"!

The very next verse gives a concrete clue of what that "more" might entail: Paul wants a room prepared for him so he can come and visit his old friend and brother, as well as his partner Onesimus. This remark has a double effect: (1) it puts one more bit of pressure on Philemon to comply with Paul's wishes, yet (2) it also places Paul even further in Philemon's debt. It shows thus that Paul wants the reciprocity and the partnership to endure. He does not want Philemon to come out of this encounter shamed, and so he gives him the opportunity to continue to be a patron or host to other Christians. He gives him the chance to come out of this honor challenge without damage to his own position and authority.

Finally, he reminds Philemon of his own prayers for Paul. After this rhetorical tour de force, however, Philemon may well have needed verse 25—"The grace of the Lord be with your spirit."

---

[74]See earlier discussions of these conventions and patronage.

[75]On the rhetorical structure of this letter see F. F. Church, "Rhetorical Structure and Design in Paul's Letter to Philemon," *Harvard Theological Review* 71 (1978): 17-33. Here surely is deliberative rhetoric from start to finish. Paul wants some advantage or benefit from Philemon and must persuade him to give it. As Church admits, the key to deliberative rhetoric "is to demonstrate love or friendship and to induce sympathy or goodwill, in order to dispose the hearer favorably to the merits of one's case" (pp. 19-20). Church divides the letter into exordium (vv. 4-7), proofs (vv. 8-16) and peroration (vv. 17-22).

The letter to Philemon, then, is an excellent case study revealing the interface between Paul's authority and his acts of persuasion, between his apostolicity and his desire to work collegially with his ministerial partners. In the end, Paul sees himself as being at the top of the hierarchically arranged set of relationships in his churches. He can command and he does expect obedience, even when need be from his partners. And certainly he was capable of using all the weapons in his rhetorical arsenal to accomplish his aims.

Imagine being present in Philemon's house when Tychicus or another Pauline associate orally performed or delivered the contents of this document. It would have revealed that even while under house arrest a good distance away, Paul could still exercise his apostolic authority. His apostolic reach through his network of associates was considerable.

Networks of Leadership

Social network theory is only just being developed in relationship to the analysis of Paul and his communities.[76] Such studies show that social factors (such as who was the head of home where the *ekklēsia* met) as well as spiritual factors must be taken into consideration in evaluating Paul's relationship to his converts. Social bonds in fact often determine ideological commitments—for example, when the head of a family converted to a new religion and his family was obliged or required to follow. Philemon's household may be used as an example. The address in this letter (vv. 1-2) suggests a family with Philemon as husband, and Apphia as wife, and possibly Archippus as son or member of Philemon's extended *familia*.[77] The letter suggests, however, that while these family members were all Christians, Onesimus was not prior to his encounter with Paul. Nevertheless, the dominant members of the household are united by bonds that are both social and spiritual, and Paul can appeal to both. It seems clear that Paul did aim to cultivate certain high-status persons as Christians and then as ministerial partners in part to establish a venue for Christians.

Leadership among Paul's coworkers would be partly determined by spiritual gifts and partly by sociological factors. We see this same phenomenon in the case of Stephanas in Corinth. In 1 Corinthians 1:16 we learn that Paul has baptized the household of Stephanas; 1 Corinthians 16:15 tells us that these were the first converts in all Achaia. This means Paul deliberately

---

[76]See L. M. White, ed., *Social Networks in Early Christian Enviroment: Issues and Methods for Social History* (Atlanta: Scholars Press, 1992).

[77]See the earlier discussion of ancient family structure.

targeted these more high-status persons when he came into the region. First Corinthians 16:15 tells us part of the reason—"they have devoted themselves to the service of the saints." The next verse then provides them a commendation to be recognized and assisted as leaders of the church in Corinth, and in fact any who work with them in ministry should be commended. Finally, we notice that Paul was visited in Ephesus by Stephanas himself (16:17). The context suggests that he had come to consult with Paul about ministerial work, and perhaps the lack of recognition of his authority (and thus Paul's), in Corinth. Surely he brought Paul much news about the condition of the Christian church in Corinth.

We see here how Paul's networks of power actually work. He relies on not only itinerant coworkers who travel regularly with him, such as Timothy and Titus, but also on local leaders who occasionally take trips to consult with him.

Paul sees himself as the authorized agent of Christ, and as such the dispenser of Christ's largesse and the implementer of Christ's will. Christ is the benefactor, but Paul is his agent. In 2 Corinthians 11:2 he calls himself a friend of the bridegroom who has specific tasks to undertake for the bride. Because Paul is in fact a patron of his converts, it is not appropriate for him to become simply their client. This would undercut his apostolic authority over them and prevent him from traveling and offering the gospel free of charge to all. Holland Hendrix reminds us that "benefactor-beneficiary and patron-client networks are operative in establishing and reinforcing the mutual status of persons involved. Balanced discharge of the obligations (expected behavior [cf., e.g., Philemon]) . . . maintains and reinforces their respective powers."[78]

Paul took part in an ongoing cultural struggle for status, power and control in a world in which power was clutched in the hands of a few. Paul's gospel brought empowerment to many, especially those of lower status who in church might become more nearly on par with their societal superiors, relating to them as brothers and sisters. As an apostle, Paul aimed to change the primary socializing agent in the lives of his converts by means of God's grace. He hoped to bind them into a close-knit community involving fellow converts locally and elsewhere in the Mediterranean, but also involving an ongoing relationship with Paul and his traveling coworkers. Most of all, he sought to encourage a vital relationship between the converts and Christ, so they would see that Christ was their ultimate

---

[78]Holland Hendrix, "Benefactor/Patron Networks in the Urban Environment: Evidence from Thessalonica," in *Social Networks in Early Christian Environment*, p. 55.

patron and benefactor and that Paul was the facilitator (agent) of that relationship.

Thus Paul sought to create a social and religious subunit within the larger society. It was not a separate society, for Paul did not seek to dictate all cultural values but to modify, mold or create values that would reflect some fundamental Christian reality or value (e.g., monotheism).[79]

Though there is no evidence that Paul's communities were ever nonhierarchical in leadership structure (Paul never resigned as the apostle of any of these churches), it must be stressed that his vision of authority, including apostolic authority, was not essentially based on gender, race or social status, but rather on whether a person was called and gifted by the Spirit to perform certain tasks, and as a secondary consideration, whether their social situation permitted them to do these tasks effectively. This latter factor would have tended to favor men in positions of power in the church, but it was not a determining factor. Among Paul's coworkers there were ministerial couples like Priscilla and Aquila (Rom 16:3) and also high-status women like Phoebe (Rom 16:1-2), Euodia and Syntyche (Phil 4:2-3). There may have even been female apostles (see Rom 16:7—Junia). To judge from Philemon, Paul was also prepared to use slaves or former slaves such as Onesimus as coworkers. A simple survey of the names of his coworkers shows as well that he was happy to partner with either Jews or Gentiles.

Paul as a Servant

Paul was an authority figure in the church, one who exercised leadership. Yet his authority was exercised as "servant leadership"—a phrase that would have seemed an oxymoron to most ancient persons. That is, Paul saw himself as a servant or slave of Jesus Christ and also ultimately of his converts.[80] One could almost say that Paul envisioned himself as the head servant or estate manager within the household of the Lord, one called upon to be a good steward of the Master's word (see 1 Cor 3), who tended

---

[79]This and other observations appear in another form in Witherington, *Conflict and Community*, pp. 455-65.

[80]When a slave was freed through sacral manumission, the god was considered the actual purchaser or ransomer, even though the payment came from the slave or another source. The slave then became property of the god, but was otherwise free. Similarly, Paul sees himself as free in relationship to other humans, but the slave of Christ who ransomed him. See Deissmann, *Paul*, p. 173. Deissmann is also right that the different metaphors Paul uses for salvation are describing the same conversion event or its benefits, but from different angles— justification, the person stands before God as accused; ransom, the person stands before God as enslaved; reconciliation, the person stands before God as alienated; grace, the person stands before God as indebted. See Deissmann, *Paul*, p. 168.

to the Master's business and carried out his orders.[81] "So let no one boast about human leaders. For all things are yours, whether Paul or Apollos or Cephas . . . all belong to you, and you belong to Christ, and Christ belongs to God" (1 Cor 3:21-23). The leaders belong to the body of Christ, the body belongs to Christ, and Christ belongs to God. Servant and apostle/agent converge in that both are implementers of another's will and plans.

Philippians 2:4-11 makes evident that Paul modeled himself on the ultimate servant leader, Christ, whose very coming to earth was a fundamental and deliberate stepping down, a stooping to conquer. Paul's leadership style, then, took the form of servanthood. It needs to be understood that this was not a goal of Greco-Roman society. People were not eager to be others' servants; indeed they deprecated and ridiculed slavish behavior. *Tapeinophrosynē* in Philippians 2:3, which we might translate "humility," literally means to be base-minded or act like a slave, neither being a complimentary description.[82] Humility was not seen as a virtue in Greco-Roman antiquity, especially if it meant acting in a slavish or subservient fashion—unless of course one *was* a slave.

If, following the example of Christ, Paul modeled this "virtue" and inculcated it in his audience, he was deconstructing certain key attitudes about status and power in his society. Those of higher status in the church would have to stop relating to others on the basis of social pecking orders or the honor rolls of society. They would have to stop assuming that standing social conventions, distinctions and customs ought to determine their behavior and way of relating to others. Cutting across the gap between Roman citizens and noncitizens, patricians and plebeians, *honestiores* (more honorable) and *humiliores* (less honorable) was the fact that all believers were citizens of a heavenly commonwealth, and the social means of making clear that reality was serving one another in love.

Paul, leading the way, would outdo all others in self-sacrificial and loving service, and on this basis implore, "Be imitators of me, as I of Christ" (see 1 Cor 10:33—11:1). This did not mean "become apostles like me," for that was a matter not of personal choice but of divine commission. But it was perfectly possible for Paul's converts to imitate his acts of public service, his "liturgies," and in an interesting way this seeking to do "liturgies" could mirror a dominant value of the culture. The difference was, the reason for Christians to perform such actions was to help others, not to promote themselves.

---

[81]On this see Hengel and Schwemer, *Paul Between Damascus and Antioch,* p. 96.
[82]See Witherington, *Friendship and Finances,* pp. 63-64.

Why would Paul introduce himself as a servant in some letters (Rom 1:1; Phil 1:1) alternately with introducing himself in other letters as the apostle of Christ (1 Cor 1:1; 2 Cor 1:1; Gal 1:1)? Perhaps here we have clues about the character of the documents which follow. When Paul introduces himself as a servant, he is not concerned that the audience recognize his authority and leadership. He feels no need to assert it, and of course in Romans it would be somewhat inappropriate for him to do so, since he did not found the church in Rome. When he introduces himself as servant, he wishes to provide an example for the audience to follow. In Philippians we have an entire document based on the notion of following good Christlike examples and avoiding bad ones.[83] In Romans Paul is providing a sample or example of his essential gospel or teaching, with hopes that the Roman Christians will follow his lead and in fact help him to go farther west serving the cause of Christ. So the term *apostle* indicates the need to assert authority, while *servant* indicates the desire to have one's leadership style and example followed.

There may also be something to the suggestion that in the letters where Paul introduces himself as a servant, he wishes to emphasize that he stands in the prophetic tradition (see, e.g., Jer 7:25). Given Galatians 1's indebtedness to the description of Jeremiah, it is very believable that Paul not only saw himself in the suffering figure of Jeremiah who was rejected by his fellow Jews, but also saw his often controverted and rejected ministry efforts reflected in the word of affirmation from the Lord in Jeremiah 7:25— "From the day that your ancestors came out of the land of Egypt until this day, I have persistently sent all my servants the prophets to them, day after day; yet they did not listen to me, or pay attention . . ." Even as late as his writing of Romans, Paul was still stressing that the gospel was for the Jews first, whether they accepted it or not (Rom 1:16). In Jeremiah he had a model of persistence and faithfulness even in the midst of rejection, suffering and tragedy.

Paul's use of the "servant of God" concept and mentality, of course, was based on Christ's example. But standing in the background is the servant of Isaiah 40—55. That servant was called upon either as or for Israel to be a light to the Gentile nations:

> Here is my servant, whom I uphold,
>   my chosen one, in whom my soul delights;
> I have put my spirit upon him;
>   he will bring forth justice to the nations. . . .

---

[83]See the earlier discussion.

He will not grow faint or be crushed
    until he has established justice in the earth. . . .
Thus says God, the LORD, . . .
I have given you as a covenant to the people,
    a light to the nations,
    to open the eyes that are blind,
to bring out the prisoners from the dungeon,
    from the prison those who sit in darkness. (Is 42:1-7)

Could Paul, following in Christ's footsteps and seeing himself as Christ's agent, have seen himself as the servant of Isaiah, and for this reason seen himself as called upon to spread the light among the Gentile nations? Paul knew that Christ during his own life had basically been unable to carry out such a task. But Christ could get the job done through his agent or ambassador Paul. Does this also explain why Paul talks about filling up the sufferings of Christ or sharing his sufferings (cf. Phil. 3:10)? Is it Paul's memory of texts like Isaiah 49 and 53 that leads him to first quote Isaiah 49:8 in 2 Corinthians 6:2 and then go on to say in verses 4-10,

But as servants of God we have commended ourselves in every way: through great endurance, in afflictions, hardships, calamities, beatings, imprisonments, . . . by purity, knowledge, patience, kindness, holiness of spirit, genuine love, truthful speech, and the power of God; with the weapons of righteousness for the right hand and for the left. . . . We are treated . . . as unknown, and yet well known; as dying, and see—we are alive; as punished, and yet not killed; as sorrowful, yet always rejoicing; as poor, yet making many rich; as having nothing, and yet possessing everything.

The meekness and gentleness of Christ the suffering servant are replicated in the meekness and gentleness of his servant Paul (2 Cor. 10:1), who sees himself as the agent of Christ, the extension of the Master, who shares the Master's modus operandi and is treated as the Master was treated. What links Paul's understanding of himself as apostle and servant are Christ and the figure of the servant of Isaiah. Paul saw himself as an extension of his Master and his experiences an extension of Christ's precisely because he saw himself as Christ's authorized agent. Like Master, like servant—or in this case like Servant, like servant.

CONCLUSIONS: PROPHET AND APOSTLE

Paul was an authority figure, a leader. Yet he embodied the example of servanthood, suffering for what he believed in. Like his Master, he was a man of sorrows and well acquainted with grief.

Paul saw himself not only as a purveyor of prophecies but also as one in whom prophetic words came to pass. His social and religious values would have seemed strange to many Gentiles, while his powerful works and words would have attracted a crowd. In short, he would have been seen as not merely charismatic but also enigmatic.

But Paul's role as a prophet cannot be separated from his apostleship. He was an apostle—an envoy or ambassador—of Christ, a commission and status that was disputed in the early church. How was it that Paul, who was not a traveling companion or emissary of the earthly Jesus or of the Twelve, could claim apostleship? In 1 Corinthians 15 Paul admits the irregularity of his apostolic call, but he believed the outcome of the process was the same. In the face of challenges to his apostolic authority, he steadfastly maintained that his authority did not derive from below: he was not merely an agent of a particular church, commissioned to a limited missionary task. Paul's exercise of apostolic authority included not only commands but the effective use of rhetoric and social persuasion. In his absence he relied on local church leaders and his coworkers to carry out his authority. Although his vision of the structure of power was somewhat hierarchical, with apostles at the top, Paul was an empowerer of the disfranchised, including the poor and women. As prophet and apostle Paul modeled himself after his Master, the ultimate servant leader.

CHAPTER 5

PAUL THE REALIST
AND RADICAL

While the previous two chapters examined Paul in some of his major roles, this chapter begins to analyze how Paul functioned in these various roles. The evidence suggests he was in some ways a pragmatist and in other ways a pioneer. When he was a Pharisee, Paul was radical enough to be prepared to resort to violence; when he became a Christian he did not cease to be a radical, he just became a nonviolent one.

Paul's religion was not of the world-negating or world-withdrawing sort. Rather he advocated the transformation of a world whose old form was already passing away. Yet the means by which this change was to transpire was through placing the leaven of the gospel in a particular subculture of the Greco-Roman world—the Christian subculture. Hence though there was a definite social and political dimension to Paul's gospel, he was not a revolutionary who advocated violent overthrow of the existing government or the world's structures. Rather these were to be transformed by grace within the context of the Christian community. This meant the reformation of social networks and relationships within the community but also as Christians interacted with the world.

A crucial text in the entire discussion of whether Paul was a revolutionary is Romans 13. In this text Paul is not advocating Christian participation in government or Christian acquiescence to immorality, nor does he offer a Christian endorsement of the use of force. Paul is dealing with an existing reality and suggesting that Christians need to respect and submit to the powers that be, even if they be a Nero. Yet there is a distinction between submission and obedience. Recognition of legitimate authority given by God is not the same as acceptance of all that is done with this power and authority. Yet Paul is counseling critical realism here, for he wants the fragile and small Christian community in Rome to survive and thrive. His purpose may be primarily that Christians accept their tax responsibilities when the tax police, wearing the short sword of their office, come around. This is not surprising advice from a Roman citizen, but its intent is to protect Christians from governmental intrusion and difficulties. This passage provides no support for Christians' serving in the military; in fact, the immediately preceding passage (12:14-21) commits Christians to an ethic of nonviolence and nonretaliation. Yet Paul is not simply advocating quietism: he advocates being proactive in loving even one's enemies.

The preceding discussion may give the impression that Paul was not a social engineer at all, but this is incorrect. He directed his social advocacy and directives to a community over which he had authority—the community of Christians. Surprisingly enough, it is in Paul's remarks about the Christian family and the family of faith that we see just how radical he can be, going against the status quo or the general direction of the culture. Paul's advice in Colossians 3—4 and parallels must be judged against the backdrop of the highly patriarchal world in which he lived. When this is done, it becomes clear that Paul is setting about to modify patriarchal family structures to make them more equitable for the subordinate members of the household. For example, he places restrictions on the father/husband/master in the family, requiring that he love and respect the other family members, treating them in Christlike fashion. Not only Paul's position but his direction and aim in comparison to the remarks of his contemporaries must be taken into account.

Paul's teaching about slavery shows the delicate way he seeks to reform social structures within the Christian community. Freedom is advocated if it can be obtained, and in any case Paul urges that Christian slaves be treated as brothers and sisters, not as property. As Philemon makes especially clear, Paul is not endorsing the institution of slavery, and he does not advocate that a person choose slavery, as many in his day did for economic reasons. Nor does Paul's love ethic aim to make it easier for masters to take advantage of their slaves; instead he is trying to constrain owners from such opportunistic behavior. Yet Paul believes it is possible to be a Christian even as a slave, and for him that social relationship is more real and important than any other. He sees government, family and work as good gifts from God, but he realizes that in a fallen world they can be misused. So he works to restrain the effects of fallenness on these institutions by developing a strategy of reform within the Christian community. This is why he can be seen as both a realist and a radical.

WAS PAUL A REVOLUTIONARY? IT DEPENDS ON HOW THE TERM IS DEFINED. Certainly he did not lead an open revolt against the body politic or against any ruler in the Roman Empire. Indeed, taking up arms seems to have been against his religion (see below). We also have no evidence of Paul's working to change laws or publicly protesting oppressive social structures. Thus the term *revolutionary* may be too extreme to describe Paul. Yet he had a decidedly public face and was well known in various places in the Empire. Paul worked—and worked hard—to change the world by creating a Christian enclave within it, made up of those who had responded positively to the gospel. Yet his was not the Amish approach of withdrawal from the world, with only limited and occasional engagement and contact with that world. His was ultimately a world-transforming, not a world-negating, vision. This chapter will argue that Paul was some sort of radical, yet he was also in many ways a realist, willing to be a Jew to the Jew and a Gentile to the Gentile so that by various means he might win some.

A radical is a person who is by no means satisfied with the status quo and has set out to change things by a variety of means. A radical is a boat-rocker, a reformer, but not a revolutionary, if by revolutionary one means a person willing to resort to violence to achieve his ends. Paul had been a revolutionary, as his persecution of the church before his conversion showed, but his encounter with Christ in one sense domesticated him, so that he became a nonviolent radical.[1] Indeed, he was so radical that he believed that the form and structures of the world were already passing away as a result of the Christ event, even though the world was oblivious to this fact.

Yet as a realist, Paul the Christian was prepared to begin with people where they were, use persuasion and count on the silent work of grace to change people's hearts and lives. Part of slipping leaven into the dough of fallen human society meant taking societal structures as they were and subtly and gradually modifying and Christianizing them. In some cases this meant placing a time bomb within an institution like slavery, so that if the bomb had not been removed from the premises, it would in due course dismantle the institution.

Yet note that the leaven was not placed directly into society at large but into a subculture within it, the Christian community. Furthermore, Paul was prepared to adapt his own lifestyle and style of interaction with the world for the sake of effective gospel ministry, so that he became a Jew to the Jew and a Gentile to the Gentile. He also used the existing social structures and his privileges as a Roman citizen for the sake of the gospel. As we shall see, Paul acted on principle, but often in a pragmatic or realistic way.

PAUL THE REALIST

Recent studies of Paul have shown that a purely apolitical or nonpolitical reading of the apostle will not do. Moreover, we must be able to distinguish between the politics of Paul and the political use—or more often misuse—of some material in his letters. Neil Elliott has chronicled in detail how Paul's teaching was used against women in New England in 1637, against slaves'

---

[1]Some will not be happy with calling Saul the Pharisee a revolutionary, since his persecution of Christians was an act of violence against a minority sect rather than against the ruling governmental structures. I however use the term deliberately, because Paul's theocratic worldview was such that he believed like the Maccabees before him and the Zealots after him that he was on a mission from God which required violence. The fact that the object of his violence was not Roman or Jewish authorities does not change the radical, revolutionary nature of his actions.

freedom in 1709 in South Carolina (and of course later during the Civil War), against Jews during World War II in Germany, Poland and elsewhere, and in Guatemala in 1982 against the poor.[2] Such abuses could summarily be condemned and dismissed, except that Elliott proposes that it is the "canonical" Paul as opposed to the real Paul who has facilitated such abuse. He argues that the later Paulines (Colossians, Ephesians, the Pastorals) have fostered a false image of Paul and that this image has been read back into the earlier, less disputed Paulines. Very unlike those who see the later Paulines as the quintessence of Paul, or a logical development by one or more faithful disciples of Paul, Elliott sees no such natural development.

This chapter will deal with some of these arguments about the household codes and Paul's views on women, but our first task is to consider Paul's primary discussion of the believer's relationship with governing authorities—Romans 13:1-7.

In the first place, we are certainly helped by Elliott's argument that part of Paul's purpose in Romans (especially Rom 9—11) is to address largely Gentile Christians in Rome (see Rom 11:13), to rebuke Roman anti-Semitism and to demonstrate that God has not given up hope of the salvation of all Israel.[3] Elliott fails to note, however, that this also implies that Paul thinks that non-Christian Jews are now temporarily broken off from the people of God until the full number of the Gentiles can come in, and then they will reenter by faith in Christ. In short, Elliott's following of the arguments of Krister Stendahl, Lloyd Gaston and John Gager on this front is a weakness, not a strength, of his study.[4]

If anti-Semitism is ruled out, are other pro-Roman attitudes nevertheless ruled in by Romans 13:1-7? If, as I have already argued, Paul is opposing Christian eschatology to imperial eschatology in Corinth, and in Thessalonica is prepared to critique the Caligula—or Antiochus—like ruler called "the man of lawlessness," does this mean Paul sees human governments as inherently evil and always a tool of the powers of darkness?

Romans was probably written by Paul sometime during the last five years of the 50s A.D.[5] Thus it was written while Nero was emperor, though before he declined into tyranny and the persecuting of Christians (which

---

[2]Neil Elliott, *Liberating Paul: The Justice of God and the Politics of the Apostle* (Maryknoll, N.Y.: Orbis, 1994).

[3]Cf. ibid., pp. 179-85, and Ben Witherington III, *Jesus, Paul and the End of the World* (Downers Grove, Ill.: InterVarsity Press, 1992), pp. 99-128.

[4]On these views, which entail a two-track model of salvation—Gentiles through faith in Christ, Jews through the law—see the earlier discussion.

[5]See, e.g., J. Fitzmyer, *Romans* (New York: Doubleday, 1993), pp. 86-87.

came at least seven or eight years later). Paul's comments, then, must be taken in this context, when by and large Christians could judge the emperor and the government to be acting as they ought to do.

Note too that this text says absolutely nothing about Christians' participating in government activities such as war or police actions. Christians were not themselves rulers during this period, and the Roman government was not a participatory democracy. Even soldiers were not enlisted through a lottery of citizens. In short, this text is about pagan rulers and their right to govern and bear the sword for some purposes. The text says nothing about a Christian's right, much less duty, to bear arms.[6]

Christians and Governing Authorities

Verse 1 directs these comments to every living person *(pasa psyche)*, which likely means every Roman Christian Paul is now addressing. It may be that some Christians were thinking of rebelling against the Roman authorities, especially given the burgeoning growth of the emperor cult. A very specific crisis in Rome may have prompted this exhortation. Tacitus *(Annals* 13.50-51) tells us that in A.D. 58, due to numerous complaints about *publicani* engaging in unscrupulous tax-farming practices (the collecting of indirect taxes), Nero contemplated abolishing all indirect taxation. In due course, senators persuaded him simply to post and strictly enforce the taxation regulations. It is possible that when the taxes were most excessive and oppressive, shortly before matters reached their resolution, various Roman Gentile Christians were restive about the situation.[7]

Hypotasso, "to submit," is the same verb we will find applied to relationships within the body of Christ in Colossians 3—4 and Ephesians 5—6.[8] This verb is not identical with *hypakuo,* which means "to obey," as can be seen in the differing subjects these two verbs are applied to in Colossians 3—4. Submitting to the governing powers, which among other things means recognizing that they have a God-given authority, is not quite the same as obeying them. In other words, this text would not rule out a civil disobedience undertaken with due respect of government's authority, for instance if the government should require the worship of the emperor. The reason given in verse 1 for this submission is that there is no human "power" *(exousia)* except from God. The existing authorities are so by God.

---

[6]On all of this see especially J. H. Yoder, *The Politics of Jesus* (Grand Rapids, Mich.: Eerdmans, 1972), pp. 193-214.

[7]See on this J. W. Friedrich and P. Stuhlmacher, "Zur historischen Situation und Intention von Rom. 13.1-7," *Zeitschrift für Theologie und Kirche* 73 (1976): 131-66.

[8]See a later discussion in this book.

It is quite possible that *tetagmenai*, when coupled with *exousia*, refers to prominent Roman officials.

Walter Wink offers an intriguing and fresh way of reading Paul's discussion of the powers that be here. His view is that whenever Paul discusses such powers, he means both the human powers and the supernatural powers that influence, guide and use them. Wink is right that in various places the New Testament acknowledges a relationship between human and supernatural forces or authorities, but we cannot simply assume that when one is spoken of the other is also always meant or implied. Nothing in Romans 13:1-7 suggests Paul is talking about the supernatural "powers behind the throne," other than the very clear connection he makes between God and the ordained human authorities. While elsewhere Paul sometimes does use *exousia* in a negative sense to refer to malign angelic forces, this hardly suits the context here, and Paul would not counsel submission to such forces in any case.[9] Not all new views of the historical Paul and his thought world are plausible ones.

Paul's discussion is about submitting not just to the emperor but also to lesser governing authorities. This point must be kept clearly in mind, for as we shall see, it appears Paul may have tax officials particularly in view. On a broader front, the point is that God raises up and disposes all rulers, but this by no means implies an endorsement of all policies of human governments.

Verse 2 draws a conclusion on the basis of verse 1. If such authorities are God-ordained and -endowed, then those who resist such authority resist God's ordering, and in the end they will incur legal judgment. Paul goes on to add in verse 3 that rulers *(archontes)* are not a terror to good works but to evil ones. The assumption is of course that the officials are working properly and justice is being done. Paul then asks in verse 3, "Do you wish to have no fear of the authority?" He responds, in effect, "Then do what is good, and far from judgment, you will actually receive praise from the authorities. They are servants of God for the good of all, including Christians" (see vv. 3-4).

Archē was a term regularly used for local or municipal officials. If people do what is evil, they should be afraid, because these officials do not wear and bear the sword for nothing. When the authority "executes wrath" on wrongdoers, he is acting as the servant of God.

---

[9]This is characteristic of Walter Wink's treatment of this material in *Naming the Powers* (Philadelphia: Fortress, 1984), pp. 6-47. He does not distinguish between supernatural and natural powers adequately. See especially pp. 45-47.

Paul is not offering a discourse on capital punishment. Were he discussing that subject, we would expect him to say something about crucifixion at this juncture. Paul may have agreed in principle that the governing authorities have the right to use lethal force to maintain order. Nonetheless, the focus here is on curbing resistance or evildoing. Paul could have used other terms had he wanted to speak about capital punishment. In view of verses 6-7, it is possible that here he has in mind the tax police who wore the Roman short sword, but we cannot be sure. I suspect that Paul is talking in general terms up through verse 5 and turns to a specific illustration, perhaps one that is very germane for Roman Christians, in verses 6-7. Tax police would be but one illustration of a governing authority's right to bear the sword.

Verse 5 rounds out the discussion and stresses two reasons one should have a healthy respect for the governing authorities. First, one could indeed be subject to lethal force. Second, there is one's Christian conscience. Here "conscience" probably does not focus on guilty feelings but rather refers to prudence, critical realism, being wise as serpents and innocent as doves. Paul the realist does not wish Christians to come to harm and counsels what would amount to Christian wisdom.

Verse 6 begins "Because of this" (NRSV "for the same reason"), which would seem to have verse 5 in view. Wise critical reflection leads one to pay tribute, by which is meant taxes and customs fees. Jews, and presumably Jewish Christians, were exempt from some taxes. They were able to pay taxes to their own temple in Jerusalem in lieu of some Roman taxes, since as monotheists they would not contribute to funds dedicated to pagan religion or the emperor cult. This policy caused no end of irritation and anger to those Romans who had to pay such taxes directly (cf. Cicero *For Flaccus* 28.67; Tacitus *Historiae* 5.5.1; Josephus *Antiquities of the Jews* 16.45, 160-61). Furthermore, Roman citizens were exempt from such taxes, which left ordinary Roman Gentiles bearing the burden. In this situation it is understandable that Paul might have to exhort his mostly Gentile audience in Rome not only to respect Jews, whom God had not forsaken (Rom 9— 11), but also to pay their taxes as a sign of respect to the God-ordained authority.

Paul actually says in verse 6 that tax collectors are not only public servants but servants of God engaged in this task of making sure that proper tribute money is paid. Verse 7 may have an echo of Mark 12:17. There are two technical terms used here. *Phoros* corresponds to *tributum*— direct taxes from which Roman citizens likely would be exempt. *Telos* refers to *vectigalia*—direct taxes, which would have included rents from government properties and also customs duties, death duties and taxes on the sale of slaves.[10] Christians, then, should owe no one anything. Taxes and proper honor should be given to all to whom they are due.

What does this teaching tell us about the historical Paul? Clearly Paul was no revolutionary. Yet this passage should not be seen as a manifesto suggesting that Christians should obey the government in all things. "Submitting" is not the same as blind obedience. Paul is suggesting a policy of critical realism, to avoid clashes with governing authorities and also to avoid the judgment that Christians are subversive because they will not pay taxes. These were not incidental issues; Paul would have known about the expulsion of Jews from Rome a few years before this letter was written (A.D. 49), and to judge from Acts 18 this involved Jewish Christians as well. Christians in Rome were in a somewhat precarious position, and so Paul is counseling a form of political quietism and nonresistance.[11]

In some ways this pragmatic approach is to be expected of one who was a Roman citizen, one who had benefited in various ways from the order that governing authorities could bring. Like most ancient persons, Paul takes it for granted that governing authorities have their authority from God. Since the primary group he is embedded in is the Christian community, he is trying to do what he can to protect that community from harm or governmental intrusion. Paul is a community-oriented person who values community preservation over personal privilege.

Paul personally could have claimed exemption from various of these taxes, but he says nothing about such a thing here. Of more interest to us are his views about Christians and the use of force, evident in the text that immediately precedes this one—Romans 12:14-21.

The Way of Nonviolence

It appears that in the first century A.D. pacifism was not considered a live option by any significant group of persons except perhaps various of the followers of Jesus. Paul, a sectarian person, did not simply bring over into Christianity all the ethical values he had upheld as a Pharisee. Nothing in the Pauline corpus calls for "an eye for an eye" or the like, even if the *lex talionis* was intended to limit rather than license revenge or retaliation. We may take it as virtually certain that since Paul admits he was a persecutor

---

[10]See the discussion in J. D. G. Dunn, *Romans 9—16* (Waco, Tex.: Word, 1988), pp. 766-67.

[11]It should be seen that nonresistance is not the same as passive resistance to authority. Amish separatism would be an example of nonresistance; Martin Luther King's civil rights tactics or those of Mohandas Gandhi could be called passive resistance.

of Christians, he had indeed been prepared to use force to make Jewish Christians conform to a particular form of Jewish orthopraxy and/or orthodoxy. Wherever Paul got the ideas we find expressed in Romans 12:14-21, they certainly did not come from the Old Testament, nor were they derived from Pharisaism. While for a sectarian person the new thing, the new agenda, the new beliefs are central and determinative of his faith and symbolic universe, he will reconfigure elements of the old belief system, using them in new ways to support the new faith posture. We see this very process in Romans 12:14-21.

This passage is important because here Paul discusses how Christians are to deal with those outside the community, having already said a good deal earlier in the chapter about dealing with fellow believers. It is in this context that Paul goes on in Romans 13:1-7 to talk about how to respond to particular outsiders, governing officials, who might be contacting and engaging them. In short, Romans 13:1-7 should not be read apart from what has already been said about Christian behavior in chapter 12.

The gist of Paul's teaching in 12:14-21 is that nonretaliation is the proper response of a Christian being attacked, and that Christians are actually to love their enemies, and do good to and for them, in response to all hostile acts (cf. vv. 14, 17, 19, 21). As J. D. G. Dunn says, this stress on doing good to those who have done you harm is repeated four times, buttressed by Scripture (v. 20) and given the place of emphasis at the beginning and end of the passage (vv. 14, 21).[12] Paul seems to take for granted that persecution and acts of malice have been happening and will happen to Christians in Rome, and he stresses that while they cannot prevent such actions, they can determine how they will respond to them. The teaching here is far from hypothetical. Paul outlines a battle plan for responding to persecution in a Christian manner. Thus the former persecutor advocates a form of pacifism, drawing on the teaching of his Master as well as Jewish wisdom literature and the Pentateuch.

The echo of the Jesus tradition is particularly strong in verse 14, the theme verse for the whole section. Paul uses all his sources here allusively, assuming the authority of it all, but it is the Jesus teaching that sets the agenda (cf. below on vv. 14, 18).[13] No doubt Jesus' personal example is also setting the agenda here, as well as Paul's own following of that example (1 Cor 4:12). Paul believed that one must take every thought and action captive so as to obey both Christ's teaching and his example (2 Cor 10:5).

---

[12]Dunn, *Romans 9—16*, p. 755.
[13]Ibid.

This subsection begins with a beatitude in verse 14. Blessing someone was desiring that God bestow favor on that person, as opposed to cursing—wanting God to blight or punish them. Paul's words here are close to the Q saying of Jesus found in Luke 6:27-28, with a variant in Matthew 5:44. Luke's form is closest—"Love your enemies, and bless those who curse you" (my translation). In fact, nowhere else in the New Testament other than Luke 6:28 and Romans 12:14 do we find this specific contrast between cursing and blessing—which suggests strongly that Paul is indeed drawing on the Jesus tradition. This teaching comports neither with the Jewish (and Old Testament) idea that God would curse those who curse God's people nor with Greco-Roman notions of appropriate response to attacks and curses.[14]

Romans 12:17 admonishes, "Do not repay anyone evil for evil." This is a strong qualification of the Old Testament's law of retaliation, which is somewhat close to other early Jewish ideas (cf. Prov 20:22; 24:29; *Joseph and Asenath* 23:9; 28:5; cf. also the "don't return good with evil" exhortation in Prov 17:13). Verse 18 adds that if at all possible, Christians should live at peace with everyone. As Dunn says, Paul is not advocating a quiet and peaceable life at all costs, in particular not at the cost of compromising one's faith. This quietism is taught not as an ultimate good but as part of the larger strategy of nonretaliation.

Verse 19 says explicitly, "Do not yourselves take revenge, beloved, but give room for wrath" (my translation). "Wrath" here presumably refers to God's wrath, though in view of Romans 13:4 it is possible that Paul has in mind the governing authorities as executors of God's justice. As Romans 1:18 shows, Paul believed God's wrath was already being revealed against ungodliness prior to the final judgment. Paul then quotes Deuteronomy 32:25 to argue that since God will make sure justice is done one way or another, sooner or later, Christians must not take matters, or weapons, into their own hands.

Indeed the proper response is just the opposite of vengeance. In verse 20 Paul again quotes the Old Testament, in this case the Septuagint form of Proverbs 25:21-22. Christians are to respond to hostility with hospitality, to

---

[14]See P. Stulhmacher, "Paul's Understanding of the Law in the Letter to the Romans," *Svensk exegetisk årsbok* 50 (1985): 100. See also his "Jesus tradition im Romerbrief," *Theologische Beit* 14 (1983): 240-50. Paul immediately draws on the Jewish wisdom tradition, showing that he gives the Jesus tradition the same authority as earlier Jewish traditions and even the Hebrew Scriptures. The closest parallel is found in Sirach 7:34—"do not fail those who weep, but mourn with those who mourn" (cf. Job 30:25 LXX). Paul is not quoting in either 12:14 or 12:15 but rather citing the gist of the tradition, no doubt from memory. This verse may have the Christian community mainly in mind, but it probably also has a broader reference.

hatred with kindness. It is improbable that Paul uses this saying to mean "Do kindness to your enemies so their guilt will be even greater and their punishment more severe." He may mean, however, that responding in Christlike fashion may produce repentance, remorse, a seared conscience, and so in fact do some spiritual good to the enemy.[15]

Verse 21 continues in this same train of thought, of not being negatively reactive but rather being proactive, acting even in negative situations in a Christlike manner. Christians should not be overwhelmed by evil and simply resign themselves to it; rather they should overcome wrongs with goodness. This nicely brings us back to verse 14 and rounds off this section of Paul's instructions. The present-tense verbs here indicate an ongoing approach Christians should adopt, even when under persecution.

The verses that frame this section, 14 and 21, show that Paul is counseling not a simple quietism but a positive program of good works, even to enemies. Not only are believers not to retaliate or take revenge, they are to do the very opposite—love their enemy. For Paul this is not simply good strategy or tactics for an imperiled minority; it is what he takes to be proper Christian conduct, following the example of Christ and his teaching. Thus though there is a pragmatic dimension to this pacifism, Paul doesn't want his converts just to be peaceful and not resist; he wants them to perform deeds of love on an ongoing basis even to enemies. Again, this constitutes a social program, not just a survival tactic. It entails a radical ethic that no other known community in the first century was advocating. Today this ethic is still rare, even in the so-called Christian West. Paul was not merely ahead of his time: he was ahead of all our times, living in the shadow of Christ and in the light of the coming eschaton.

PAUL THE RADICAL

The advice Paul gives in Romans 12—13 does not make him a social engineer, if by social engineer one means a person who tinkers directly with the existing structures of society. Rather, he is building a certain approach to life in the world and in interaction with the world by the Christian community. The Christian movement was a new phenomenon, and the Christian communities it spawned were hardly yet manifesting

---

[15]See the discussion by J. Zeisler, *Paul's Letter to the Romans* (Philadelphia: Trinity, 1989), pp. 306-7. The practice mentioned seems to have been an actual ancient Egyptian rite of repentance, in which hot coals were placed in a pan on the head of someone who had done wrong. Paul may well have known of this ritual, but would the Gentile Christians in Rome?

anything that could be called institutional structures. Few took notice of what was happening in the mostly private Christian meetings, and many would have seen them as just another association, *collegia* or burial society that met in private homes.[16] In antiquity, a religion without temples, priests or sacrifices would hardly have been seen as a religion at all. It was just another new philosophy.

But when Paul turns to the household structure itself, he is dealing with a long-standing patriarchal and social institution of ancient culture. Romans, Greeks and Jews alike had long histories of customs and traditions associated with this institution and clear cultural expectations surrounding it. For Paul to comment on and try to tinker with the household was indeed a form of social engineering, even if he was dealing only with Christian households, or those of a mixed religion (see 1 Cor 7). On the subject of the new Christian community and its structure he would be seen as preaching and persuading; on the subject of the household many would have seen him as meddling.[17] Yet meddle he does, as we shall see.

Some may find it surprising that I place Paul's discussion of household codes and his view of men, women and slaves under the heading "Paul the Radical." When compared with what was being said in the larger culture, however, we see in these texts how committed Paul was to transforming the status quo within the Christian community.

Household Codes
Household codes were advice or instructions originally given to heads of households about how to manage their households. Such advice in the Greco-Roman world goes back at least to Aristotle, and by the first century A.D. Stoics, Jewish sages and early Christian teachers were weighing in with their versions of these codes.

Some scholars have taken the appearance of household codes in

---

[16] A collegia, a burial society or an association was a means by which mostly nonelite members of Greco-Roman society could find friendship, fellowship and support, especially in a time of need. The burial society, as the name implies, was a group which met regularly not just to remember and celebrate the lives of their deceased friends, though this was a part of the function of such a group, but also to support one another in burial expenses or support of a deceased person's family and the like. Collegia and associations were groups that met together on the basis of some common philosophy or interest, and in some cases the associations were rather like trade unions, with all the tentmakers or bricklayers in a particular locale meeting together for support and political planning.

[17] There was of course some overlap between the structure of the household and of the Christian community, not least because the latter met in the social setting of the former. But the two entities can be distinguished, and Paul is particularly addressing roles in the physical family here.

Colossians and Ephesians as indicators of the non-Pauline authorship of these letters. This view is usually argued as follows. Paul took a more egalitarian view of women and their roles than we find in the household codes, for these codes reflect the Greco-Roman and/or Jewish status quo. Therefore the codes provide one more piece of evidence that these letters are not by Paul.

There are difficulties on two counts with such arguments. First, it should not be taken for granted that the codes represent a baptism of the patriarchal status quo.[18] But second, texts like 1 Corinthians 11:2-16 (and for that matter 1 Cor 7) show that in discoursing on male-female relationships, Paul does support the importance of even symbolic representations of husband-wife differentiation. Paul never was a modern egalitarian, but he was also not like modern advocates of strong forms of patriarchy in the home and in the church.

In Pauline authorship debates it is too seldom noted that the Ephesian form of the code is far more Christianized and "enlightened" in form, and far more like Paul's earlier remarks on women, than the Colossian code; yet more scholars think Paul wrote Colossians than Ephesians! One can only conclude that the household codes do not provide clear evidence regarding whether Paul wrote these letters. Certainly arguments against Pauline authorship based on the codes are not compelling, and indeed to judge from the two most recent treatments by J. D. G. Dunn and Jerome Murphy-O'Connor, they are not even very convincing.[19]

Furthermore, what Paul says about married men and women should not be equated with what he says about women and men in general. Nor is it proper to equate what he says about household management with his views about women taking on what we would call ministerial roles in and for the church. The family and the family of faith are related but distinguishable topics, and Paul is concerned to deal with the family in the "household codes." Finally, it is even possible to argue, as Dunn has, that these codes are provided to help Christians find a modus vivendi, a means of living within society, demonstrating they are good members of that society. If so, it is the kind of apologetic and pragmatic advice that Paul, himself a Jew to the Jew and a Gentile to the Gentile, and very concerned

---

[18]Against Jerome Murphy-O'Connor, *Paul: A Critical Life* (Oxford: Oxford University Press, 1996), p. 249, who nevertheless finds a way to argue for Pauline authorship of this document, seeing the household code as a tactic to bring Christian mystics in Colossae back down to earth.

[19]On the evaluation of Colossians and Ephesians as non-Pauline on other grounds see the earlier discussion.

not to offer any offense to the world except the offense of the gospel, would indeed have given in such a situation.[20] Yet I will argue shortly that these codes are more radical than Dunn thinks, pointing to the reformation of social structures within Christian households.

I have addressed elsewhere the origins of the so-called household codes in Colossians 3—4 and Ephesians 5—6; suffice it to say here that this material does not appear to be drawn chiefly from the Old Testament, or chiefly from Greco-Roman sources, but perhaps partly from late Hellenistic Jewish discussions of these matters, with key Christian modifications based in part on the teachings of Jesus. While discussing household management was common in Paul's world, we can find no direct evidence of household *tables* involving paired opposites that are the clear basis of what Paul says here.[21] And as David Schroeder has shown, there are substantial differences between the New Testament codes and the Stoic and Hellenistic Jewish materials.

The Colossians code: the family. Colossians 3:18—4:1 has been argued to be a pre-set piece, in part because one could read straight from 3:17 to 4:2 without noticing anything missing. Furthermore, the sentences in the household code are short and to the point, unlike the long sentences of Colossians 1—2. And there are enough similarities between 1 Peter 2:18—3:7 and the code in Colossians to suggest that both authors are drawing on common early Christian material. Yet even if this is largely traditional material, we must assume that Paul has made it his own and endorses what it says.

The passage contains several notable structural elements in our passage. (1) The subordinate member of each pair is addressed first—wives, children, slaves. (2) Each exhortation consists of an address, an admonition, and sometimes a motive or reason, occasionally a specifically Christian one. (3) The members are arranged according to their degree of closeness to and similarity of social position with the head of the household—wives, children, slaves. (4) The same person is referred to by the various terms *husband, father* and *master,* whereas the three subordinate members or

---

[20]See J. D. G. Dunn, *The Epistles to the Colossians and to Philemon* (Grand Rapids, Mich.: Eerdmans, 1996), pp. 242-45.

[21]See Ben Witherington III, *Women in the Earliest Churches* (Cambridge: Cambridge University Press, 1988), pp. 45-60. On the entire discussion of the household table and the search for its origins see J. E. Crouch, *The Origin and Intention of the Colossian Haustafeln* (Gottingen: Vandenhoeck and Ruprecht, 1972); David Schroeder, "Die Haustafeln des Neuen Testaments (ihre Herkunft und Theologischer Sinn)" (Ph.D. diss., Hamburg: Mikrocopie, 1959); G. E. Cannon, *The Use of Traditional Materials in Colossians* (Macon, Ga.: Mercer University Press, 1983).

groups involve different people.

In Paul's discussion of the relationship of wives and husbands, we are told nothing about his views of single women, widows or female minors, or about the relationship between women and men in general. Nor does he address here the roles of women in the family of faith or the house church. His focus is the structure of the Christian family. Notice that here, as throughout these household codes, the subordinate members of the household *are* addressed as persons who are expected to be able to be morally responsible. We can assume that Paul is addressing households where all the members are Christians and can be addressed personally by the apostle.

The key verb *hypotassō* is in the present continual tense, referring to an ongoing activity. Notice that Paul does not instruct the husbands to tell the wives to submit; this is something they are called upon to do on their own. This verb is the same one used in Romans 13:1 to refer to everyone's relationship to the governing authorities, and clearly it does not imply anything about the inherent inferiority of the subordinate member in the relationship. The term is also used in Ephesians 5:21 to speak of the mutual submission of all believers, both male and female, to each other. It is used to speak of Christ in relationship to God in 1 Corinthians 15:28.

The term is relational, not ontological, in character, describing a certain way one person or group should freely relate to another. It describes the shape of Christian humble service, which in Colossians 3 is especially predicated of the wife, but in Ephesians 5:21-22 can be seen as appropriate for husband and wife toward each other. Paul says this sort of behavior is fitting *in the Lord.* This is presumably because Christ himself modeled this behavior by taking on the form of a servant, submitting to serve others while on earth. Paul is not urging conformity to society's norms, or what is seen as natural, but rather conformity to Christ.

The parallel exhortation to husbands is marked by the word *love.* We have no evidence that this term was used to discuss household duties in Hellenistic literature prior to this time.[22] Paul wishes to stress the husband's responsibility to love his wife. Significantly too, pagan household codes regularly gave exhortations only to the subordinate members of the household; here, however, the responsibilities of the head of the household are equally stressed. Love here must mean more than mere feelings, since it can be commanded. It must be love in action, a particular way of relating to and

---

[22]See Wolfgang Schrage, "Zur Ethik der neutestamentlichen Haustafeln," *New Testament Studies* 21 (1974-1975): 12-13.

serving the wife.[23] Interestingly, nowhere in the New Testament household codes are wives exhorted to love their husbands.

The husband is also exhorted never to treat his wife harshly. This is the negative corollary of the exhortation to love. In any case, the combination of these two exhortations in Colossians 3:19 makes evident that the husband is not free to treat his wife as he pleases; indeed he owes her love in action.

Verse 20 calls on children to obey parents in all things. No distinction is made between what is owed the father and what is owed the mother. Notice that while children are expected to obey *(hypakuō)*, this is not the command given to the wife. The verb *obey* here is in the active imperative, unlike *submit* in verse 18. This suggests not merely an allowing or assuming of a position but an endeavor to render ongoing obedience. Possibly this exhortation is derived in part from the Old Testament and the teaching of Jesus (cf., e.g., Ex 20:12; Deut 5:16; Mk 10:19). The non-Christian parallels demand honor rather than obedience from children (cf. Eph 6:2).[24] The command to obey in all things must be taken in the context of Paul's address to a *Christian* family, the assumption being that Christian parents would not demand something contrary to Christian love and teaching.[25]

Verse 21 reflects the general patriarchal character of the ancient household: the father had final authority over all that transpired in the home. Yet Paul chooses to stress that this power and authority involve responsibility. It is not a blank check to treat others as one wishes. Thus he exhorts fathers not to provoke their children and so break their spirits. Coupling this with the command not to be harsh to one's wife, we see clearly that the thrust of Paul's remarks is to ameliorate the potentially damaging effects of the patriarchal family structure. This is also the thrust of Paul's emphasis on love and service. His aim is to construct a more humane situation within the Christian community, rather than trying to change society at large.

Paul starts with these social structures where they are. What is crucial is the *direction* in which he seeks to move them. Paul hopes actually to reform the existing patriarchal structure of the family. If his exhortations were fully implemented, and if a household "head" indeed acted as a head servant in self-sacrificial service to others, would ancients have recognized such a family as a "traditional patriarchal family"? I think not. It would not look like modern egalitarian models of the family, but in its own way and time it would have been novel, indeed in some respects radical. Paul's

---

[23]See on this subject V. P. Furnish, *The Love Commandment in the New Testament* (Nashville: Abingdon, 1972).

[24]See Crouch, *Origin*, p. 114.

[25]See P. T. O'Brien, *Colossians, Philemon* (Waco, Tex.: Word, 1982), pp. 224-25.

commands would have been seen as particularly restrictive and demand-
ing of the head of the household, and his call for the husband to act as a
servant toward other members of the family would have been offensive,
especially among the Greco-Roman social elite.

The Ephesians code: the family. Ephesians 5:21—6:9 is the New Testament's
longest single household code. It is almost twice as long as that of
Colossians 3—4, and it includes various new features as well. Since it is
very possible that this material is Pauline or ultimately goes back to Paul,
we must examine it closely.

Ancient marriages were arranged,[26] and so exhortations about loving
one's partner might certainly be needed, but in some quarters of the Greco-
Roman world they would have been seen as excessive or strange. Greeks
and Romans were accustomed to hearing how to get along or put up with
one's mate, or how to have a peaceful household characterized by unity
and harmony. In other words, most Greco-Roman advice was geared to
preserving the status quo and making it tolerable (cf. Plutarch's *Advice to
Bride and Groom* 142E; Aristotle *Politics* 1254ab, 1255b).[27] This is clearly not
the function of Paul's remarks. Paul is interested in modifying the status
quo.

Some 60 percent of the Ephesian household code is devoted to the
husband-wife pair—a clear indication of Paul's central concern here. Like
the Colossian code, to which it may be indebted, the order of exhortations
is wives, then husbands; children, then fathers; slaves, then masters. As in
Colossians, this code has a variety of Christianizing phrases attached to it;
in fact such contextualizing and modification are more in evidence in
Ephesians than in Colossians. For example, Christ is used as a clear
paradigm for the husband's behavior (5:25, 29) and for that of masters (6:9).
Paul again uses the Old Testament explicitly and implicitly to give a biblical orientation to his commands (5:28, 31, alluding to Lev 19:18, 34). If Paul
is using traditional material here, it has been transformed to address the
same theme as the rest of the Ephesian homily: praise of the church and its
unity in Christ, as well as praise of the union between Christ and the
church. The Christian household is exhorted not merely to be a part of this
unity but to be an exemplary model of it.

Ephesians 5:21 must be seen as the introduction to the discussion that
follows. *Submit* in verse 21 (NRSV "be subject") is carried over into verse

---

[26]See the earlier discussion.
[27]See the lengthy helpful discussion in M. Barth, *Ephesians 4—6* (Garden City, N.Y.: Doubleday,
   1974), pp. 612-40.

22, serving as the main verb for the exhortation to wives as well. This is of considerable significance. Even if beginning in verse 22 Paul is taking over a traditional household code, the connecting of verse 22 to 21 means that whatever *submit* means in the relationship of all Christians to each other, including males to females ("submit to one another"), is also what it means for a Christian wife in relationship to her husband. Put another way, the submission of wives to husbands is simply a particular example of how all Christians should submit to one another out of respect. When the text goes on to say, "Husbands, love your wives . . ." and then describes Christ's self-sacrificial act, even submitting to death, as the model of this love, we see that the husband also is submitting to the wife, though the roles each fulfill are somewhat distinct. Thus in fact verses 22-33 serve as one large explication of how husband and wife submit to each other and serve each other.

True, given the family as it existed in Paul's day, the husband is seen as de facto in the superior social position, and this is why Paul spends much more time defining and refining what the husband should and should not do, lest he take un-Christian advantage of his position and of his wife. The exhortation to nourish and tenderly care for the wife, just as Christ does the church, is actually the sort of command one would expect to be given to the wife as caregiver of the husband, or to parents in relationship to children. But here it is given to the Christian husband so that he will make an extra effort to love and look out for his wife. This exhortation goes somewhat against the flow of normal family life at that time, for the husband was often free to be a public figure, to travel, and quite frankly to neglect the wife he had obtained through arranged marriage. Consider again the letter from the irate wife quoted in chapter three.[28] Paul is not interested in simply baptizing the status quo.

The quotation of Genesis 2:24 in Ephesians 5:31 suggests a situation where the wife is not simply incorporated into the extended family of the husband, as was the normal practice in a patriarchal culture full of arranged marriages. The Genesis emphasis is not on what the wife does but on what the husband does—he leaves father and mother and cleaves to the wife, and the two begin a new unit based on the one-flesh union they share. Is Paul suggesting some Christian critique of the traditional extended-family insofar as it might involve several generations of the husband's family under one roof?

Paul immediately goes on to parallel this new relationship of husband and wife with the relationship of Christ and the church. Christ left the

---

[28]See the earlier discussion.

heavenly realm and his heavenly Father (see Phil 2:4-11), came down and joined himself with a group of people, the church, and he was even prepared to die for his bride, showing the last full measure of devotion and loving self-sacrifice (v. 25). There is a cross-fertilization of ideas and images here; the flow of thought and analogy is not simply in one direction, from husband and wife to Christ and the church or vice versa. But verse 32, "This is a great mystery, and I am applying it to Christ and the church," suggests that the pair that controls and contours the character of the discussion is Christ and the church. In other words, Paul has lessons to apply to the relationship of husband and wife that he has learned from reflecting on Christ's relationship to the church. Here we see a definite and intentional placing of marriage in a specific Christian theological and ethical context.

Finally, in verse 33 Paul stresses again what has already been intimated in verse 28—that not only is the wife a person, one's nearest neighbor to be loved according to God's dictum about loving neighbors, but she is to be loved as one loves oneself. In a world full of self-serving husbands seeking to improve their honor ratings in the world and using family connections to do so, this exhortation must have come as something of a shock. Paul does not say, "Love your *familia* as yourself"—in other words, continue to nurture the kinship ties you have always shared with your father's family. He does not say, "Embed yourself further in your extended family." What he says is, in essence, start a new family unit (v. 31), and in that unit your prime duty of love and service is to your wife, not to your parents and relatives. Indeed, he suggests, your wife is as valuable as your self.

It is also striking that Paul does not exhort the wife to love the husband but to respect him (v. 33). This exhortation no doubt may have been necessary especially when a husband was not following the example of Christ very well. I submit that while some of this teaching would seem familiar to Paul's first audience, a good deal of it was a novel, even radical teaching, however tame and ordinary it may seem to us today.

The exhortations to fathers and children in Ephesians 6:1-4 are given more of a Judeo-Christian foundation in several ways than the parallel admonitions in Colossians. First, there is the phrase "in the Lord" in 6:1.[29] Unlike Colossians 3:20, which simply speaks of duty in the Lord, here the phrase qualifies either *parents* or the verb *obey*. In either case, such obedi-

---

[29]The phrase is absent in some important witnesses (e.g., B, D*), but the support of P[46], A and a host of other manuscripts suggests it is original. Its position in the sentence does not favor the suggestion that it was a later scribe's addition on the basis of Colossians 3:20. See B. M. Metzger, *A Textual Commentary on the Greek New Testament* (London: United Bible Society, 1971), p. 609.

ence presupposes a Christian context where parents will not abuse their children or their children's loyalty and subordinate position. Paul says nothing here about children's obedience to non-Christian parents. Thus the advice given in Ephesians 5—6, like that of Colossians 3—4, given assumes a Christian household, not a religiously mixed marriage.

Ephesians 6:2-3 provides Old Testament support for verse 1's exhortation. Exodus 20:12 says that children should honor their parents so they will live long in the land. This is modified here in a significant way, for the inducement is said to be "so that it may be well with you and you may live long on the earth." The latter is called a promise from God, the exhortation a divine commandment. There are probably no ominous suggestions here that misbehavior could lead to the death of the child, but that is not impossible in view of what follows in 6:4—"Fathers, do not provoke your children to anger, but bring them up in the discipline and instruction of the Lord."

Instead of exercising the *patria potesta* in some arbitrary fashion when children get unruly, the father should take the time to give his children Christian instruction and correction. Here again we see Paul limiting the powers of the head of household and requiring husbands to act in a Christian manner, not merely in accord with what the culture allowed or encouraged.

The obligation for fathers to instruct their children was of course known in the Greco-Roman world, but in large houses it was left to a slave guardian, the *paidagōgos,* or to the wife, or even to the older children.[30] So Paul is adding or emphasizing extra responsibilities rather than extra privileges for the traditional head of household. He must assume the tasks of religious instruction with his children.[31]

Summary: Paul on the family. What do we learn from a scrutiny of Colossians 3—4 and Ephesians 5—6 about Paul's views on Christian husbands, wives and children? While he begins with the traditional family

---

[30]See discussion of the *paidagōgos* in Ben Witherington III, *Grace in Galatia* (Edinburgh: T & T Clark, 1998), pp. 262-71.

[31]Here in 6:1-4 as with Colossians 3:20-21, I am translating *pateres* literally as fathers, not as parents for two very good reasons: (1) in both texts the parallelism would be broken if the superordinate side of the pairs were read husbands-parents-masters instead of husbands-fathers-masters; (2) in the patriarchal family structure it was far more likely that the father, having the *patria potestas,* would use unnecessarily harsh measures in punishing the children, or by other means provoke them to anger. For example, a father would arrange marriages for his daughters even while they were quite young. This could provoke all kinds of anger and wrath (cf. the earlier discussion). Paul is trying hard to guard against such abuse of position and power here as he reforms the patriarchal family structure in a Christian manner.

structure where he finds it, he by no means simply baptizes the existing
patriarchal status quo. Instead he works to Christianize all these relationships and eliminate the possibility of abuse. He also, while using traditional terms, redefines notions of headship and submission. All Christians
should submit to one another and serve one another out of reverence for
Christ. In other words, it is not simply something a wife should do in
relationship to her husband. Paul has eliminated the notion that simple
gender determines who should submit. Headship is redefined in the light
of the way Christ is head servant of the church. The sacrificial behavior of
Christ, even to the point of dying for the church, sets up the paradigm for
the exercise of headship in the Christian family.

What stands out in Paul's household codes is not his use of familiar
terms and concepts but the way he modifies those terms and concepts.
Given the context in which they were read, the direction in which his
modifications tended is as crucial as what he actually says. And this leads
us to the thorny issue of Paul's views on slavery.[32]

Paul and Slavery

The Roman Empire was able to exist and expand in large measure because
of slave labor. The enslaving of provincials and "barbarians" was a growth
industry in the first century A.D. Some estimates even suggest that at the
Empire's height as many as 85 percent of the people dwelling within the
Roman Empire were slaves. This is surely far too high. Fifty percent would
probably be a better guess for some parts of the Empire, particularly Rome
of the first century if we are counting both slaves and former slaves (freedmen and freedwomen). A reasonable estimate of those who in a particular
year were slaves around the middle of the first century A.D. would be about
33 percent. Still, we are talking about an enormous number of people, and
these people drove the economic engine of the Empire, which depended on
manual labor.[33]

The more territory the Romans captured, the more prisoners they took
and thus the more they sold into slavery. Surprising as it may be to us
today, many people in fact sold themselves into slavery in order to gain a
stable economic situation or a decent living. And slaves were often not keen
on manumission when they found out the cost of being a free and

---

[32]The basic study is H. Guzlow, *Christentum und Sklaverei in den ersten drei Jahrhunderten* (Bonn:
Habelt, 1969). The best survey in English is T. Wiedemann, *Greek and Roman Slavery*
(Baltimore, Md.: John Hopkins University Press, 1981).

[33]See the discussion in O. Patterson, *Slavery and Social Death: A Comparative Study* (Cambridge,
Mass.: Harvard University Press, 1982).

independent person. One inscription on the tomb of a freed slave says, "Slavery was never unkind to me" (*Corpus Inscriptionem Latinae* 13.71119). Most of the slaves in Paul's day, including some Jews, came from the eastern end of the Roman Empire. Jews were viewed as good workers and a stable group of people, so Jewish slaves had been settled in various key cities in the Empire, including Antioch and Corinth (see Philo *Legatio ad Gaium* 281-82 on the Jewish colony in Corinth). As a Jew from the eastern end of the Empire, Paul was surely in a position to know something about slavery. For instance, he would have known well that Torah included laws meant to protect slaves from mistreatment, but that Roman laws were far less strict regarding such matters.

Slaves were "living property," as Aristotle had once defined them, and had no legal rights. They were basically subject to the will and whims of their owners. However, there is considerable evidence from the early Empire of slaves' being allowed to save their money and buy themselves out of slavery. Furthermore, Seneca says that during the reign of Claudius in the 40s and 50s slaves had a great Saturnalia:[34] many were gaining their freedom, and through thrift and good business practices others were rising high in society even without manumission (Seneca *Apocolocyntosis* 3.12, and cf. his *On Benefits* 28.5-10, where he complains about a free man running off to pay an obligatory social call on a wealthy slave). Keep in mind that many of the slaves in the Empire were not rustics but had formerly been well-off, well-educated members of their own cities or tribes. When such persons were sold into slavery, they generally became estate managers or guardians and tutors of a wealthy master's children.

Americans, given the history of Southern antebellum slavery, tend to picture slaves as working on plantations or in other agricultural settings, or perhaps as indentured servants in wealthy European homes of a bygone era. The slaves Paul discusses would be closer to the latter than to the plantation worker, for he discusses slaves only in the context of a household. A good deal could be said about slaves laboring in the Roman mines, building major structures and roads in the Empire, or even working as civil servants—including the famous imperial slaves, some of whom Paul seems to encountered and converted while in Rome (see Phil 4:22, though these may have been Christians before he arrived). The focus of Paul's discussion, however, is slaves in the home situation, particularly in urban homes.

The slaves Paul met were household servants: artisans, businesspersons,

---

[34]The Saturnalia was an annual festival in which people would reverse roles, with the slaves becoming masters and vice versa.

pedagogues and the like. If Paul indeed converted several entire house-holds in cities he visited, likely some slaves were among these first converts in Roman colony cities like Philippi (the household of Lydia or of the jailer—Acts 16) or Corinth (the household of Stephanas—1 Cor 16:15). It is not surprising, then, that Paul feels called upon to address issues surround-ing slavery in a variety of his letters (1 Corinthians, Colossians, Philemon, Ephesians). Corinth in particular was the great central clearinghouse for the Empire's slave trade. Conservative estimates strongly suggest that in the A.D. 50s at least one-third of the city's population were slaves of one kind or another.[35]

An attempt to uncover ancient attitudes about slavery would reveal the following. (1) No ancient government, not even a Jewish one, sought to abolish slavery. (2) No former slaves who later became writers ever attacked the institution. (3) Slave revolts do not appear to have been aimed at abolishing the institution but at protesting abuses—or at turning slaves into masters, even in the case of the Spartacus revolt.[36] (4) The evidence we have suggests that poor free workers were more likely to be abused than slaves, since an owner stood to take a financial loss if he mistreated a slave. (5) Unlike in the American South just prior to the Civil War, in the first century A.D. manumission of slaves was so common that Augustus set up laws to restrict the practice (see above on Claudius). There is evidence that it became a regular practice of Christians to purchase the freedom of some of their slave church members (cf. *1 Clement* 55.2; Ignatius *Letter to Polycarp* 4.3; Hermas *Mandates* 8.10, *Similitudes* 10.8). None of this negates the perni-cious character of the institution of slavery, but it is important that we discuss Paul's response to slavery in its proper historical context.

First Corinthians 7:21-23. Roman law did not allow slaves to *choose* freedom, as if they were masters of their own fate. Whatever Paul means in 1 Corinthians 7:21, he cannot be saying, "If you have a chance to choose freedom, do not avail yourself of it." Slaves could work hard, save their money (a nest egg, called a *peculium*) and then make a strong case for freedom, but they could not force the issue. It was not the slave's choice but the master's. Furthermore, apparently a slave had no right to refuse manumission if the owner was determined to manumit.[37]

Manumission could take several forms. In sacral manumission, the slave

---

[35]See the discussion in Ben Witherington III, *Conflict and Community in Corinth* (Grand Rapids, Mich.: Eerdmans, 1994), pp. 181-85.

[36]See the helpful discussion in S. Scott Bartchy, *Mallon Chresai: First Century Slavery and the Interpretation of 1 Cor. 7.21* (Missoula, Mont.: Scholars Press, 1973), pp. 60-65.

[37]Ibid., pp. 63-67.

or another person purchased freedom in a temple in the name of a deity. The deity was seen as the mediator of the transaction. More commonly, a master would stipulate in his will that a slave was to be freed upon the master's death. Manumission could also be readily performed before a magistrate or even informally in a ceremony before friends. What ensued thereafter is interesting.

> When a Roman manumitted his slave, [the slave] would (if the correct formalities had been observed) attain restricted citizenship status, extending even to the right to inherit his patron's estate. There is evidence that the feeling that a loyal domestic servant ought automatically to be granted freedom and civic rights after a number of years was so widespread that the "model" of slavery as a process of integration [into free society] may be useful here. . . . Roman jurists recognized a slave's right to use his *peculium* to buy himself free from his owner.[38]

Paul has stated as a general principle that it is all right for persons to stay in the social status and situation they find themselves in when they come to Christ, for social status neither commends nor condemns a person before God. Yet in 1 Corinthians 7:21 he makes an exception to such a rule. He is saying, "If indeed you are to become free, by all means make use of it!" While social status or position is of no major importance and has no eternal significance in Christ (see Gal 3:28), Paul understands that some social conditions are far better than others, especially if one wishes to serve the Lord. Among those advantageous social conditions would be being free and being single, as a close study of 1 Corinthians 7 will show. However, Paul does not want his converts to evaluate themselves on the basis of society's values.

In fact, in Christ there is a complete transvaluation, or reversal of values. A Christian slave is already the Lord's freedman or freedwoman in regard to sin, yet the free or freed person in Christ is the Lord's servant and the servant of fellow believers. In Christ something like a Saturnalia happens.[39] A close study of Paul's metaphorical use of the language of slavery shows that he can use it in a positive manner to refer to his own tasks and condition and that of other Christians as well. As Dale B. Martin has shown, to some extent this slavery language can even be used to describe a certain leadership style, servant leadership.[40] One thus must distinguish between

---

[38]T. Wiedemann, *Greek and Roman Slavery* (Baltimore, Md.: John Hopkins University Press, 1981), p. 3.

[39]On which see earlier discussion in this book.

[40]See Dale B. Martin, *Slavery as Salvation: The Metaphor of Slavery in Pauline Christianity* (New Haven, Conn.: Yale University Press, 1990).

Paul's metaphorical use of slave language and what he says about the social institution itself.

According to 1 Corinthians 7:23, Paul opposes the trend for people, particularly Christians, to sell themselves into slavery to support their family or pay off debts. In Paul's view, there was no point to making such a change. One of the major themes of 1 Corinthians 7 is that one should not change one's social condition *just because* one has become a Christian. No social status of any kind hinders conversion or being a Christian, and therefore a change in status is not required when there is a spiritual change in one's life. Yet when it was possible to do both—change spiritually and socially—in a positive way, believers could and should avail themselves of the opportunity.

Paul does consider that slavery makes things more difficult for a Christian, and so he advises taking opportunities for freedom when they arise. While his general tendency in this chapter is to minimize the significance of social status, he understands that in reality not all social conditions are the same. Social status and standing becomes a significant issue if the gospel and its advancement in an individual's life, or that of a family or church, is impeded.

Philemon. Paul's feelings about slavery are certainly made clearer in Philemon, where he pleads for Onesimus's manumission.[41] Unlike in 1 Corinthians 7, where Paul does not address masters, in this gem of a letter his feelings about the responsibility of Christian masters become much clearer.[42] Paul does not violate Roman law, but he does do some rather powerful rhetorical arm-twisting to accomplish his aims. And in Philemon he sets forth a principle—all persons in Christ, of whatever social status, are brothers and sisters—that eventually led to the realization that slavery and Christianity (with its views about human dignity, freedom and serving only one Master) are basically two incompatible institutions.[43]

The radical implications of Paul's words in Philemon were not immediately understood. Indeed, in many quarters and for many centuries they were not understood at all.

Colossians 3:22—4:1. This passage's somewhat lengthy advice to slaves, coupled with its brief advice to masters, must not be read in isolation from

---

[41]On which see the earlier discussion.

[42]See Norman Petersen, *Rediscovering Paul: Philemon and the Sociology of Paul's Narrative World* (Philadelphia: Fortress, 1985), p. 175.

[43]See the discussion by C. F. D. Moule, *The Epistle of Paul the Apostle to the Colossians and to Philemon* (Cambridge: Cambridge University Press, 1957), pp. 11-14.

what Paul has already said in 1 Corinthians and Philemon. Indeed, in all likelihood Colossians was written and delivered at the same time as Philemon, and in part at least to the same audience. It also must not be read in isolation from Colossians 3:11, where Paul says that in Christ there is no slave or free any more than there is any Greek or Jew. All are one and have the same status in Christ.

In this passage Paul places the behavior of both slaves and masters in the context of their relationship to the Lord. The slave should serve as if serving the Lord; the master should act always cognizant that he has a Master in heaven. Both slaves and masters thus should be on their best behavior, indeed their best Christian behavior, because the Lord is not just watching but preparing for final judgment with its rewards and punishments.[44] The slave needs to know that an eternal reward will be given for the years of good and godly service. It has not been for naught, nor has it been done just for the earthly master.

Again, Paul is assuming that both masters and slaves in this situation are Christians; otherwise the Christian sanctions and exhortations he gives to each in turn are pointless. Thus when he says, "Slaves, obey your earthly masters in everything, . . . fearing the Lord" (which is to say, knowing he is watching and evaluating things), Paul is assuming a Christian context, with Christians acting in a Christian fashion, aware that the Lord will hold them accountable for their actions. Notice too that Paul does not direct masters to tell slaves to obey. Rather, he addresses slaves directly as persons in Christ.

The key hinge verse of the Colossian code's slavery section is 3:25, with its warning that the wrongdoer will be punished and that there will be no partiality. This final clause is surely linked with verse 24 and provides a sanction to make sure Christian slaves will do their best in their work. Yet probably it also prepares for what follows in the next verse, where Paul says, "Masters, treat your slaves justly and fairly, for you know that you also have a Master [and a judge] in heaven" (4:1). God indeed will not be partial or show favoritism to masters any more than to slaves if they do wrong. In fact, the biblical principle enunciated elsewhere is that God will require more of those to whom more rights and responsibilities have been given.

What are we to make of this teaching? It must be seen for what it is. Paul is not baptizing the institution of slavery, much less making it easier for masters to take advantage of their slaves due to their Christian faith. If

---

[44]See the earlier discussion of Paul's eschatology.

anything, he is trying to limit the master's power by invoking Christ as Master and Judge of all as a sanction. Paul is concerned that even in all-too-fallen relationships persons act in a Christian fashion and so be good witnesses to one and all. He is trying to inject the leaven of the gospel into this situation so that relationships between slaves and masters might improve—indeed, so that they might treat each other not just as fellow human beings but as brothers and sisters in Christ.

Ephesians 6:5-9. This text can be profitably studied in parallel to the one we have just examined, especially at certain key points (see table 1).

Table 1

Colossians 3:22—4:1	Ephesians 6:5-9
Slaves, obey your earthly masters in everything,	Slaves, obey your earthly masters
not only while being watched and in order to please them, but wholeheartedly, fearing the Lord.	with fear and trembling, in singleness of heart, as you obey Christ, not only while being watched, and in order to please them, but as slaves of Christ.
Whatever your task, put yourselves into it, as done for the Lord and not for your masters,	Render service with enthusiasm, as to the Lord and not to men and women,
since you know that from the Lord you will receive the inheritance as your reward; you serve the Lord Christ.	knowing that whatever good we do, we will receive the same again from the Lord, whether we are slaves or free.
For the wrongdoer will be paid back for whatever wrong has been done, and there is no partiality.	And masters, do the same to them.
Masters, treat your slaves justly and fairly, for you know that you also have a Master in heaven.	Stop threatening them, for you know that both of you have the same Master in heaven, and with him there is no partiality.

Even a cursory examination of the parallels reveals that there is some sort of relationship, possibly literary, between these two passages. Likely the Ephesian text is the later of the two and dependent on the Colossian one, unless they were composed at the same time for different purposes and different audiences.

The Ephesian version of the code places more demands on the master than the Colossian one. The "no partiality" clause is clearly placed with the exhortation to the master in Ephesians (whereas it is connected to the end of the slave exhortation in Colossians); also masters are explicitly commanded to stop threatening their slaves. Furthermore, Ephesians 6:9

calls for reciprocity between masters and slaves. Here this call is directed to masters and may mean not merely that they are to have the same attitude as the slaves about seeing their work as being for the Lord, but that they are to serve their slaves with the same enthusiasm as their slaves serve them![45] At the very least, masters are to do good to their slaves as the latter are doing good to them.[46]

Once again we see Paul attempting to reform and modify an existing social structure and ameliorate the harm such structures can do to both the subordinate and superordinate persons in the relationship. Paul is not providing a Christian rationale for the indefensible. He is clear about the humanity of all involved, the impartiality of God toward all, and the equal obligation to mutual service as to the Lord in all relationships. Thus what is significant is the way Paul modifies traditional advice for slaves and masters. Andrew Lincoln puts it well:

> What is perhaps most striking about the codes of Colossians and Ephesians, however, is that slaves are addressed not simply as members of the household but as full members of the church. Nor is it simply, as in some other societies or cults, that there was no distinction between masters and slaves in the ritual activities, but these codes reflect the life of a community in which, despite the differences in their duties, both slaves and free can equally fully practice their faith in everyday life.[47]

We are a long way from Aristotle's or Plutarch's advice on household management here.

The overlap between household and house church is important for understanding Paul's advice in his household codes. First-century Christian worship and fellowship were virtually confined to houses, and thus in the Greco-Roman world would have been seen as an extension of the religion of and in the household. Paul clearly believed that "in-house" and "in-community" Christianity could make a difference in the first-

---

[45] Adolf Deissmann, *Paul: A Study of Social and Religious History* (New York: Harper & Brothers, 1957), p. 243, suggests that the longer exhortations to slaves reflect the larger number of slaves than masters in these churches. But it seems more likely that this reflects where problems were, especially in light of the heightened social expectations Christian preaching inspired. Deissmann is correct however that the social situation was complex. For example, we probably must imagine former slaves and their relationships to their former masters, and also those who had been Gentiles, became Jewish proselytes and then finished as Christians. Cf. Deissmann, *Paul*, p. 238.

[46] Andrew Lincoln, *Ephesians* (Waco, Tex.: Word, 1990), p. 423, is probably wrong to deny that the focus here is on reciprocal doing, rather than just having the same attitude about doing. "Do the same to them" seems a reasonably clear call to action.

[47] Ibid., p. 419.

century world. Change could come in households—not just in individuals'
lives but in the social networks of the extended family. Relationships, not
just individuals, were expected to change.

Paul's household codes reveal the way he aimed to change and so
Christianize the household. As I have stressed elsewhere, apart from
proclamation to all and sundry, Paul's basic strategy for social and spiritual
change of the world was to put the leaven of the gospel into the structure
of the Christian community, and as a subset of that the structure of the
Christian household, and let it do its work over the course of time. The
community was to be a witness to all. This focus on the community was for
the most part in lieu of placing the gospel leaven directly into secular
society.[48] Paul believed in living a true Christian life and letting the implications of that bring reformation to the patriarchal and slave society in
which he lived. He insisted that Christians live out their new freedom in
Christ as brothers and sisters and as equals (see Gal 3:28). Colossians 3:11
and Galatians 3:28 were not merely slogans without social and spiritual
implications, but the implications were played out *in Christ,* which meant
in community, which in turn meant *in house* and *in households.* Living as a
new community, a model of how the new creation changes things,
Christians bore good witness to a new worldview.

CONCLUSIONS

Paul was no mere baptizer of the status quo. Nor did he believe in taking
up arms to resist evil. He was both a realist and a radical. He showed
respect for existing structures of society—government, family, business—
but he did not encourage his converts to serve them in some idolatrous
fashion. He recognized that social structures are fallen and can even be
demonized if a truly wicked person becomes emperor, governor, owner or
parent. But he also believed that government, family and work are in the
first place good gifts from God.

Paul retained his theocratic worldview throughout his life. In his view
all genuine authority and power come from God. The emperor and his
minions rule by permission and empowerment from God. The emperor
himself is not God. Even the devil is God's devil, and God finally will
exercise his sovereignty over him as well. In fact, the decisive victory over
the powers of darkness has already been won by Christ on the cross.

Paul was not shy about criticizing social structures when it was needful,

---

[48]See the discussion in Witherington, *Conflict and Community,* p. 185.

but since he saw them as part of the form of this world which is passing away, he did not spend most of his time engaged with such matters. Better to emphasize the new creation as it was coming into expression in the Christian community and the Christian household. Yet this necessarily entailed reforming structures within the Christian household and house church. The next chapter will take a rather different tack in discussing Paul's moral vision and especially how it impinged on the roles of women and men in the church. Yet what has been said in this chapter must be kept steadily in view. For Paul, the spiritual roles and realities involved in ministry and social structures are all part of one larger whole.

CHAPTER 6

PAUL THE ANTHROPOLOGIST AND ADVOCATE

Paul's view of human nature and human relationships was clearly different from that of modern Westerners. This can be seen, for example in the way Paul uses anthropological terms: he uses **kardia** *(heart) to refer to the seat of thought, will and emotion—the control center of the human personality—which frequently overlaps with "mind." Though Paul seems to be using "heart" metaphorically, he seems to operate with an integrated view of the self: a person has emotion-charged reason or rational will.*

Paul does not simplistically consider the mind the higher side of the human personality and the flesh the lower, more animal side, for he can speak of the mind of the flesh. He is not locked into the Greek notion of body-soul dualism, for he does not really speak of a soul, preferring to speak of the human spirit as the less material, or nonmaterial, part of human personality. This human spirit is distinguishable from the Holy Spirit, which does not indwell every person inherently. Like other Jews of his time, Paul does not see human flesh or materiality as inherently evil and spirit as inherently good. He has a basically positive view of God's material creation, believing it can and should be renewed, through new creation and in the end through resurrection.

Paul is not a radical dualist, yet he describes a tension in the Christian life between the Holy Spirit and fallen human inclinations (called "flesh"). For him there is no such thing as purely private social or sexual relationships, for he is convinced that what one does with one's body in fact affects the body of Christ. Thus his body metaphor is not just a metaphor. Paul envisions Christian relationships as spiritually and socially intertwined, such that the part affects the whole, the microcosm's behavior affects the macrocosm. For Paul, persons are not primarily individuals but beings in relationship, with identity and responsibilities defined by relationships. Most important, since the Spirit dwells both in the believer and in the corporate body of Christ, Christians must not defile the presence of God through their actions and in their person.

Paul's vision of Christian community is aptly summed up in Galatians 3:28: Christ—not social, sexual or racial factors—determines one's existence and proper relationships. Christ overcomes the factors that are apt to divide humanity. This is not to say Paul thinks that sexual, social or racial differences are obliterated in Christ—rather they are transformed and redeemed. In particular, the creation-order distinction between man and woman is seen as redeemed and renewed rather than abolished in Christ. Paul advocates new roles in the Christian community for women, slaves and Gentiles.

Though Paul assumes a relationship between the physical family and the family of faith, he does not simply identify the two, nor is his advice the same when it comes to roles in these two different but related social entities. For example, Paul's advice to wives is not the same as his advice to women in general. The apostle appears to assume no gender hierarchy at all as the appropriate structure for the family of faith; in regard to the physical family, he is busily reforming its patriarchal structure. His discussions of both the physical family and the family of faith fall within a context of specific Christian norms and theological beliefs.

It is a particular mistake to assume that Paul's corrective remarks, when he is addressing abuses (such as in 1 Cor 11 and 14), can be globalized to represent his full evaluation of women and their roles in the church. A simple survey of the actual roles played by women in communities to whom he wrote makes clear that neither "chauvinist" nor "modern radical feminist" is an appropriate label for his views. Nor is he an advocate of "love patriarchalism." Especially freeing for women was his championing of the legitimacy of remaining single for the sake of the Lord and his work. Equality for Paul meant that all persons are equally created in the image of God, equally the objects of God's love, equally capable of being gifted and graced to serve God. Paul deconstructs society's stratification in the Christian community, without arguing for nonhierarchical leadership structures.

Paul was not a modern person, but neither was he a normal ancient person. He took a sectarian approach to life and his world and as a result was often seen as a deviant or an outcast.

CONTEMPORARY WESTERN CULTURE IS OBSESSED WITH THE HUMAN BODY AND human sexuality. The bestseller list in any given month is likely to carry at least one title such as *Our Bodies, Our Selves*. Given that "image is everything," millions of dollars are spent on exercise equipment, body sculpting, men's and women's magazines providing tips on improving one's health, sex life and appearance. We can augment, enhance or otherwise alter our physical appearance through liposuction, body building and sex-change operations; we can reproduce ourselves through in vitro fertilization and even cloning.

The ancients were just as interested, however, in the subject of human embodied existence, and they had their own views of the body, its possibilities and processes, unions and distinctions, intake and output. Many of our "new" forms of using the body for pleasure or perversity were actually practiced in their day. How did Paul live in and react to a world of gender bending and gender blending, a world that alternately exalted and despised the human body? What do his pronouncements tell us about Paul himself?

This study has already discussed the way ancient persons viewed human personality and human nature; let us now consider Paul's views on human nature and the place of humankind in the hierarchy of being, including the world of spiritual forces. We will discover once more, if we needed reminding, that Paul was not a modern person in his views on these matters. The second part of this chapter considers the way Paul viewed roles and functions within the body of Christ. Do contemporary evaluations of Paul as either a chauvinist or a feminist have any basis in fact?

PAUL THE ANTHROPOLOGIST

A careful reading of 1 Corinthians 5:1-8 and 6:14-20 reveals that Paul's notions about human beings and human nature differ from those of the vast majority of modern persons. We could almost ignore "though absent in body, I am present in spirit" in 5:3 as a pure metaphor meaning something like "I'm thinking about you"—but what about "hand this man over to Satan for the destruction of the flesh, so his spirit may be saved at the day of the Lord"? Both texts contrast flesh or body with the human (rather than the Holy) spirit, but what are we to make of this?

Even more puzzling is Paul's diatribe against visiting a prostitute in 6:14-20, where he insists, "Don't you know that your bodies are members of Christ?" (v. 15), and later says, "Anyone united to the Lord becomes one spirit with him" (v. 17). Even more amazingly, he asks rhetorically, "Should I take the members of Christ and make them members of a prostitute?" (v. 15). Is Paul really saying the Christian's body is actually connected in some way to the body of Christ and therefore to Christ, such that frequenting a prostitute could actually result in Christ's being coupled with a prostitute? Given that this seems to be the logic of the argument, a review of first-century anthropology is needed if we are to make sense of either of these texts. At the end of this section, after we have surveyed some of Paul's key anthropological terms, we will return to these 1 Corinthians passages.[1]

Parts Is Parts
John Donne, the great English cleric and poet, once said, "I am a little world made cunningly of elements, and an angelic sprite" (*Divine*

[1]For a fresh reading of these two texts see Dale B. Martin, *The Corinthian Body* (New Haven, Conn.: Yale University Press, 1995), pp. 168-78.

Meditations 5).[2] Paul never discusses human anthropology in the abstract, and indeed the subject always is colored by his belief that outside of Christ "sin exercise[s] dominion in your mortal bodies" (Rom 6:12; cf. 6:6, 17). For Paul, sin entered the human race with Adam and has been present to bedevil humans and human nature ever since. Paul was not an early advocate of the "I'm OK, you're OK" school of thinking about human nature. In the apostle's mind, no persons are born sinless or blameless, for human nature as we now find it is sinful (Rom 3:9).[3] If God is the source of life, and if sin separates a person from God, then sin's ultimate consequence is death. Sin, like death, affects the entire person. With this backdrop we can make some sense of Paul's anthropological terms, but bear in mind that Paul is not interested in mere anthropology; his is a theologically not medically oriented evaluation of human nature.

Not surprisingly, there has long been interest in Paul's anthropological discussions. In fact, a study that set the agenda for all subsequent efforts, the work of Rudolf Bultmann, in effect approaches the whole of Paul's thought through his anthropological remarks.[4] Paul's anthropological remarks are indeed crucial, but I do not see them as the key to his whole thought world. Instead, as the next chapter will argue, certain fundamental narratives, rather than just interesting ideas, seem to provide the framework and key to Paul's thought world.

Bultmann brought to his discussion of Paul's anthropological terms certain assumptions about human nature that were highly influenced not merely by the "introspective consciousness of the West"[5] but more particularly by philosophical existentialism, a tradition indebted to various people ranging from Kierkegaard to Sartre. Bultmann in fact uses existentialism as something of a hermeneutical key to unlock the Pauline mysteries for modern human beings, or better said, to contemporize Paul's discussion by making it a dialogue partner with modern Western society, fixated as it is on the psychological dimension of the individual. This leads to certain key Bultmannian slogans meant to encapsulate Paul's thought, such as "Become what you already are," which assumes that ancients were as

---

[2]What follows here appears in another form in Ben Witherington III, *Paul's Narrative Thought World* (Louisville, Ky.: Westminster John Knox, 1994), pp. 290-300.

[3]One may wish to distinguish between the concept of an infant being innocent—that is, having not yet consciously chosen to sin—and being faultless. Both Jew and Gentile are said to be born with a fallen nature, and are therefore not born faultless (Rom 3:9). Furthermore, if one is not faultless, one is not blameless.

[4]See Rudolf Bultmann, *Theology of the New Testament*, vol. 1 (New York: Scribner's, 1951).

[5]A phrase we owe to Krister Stendahl. See the earlier discussion.

identity-conscious as moderns.

Not surprisingly, given his Lutheran environment, Bultmann interprets *sarx*, "flesh," not as the lower, sensual part of the self but as the whole self oriented toward itself, setting itself up as independent from God and therefore truly self-centered (Luther's "the heart turned in upon itself"). Bultmann also interpreted *sōma*, "body," as meaning not the outer physical part of a human being but as a term for the whole person (one does not *have* a body, one *is* a body).[6] He was rightly critiqued on these points by Robert Gundry, who showed that even at the exegetical level, such an interpretation of Paul's use of *sōma* (and of *sarx*) could not pass muster.[7]

Bultmann had done no detailed anthropological research on ancient views of human personality, but he should not be faulted for this. Few if any New Testament scholars had done such study, and even now such historical-anthropological research of the New Testament period has only just begun. Robert Jewett's important study of Paul's anthropological terms basically follows in Bultmann's footsteps in its assumptions about human nature, with the additional problem that Jewett tries to read Paul as if he were reacting to pervasive early Gnosticism.[8]

A fascinating study by Gerd Theissen analyzes and interprets Paul through psychological exegesis, revealing that the apostle has much to say about the subconscious and what is submerged therein. Theissen's study aims to make Paul a dialogue partner with modern psychological analysis,[9] but here again the assumption seems to be that modern approaches to human nature are necessarily correct, revealing the truth about human character, and we need not be too concerned about the difference between modern and ancient views of human personality.

It is telling that the monumental *Anchor Bible Dictionary* includes a lengthy article on anthropology and the Old Testament but none on anthropology and the New Testament. The work of Bruce Malina and Jerome Neyrey and a few others is just beginning to be processed, let alone assessed,[10] and some scholars persist in simply ignoring the insights of cultural anthropological research that have bearing on Paul's discussions of human nature.[11]

---

[6]Bultmann, *Theology*, pp. 232-48. For the famous quote about the body see pp. 192-94.

[7]Robert H. Gundry, *"Sōma" in Biblical Theology with Special Emphasis on Pauline Anthropology* (Cambridge: Cambridge University Press, 1976).

[8]Robert Jewett, *Paul's Anthropological Terms* (Leiden: Brill, 1971).

[9]See Gerd Theissen, *Psychological Aspects of Pauline Theology* (Philadelphia: Fortress, 1987).

[10]See earlier discussions of these scholars.

[11]I am referring to J. K. Chamblin, "Psychology," in *Dictionary of Paul and His Letters*, ed. Gerald F. Hawthorne, Ralph P. Martin and Daniel G. Reid (Downers Grove, Ill.: InterVarsity Press, 1993), pp. 765-75, where no acknowledgment is made that the work of Malina and others

This chapter will draw on some of the concepts discussed in the first chapter and will also interact with some major recent contributors to the discussion, such as Dale B. Martin, J. D. G. Dunn and Jerome Neyrey. Much has transpired since Bultmann and Jewett first led us on guided tours of Paul's anthropological terms.

Those who are questing for the historical Paul today must be very wary of discussions of Paul's anthropological terms that (1) do not deal with sociological and anthropological data about ancient persons, (2) use modern psychological or philosophical categories to "contemporize" Paul, or (3) simply assume that Paul's terminology can be analyzed theologically with no consideration of ancient theories of human personality. Here I will analyze a few of Paul's terms in the context of both his Jewish background and his audience's Greco-Roman foreground, keeping steadily in view the typical ancient collectivist approaches to human individuals, including the assumption that the group and its values delimit and define individual personality.[12]

The term kardia, or "heart," means for Paul much the same as what it meant for the Old Testament writers. The heart is not a mere pump that sends blood throughout the body, nor merely the locale of feelings, but rather the control center of human personality—the seat of thought, will and affections. The heart can be either good or bad (Rom 10:8). In Romans 1:21 the "heart" is the place where thinking happens (even though many translations render kardia as "mind" here), but in 1:24 it is associated with lusts and desires. Romans 1:21 also indicates that all outside of Christ have a heart that is darkened. Romans 2:5 speaks of spiritual hardening of the arteries, while in 2:29 circumcision of the heart has to do with the heart's disposition, the cutting away of calloused or hardened tissue. The heart is furthermore said to be the locale of good desires and even belief (Rom 10:1, 10), and in fact is said to be the place where the Spirit resides within a person (2 Cor 1:22). The flexibility of Paul's use of kardia shows that he is not referring to the physical organ; he uses the term metaphorically. It would appear that the heart is an instrument of one's ego or personality and so can be either good or bad, depending on one's own condition.

Paul uses nous, or "mind," in rather similar fashion. It too is an instrument of the entire person and so can be the tool of either the "flesh" or the Spirit. It would probably be a mistake to think that Paul sees "mind"

---

might be illuminating. Rather the discussion suggests that we need only to further refine the Western interpretation of Paul that goes back to Luther (e.g., on Rom 7, p. 774).

[12]See the earlier discussion.

(reasoning faculty, storehouse of knowledge—1 Cor 14:14-19) as the higher side of human personality, with flesh being the lower or more animalistic side, because he can speak of a fleshly mind or "the mind of his flesh" (Col 2:18 mg). The point of this last text is that the mind can be carnal. A near synonym to *nous* is *phronēma* ("mind"), and it too can be said to be carnal (Rom 8:5).[13]

In Romans 7:22-25 mind is contrasted with flesh. Flesh in this passage is associated with sin that dwells in one's members, while mind is associated with the inner self or conscience attempting to serve the law of God. This passage suggests, then, that mind involves the inner being, the self, the conscience, and is seen here as a good thing as opposed to flesh, which involves sinful desires grounded in a fallen physical nature. What Paul calls a "fleshly mind" or "mind set on the flesh" is a conscious orientation that follows this fallen nature. Paul thinks the mind is the key to one's orientation; hence he can discuss the renewal of the mind in Christ (Rom 12:2).

Paul uses the term *pneuma* for the human spirit, albeit sparingly. First Corinthians 14:14 (cf. v. 32) speaks of "my spirit," and in the very next verse spirit and mind are contrasted. Second Corinthians 7:1 must surely also be a reference to the human spirit, referring to defilers of the flesh and the spirit. Spirit would seem to be the suprarational or noncognitive aspects of human experience—that which goes beyond the flesh.

Dale B. Martin has provided some reason to rethink the notion that Paul means something immaterial by *pneuma*. For one thing, the term also means wind or air, which in antiquity was certainly not viewed as nonmaterial. "For most ancient theorists, pneuma is a kind of 'stuff' that is the agent of perception, motion and life itself; it pervades other forms of stuff and, together with those other forms, constitutes the self."[14] It may be that this is the case with Paul as well. Among other things, this would mean that a "spiritual body" in 1 Corinthians 15:44-49 does not mean a nonmaterial body, but either a body made out of the stuff known as *pneuma* or a body completely empowered by the Holy Spirit.

First Corinthians 2:11-12, where Paul parallels the human spirit and the Holy Spirit, shows that though he sees the two in similar ways, they are clearly distinguishable (cf. 1 Cor 5:5—the Holy Spirit needs no salvation). The Holy Spirit does not inherently dwell within a human person; this

---

[13]On these two terms see J. D. G. Dunn, *The Theology of Paul the Apostle* (Grand Rapids, Mich.: Eerdmans, 1997), pp. 73-75.

[14]Martin, *The Corinthian Body*, p. 21. Compare for example Dio Chrysostom, who says *pneuma* is the substance that is sucked in by people for nourishment (*Discourse* 12.30).

happens only through faith in Christ. Dunn is right to stress that Paul's references to the human spirit are sparse but those to the Holy Spirit are plentiful. He correctly concludes from this that "for Paul the gospel is not about an innate spirituality awaiting release, but about the divine Spirit acting upon and in a person from without. . . . [But the human] spirit is evidently that dimension of the human person by means of which the person relates most directly to God."[15] Paul sometimes does use *pneuma* metaphorically (Rom 8:15—the spirit of slavery or of adoption). In Romans 11:8 the term seems to mean an attitude or orientation of stupor.

Paul also uses *psychē* sparingly, even if we include the cognate *psychikos*. "Soul" is not a good translation for this term in the Pauline corpus. For example, in Romans 13:1 the term simply means every living person. In Romans 1, where *psychē* is used in its Old Testament sense, it simply means life or self, as in 1 Corinthians 15:45, where Adam is said to be a living being (a living *psychē*), and Romans 16:4, where Paul speaks of those who risked their "lives" (similarly Phil 2:30). At times the term is simply synonymous with "human being" (Rom 2:9; cf. 13:1). While 1 Thessalonians 5:23 has sometimes been used to suggest that Paul had a trichotomous view of human nature (body, soul, spirit), this is very unlikely. Probably *psychē* here refers to the natural life principle that animates the body.

Paul uses the adjective *psychikos* in its normal sense of "physical" or "natural"—in other words, just the opposite of soul. It stands on the side of the unspiritual rather than the spiritual (cf. 1 Cor 2:14; 15:44, 46). The *psychikos* person is one without the Holy Spirit, and so one who lives on the basis of natural life and natural life principles alone.

Paul's use of *psychē* shows quite clearly that it is not adequate to read his anthropological terms purely from the perspective of the Greco-Roman philosophical dualism separating body and soul. His usage is far closer to the Hebrew concept of *nephesh*, which ranges in meaning from life breath (the natural animating principle) to the human being so animated (living *nephesh* = living person). For Paul the spirit and heart, not the *psychē*, represent the depths of the human personality.[16]

The Body
There is a limited anthropological dualism in Paul's letters. We hear of

---

[15]Dunn, *Theology*, pp. 76-77.
[16]See the salutary remark by Dunn, *Theology*, p. 78, warning against the Freudian and Jungian assumption that when one plumbs the depths of the human psyche one has said all that one needs to say about the innermost dimensions of human personality.

spirit versus mind, or spirit versus flesh, or even spirit versus body. Such terms lead us to question Paul's inner person/outer person terminology (see, e.g., 2 Cor. 4) and old person/new person terminology. In Romans 7:22-23 the innermost self is either identified or closely associated with the mind. Paul does not see the body as the prison house of the soul, nor does he denigrate the physical body. He is a Jew with a strong creation theology based in Genesis 1—2. Paul does not simply adopt the Hellenistic contrast between inner and outer person; he adapts this terminology for his own purposes. For example, in 2 Corinthians 4:16 it is the inner person who is being renewed (see Rom 12:2). So the inner person cannot simply be identified with the "new creature in Christ" or the "new person."[17] Rather, "inner person" refers to the mind and/or the human spirit, both of which need renewal, being part of fallen human nature. Paul repeatedly says that the "old person" or the old nature has been crucified and put off at the point of conversion (cf. Rom 6:6; Eph 4:22; Col 3:9).

This means that the "outer person" must be seen as the physical body, subject as it is to disease, decay and death. The "inner person" has to do with the nonphysical (though not necessarily nonmaterial) aspects of human personality. The human mind or spirit or heart is revived at conversion, but the body is not (Eph 3:16). This internal revival is what Paul means by being a new creature or putting on the new creation (Eph 4:24; Col 3:10).

Yet this limited dualism does not lead Paul to view the body as evil (as the real problem) or the mind as good (as the higher nature). As we have seen, sometimes he speaks of carnal minds or defiled spirits. In fact, the body is caught in the middle of a struggle between the inner person and the reign of sin, in the case of the nonbeliever (Rom 7), and between flesh and Holy Spirit, in the believer (Gal 5:16-25).

While the new creation in principle involves the whole person (body, mind, spirit, heart), until the day of resurrection the body does not experience new creation. Even miracles are not seen as any sort of permanent renewal of the body, and no doubt this is why Paul does not refer often to healing miracles. It would be inappropriate to call miracles new creation in the body, since only resurrection will provide a lasting form of newness in the flesh. In fact Paul emphasizes the opposite about the body in the here and now—it is wasting away (2 Cor 4—5).

---

[17]See Gundry, "Sōma" in Biblical Theology, pp. 79-100. He refutes the views of Bultmann, Furnish and others who wish to identify the inner person with the new person (cf. Col 3:10; Eph 4:24).

What of *sōma* and *sarx?* Paul can use both of these terms to refer to an individual's physical body or nature. Notice the rapid succession of synonyms in Romans 7:23-25—his members, this body, his flesh. Paul sometimes also uses *sōma* in a more metaphorical way. As we might speak of a body of beliefs, Paul speaks of a principle ("body"), or proneness or inclination, to evil or sin (Rom 8:4-13). Furthermore, there is a metaphorical use of "flesh" in Romans 7:5, where the believer is said to live no longer in the flesh. This does not mean one sheds one's skin; rather, it refers to not being controlled by one's sinful inclinations or desires (see Rom 8:9). So Christians do not walk according to the flesh—they do not live and act on the basis of sinful inclinations and desires. Living according to the flesh involves setting one's mind on fleshly things (Rom 8:5). Paul does not see the physical flesh as evil in itself, but he does see it as easy prey for sinful desires. It is also weak because it has needs and strong desires. Sin is seen as more powerful than the physical flesh—or, for that matter, the human mind if it is not renewed in Christ. Sin in a fallen person can stifle even the best intentions (Rom 7:22-23).

Sōma can be used simply of the human physical body (1 Cor 15:34-39; 2 Cor 5:8). But can it also refer to the whole person, for instance in 1 Corinthians 6:12-20? While one cannot radically separate body from personhood and human spirit in this life, even in this text Paul is not identifying the *sōma* with the whole person. Rather, how one uses one's body affects the whole person. The physical body, being the weak link in the human armor, can be dominated and even destroyed by sinful desires (Rom 6:6). That domination is what has been cut off or circumcised in Christ. While sin still remains, it does not reign in the life of the believer. Notice the progression in Romans 6:6—the old self has been crucified, with the result that the body of sin (i.e., the body as dominated by sin) might be destroyed. The speaker in Romans 7:14-25 does not wish to be delivered from the self, or even from the body per se, but rather from the physical body as it is dominated by sin, and as it is heading for both spiritual and physical death.

Dunn has stressed that when Paul uses the term *body* his focus is on embodied existence, with particular concern for social relationships that are made possible by having a body. He takes 1 Corinthians 6:13-20 to deal with "the interplay between body corporate and body corporeal, between church as body and mutual (bodily, that is, also social) relationships."[18] But more needs to be said at this point. Paul does not think of his converts as

---

[18]Dunn, *Theology,* p. 59.

isolated individuals who then as an aggregate make up the body of Christ, as individual billiard balls make up a rack when all of them are placed within the triangular frame. For Paul, Christians are actually spiritually a part of each other and spiritually united to Christ the head through their corporate existence. When it comes to the body of Christ, the whole is greater than the sum of the parts. There is an interactive dimension and interconnectedness between individuals and with the living Christ in heaven. Thus what happens to and with the microcosmic body of the individual Christian can affect not only the macrocosmic body of Christ but even in some sense Christ himself (see discussion of 1 Cor 6:15 below).

Neyrey has rightly stressed that the human body was seen as a microcosm of the larger community. Getting rid of pollution in the community was parallel to dealing with pollution in an individual's body. So for example, if a community had been violated by an enemy and damaged or destroyed, individuals would go through ritual cleansing of their bodies, particularly the orifices, to rid themselves of the effects of pollution. Pollution of the individual could lead to or be part of pollution of the community and vice versa, and cleansing of the community could require cleansing of all its individuals. In a world where communicable diseases were little understood, and microscopic bacteria and viruses unknown, the ancients nevertheless believed firmly in the interconnectedness and interactive nature of individual and community and gave far more weight to environmental factors affecting human life than some moderns do.[19]

This leads us to Paul's paradigmatic statement of the moral struggle of the Christian life—Galatians 5:16-25.[20] Notice that the tension in the Christian life is not said to be between the human spirit and the human flesh, but between the Holy Spirit and the flesh, with the latter having primarily a metaphorical sense, though of course it entails deeds done in and by the body. It is not the flesh as mere flesh that goads the person into sin, but the flesh as sinful inclination. All the "works of the flesh" listed in verse 19 are negative; such would not be the case if Paul were talking about works of the body or physical activities. "Flesh," then, is not just mortal frailty but a perverse inclination. Here and elsewhere, it is a major mistake to see Paul as some sort of ascetic.[21] This text reminds us that there is an

---

[19]See Jerome Neyrey, chap. 5 in *Paul in Other Words: A Cultural Reading of His Letters* (Louisville, Ky.: Westminister John Knox, 1990).

[20]On this see Ben Witherington III, *Grace in Galatia* (Edinburgh: T & T Clark, 1998), pp. 389-413.

[21]Against the reading of 1 Corinthians 7 by Vincent Wimbush, *Paul the Worldly Ascetic: Response to the World and Self-Understanding According to 1 Corinthians 7* (Macon, Ga.: Mercer University Press, 1987).

eschatological tension between the leading of the Spirit in the Christian life and the goading of the "flesh." The Holy Spirit is pulling in one direction, the sinful inclinations in another. Literally the text here speaks of the Spirit "desiring" against the flesh and vice versa (v. 17).

This highlights a major difference between Galatians 5:16-25 and Romans 7:7-25. "In Rom. 7.7-25 the power of indwelling sin *prevents* the person existing under the law from fulfilling the divine law in which his inmost self delights; the 'law of sin' in his members wages war against the 'law of the mind' (Rom. 7:22f), and at this stage no mention is made of the Spirit, whereas the conflict in the present text is between flesh and Spirit."[22] Galatians 5:16 is properly translated "Walk by the Spirit and you will not fulfill the desires of the flesh." A means of victory over sinful inclinations is stressed here. Romans 7 is the cry of one who cannot do what he in his mind would like to do. In Galatians 5 the battle is real but not hopeless. If Christians live and act according to the leading of the Spirit, they will not be fulfilling fleshly desires. This implies the Christian must actively will and do the good, but it also implies that such willing and doing are quite possible. Submitting to the Spirit repeatedly leads to liberation from such desires and inclination. Indeed, submitting to the Spirit leads to character formation in the image of Christ, such that love, joy peace, patience, kindness come to characterize one's life.

But here again the Christian is enmeshed in a social network. The Christian has a relationship with God, and in particular with the Holy Spirit who dwells both within one's individual body and in the midst of the community as a whole (cf. 1 Cor 3:16-17 to 1 Cor 6:19). The Christian is not able to manifest the fruit of the Spirit apart from relationship with the Spirit or the resources of the Spirit within the life of the Christian community. Individual Christian life, then, is marked by thorough dependence on God in the person of the Holy Spirit and on one's brothers and sisters as the body of Christ. It is not just a matter of the individual's relationship to Jesus Christ, for even that relationship is mediated to a large degree through the body of Christ. Corporate identity is primary; individual identity is derived from it.

The Corinthian Dilemma

This brief survey of Pauline anthropological terms brings us back to 1 Corinthians 5—6. Modern readers of these chapters find themselves in a conceptual world vastly different from their own. First of all, Paul's

---

[22]F. F. Bruce, *Commentary on Galatians* (Grand Rapids, Mich.: Eerdmans, 1982), p. 244.

primary concern in these chapters is upholding the moral purity of the body of Christ and protecting it from pollution. Such pollution can happen when a church member either sins within the community or goes outside of it to sin. Analogy is drawn with leaven and dough, with leaven being rotten matter that can pollute dough. Paul demands that the Corinthian Christians cleanse the body of Christ by expelling the polluting agent.

In the words of Martin, what we see here is

> a modified sectarianism. Although [Paul] insists on maintaining firm bound-aries between those inside and outside the church, socially those boundaries are permeable. Paul is not afraid that social contact between a Christian and a non-Christian will pollute the church but he does think that the disguised presence within the church of a representative from the outside, from the "cosmos" that should be "out there," threatens the whole body. The body of Christ is not polluted by mere contact with the cosmos, but it may be polluted if its boundaries are permeated and an element of the cosmos gains entry into the body.[23]

This explanation raises some questions about 1 Corinthians 5—6. What does Paul mean by "being present in spirit" (see 5:3)? Apparently, since 1 Corinthians was to be read in the worship and acted upon by the congregation, Paul sees himself as present by proxy in his letter.[24] He has expressed his heart in the letter, and when it is properly delivered his spirit-filled words will come alive and *they* will be with the congregation, speaking to them and their situation directly. Paul meanwhile will be praying fervently for the good effect of this letter, even praying in the spirit. By his words Paul has already passed judgment on this offender. Paul believes that when his words are read, "my spirit is present with the power of our Lord Jesus." Like Jesus' healing words spoken at a distance for the daughter of the Syrophoenician woman, Paul's words make him present by extension, and they are invested with the power of the omnipresent Christ.

How then will Satan destroy the "flesh" of the offending man? One might reason that Satan is more likely to encourage than destroy sinful inclina-tions. Could Paul be talking about the man's death? This is quite possible, especially since he refers to the saving of the man's "spirit" only at the day of the Lord. Or is he? Martin suggests that the spirit saved at the day of the Lord could be the congregation's "spirit" rather than the individual's.[25] This

---

[23]Martin, *The Corinthian Body*, p. 170.

[24]The so-called apostolic parousia in the spoken word, or in this case in the orally delivered letter.

[25]Martin, *The Corinthian Body*, pp. 170-75.

is quite possible. Still, it is also possible that Paul has in mind the ultimate salvation of the man, after a sort of shock therapy and shaming have been administered to him.

Since there was only one Christian group in Corinth, such an expulsion might very well bring offending persons to their senses if they wished to continue to be Christians. The Qumran community had a parallel practice: offenders were expelled as sinners who belonged "outside the camp." Especially if the woman involved had been a part of and remained in the Christian community, the man's expulsion might be effective discipline. Perhaps Paul hoped for repentance on the near horizon, but at least repentance before death to enable the salvation of the man's self, his spirit. In other words, church discipline was necessary for the health of the church, but also if there was to be hope of salvation for the man. It was not punitive but intended to bring health both to the body and to the individual offender. His sinful inclinations must be doused.

This text offers a very clear example of Paul as a sectarian person drawing careful moral boundaries around his community.[26] He is quite ready to exercise church discipline, believing that the good of the community is more important than the social well-being of the individual. He is a collectivist. Paul is quite prepared to upset the status quo and ruffle various elite feathers to maintain a body of Christ with moral integrity.

Let us turn briefly to 1 Corinthians 6:12-20, which affirms certain truths about the individual body of the believer. Whereas 1 Corinthians 5 speaks of the congregation as body (see also 3:16-17), the end of this passage refers to the body of an individual Christian as a temple in which the Holy Spirit is meant to dwell. There is a spiritual connection between the body of the individual believer and the body of Christ, such that when an individual believer couples with a prostitute he unites the member of Christ with a harlot, and so the body of Christ is polluted. By being connected to the body of Christ, a believer is one spirit with the Lord. Sharing a one-flesh union with a prostitute pollutes one's spirit—but also one's relationship with the Lord *and* one's relationship with Christ's people. A spiritual bond is created between two human beings who couple, and this bond can pollute the bond one has with the Lord and his people. It can cause spiritual alienation from both Christ and the body, and so ultimately spiritual death.

The situation seems similar to that described in 1 Corinthians 5, though

---

[26]See Ben Witherington III, *Conflict and Community in Corinth* (Grand Rapids, Mich.: Eerdmans, 1994), pp. 156-59.

the terminology varies a bit. In both cases Paul speaks of bodies and spirits on the personal, microcosmic level and bodies and the Spirit on the macrocosmic level. Evidently Paul thinks these terms are far more than metaphors. He assumes there are real spiritual fellowships, connections, unions, pollution.

To be in Christ is a good deal more than to simply be in an association or society. It is to be spiritually linked with Christ and his body. This means that what one's does with one's own body, linked as it is to one's spirit, also affects Christ's body, and ultimately the Lord.

Here is very clear proof, if any more were needed, that Paul did not espouse radical individualism, much less the private character of one's relationship with Christ. One is joined to Christ only in connection with being joined to Christ's body, so that "no man is an island, entire of itself; every man is a piece of the continent, a part of the main. If a clod be washed away from Europe, Europe is the less. . . . Any man's death diminishes me, for I am a part of mankind. . . . Therefore do not seek to know for whom the bell tolls, it tolls for thee" (John Donne).

Pollution of Christ's body is possible only if there is real spiritual koinonia and union between the members of the body, as well as between the members and the head, Christ himself. Paul sees himself and others as integrally embedded in the collective entity known as the body of Christ. Individuals are limbs of the larger entity, not like individual units within a box. Paul the anthropologist turns out to be Paul the ecclesiologist as well. This leads us to an exploration of Paul's views of body life, particularly in regard to the roles and status of women and men in the church.

PAUL THE ADVOCATE

In antiquity, an advocate represented others—whether in a legal dispute, in a business negotiation, in a series of negotiations during wartime, or before an assembly promoting some particular group's cause. Paul was such an advocate, and while in his public preaching he was an apologete for the gospel discoursing with mostly nonbelievers, in his letters his audience was his own converts and his fellow Christians. Still, over and over again he attempts to persuade these converts to do or be one thing or another. This is because his converts had thus far only caught a slight case of Christianity—they were only partially socialized—and they still needed to work out the implications of the gospel for their daily life, their beliefs and behavior.

Paul was like contemporary advocates for various minority groups seeking their rightful recognition and fair treatment in society. Paul's advocacy was primarily on behalf of women, slaves and whichever ethnic group in a particular locale was likely to be neglected, taken advantage of or discriminated against.[27] We will discover that Paul is an advocate of not just new individuals but a new society known as the body of Christ, where prejudice, hatred, bigotry and discrimination are done away with, and fear of the unknown and the dark powers are overcome by faith and light.[28]

Human nature, according to Paul, consists of body and spirit, or body and mind, and a natural animating principle. For the Christian, however, there is a further factor, the Holy Spirit, and that Spirit can renew the mind, purify the spirit, even heal the body. The Spirit's power is such that Paul believes a Spirit-filled person can not only *be* better—manifesting the character of Christ and the fruit of the Spirit—but also *do* better. Christians can have victory over sinful inclinations and can use their gifts and graces for the glory of God. But an individual can do any of this only within the community of God, the body of Christ. A new person has to be a part of a new creation, embedded in a particular people. So what does it really mean to be in Christ, and how is that different from being a part of any other group in the Greco-Roman world?

In part Paul expresses his vision of Christian community by explaining what it is not. This is a significant concern for him, for he says the same thing, with a few variations, to four separate group of converts—the Galatians, the Corinthians, the Romans and finally the Colossians. Paul himself did not found the latter two of these churches.[29] Table 2 allows ready comparison of his teachings to these churches by arranging them in parallel columns.

The male-female pair occurs only in Galatians 3:28, and the slave-free pair shows up in Galatians, Corinthians and Colossians. The one pair that is common to all four texts is Jew-Greek, which Paul probably considered the most significant of the three pairs. I have dealt at length with Galatians 3:28 elsewhere,[30] so here I will mainly summarize that earlier discussion. What is crucial about these texts is not their source, nor how some of these pairs were used elsewhere and in later contexts, but how Paul is using them

---

[27]For example, in Romans 9—11 Paul's advocacy is on behalf of non-Christian Jews and is addressed to Gentiles, whereas in Galatians 1—2 we hear of Paul's advocacy on behalf of his Gentile converts with the Jewish Christian authorities in Jerusalem.

[28]We have already discovered this in two previous passages discussing Paul's views of slavery.

[29]Which leads to the suggestion that he is citing a familiar formula.

[30]See Ben Witherington III, "Rite and Rights for Women—Gal 3:28," *New Testament Studies* 275 (1981): 593-604.

in his letters. The earliest of the texts is the fullest and the most revealing.

Table 2. The body united in Christ in Paul's teaching (author's translations)

Romans 10:12	1 Corinthians 12:13	Galatians 3:28	Colossians 3:11
For there is not a distinction between Jew and Greek, for the same [is] Lord of all.	In one Spirit we were all baptized into one body, Jews or Greeks, slave or free.	Not any Jew or Greek, not any slave or free, not any male and female; for you all are one person in Christ.	Not any Greek and Jew, circumcised and uncircumcised, barbarian, Scythian, slave, free, but Christ is all and in all.

Galatians 3:28

This text deals with ethnic, social and sexual divisions in society. Paul is saying here that all that divided the society of his day could be united in Christ. The basic markers people used to determine identity and status were no longer to do so. What was to determine identity and status was Christ and whether one was in his body. Notice how Colossians 3:11 puts it—Christ is everything and in everyone in his body. He is the definer of his people. Romans 10:12 insists that there is no distinction between Jew and Greek, not because of anything inherent in them but because the same Lord is Lord of them all.

It has been suggested, especially in regard to Galatians 3:28, that we are dealing with a baptismal formula. This view can be strongly supported from the 1 Corinthians 12:13 form of this saying.[31] The point then would be that identity and boundary markers left behind when one is baptized are replaced by one's new identity in Christ. Especially the end of Galatians 3:28 makes clear how collectivist is Paul's vision of Christian identity. The formula does not say merely that all are united in Christ; it says all become *one person* in Christ.[32] If we ask which person, and take a clue from the masculine form of the word *one*, the answer must surely be Christ

---

[31]This version of the formula also makes clear that Paul is not just talking about adherence or joining but rather about a spiritual transaction. The Holy Spirit unites one with or immerses one in Christ's body and then becomes the resident inward resource providing ongoing spiritual life and guidance for the believer. It is interesting that Paul uses the language of water baptism here but does not specifically mention the rite. This is probably because, as 1 Corinthians 1:14-15 shows, Paul believed that conversion—spiritual transformation—was what was crucial. Initiation was not absolutely necessary, though perhaps ideally the rite and the reality ought to go closely together. In other words, the spiritual transaction—not the water rite—is what joins one to the body of Christ, though doubtless the two can and sometimes do come together in close sequence or even simultaneously.

[32]The masculine form of the word *one* makes clear that Paul is not talking about one thing, force or union, but rather one person.

himself—or better, the extension of him on earth known as his body. Jews, Gentiles, slaves, free, women, men have all become part of the one body of the person Christ, and Christ now defines who they are. They are Christians—those who model, manifest, make known and follow the Christ.

Galatians 3:28 does have one peculiar feature. Paul goes out of his way to break up what would otherwise be a threefold parallelism when he makes the last pair "no male *and* female." Some commentators simply ignore this change; some simply say Paul is quoting Genesis 1:27 but draw no conclusions from this. I would suggest several possible meanings.

First, Paul may be denying that there is any androgyny in Christ. Christ is not the creator of an androgynous person representing him on earth. This would be in response to those who suggested such a thing, for some Jewish traditions, mentioned for example by Philo, suggested that the original Adam was both male and female. Paul's point would be that the final "person" in Christ will not be like that, whatever one may think of the first Adam.[33]

Second, another possibility takes more seriously the allusion to the Septuagint of Genesis 1:27-28 and suggests that Paul is saying that in Christ there need be no necessary coupling of male and female. In other words, the Genesis mandate to be fruitful and multiply, connected as it is to the male and female division of humanity, is no longer required of humanity. It is even possible that some of the Judaizers in Galatia had suggested that since women could not be circumcised, they could become full members of the Christian community only by being married to a circumcised Christian male. Paul, as we know from 1 Corinthians 7, not only was prepared to say that Christians need not marry, but even says that singleness, if one has the gift and calling for it from God, is preferable, as the single person has more time for the things of the Lord.

If either of these suggestions is correct, Paul is not at all suggesting that sexual differences disappear or are unimportant in Christ. Texts like 1 Corinthians 11 certainly do not give the impression that this is Paul's position. Paul *is* saying that ethnic differences and the social relationships of slave and free, male and female, are not constitutive of the body of Christ and its identity. Rather, all are members of the one body as brothers and sisters in Christ. This is the fundamental reality in Christ. One's ethnic origins, social condition and marital status neither add to nor subtract from

---

[33]See Wayne A. Meeks, "The Image of the Androgyne: Some Uses of a Symbol in Earliest Christianity," *History of Religions* 13 (1974): 165-208, on these issues.

that reality and the status it conveys.

Colossians 3:11

The one factor Colossians 3:11 adds to Paul's statement in Galatians is that even non-Greek-speaking persons (the *barbaroi*) and those at the edge of the Empire who were much feared (Scythians) could be in Christ and would have the same status as everyone else in Christ. Christ provides an all-encompassing identity for the human race, and no group is excluded.

It may also be added, as Dunn notes, that the conclusion of this verse no doubt echoes the emphasis in the hymnic material in Colossians 1:16-20.

> It is precisely because of the cosmic scope of Christ's work, including above all his act of reconciliation (1:20), that such internal divisions and ways of categorizing peoples and individuals have ceased to have meaning as determinants of Christian self-perception, conduct and relationships. . . . If "Christ is everything and in everything," then nothing can diminish or disparage the standing of any one human in relationship to another or to God.[34]

Here again the ancient collectivist culture suggests that the group defines the identity of the individuals in it, not the other way around.[35]

Paul's Social Program

Yet we need to ask whether this is simply an ideal or whether it in fact involved a social program. Did Paul really advocate the breaking down of these barriers and the revaluation of basic social values in the Christian community? Was he really an advocate for new roles for slaves, Gentiles, women? The answer to this question is yes, as we shall see, but there is a reason Paul believed such a new vision of the humankind *could* be implemented. Christ's work has set those in Christ free: free from the powers and principalities, the customs and older traditions, the elementary principles of the universe, the pagan national deities and emperor cult, and the reign of sin within the human heart. The things that enslave people have all been dealt with through the death and resurrection and Spirit sending of Christ. Though these enslaving forces have not ceased to exist, in community and in Christ there is freedom to be all one is called and meant to be. Galatians 3:28 is not just a manifesto or a goal but something Paul saw as coming to pass, at least in part, in the here and now. There really is already a new community, and thus new roles and opportunities for Gentiles and Jews,

---

[34]J. D. G. Dunn, *The Epistles to the Colossians and Philemon* (Grand Rapids, Mich.: Eerdmans, 1996), p. 227.
[35]See the earlier discussion.

slaves and free, men and women are now possible in Christ.

We can see this new agenda already working itself out, for instance, in the roles Titus and other Gentiles were being allowed to play in the body of Christ and as part of the group of Paul's coworkers. As noted earlier, Paul valued the service of the slave Onesimus as a newfound brother and fellow worker in Christ and argued in Philemon for his manumission.[36] Clearly Paul envisioned a change of social status and roles within the new people of God for such persons. What then about Paul's view of women and their roles?

Women in the Church

The teaching of Galatians 3:28, amplified in 1 Corinthians 7, makes it clear that neither women nor men in Christ were to be obligated to marry. Thus women could assume roles other than wife or mother in the Christian community. What roles do we find them playing in Paul's letters?

It is clear that some women were among Paul's coworkers in ministry—as is evident, for example, in Philippians 4:2-3. Paul would hardly settle a private squabble in such a public letter, but a struggle between two coworkers and leaders in Philippi was another matter. Romans 16:1 speaks of Phoebe the deacon of the church at Cenchreae near Corinth, who also seems to be the bearer and deliverer of Romans to Rome. *Diakonos* here is the same term Paul uses of his own ministerial role in 1 Corinthians 3:5 and 2 Corinthians 3:6. Phoebe is also seen as a benefactor or even a supervising leader, depending on how one renders *prostatis*. Priscilla and Aquila, a husband-and-wife ministerial team, are repeatedly presented as Paul's coworkers for the gospel (Rom 16:3-4; 1 Cor 16:9—note the church in their house). Then there are Andronicus and Junia, who are said to be prominent among the apostles (Rom 16:7); this is most naturally taken to mean that they are both apostles.

Such passages raise serious doubts about whether Paul deserves the chauvinist label he has sometimes been saddled with. Antoinette C. Wire, for example, presents Paul as a repressive figure whose main opponents in Corinth are the Corinthian women prophets.[37] This view does not work, not only because clearly Paul is more often criticizing men in 1 Corinthians (see, e.g., 1 Cor 5—6 and 8—10) but also because 1 Corinthians 11:2-16 would be entirely pointless if in fact Paul were attempting to prevent rather than authorize women's speaking in Christian worship. Furthermore, Paul

---

[36]See the earlier discussion.

[37]Antoinette C. Wire, *The Corinthian Women Prophets: A Reconstruction Through Paul's Rhetoric* (Minneapolis: Fortress, 1990).

corrects men as well in 1 Corinthians 11:2-16. Yet Wire is simply following the lead of earlier feminist interpreters of Paul's discussions of women's head coverings in Corinth, such as Elisabeth Schüssler Fiorenza. Schüssler Fiorenza's argument is even less plausible, for she recognizes that some of Paul's coworkers in ministry were indeed women.[38] Interestingly, some of the same arguments show up in the work of Wayne Grudem and others who see Paul as taking a strongly traditional, patriarchal view of women and their roles.[39]

On the other end of the spectrum are those who in essence see Paul as a strong feminist. The strategy of these scholars, such as William O. Walker, is to suggest that texts like 1 Corinthians 11:2-16 and 14:33b-36 are interpolations,[40] or are post-Pauline, or have been badly misunderstood, as in the reading of Alan Padgett and Catherine Clark Kroeger.[41] Missing from all these discussions is the factor discussed in the last chapter: Paul was pragmatic and worked with social structures and networks as he found them, seeking to reform them within the Christian community.

We need to take account of not only Paul's position but also the direction of his remarks given the context in which he operated. The categories "chauvinist" and "feminist" are both anachronistic if we are looking for the historical Paul and his views on women's roles. Paul plays with the social cards he is dealt, but he seeks to slip some new cards into the deck and to rewrite the rules for those who play the game in his communities. The cards Paul was dealt reflect a strongly patriarchal culture which often had highly schematized roles for men and women. It is hardly surprising under these circumstances that when he discusses household management he bears witness to the existing patriarchal structure of the home and to exist-

---

[38]See Elisabeth Schüssler Fiorenza, "Women in the Pre-Pauline and Pauline Churches," *Union Seminary Quarterly* 33 (1978): 153-66; and *In Memory of Her* (New York: Crossroad, 1984), pp. 170-80.

[39]See Wayne Grudem, *The Gift of Prophecy in 1 Corinthians* (Lanham, Penn.: University Press of America, 1982), and more recently his "Does *kephalē* mean 'Source' or 'Authority Over' in Greek Literature? A Survey of 2,336 Examples," *Trinity Journal* 6 (1985): 38-59; and the older study by George W. Knight, *The New Testament Teaching on the Role Relationship of Men and Women* (Grand Rapids, Mich.: Baker, 1977).

[40]See William O. Walker, "The Burden of Proof in Identifying Pauline Letters Are Interpolations," *New Testament Studies* 33 (1987): 610-18, and see the convincing refutation by Jerome Murphy O'Connor, "1 Corinthians 11:2-16 Once Again," *Catholic Biblical Quarterly* 50 (1988): 265-74.

[41]Alan Padgett, "The Pauline Rationale for Submission: Biblical Feminism and the *Hina* Clauses of Titus 2:1-10," *Evangelical Quarterly* 59 (1987): 39-52; Richard Clark Kroeger and Catherine Clark Kroeger, *I Suffer Not a Woman: Rethinking 1 Timothy 2:11-15 in Light of Ancient Evidence* (Grand Rapids, Mich.: Baker, 1992).

ing male-female distinctions in forms of dress and ritual practices. The question is, What does Paul *do* with these preexisting structures and customs? Does he simply endorse them, or does he modify them? And if he modifies them, what is the aim or effect of his remarks? How would they have been heard in his own culture and time? We must consider the social effect of Paul's remarks in his own culture, not in our own culture, if we are to assess whether he was a reformer or a traditionalist in regard to women and their roles.

Considerable evidence about women in the Pauline churches[42] indicates that Paul was indeed open to women's playing a variety of roles in the church. Still, the discussion usually comes down to texts like 1 Corinthians 11:2-16, 14:33b-36 and 1 Timothy 2 (for those who think the latter is by Paul). Whatever 1 Corinthians 14:33b-36 (which says women should keep silence as even the law says) may mean, if it is not (as many suggest) an interpolation, it cannot entail an absolute prohibition of women's speech in worship. Were that the case, 1 Corinthians 11:2-16 would make no sense. First Corinthians 11:2-16 aims to make clear under what conditions a woman and a man could pray and prophesy during worship. There would be no point to such arguments if in fact Paul forbids such activities. Had he wanted to prevent women from speaking in worship altogether, he could have spared himself the variety of twists and turns he goes through to make his point in 1 Corinthians 11. He could have simply said, "No praying or prophesying by women—period."

Furthermore, prophecy as Paul defines it is a sort of speech that he himself offers to his converts time and again.[43] It is not readily distinguishable in importance from teaching and preaching, and on a list of church functionaries Paul ranks those who prophesy right behind apostles (1 Cor 12:27, 29). So one cannot argue that prophesying—whether by women or by men—is less important, less enduring or less official than teaching or preaching. Notice that preachers and evangelists are not even listed in 1 Corinthians 12:27, 29.

Thus whatever the limitations Paul is imposing in 1 Corinthians 14:33b-36 and even in 1 Timothy 2, these texts cannot be interpreted to refer to a global silencing of women in church. Rather, they must entail Paul's correction of specific abuses of legitimate gifts that women had and were expected to use.

Finally, as Richard B. Hays has pointed out, Paul's advocacy of women's

---

[42]See Ben Witherington III, *Women in the Earliest Churches* (Cambridge: Cambridge University Press, 1988), pp. 76-127 and the notes; also Richard B. Hays, *The Moral Vision of the New Testament* (San Francisco: Harper & Row, 1996), pp. 52-60.

[43]See the earlier discussion of Paul the prophet.

praying and prophesying in worship does not mean Paul was a modern egalitarian who denied that gender makes any difference in the body of Christ.[44] He was an ancient who in his own day would have been seen as working toward what *we* would call a more egalitarian position. Nevertheless, Paul believes that symbolic representations of the goodness and reality of sexual differentiation should be maintained. This is the point of the whole argument about head coverings for women and lack of head coverings for men. There is a reason for this.

The Image of God in Male and Female

Unlike ethnic differences, such as that between Gentile or Jew, or social differences, like that between slave and free, only gender differences are mentioned in the creation narrative as connected to, grounded in and definitive of the image of God (Gen 1:27). In Paul's view sexual differences, unlike these other differences, do not result from human fallenness but are a part of God's original good plan for humankind. Thus while the image of God as male and female needs to be renewed in Christ, it should not be replaced or obliterated by some sort of androgynous identity.

Furthermore, Paul would not have subscribed to the modern theory that human personality can be abstracted from gendered existence. He would not have seen humanness as a neutral core of being that can be distinguished from one's maleness or femaleness. To be truly human is to be male and female in the image of God. Thus Paul looks for a way that men and women can use their God-given spiritual gifts and at the same time affirm the goodness of the image of God as male and female in worship. To his credit, he finds a creative way of doing this that involves not simply endorsing an older Jewish or Greco-Roman custom of head covering but creating a new one for Christians.[45]

Paul does not advocate that women's participation in worship be minimal or eradicated, but at the same time he is perfectly prepared to speak about a difference between man and woman having to do with issues of headship and glory. In his understanding equality has to do with both men and women being created in the image of God. It does not mean absolute sameness of nature, sameness in symbolic worship apparatus, sameness in all purposes for one's creation or sameness in all tasks.[46]

---

[44]See Hays, *Moral Vision*, pp. 52-55.

[45]See Witherington, *Conflict and Community*, pp. 231-40.

[46]For example, note Paul's stress in 1 Corinthians 11 on men coming forth from women ever since the creation of the first woman from the first man. The roles are not seen as interchangable at any one point in time.

Indeed for Paul, it is difference, and the insufficiency of each sex by itself, that makes both male and female important and necessary. Were men and women exactly identical, the existence of two sexes would be redundant. Neither man nor woman completely represents the image of God—it is both male and female.

Thus it is no accident that in Galatians 3:28 Paul says "no male *and* female," breaking up the parallelism. Men and women do not have to be coupled in Christ. Women do not need to be joined to men to be in Christ. Androgyny is not the goal or the reality in Christ. The only all-encompassing oneness is the collectivist vision of oneness involving the identity of Christ himself, which transcends and transforms all human identities. The one person in "all are one person in Christ" is Christ himself. That is, Christian identity is most profoundly determined by One who transcends and transforms us—Christ. Christian identity is not just about being all that we can be as individuals. It is about becoming more and more Christlike as we are molded by him. This transformation does not take place in isolation but in the context of Christ's body.

An important balanced study by D. G. Horrell has provided further evidence of Paul's radical social agendas as he instructed and constructed the body of Christ.[47] In a careful analysis of 1 Corinthians, Horrell shows how Paul seeks to systematically deconstruct the system of social stratification that those of higher social status imported into the body of Christ. He puts the matter as follows:

> Paul's criticism of the socially strong, coupled with the absence of any explicit demand for the subordination of weaker social groups, should surely lead us to question the appropriateness of the term love patriarchalism as a summary of the social ethos of Paul's teaching in 1 Corinthians. . . . In 1 Corinthians he particularly attacks the socially prominent members of the community, requiring that their behaviour change, and demonstrating that God's way of achieving unity is to elect and honour the lowly and to call the strong to self-lowering. While . . . Paul does not legitimate the dominant *social* order—on the contrary he undermines and inverts it—he does legitimate an ecclesiastical hierarchy in which he is at the top. . . . He outlines a hierarchy of leading functions (12.28-30), calls for submission to particular leaders (16.16), and presents himself as the Corinthians' only father—a position from which he is able (and willing) to threaten them with punishment (4.14-21).[48]

---

[47]See D. G. Horrell, *The Social Ethos of the Corinthian Correspondence: Interests and Ideology from 1 Corinthians to 1 Clement* (Edinburgh: T & T Clark, 1996).

[48]Ibid., pp. 196-97.

"Love patriarchalism" is a term coined by Gerd Theissen to characterize Paul's vision of how the body of Christ ought to operate. Theissen meant to suggest that the harsh aspects of the existing patriarchal social structures were ameliorated by Paul's appeal to the dominant to love and respect the weaker members of the body of Christ, though he did not significantly change those structures. Horrell, however, is right to consider this an inadequate assessment of Paul's social strategy, an underestimation of the radicality of his social program.

Horrell demonstrates at some length that when Paul prohibited going to idol temples, or going to court against fellow Christians, or when he criticized sexual immorality or insisted on equal sharing at the Lord's Table, or advocated that Christian slaves take an opportunity to gain freedom, he was taking away privileges of the social elite, in particular elite males, in a congregation. Yet his siding with the weak and inculcating an ethic of self-sacrificial service and a focus on Christ crucified—antithetical to self-glorification or self-aggrandizing—created a very different ethos in the Christian community from that which existed in the world.

As Horrell rightly points out, this social critique did not mean that Paul was advocating a nonhierarchical vision of church leadership. Yet the basis of this hierarchy was not gender, social status or race but rather one's call and gifts. The world's social status quo was not to govern those who are in Christ, but Paul was no Quaker in his vision of the structuring of Christ's body. He will undoubtedly continue to seem a enigma to those who do not see how social, sexual and racial egalitarianism and hierarchical church structure can be spoken of in the same breath.

CONCLUSIONS

Paul had some definite views about human nature. He was convinced that there is an inner and outer dimension to being human. The inner person has to do with the mind or heart or spirit; the outer person has to do with the body. These two dimensions of human nature affect each other, and both need renewal and regeneration in Christ. In Paul's view new creation happens now in the mind or spirit but later, at the resurrection, in the body. This means that while the inner person is being steadily renewed, the outer person, except in the occasional healing miracle, is wasting away (2 Cor 4:16-18).

Paul does not envision humans as isolated individuals. First Corinthians 5—6 reflects his view that what happens in the microcosm of an individual Christian life spiritually affects the condition of the macrocosmic body of

Christ. Each Christian is so embedded in Christ and his body that an individual's sin can pollute or tarnish the purity of that body. Given this, drastic actions needed to be taken to protect the spiritual health of the body in Corinth, but not without concern for the ultimate salvation of the sinning individual's spirit.

Without question Paul was an advocate, and his advocacy involved urging social change within the church context. He argued long and passionately about and for women and their roles in his churches. He encouraged and promoted the work of women who were his coworkers. He stressed that in Christ there can be real social and spiritual change, reforming the old structures of the world. In Christ, Jew and Gentile can have fellowship and treat each other as partners and equals. Even barbarians and real foreigners like the Scythians can be seen as fully human and full brothers and sisters in Christ. In Christ, slaves can be manumitted and seen as brothers or sisters. Newness is possible on all these fronts because Christ's death has set his followers free from the things that prevent new life, new roles, new community—namely domination by sin, social custom, spiritual powers and principalities.

In Christ, women can assume new religious roles; and if they are not gifted for marriage and children, they are not expected to be married.[49] First Corinthians 7 furthermore shows how much mutuality Paul believed can be structured into a Christian marriage relationship. It also shows that Paul was no ascetic. Moreover, singleness for the sake of the gospel is preferable to marriage for those who are given the ability to remain single—a subject that will be considered further as we look at Paul the storyteller and exegete.

---

[49]See the analysis by A. N. Wilson, *Paul: The Mind of the Apostle* (New York: Norton, 1997), p. 172, on Paul as the great early Christian libertarian. For a more specific discussion on Paul's view of women, see Wilson, *Paul*, pp. 140-43 ("His writings do not suggest misogyny," p. 140).

CHAPTER 7

PAUL THE
STORYTELLER AND
EXEGETE

Narrative and story are fundamental to the very fabric of oral cultures. This was certainly true of the Jewish culture in which Paul was nourished, as a brief glance at the Jesus tradition will show. In fact, Paul's symbolic universe or mental furniture was essentially made up of a series of stories. These sacred stories shaped the way he thought about life and its meaning.

Paul does not recount these stories in his letters in any full way. Yet his thought world is essentially a narrative one, and out of these stories comes both his gospel (his evangelistic preaching) and his theologizing in rhetorical form (his letters).

This chapter addresses the substructure of Paul's thought, the thought world out of which he does his theologizing. A structuralist approach to Paul's thought world would assemble a collection of logically or hierarchically arranged thoughts; instead, here we see his thought world as inhabited by narratives. Paul theologizes in response to particular situations, but he does it out of—and in part by articulating—his narrative thought world.

For Paul there are five interwoven stories making up one large drama: (1) the story of God; (2) the story of the world gone wrong in Adam; (3) the story of God's people in that world, from Abraham to Moses and beyond; (4) the story of the Jewish Messiah, Christ; (5) the story of Christians, which arises out of stories 2-4.

The stories of Christ and Christians are closely knit together, representing the beginning of the tale of how the world is being set right again. Christ's story is the center of this narrative tapestry; to use a different image, it is the hinge, the crucial turning point, bringing to a climax the previous stories and determining how the rest of the story will play out and turn out. The story of God's people in effect contracts to that of the Christ, the seed of Abraham, but expands again to include Christ's followers. Thus the first half of this chapter briefly recounts and analyzes these important stories and their interconnection.

When Paul thinks of sin he thinks of the story of Adam; when he thinks of justifying faith he thinks of the story of Abraham; when he thinks of law he thinks of the story of Moses; and when he thinks of grace and redemption he thinks of the story of Christ, which is in various ways the template for the story of Christians, the story of faithful living according to the will and plan of God. This discussion reveals that while Abraham is seen as the paradigm for Christians of justifying faith, Christ is the paradigm of Christian humility and faithful servanthood, of self-sacrificial love even unto death.

In a sense Paul sees the whole of the Hebrew Scriptures as a giant repository of prophetic texts that have key lessons to teach Christians. Paul was a creative exegete of Scripture, with an approach that varied from that of his Jewish contemporaries. His hermeneutic is christo-centric in its guiding force and ecclesiocentric in its scope and application. Christ is the hermeneutical key to a right reading of the Scriptures; the church is the right audience for hearing this rereading. Thus Paul reads the sacred traditions through the eyes of Christ for the sake of the Christian community and its edification. He sees all the Hebrew Scriptures, including the law, as God's Word and therefore profitable for learning and teaching. Even the ritual law (cf. 1 Cor 9:8-9) has lessons for the Christian. Paul believed it is crucial to know where God's people are in the working out of the story of salvation history (beyond the era of the law and under the reign of Christ) if they are to properly understand the significance of Scripture for them. While Christians are not under the Mosaic covenant, they are under the guidance of the Scriptures which are fulfilled in the messianic age.

Scholars treating Paul's handling of the Scriptures routinely note that he employed standard Jewish techniques of exegesis. As a result, in the modern era Paul has often been accused of exegetical legerdemain, given the creative way he often handles the biblical text. Yet we must distinguish between when Paul is actually doing exegesis and when he is making a homiletical use of a text. More often than we might realize, Paul the pastor is busy using and applying biblical texts in creative ways, rather than simply interpreting them. In other words, he is engaging in what has been called a pesher or contemporizing handling of the text, a skill he may have learned while he was a Pharisee.

There is a danger of anachronism when one compares Paul's handling of Scripture to later techniques reflected in the Mishnah and the Talmuds. It is more appropriate to compare his techniques to those found at Qumran, an eschatological community reading the text prophet-ically. In any case we must be able to distinguish, as Paul himself does, between the original meaning of the text and its larger significance and relevance to the eschatological community of God's people in Christ.

Paul's allusive handling of Scripture shows that he believed one needs to know the whole story to appreciate the parts. As an exegete and applier of the text, Paul was creative, using typology and even allegorizing to relate Scripture to the situations of his converts. Yet it would be a mistake to see him as an early predecessor of Augustine or others who were constantly looking for a sensus plenior, a deeper or hidden sense to Scripture. Paul believed he lived in an age when the hidden had been brought to light and the meaning and truth of Scripture made plain. He believed he lived in the eschatological age, when the ends and goals and aims of all the ages were coming to fruition through Christ and his body. He sought new ways to apply the old meanings to his converts, and his hermeneutical creativity helped him find these ways.

IN VARIOUS WAYS THIS BOOK HAS ALREADY ADDRESSED THE SUBJECT MATTER OF Paul's story and stories. Here, however, our aim will be to learn what we can about Paul as an ancient person by examining the way he handles sacred traditions. The key to understanding Paul the exegete and applier of Scripture is knowing that he lives in and out of a storied world. It affects everything he says and does and everything he thinks about Scripture.

PAUL'S NARRATIVE THOUGHT WORLD

Oral culture is marked by storytelling. When only 10 percent of a population is literate, most people learn orally and aurally, and largely through stories, parables, proverbs, maxims and other forms of literature. While it is easy to place Jesus in this sort of pedagogical context (according to the Synoptics, the bulk of his public teaching took the form of parables), on the surface it may seem more difficult to put the apostle to the Gentiles in this category. Yet numerous scholars today are suggesting that in Paul's case the storied world operates as the essential backdrop, framework or underpinning for what we find in his letters.

Occasionally Paul retells stories, or they emerge in a relatively full form (see, e.g., 1 Cor 10; Gal 4), but by and large they function as the presupposition or subtext. Like a tune always playing in Paul's head, which occasionally we hear the apostle humming or singing, his storied world provides the inspiration of and for his life and thought processes. Just as we might overlook a tune someone was humming as we walked or talked with them, in the past many have overlooked this important and revealing dimension of the apostle's thought world. This oversight is now being remedied by a variety of scholars.

Significantly, this approach to Paul does not simply arise out of the postmodern interest in story and the logic and discourse of narratives, though that is surely a contributing factor in some cases. Largely the trend arises simply out of the recognition that Paul was an ancient person. He was not a post-Enlightenment theologian or ethicist or philosopher, and the attempt to reduce his letters to these sorts of categories is anachronistic. This is not to say that Paul did not use ancient Greek forms of syllogistic logic from time to time (see, e.g., 1 Cor 15:12-19), but by and large his logic is narrative. It has to do with stories about Adam, Abraham, Moses, Israel, Christ, himself, Christians.[1]

---

[1] A fuller form of some of this discussion can be found in Ben Witherington III, *Paul's Narrative Thought World* (Louisville, Ky.: Westminster John Knox, 1994).

So without a sense of the scope and dimensions of the drama out of which Paul lives and thinks, it is difficult to understand how the individual parts or details of his thought world fit together.

Prior to the rise of narratological studies of Paul, Pauline scholars had often suggested that his thought is essentially ad hoc, essentially responses to situations in the life of some church which he finds he must address. The narratological approach to Paul's letters suggests that this notion, though partially correct, is also somewhat misleading.[2] The situations Paul addresses prompt him to articulate his thoughts, but those thoughts by and large have arisen as a result of his deep and profound reflection on key narratives.

Paul had been a mature Christian for many years before his extant letters were written. Even in the case of the earliest of these letters, say Galatians or 1 Thessalonians,[3] he had been a Christian for more than a decade and had undergone a wide array of experiences, many of them difficult and dangerous, during that time. Whatever development of Paul's thought that may have taken place appears for the most part to have taken place before any of the extant letters were written.[4] Even in the crucial matter of Christology, there is precious little development that can be traced in Paul's later letters, apart perhaps from greater emphasis on the role of Christ in relationship to the cosmos. Thus a narratological approach would stress that the contingent situations Paul faced affected how and when he articulated different aspects of his thought.

Here Norman R. Petersen is close to the mark:

> Paul integrates his social instructions within a symbolic universe [read storied world] rather than a social one, for the consequences of compliance or non-compliance are not determined socially, that is by social actors, but eschatologically by the Lord. In this respect, therefore the force of Paul's instructions is derived from the symbolic universe which makes them non-negotiable and gives them the status of commands.[5]

These comments address Pauline ethics, but Petersen rightly goes on to

---

[2]I know of no one who denies that Paul's letters respond to concerns raised by his audience. The issue here is what resources Paul draws on when he responds. Does Paul react purely to the stimulus of his audience, or does he draw on images, stories, metaphors and ideas that he had previously considered and developed?

[3]See the later discussion of chronological matters.

[4]See especially Martin Hengel and Anne-Maria Schwemer, *Paul Between Damascus and Antioch* (Louisville, Ky.: Westminster John Knox, 1997), pp. 10-12.

[5]Norman R. Petersen, *Rediscovering Paul: Philemon and the Sociology of Paul's Narrative World* (Philadelphia: Fortress, 1985), p. 135.

add that for Paul "theology is a form of systematic reflection upon prior knowledge."[6] To this remark it can be added that Paul's storehouse of knowledge involves certain paradigmatic stories. Though Paul's theology proper will not be discussed until the next chapter of this study, it can be stated here that the narratological approach to Paul's thought has important implications for discussion of his theology. Making a distinction between a coherent core and a contingent fringe of Paul's thought is not a very useful model.[7] Contingency has to do with the mode or manner of Paul's expression, *not* for the most part the substance of his thought.

The narratological approach to Paul's thought can be distinguished from another recent approach that is also nontraditional. Daniel Patte has provided us with an interesting study of Paul's "faith."[8] Approaching Paul's letters from a structuralist standpoint—which assumes that a text's surface elements have meaning largely because of their connection to an underlying substructure that provides the organizing principle linking semantic units—Patte seeks to get at Paul's undergirding convictional system. A structuralist approach, however, assumes that "Paul's letters consist of a string of ideas hierarchically organized in order to perform a rhetorical function appropriate to the epistolary occasion."[9] In other words, structuralism still operates with the old paradigm of Paul's thought world as a somewhat random collection of ideas which he organizes when discourse is required. While this approach, like narratological studies, takes seriously the important substructure of Paul's thought, it does not agree on the nature of that substructure. The narratological approach suggests that the substructure already has a story line; it does not envision Paul arranging disparate ideas in some hierarchical pattern.

The Narratological Approach in Recent Scholarship

The narratological approach to Paul's letters is a rather recent trend in Pauline studies, so it is not surprising that there are few full-dress attempts to read his thought this way. Though it is clear from his magisterial study *The Theology of Paul the Apostle* that J. D. G. Dunn basically takes the older history-

---

[6]Ibid., p. 202.

[7]Against J. Christiaan Beker, *Paul the Apostle* (Philadelphia: Fortress, 1980), and also his "Recasting Pauline Theology: The Coherency-Contingency Scheme as Interpretive Model," in *Pauline Theology*, vol. 1, *Thessalonians, Philippians, Galatians, Philemon*, ed. J. M. Bassler (Minneapolis: Fortress, 1991), pp. 15-24, and the response by Paul J. Achtemeier, pp. 25-36.

[8]Daniel Patte, *Paul's Faith and the Power of the Gospel* (Philadelphia: Fortress, 1983).

[9]T. L. Donaldson, *Paul and the Gentiles: Remapping the Apostle's Convictional World* (Minneapolis: Fortress, 1997), p. 39. Donaldson adopts and adapts such an approach in this recent stimulating study.

of-ideas approach to Paul's thought, he gives some due to a narratological approach in his *Theology of Paul's Letter to the Galatians,* not least because the narrative substructure of Paul's thought surfaces in Galatians 4:21-5:1.[10]

We can certainly see something of a narratological approach to the study of New Testament material in N. T. Wright's *The New Testament and the People of God,*[11] where he says, "Human writing is best conceived as . . . the telling of stories which bring worldviews into articulation."[12] Wright goes on to say, following Norman Petersen, that each of Paul's letters has a narrative world that is presupposed by the text; then he asks, "What were the stories which give narrative depth to Paul's worldview, *which formed an irreducible part of his symbolic universe?*"[13] He goes on to stress, "It is arguable that we can only understand the more limited narrative worlds of the different letters if we locate them at their appropriate points *within* this overall story-world, and indeed within the symbolic universe that accompanies it."[14]

Wright then gives a very brief sketch of his reading of Paul's narrative thought world, with a promise that he intends to elucidate it more fully in the third volume of the trilogy of which *The New Testament and the People of God* is only the first. Wright's reading of Paul's thought world stresses that it is a thoroughly Jewish thought world, without significant indebtedness to Greco-Roman thought, and that Israel is at the heart of the story, though there is a key twist to the story that most early Jews would not have expected—that only in and through Jesus of Nazareth are the role of Abraham in relationship to the world and the promises to Abraham fulfilled. The "story of Jesus, interpreted precisely within the wider Jewish narrative world, was the hinge upon which Paul's re-reading of that larger story [of Israel] turned."[15] Wright's analysis is a work in progress, so it remains to be seen how he will more fully elucidate the Pauline data.

A fuller version of such an approach to Paul surfaces in two works of Richard B. Hays: *The Faith of Jesus Christ* and (more fully) *Echoes of Scripture in the Letters of Paul.*[16] The burden of Hays's earlier work is to establish that

---

[10]J. D. G. Dunn, *The Theology of Paul's Letter to the Galatians* (Cambridge: Cambridge University Press, 1993), pp. 36-46.

[11]N. T. Wright, *The New Testament and the People of God* (Minneapolis: Fortress, 1992).

[12]Ibid., p. 65.

[13]Ibid., p. 404.

[14]Ibid., p. 405.

[15]Ibid., p. 407.

[16]Richard B. Hays, *The Faith of Jesus Christ,* has as its subtitle *An Investigation of the Narrative Substructure of Galatians 3:1-4:11* (Chico, Calif.: Scholars Press, 1983), and is a revision of Hays's doctoral dissertation. Hays, *Echoes of Scripture in the Letters of Paul* (New Haven, Conn.: Yale University Press, 1989), is the much-celebrated sequel to that work.

a story about Jesus is foundational for Paul's theological and ethical formulations in his letters.[17] The story Hays has in mind includes not only the
earthly existence of Jesus and his death and resurrection but also his preexistence, such that the Christ story follows a decided V pattern—preexistence, earthly existence and exaltation to God's right hand after resurrection. Hays also stresses that because Paul's language is "highly allusive and
. . . depends heavily on the foundational language of story, we must also
reckon with another possible implication: perhaps Paul's language is less
univocal and more 'poetic' than the Western theological tradition has
usually supposed."[18] We have seen something of the poetic character of
Paul's thought when we discussed his handling of matters eschatological
as a prophetic figure.[19]

Hays's *Echoes of Scripture in the Letters of Paul* is a study in intertextuality: he is interested in how Paul alludes to and depends on the larger
context of various passages in the Hebrew Scriptures. The focus is on Paul
as an exegete and his hermeneutical moves as he contextualizes and
contemporizes the Old Testament text for his audience. There is actually
less discussion here of the broader narrative substructure of Paul's thought
and more on the way the Old Testament's stories shape his discourse. This
study well complements Hays's earlier work focusing on the story of Jesus
himself. Most recently Ross Wagner, a doctoral student of Hays, has
followed this intertextual "echo" approach with illuminating results.[20]

Stephen Fowl has focused in a more concentrated fashion on the way
Paul's presupposed narrative about the Christ shapes his ethics.[21] His stress
on the imitation of Christ is seen to be grounded in the foundational story
of the Christ. Yet Fowl also points out how Old Testament stories, such as
the story of Abraham or of the Suffering Servant, provide not merely a
substructure or foundation but exemplars for Christians to follow.[22]

My own *Paul's Narrative Thought World* is a full-scale proposal along
these lines. I did not come at a narratological study of Paul as a result of
postmodern interest in narrative. To the contrary, my interest arose in part
because of my background as a writer and one who studied English literature, and also due to the influence of a little book my doctoral supervisor

---

[17]See Hays, *Faith of Jesus*, p. 256.

[18]Ibid., p. 265.

[19]See the earlier discussion.

[20]See Ross Wagner, "'Not Beyond the Things Which Are Written': A Call to Boast Only in the
Lord (1 Cor 4:6)," *New Testament Studies*, forthcoming.

[21]Stephen Fowl, *The Story of Christ in the Ethics of Paul* (Sheffield: JSOT, 1990).

[22]Ibid., pp. 61-63, 94.

C. K. Barrett wrote a long time ago, *From First Adam to Last.*[23]

Indeed, not all narratological studies of Paul's thought start with the same premises or take the same approach. The works of Hays and Wagner are chiefly studies in intertextuality, listening for echoes of the Old Testament texts in Paul's own texts. The approach I take is broader, seeing some of the narrative substructure of Paul's thought as coming not from a text, such as the Old Testament, but from Christian oral tradition which he has inherited and passed along (see, e.g., 1 Cor 15:3-8). I am interested in all the narratives that shape Paul's thought world, those found in the Old Testament and those originating elsewhere. Such an approach is closer to Wright's important work and Hays's earliest work, *The Faith of Jesus Christ.*

Paul's Formative Stories

The formative narratives Paul is grounded in, reflects on and uses are five interwoven stories making up one large drama: (1) the story of God, the One who existed before all worlds and made them; (2) the story of the world gone wrong in Adam; (3) the story of God's people in that world, from Abraham to Moses and beyond; (4) the story of the Jewish Messiah, the Christ, which arises out of the stories of humankind and of Israel, but also out of the larger story of God as Creator and Redeemer; (5) the story of Christians, including Paul himself, which arises out of stories 2-4.

The stories of Christ and Christians are closely knit together, constituting the beginning of the tale of how the world is being set right again. Christ's story is the hinge, the crucial turning point, bringing to a climax the previous stories and determining how the rest of the story will play out and turn out. The story of God's own people in effect contracts to that of the Christ, the seed of Abraham, but expands again to include Christ's followers.

The story of God. Paul does not spend a good deal of time on theology proper in his letters. By this I mean he does not spend nearly as much time as we might expect discussing the One whom he calls God the Father. This is in part because for Paul, Christ is part of the story of God. In fact Christ is the most crucial part for Paul, who is concerned about the salvation of the world—in contrast to, say, Philo with his abstract, philosophical reflections on the Creator God. Soteriological and eschatological urgencies dictate in large measure the way Paul deals with the story of God.

What does Paul express or assume about God's own story? First, Paul has a very clear understanding that God created the world, created it good,

---

[23]C. K. Barrett, *From First Adam to Last* (London: A & C Black, 1962).

created human beings in that world, and made them male and female in the divine image (cf. Rom 1:19-20; 1 Cor 11:8-12). As 1 Corinthians 11:12 says, all things come from God. Paul does not picture two divinities or powers in heaven, an ontological dualism with a good god and an evil one fighting for control of the universe. Nor does he make the mistake of the later Gnostics: divorcing God from the creation by making God and spirit good but matter and the material universe evil or tainted. He is firmly committed to monotheism, as shown by his adoption and modification of the Shema, the credo of Israel, "Hear O Israel, the Lord our God, the Lord is One" (see 1 Cor 8:5-6). Yet Paul's understanding of Christ and his activities have brought about a reevaluation of what or whom is included in the term *God* or *Lord*.

But for Paul it is not just a matter of "In the beginning God . . ." As he says in 1 Corinthians 15:28, when Christ has completed all his tasks after the second coming, "the Son himself will also be subjected to the one who put all things in subjection under him [cf. Eph 1:22], so that God may be all in all." Nor is it just a matter of God the Father's having a role at the beginning and at the end of the drama, with Christ and the Spirit doing everything in between. William Paley's watchmaker God who starts things going, winds up the clock and then lets it tick on its own is not the God of Paul the apostle.

Paul's God is continually involved in the work of creating and sustaining. For example, Paul stresses that it was God who raised Jesus from the dead (1 Cor 15:15); Jesus did not raise himself. This event in space and time shows that for Paul, God is still working, indeed continually so. Furthermore, the Father is the One who answers prayer, is the One whom the believer—and the Spirit within prompting the believer—seeks for succor or salvation, comfort or consolation (Rom 8:15). Galatians 4:6 informs us that God is the One who sent the Spirit of his Son into our hearts so that we might cry out "Abba!" God was in Christ reconciling the world to himself (2 Cor 5:18-19). Notice the stress that ultimately even redemption and reconciliation come from God, not just from Christ: "All this is from God, who reconciled us to himself through Christ, and has given us the ministry of reconciliation" (2 Cor 5:18). When Paul reflects on his own story, he stresses that God set him apart before his birth, called him by grace and was pleased to reveal his Son in him (Gal 1:15-16).

Throughout his letters Paul generally uses the term *theos* for God the Father, not for Christ or the Trinity, though occasionally (cf. below on Rom 9:5) he applies *theos* to Christ. In Paul's view, God the Father has always been the initiator, sustainer and redeemer; God is no absentee landlord in a universe he has left to its own devices. Not only is God continuing to create, sustain and redeem, he is also busy judging (cf. Rom 1:18), goading and guiding, and answering prayers.

The story of the Christ and of the Spirit—called the Spirit of God or of the Lord (2 Cor 3:17-18)—is to some extent a subset of the story of the Father. This needs to be borne carefully in mind. Paul did not see himself as giving up monotheism when he became a Christian. He believed that his understanding of what monotheism entailed had simply been broadened through his conversion.

The story of humankind. The story of humankind is in Paul's view the story of three universals. All live in this present age and are subject to its spiritual and even supernatural wickedness and problems. Even the creation itself experiences the Fall (Rom 8:19-22). All live in bondage to sin, so none can be justified by their works (Rom 3:23-25). All are subject to death. Outside of Christ, one experiences the unholy trinity of the world, the flesh and the devil, and that trinity rules in each unredeemed person's life. There is only lostness outside of Christ, and a complete inability to save oneself.

But how did humankind come to be in such a dark state of affairs if God created all things good? Paul's answer is to tell the story of Adam. We do not find Paul saying much about original righteousness or the prefallen condition. He focuses on the world as he finds it since Adam—the world whose form is passing away (1 Cor 7:31)—and Adam is brought into the discussion only to explain the present malaise (Rom 5:12-21; 2 Cor 11:3). Of course Paul knows the story of man created from the dust and given a natural life-animating principle (1 Cor 15:47-48) and the story of being created in the image of God, with Eve originally coming forth from Adam but man coming forth from woman ever since (1 Cor 11:7-12). But Paul does not say more about this because his audience doesn't live in that world. Their world is one of dark shadows of disease, decay, death and the devil. To be sure, humankind is not as bad as it could be—the mirror image has been bent or broken, but not entirely shattered or lost. The point, however, is that humankind has fallen and cannot get up on its own. For Paul salvation is not a human self-help program.

Of prime importance to Paul about the story of Adam and Eve is the effect they have had on the rest of the race. Paul mainly holds Adam responsible for the Fall (Rom 5:12; 1 Cor 15:21-22); as for Eve, she was deceived (2 Cor 11:2). Paul believes that the story of Adam and Eve is more than a personal tragedy; it is representative and affects those that come after them. The original couple not only committed the original sin but also passed on both the inclination and the determination to go and do likewise. Paul concludes, "Just as sin came into the world through one man, and death came through sin, . . . so death spread to all *because all have sinned*" (Rom 5:12). The progeny are like the parents in their tragedy.

One of Paul's most creative moves in telling the story of human fallenness is found in Romans 7:7-13. Here he tells the story in the midst of commenting on the law.[24] It appears that Paul saw the original sin as a violation of the Tenth Commandment, the one against coveting. In Romans 7:7-13 Paul is dealing with the paradox that while God's commandments are certainly all good, human beings would not have known what transgression amounts to had there not been commandments: "I would not have known what it is to covet if the law had not said, 'You shall not covet.'"

For dramatic purposes, Paul has chosen to retell the tale of Adam in the first person and has chosen to read the snake as a personification of sin. One can then read Romans 7:8-11 as follows: "But sin [the serpent], seizing an opportunity in the commandment, produced in me all kinds of covetousness. . . . I [Adam] was once alive apart from the law, but when the commandment came, sin sprang to life and I died, and the very commandment that promised life proved to be death to me. For sin [the serpent], seizing an opportunity in the commandment, deceived me and through it killed me." Here is the by-now-familiar primeval tale of life apart from sin, into which come a commandment, deception, disobedience and ensuing death.

There are strong reasons for reading Romans 7:7-13 in this fashion.

• Verses 7-8 make reference to one specific commandment, called the commandment in verse 8, and Adam was given only one.

• Verse 9 says, "I was once alive apart from the law," but certainly the only persons Paul believed lived before or apart from any law are Adam and Eve.

• In verse 11 sin is certainly personified as a living thing that seized an opportunity and deceived a human being. This is surely the tale of Eve and Adam and the snake.

• The same verb used for "deceived" here is the one used to speak directly about Eve's being deceived in the Garden in 2 Corinthians 11:3.

• In verse 7 Paul says sin was not known except through the commandment. But everyone since Adam has had personal or experiential knowledge of sin.

---

[24]See the earlier discussion of Paul's view of the law. A Christian ethic is discussed later in the book.

Thus the view that best makes sense of all the nuances of Romans 7:7-13 is that Paul is reflecting on the primeval story of Adam and how human sin and fallenness began.

If Romans 7:7-13, which involves all past-tense verbs, is about Adam, whose story is told in Romans 7:14-25, where we find present-tense verbs? I would suggest that it is a dramatic presentation of the present fallenness of all humanity who followed in Adam's footsteps, a story perhaps told primarily from the perspective of a Jewish person outside of Christ.

Paul has prepared for this discussion earlier in Romans 5:12, where he explained that not only did sin enter the world through Adam but all his progeny went on to sin as well, both Jews and Gentiles. As Romans 2:9 says, judgment for sin will begin with the household of God. Romans 5:17 says sin and death came to reign over all humankind, and 6:17 says those outside Christ are slaves to sin, unable to avoid sin or escape its bondage.

Again, the context of Romans 7:14-25 is a discussion of the law. Notice the important statements that prepare for this section in 7:5-6, where Paul speaks of what believers were in the past in the flesh and what they have now been made in Christ (v. 6). Believers have been released from the law, as the analogy with the death of a husband makes clear. One is no longer under its jurisdiction, no longer obligated to it. In 8:8-9 Paul uses the phrase "in the flesh," just as he did in 7:5-6 to characterize what was true of a person before becoming a Christian. Yet the person of Romans 7:14-25 is said to be fleshly and sold under sin (v. 14) and cries out for deliverance. This is not a person who is free in Christ.

There are several major options for the identity of the "I" of Romans 7:14-25,[25] but only two make sense in the context. Paul may be discussing the Jew who knows and strives to obey the law—a Jew who now has 20/20 hindsight and insight. This person knows the law of God is good, but his fallen nature leads him to do what he ought not to do. The other possibility is that Paul is describing the plight of any person outside of Christ who is under conviction, having heard God's Word, in particular his law, and yet is still in the bondage to sin. Paul earlier said (2:14-15) that the essence of what the law requires is written on Gentile hearts. Thus 7:14-25 would describe the person under conviction of sin and crying out for redemption, and 8:1-15 would be the response of God to this cry and the description of the transformation that happens once one is in Christ.

Romans 8:1-10 makes clear not only that the verdict of "no condemnation" has been pronounced but also that the Spirit has entered the person's

---

[25]See Witherington, *Paul's Narrative Thought World*, pp. 24-28.

life and has released him from bondage to sin. The spirit of slavery has been replaced by the Spirit of adoption, and this Spirit prompts the person to say not "Who will deliver me from this body of death?" but "Abba! Father!" (contrast 7:24 and 8:15). Paul is of course not saying that believers instantly become perfect or are not still tempted to sin. The point is that though the temptation to sin remains, it no longer reigns.

The story of God's people. It may seem strange that Paul, the former Pharisee, devotes considerable time and space to Abraham and his story (Rom 4; 9:6-15; 11:1; Gal 3:6-18; 4:21-31) but gives Moses far less ink. For Paul, Abraham is the critical example of faith prior to the coming of Christ. Galatians 3:8 puts it this way: "And the scripture, foreseeing that God would justify the Gentiles by faith, declared the gospel beforehand to Abraham." Abraham is the prototype—or as Stephen Fowl puts it, exemplar—of Christian faith because he heard the first preaching of the good news about justification by faith and responded appropriately. Abraham thus is seen as the ancestor of both Jew and Gentile. Even Gentiles share the faith of Abraham (Rom 4:16) and with Jewish Christians become his heirs and beneficiaries of the promises given to him through Christ (Gal 3:14).

As with all the stories of the Hebrew Scriptures, Paul looks at the story of Abraham through christological and, to a lesser degree, ecclesiological glasses. The story elements he stresses are those most germane to his Christian audience. What he omits (the sacrifice of Isaac, the Sodom and Gomorrah story, the entertainment of angels, the Melchizedek incident) is as telling as what he includes. Paul's concern is to show that Abraham is a paradigm of faith and that the promises to him are fulfilled in his seed, Christ, and by that means to those who are in Christ. So one of the most crucial aspects of the Abraham material is its chronology.

It is crucial not only that Abraham is already promised many offspring in Genesis 12:2-3 but also that God's covenant with him is already initiated in Genesis 15. The most crucial scriptural comment is "And he believed the LORD, and the LORD reckoned it to him as righteousness" (Gen 15:6). All of this transpires *prior* to any discussion of circumcision as a covenant sign, which appears in Genesis 17. Note also that the account of Hagar and Sarah does not show up until after Genesis 15:6 (see Gen 16; 21:8-21). This order of events allows Paul to appeal to God's original dealings with Abraham over against the later institution of circumcision, whether Abrahamic or Mosaic. This leads to conclusions such as the one in Romans 4:11-12: circumcision is only the seal or sign of a righteousness (or right standing) Abraham had already obtained through faith in God. Paul also sees this order of events as implying that Abraham can be the father of Gentile believers as well as Jewish ones, for like them he believed without having been circumcised and was accepted on this basis (see Rom 4:1). He is not the forefather of all believers according to the flesh but on the basis of faith. This can lead to a further corollary. Not all of Abraham's physical descendants are true children of God, true Israelites, for it is not the children of the flesh but those of the promise who are true descendants (Rom 9:6-7).

Abraham's paradigmatic character comes to the fore in Romans 4:23-24. Abraham is exhibit A of relating to God on the proper basis of eschatological faith—"Now the words, 'it was reckoned to him,' were not written for his sake alone, but for ours also. It will be reckoned to us who believe in him who raised Jesus our Lord from the dead." Of course this is not just any story but a scriptural story, and as such it provides a normative model for the people of the Book. Abraham is not merely analogous to Christians; he is their scriptural model or paradigm.[26]

The story of Abraham takes a surprising turn in Galatians 3:16, where in a tour de force argument Paul maintains that the term *seed* in the Abraham story refers in particular to Christ. Wright is correct to stress the twists that Paul adds to his foundational Jewish stories.[27] Genesis 17:6-7 seems to lie in the background here. It is this version of the promise to Abraham that refers to the fact that kings will come from him, and this version also says the covenant is between God and Abraham *and his offspring.*

Romans 9:6-7 shows that Paul knows quite well that seed is a collective noun, but the larger context of Genesis 17 has provided him with the legitimate opportunity to focus on the most important Jewish king who descended from Abraham. From this discussion we learn that in fact Paul sees the risen Christ as, like God, an inclusive or omnipresent personality, one in whom many can abide or dwell. Christ is the seed, and believers in Christ are also that seed if they are in him. They become heirs through being in the seed who is Christ. Thus seed in Galatians 3:16 has both a particular and a collective sense (Christ and those in him), just as it did in the case of Abraham (Isaac and subsequent descendants are promised). So if Galatians 3 is read carefully in the context of Genesis 17, if one hears the intertextual echo, then Paul in the end is not guilty of exegetical legerdemain. Here the discussion initiated by Hays about Galatians 3 bears good fruit.[28]

---

[26]See Stephen Fowl, *The Story of Christ in the Ethics of Paul* (Sheffield: JSOT, 1990), p. 94.
[27]Wright, *New Testament*, pp. 405-9.
[28]See Hays, *Faith of Jesus*, pp. 194-200.

Of crucial importance for understanding Paul's narrative thought world is the connection mapped out between the Abrahamic and new covenants in Galatians 3—4. The Abrahamic covenant is seen as being fulfilled in Christ, and thus the covenant he began is the consummation of the Abrahamic one. Both of these covenants involved both the circumcised and the uncircumcised. From Paul's perspective, circumcision is not the essential thing, faith is; for Genesis 15 precedes Genesis 17. Both of these covenants involve children given by the grace of God, both involve an everlasting covenant, both promise that all the nations of the earth will be blessed (see Gen 17:6).

In terms of narrative flow, Paul pays a high price for closely linking the Abrahamic and the new covenant. It means that the Mosaic covenant must be seen as an interim arrangement, a parenthesis between the promises given to Abraham and the promises fulfilled in Christ. This would not mean that the law was a bad thing, just a temporary one—a guardian to keep God's people in line until Messiah should come.

When Paul thinks of Adam he thinks of the entire story of sin and Fall; when he thinks of Abraham he thinks of a faith-based covenant and the promises that went with it; but when he thinks of Moses, he thinks of the law, and in particular the law as something given *pro tempore*.

Nowhere is this more evident than in Galatians 3—4, but Romans suggests the same thing.[29] Because Paul thinks christologically about the time line of salvation history, in his view when Christ came the relationship between the law and God's people changed: "But when the fullness of time had come, God sent his Son, . . . born under the law, in order to redeem those who were under the law, so that we might receive adoption as children" (Gal 4:4-5). The Mosaic law is not seen as opposed to the promises or as annulling the Abrahamic covenant (Gal 3:17-21); it was simply given for different times and purposes.

Perhaps Paul's views on the Mosaic covenant become clearest in 2 Corinthians 3, a retelling of Moses' visit to Mt. Sinai. The reader who does not know this story will not understand the nuances of Paul's interpretive moves. Second Corinthians 3 can be seen as a tale of two ministries of two called servants of God (Moses and Paul), which leads to comments on two covenants, the Mosaic and the new. This tale is clearly not about the Hebrew Scriptures itself, nor is Paul suggesting we should adopt a particular hermeneutic—spiritual versus literal—to interpret the text. Hays's

---

[29]See the more detailed substantiation of this line of argument in Ben Witherington III, *Grace in Galatia* (Edinburgh: T & T Clark, 1998), pp. 197-341.

suggestion that 2 Corinthians 3 is chiefly about Pauline hermeneutics goes awry.[30] Nor is Paul pitting the written word (here written in stone because the Ten Commandments are alluded to) against the Spirit or even the spoken word. Rather, he is comparing and contrasting ministries, along with the covenants on behalf of which these two ministries were undertaken.

Moses ascended Mt. Sinai and came back down with the Ten Commandments and trailing clouds of glory. Paul sees the Ten Commandments, like the law as a whole, as holy, just, good and even spiritual (Rom 7:12, 14). In no way does he dispute that the law came attended with splendor. Yet its glory, and that of Moses, has been eclipsed by the greater splendor of Christ and the new covenant. Thus not only the glory on Moses' face but the Mosaic covenant itself is being annulled (2 Cor 3:11). Unfortunately, though the intent and purpose was otherwise, the law was death-dealing rather than life-giving for fallen human beings. The problem with the law was that it could not give life—it could not enable one to obey it—which meant it could only condemn human behavior over and over again. What was to be done about this?

A crucial verb in 2 Corinthians 3:7, 11, 13, 14 is *katargeō*. Twenty-one of the twenty-seven New Testament uses of this verb are found in the Pauline corpus, and in other Pauline texts the word always refers to something replaced, invalidated or abolished, not merely something that is faded. The deliberate contrast between the ministry of life and that of death in 2 Corinthians 3 strongly suggests we must interpret the verb similarly here. The coming of the glorious Christ has put even former glories in the shade, in effect making them obsolete.

Paul's argument is grounded in his reading of the way salvation history has progressed. It is not about human attitudes or approaches toward the law, nor is the law itself seen as defective. The defect lies in fallen human beings. The law's effect on such fallen ones is contrasted with the Spirit's effect on them. The written code kills, the Spirit gives life. Galatians 3:19 then makes clear that a change of guides or guardians was needed. The law was only until Christ came.

The story of Christ. Thus again, as was true when Moses came on the scene, the story of humankind takes a decisive new turn when Christ comes. Like Moses coming down from the mountain, Christ comes trailing clouds of glory. Yet Christ chooses to leave his glory behind in order to fully take on human form—indeed the form of a servant—among human beings.

---

[30]See however Hays, *Echoes*, pp. 122-53.

The story of the Christ, the plot of his career, is most ably and nobly summed up in the christological hymn material of Philippians 2:5-11.[31]

This hymn fragment is *not* a contrast between Christ's and Adam's story. In contrast to 1 Corinthians 15:45-49, language of the last or eschatological Adam who founds a new race of persons is entirely missing from this hymn. A monotheistic Jewish Christian like Paul could have never thought it appropriate for a mere human like Adam to be worshiped as exalted Lord, as we find at the end of this hymn. Adam would also be an unsuitable parallel for the glory and status Christ had and gave up that other humans did not have. Furthermore, the Genesis story says nothing about Adam and Eve desiring absolute equality with God, only that they wished to be like God. Last, verses 5-7 speak of Christ's making choices that affect his earthly form and condition. Christ chooses to set aside one form in order to take on the form of a human, indeed a servant among humans. The phrase "being found in human form" is inexplicable if he had never been anything other than a human being.[32]

So this synopsis of the Christ story tells of a person who existed prior to taking on human form and continued to exist beyond death in heaven. Philippians 2:6-11 is a story divided in two parts. In the first half of the hymn which has a V pattern (with preexistence, earthly existence, and existence in heaven after life on earth being the three nodal points), Christ is an actor who thinks, chooses and lives out a planned earthly existence. The second half, however, tells what God did for Christ as a result of his attitude and actions leading up to and including his death. This hymn thus juxtaposes imagery of preexistence, suffering servant, wisdom, humility and exaltation.

Verse 5 does deliberately draw a parallel between the frame of mind and decision-making of the preexistent Son of God and that of Christians. As will be discussed later in this chapter, this exalted piece of theological discourse has an ethical function: it is meant to lead believers to imitate Christ. Christ deliberately stepped down, he deliberately did not draw on his divine prerogatives, he deliberately took a lower place, he deliberately submitted even to death on the cross. Of course the analogy drawn here between the behavior of Christ and that of Christians is just that—an analogy. But it is a potent one. Its message is that we ought to follow

---

[31]Here I part company with Stephen Fowl, who does not see a christological hymn in this passage. See Fowl, *Story*, pp. 31-45.

[32]See I. H. Marshall, "Incarnational Christology in the New Testament," in *Christ the Lord: Studies in Christology Presented to Donald Guthrie*, ed. Harold H. Rowden (Downers Grove, Ill.: InterVarsity Press, 1982), pp. 1-16; also Witherington, *Paul's Narrative Thought World*, pp. 97-105 and the notes.

Christ's self-sacrificial lifestyle so others may benefit.

The first half of the hymn has a paraenetic thrust. The second half may also hint that God will do for the believer what he has already done for Christ—provide a resurrection, saying, "Come up higher, brother or sister." The crucified conqueror's story is to be recapitulated in the life of his followers, as it was being recapitulated in the life of Paul himself. In this same letter Paul says, "I want to know Christ and the power of his resurrection and the sharing of his sufferings by becoming like him in his death, if somehow I may attain the resurrection from the dead" (Phil 3:10-11). Paul sees himself as modeling Christ so that his converts will do likewise. This is made very clear in 3:14-17, where he pleads directly, "Brothers and sisters, join in imitating me" (v. 17; cf. 1 Cor 11:1). It is important to remember the context. This is not hubris; it is the modeling a good teacher was expected to do. Paul is not claiming to be *the* pattern, only a good example of how one follows the pattern.[33]

It may be objected that Paul believed the Christian has obtained from God an alien righteousness through faith in Christ and apart from works (Phil 3:9). This is true, but it negates none of the ethical thrust of this telling of the Christ story. Indeed Paul assumes that the gift of right standing with God is the platform or basis for exhorting his charges to Christlikeness and promising them the completion of the process if they remain faithful to the end. To "gain Christ" (3:8) is not merely to gain right standing with God; it is to gain full Christlikeness at the resurrection (3:10-11).

Some of the details of the story are most revealing of what Paul thinks about its central protagonist. For example, *morphē*, from which we get a word such as *metamorphosis*, always signifies an outward form that truly and accurately expresses the real being that underlies it (see Phil 2:6). This must mean that Christ manifested a form that indicated he truly had the nature and being of God; thus Paul speaks of his being equal to God. The preexistent Son of God actually had such a status and condition; Christ by rights and by nature had what God had.

The much-disputed term *harpagmos* in all likelihood means taking advantage of something that one rightfully has. Christ did not take advantage of his divine prerogatives and glorious status but set them aside and took on the form of a human being. It is not likely that this means he set aside his divine nature; rather he set aside the right to draw on his divine attributes (omnipotence, omniscience, omnipresence) while on earth. In short, the incarnation meant a divine being's deliberate self-limiting in

---

[33]See the earlier discussion.

order to be truly and fully human. He lived among humans as one of us, drawing on the power of the Spirit, the Word of God and prayer, just as we must do. Thus the human career of Christ, beginning with his taking on the form of a servant and continuing through his death and resurrection, is said to be analogous to the plot of the story of Christians.

Christ not only stripped himself but also shunned any rightful human accolades or dignity, taking on the form of a servant or slave. How very differently he lived from most ancient persons, caught up in honor challenges and striving for more public recognition.[34] Yet in the end he was honored. God in fact gave him the divine name, the name for God in the Septuagint—*kyrios*. Isaiah 45:21-25 lies in the background. In this hymn, then, we see, as in 1 Corinthians 8:6, that Paul is affirming a transformed definition of Jewish monotheism. Christ is not given a purely honorific name of which he is unworthy or ill-suited by nature. Paul believes to the contrary that the name matches the nature and this is why worship is appropriate.

Christ's story is the crucial hinge in the whole human drama (as Wright stresses), which indicates how the story will end.[35] Paul is able to retell this story in many other creative forms (e.g., Col 1:15-20), but the essence of the story is the same: a preexistent divine Son of God who stooped to conquer. The means of triumph was not just taking on the form of a servant but also dying a slave's death on the cross and then being vindicated by God through the resurrection (cf. Rom 1:3-4).

The story has a sequel, involving the return of Christ to earth once more. This means that the follower of Christ during the church age must live between the advents, keeping one eye on each horizon. There is an "already and not yet" character to the story of Christ, and so to the story of his followers.

The story of Paul and of Christians. Paul is interested in the entire story of humankind from beginning to end. When he reaches the climax, the story of Christ, he focuses overwhelmingly on the end of the Christ story—the death and resurrection—though Christ's coming and true humanity are also emphasized. Paul's gospel about Christ is a passion and resurrection narrative with a short introduction. Yet he does not neglect the cosmic origin and end of the story, for the latter has direct effect on the believer's story now. If Christ has led supernatural captivity captive (Eph 4:8), and believers are no longer in the thrall of demons (though they may still be pestered or persecuted by such foes), then Christians need to know this and

---

[34]See the earlier discussion.
[35]Wright, *New Testament*, pp. 406-7.

not live as those without hope or help.[36]

The story of humankind narrowed down to the story of Israel in the persons of Abraham, Moses and their successors, which further narrowed down to the story of the Jewish Messiah, the Christ. Thereafter the story widens again to embrace the story of those who are in the Christ. Since this book's particular concern is Paul, we will focus on his story, with occasional comments on the story of Christians in general. As we have already seen, there do not seem to have been any positive antecedents or precursory events that led to Paul's conversion from a zealous opponent to a zealous proponent of the Christ.[37]

A much-neglected text in the study of Paul's conversion is 2 Corinthians 4, particularly verse 6,[38] a partial quotation of Genesis 1, God's making light to shine out of darkness. Paul wishes to connect the text with the fact that Christ has "shone in our hearts to give the light of the knowledge of the glory of God in the face of Jesus Christ." Paul is saying that conversion begins a whole new world for the convert. He or she becomes a new creature, part of a new creation. This new world of illumination dawned on Paul on the Damascus Road when he saw the risen Lord, or as he puts it here, the very presence, the very glory of God in the shape of the face of Jesus. The new creation, then, is much like the first one, a matter of God's calling into existence "the things that do not exist" (Rom 4:17)—a radical departure from the past, a truly new and fresh start. The emphasis is on discontinuity with the past. While Paul may be partly envisioning his story in terms of the story of the first Adam (see above), clearly he envisions it even more in terms of the story of the last Adam—the One who gave up much and took the form of a servant.

This is very much how Paul sees himself, as is clear from autobiographical texts like Philippians 3:4-10, and it is not an accident that in 2 Corinthians 4 Paul tells his own tale with echoes of the way he tells the story of Christ in Philippians 2. Paul's status and prerogatives in Judaism were considerable, and he was advancing in it well beyond his peers, as he tells us in Galatians 1. He was on the way up, not on the way to becoming a servant. Yet as a Christian, Paul is prepared to place all of that in the loss column given the surpassing privilege of knowing and being known by Christ and being conformed to his image. Thus in Galatians 6:15 he distin-

---

[36]See the earlier discussion.

[37]See the earlier discussion.

[38]See the helpful discussion by Martin Hengel and R. Deines, *Pre-Christian Paul* (Valley Forge, Penn.: Trinity Press International, 1991), p. 79.

guished sharply between what once mattered greatly to him, such as whether one was circumcised (cf. Phil 3:5), and what now matters: the new creation. As Richard N. Longenecker has rightly stressed, Paul is talking about not just re-creation but a *new* creation.[39] Similarly, he is talking about not simply a renewed covenant but a *new* one that eclipses, brings to closure and fulfills the old ones.

In 1 Corinthians 5:17 Paul says that those who are in Christ are new creatures. Among other things, conversion dramatically changed Paul's view of Jesus. Whereas formerly he evaluated Jesus from a fallen and worldly point of view, he certainly does so no longer. Yet it would be a mistake to think that Paul sees conversion as involving only a transvaluation of values and attitudes. He believes that conversion also entails *a change in one's spiritual makeup.* One's life takes on a christoform shape.

One of Paul's favorite self-designations is "servant" (Rom 1:1; Phil 1:1). His story is analogous to that of Christ and is modeled on it. But this is not just a matter of imitating Christ, it is also God's work of conforming him to the image of Christ. Thus in 2 Corinthians 1:5 Paul speaks of suffering the sufferings of Christ. In Paul's view the trajectory of his own life is much like that of his Master. Paul's hope is to be completely conformed to Christ's image by obtaining a resurrection like his.

It appears quite likely, in view of 1 Corinthians 15:8-9, that some believed Paul's transformation from persecutor of the church to apostle of Christ had happened with unnatural haste. Early Jews were used to a gradual process by which persons became proselytes of Judaism, having first been inquirers or God-fearers for a period of time. Paul's change of character had come much more suddenly. Ancient persons were naturally suspicious of claims that people had changed their nature or character, for character was seen as innate, something one was born with and then manifested over the course of one's life.[40] It would not be surprising, then, if some were calling Paul an *ektrōma* and therefore unfit to be or be called an apostle of Jesus due to his earlier persecuting activities (1 Cor 15:8-9). An *ektrōma* was a miscarriage, whether stillbirth or abortion—a child rushed prematurely into the world. Here Paul connects the image with his being last to see the risen Lord. The implication seems to be that had his conversion not happened quickly, it might not have happened at all.

It is not clear whether Paul means only that people saw his conversion as having happened too suddenly, with ungodly haste, or that they saw his

---

[39]Richard N. Longenecker, *Galatians* (Waco, Tex.: Word, 1990), p. 296.
[40]See the earlier discussion.

adoption of an apostolic role as also too hasty. It may also be that Paul means that his experience of seeing the risen Lord happened out of due season—well after the other appearances, to judge from Acts—but had it not happened thus, it would not have happened at all. In any case, both Paul and his critics saw him as unworthy to be an apostle. But it wasn't a matter of worth, it was a matter of grace.

Being born a new creature in midlife is no easy thing, as it means giving up much that one has worked for and loved—in a sense dying to one's past and being born again. Paul speaks for himself and other Christians when he says in Romans 6:2-4 that conversion means being buried with Christ in baptism, being baptized into his death, and so beginning to enter the story of Christ. The heart of the creed for Paul—that Christ died for our sins according to the Scriptures, was buried and was raised on the third day (1 Cor 15:3-5)—becomes in Romans 6:2-4 the central analogy for what happens and will happen to Christians. Just as Christ died for sins, so believers die to sin (v. 2). Just as Christ was buried, so the believer has been buried with Christ in his death (v. 4), and just as Christ has been raised, so too the believer can now walk in the Spirit, in newness of life, and look forward to a bodily resurrection.

Colossians 2:6-12 takes a similar tack. When Paul refers to the circumcision of Christ in verse 9, does he mean merely what happened to him or also to what happens to any believer in Christ? The believer is raised together with Christ "through faith in the effective working of God who raised him from the dead" (v. 12). Christ's story is efficacious for the believer when it is recapitulated: the believer goes from being dead in trespasses to being made alive in him. What Christ has done for the believer on the cross and in the resurrection is the basis of what he later does in the believer. Christians experience Christlikeness in the Spirit only because Christ himself first experienced death and resurrection.

The story of Paul's (and others') Christian life does not stop at justification by grace through faith, though as Galatians 2:15-21 makes clear, that is the crucial beginning point.[41] One must go on to work out one's salvation with fear and trembling, to grow in grace and holiness. One must consciously choose to walk in the Spirit and not indulge the works of the flesh (Gal 5). One must have a sense of the already but also the not yet of Christian life—suspended between new birth and new body, inner renewal and outer decay.

The Christian should not expect to be exempt from suffering in this life,

---

[41]See the discussion in Witherington, *Grace in Galatia*, pp. 169-94.

since Christ and his apostles were not. Furthermore, the Christian must have a clear vision that Christ's history is the believer's destiny. This is what Paul has in mind when he talks in 1 Corinthians 15 about believers' being the latter fruit of a crop of resurrection persons—Christ being the first fruit. This is also what he has in mind when he speaks of believers' being destined to be conformed to the glorious resurrected image of God's Son (Rom 8:29). The moral conforming is happening now, the physical conforming later. Thus Paul himself sees his life as a pilgrimage toward resurrection (Phil 3:10-11). He knows this will not happen before the Lord returns. So the present is a time for striving and pressing on toward the goal. Every Christian should have the honesty to admit with Paul, "Not that I have already obtained this or have already reached the goal; but I press on to make it my own, because Christ Jesus has made me his own" (Phil 3:12).

The mark on and of the Christian is the mark of Christ. The believer belongs to Christ, imitates the Master and is spiritually conformed to the Master's image. This involves both tragedy and triumph, sorrow and joy. The words of William Penn would have been heartily endorsed by Paul as a description of the Christlike: "No pain, no palm; no gall, no glory; no cross, no crown." And indeed no final resolution until the author of all these stories brings down the curtain on the human drama in the person of his Son when he returns. Then the human story, the story of Israel, the story of Christians will be finally and fully gathered up into the story of Christ, and every knee shall bow and every tongue confess, whether willingly or unwillingly, that Jesus Christ is Lord, and the glory will be to the Father, whose story began this discussion.

Conclusions: Paul's Storytelling

There is still much to be learned about the historical Paul from examining his fundamental stories. For now it is sufficient to say that Paul lived in and out of a storied world, and his thought cannot be understood apart from these foundational narratives. The one story by which Paul exegetes all the others is the story of Christ, which is not a story in the Old Testament but a retelling of the kerygma of the early church. This is one reason that intertextual studies will not suffice to plumb the depths of Paul's thought world. Nor do structuralist approaches do justice to the narrative substructure in which all of his thought coheres.

It probably does not make sense to confine Paul's thought world to the story of Israel, or to insist that Israel's story is *the* central one for him. Paul spends next to no time on the story of David or the Davidic character of

Christ, but much time on the Adam/last Adam tandem. He spends more time on Abraham (the forefather of Israel) than on Moses (the Hebrews as they came forth from Egypt and became a people called Israel at Sinai). When Paul does focus on Moses and the law, in Galatians and 2 Corinthians 3, the discussion is more about obsolescence than fulfillment, more about the newness of the new ministry than its continuity with the old, more about the surpassing glory than the fading glory. For Paul, all humankind stands not between Sinai and the Promised Land but between Adam and the eschatological Adam; and all must live out of the story of one or the other of these Adams. The center of Paul's story is christological not ecclesiological or "Israelogical," to coin a term.

It appears then that my reading of Paul's narrative thought world differs some from Wright's; but at this writing Wright has not yet culminated his study of Paul's narrative thought world. Daniel Boyarin, however, rightly points to Paul's strong stress on christocentric universalism as opposed to Israelogical or Israelocentric thought.[42]

This portion of our study has only confirmed that Paul saw his own identity defined primarily in relationship to Christ and his people, and he made it his personal goal to be conformed to Christ's image. This is the sort of action we would expect of an ancient person looking for a paradigm to follow and a community to be a part of, in order to understand his place in the world. Paul's identity was shaped and established not by how he stood out from the crowd and his models but by how he followed them.[43]

PAUL THE EXEGETE

It is clear at this point that we cannot understand Paul the exegete, or for that matter Paul the ethicist or theologian,[44] unless we have an understanding of Paul's narrative thought world. His stories are sacred stories from the Hebrew Scriptures and the Christian tradition. Yet Paul sees the old, old stories as reconfigured in light of the Christ story.

Paul's Hermeneutic
Paul's hermeneutic is christocentric in its guiding force and aim and eccle-

---

[42]See the earlier discussion of Daniel Boyarin, *A Radical Jew: Paul and the Politics of Identity* (Berkeley: University of California Press, 1994).

[43]For more along these lines see Ben Witherington III, "Christ" and "Christology," in *Dictionary of Paul and His Letters*, ed. Gerald F. Hawthorne, Ralph P. Martin and Daniel G. Reid (Downers Grove, Ill.: InterVarsity Press, 1993), pp. 100-15.

[44]See chapter eight.

siocentric in its scope and application. Christ is the hermeneutical key to a
right reading of the Scriptures, and the church is the right audience for
hearing this rereading. Thus Paul reads the sacred traditions through the
eyes of the Christ for the sake of the Christian community and its
edification.

Interest in intertextual studies of Paul's letters has never been higher, in
large measure due to the impact of Richard Hays's important work *Echoes
of Scripture in the Letters of Paul.* The discussion below will take into account
several of Hays's major proposals and assumptions, but some preliminary
remarks are in order.

Paul sees all of the Hebrew Scriptures, including the law, as God's Word
and therefore profitable for learning and teaching. Even the ritual law (cf.
1 Cor 9:8-9) has lessons for the Christian. Paul believed it was crucial to
know where God's people were in the working out of salvation history—
that is, beyond the era of the law and under the reign of Christ—if they are
to properly understand the significance of Scripture for them. While they
are not under the Mosaic covenant, they are under the guidance of the
Scriptures which are fulfilled in the messianic age.

Scholars treating Paul's handling of the Scriptures frequently comment
to the effect that he "employed standard techniques of Scriptural exegesis,
occasionally even using rules of 'rabbinic' hermeneutics."[45] In the modern
era Paul has often been accused of exegetical legerdemain because of the
creative way he sometimes handles the biblical text. Yet one must distinguish between when Paul is actually doing exegesis and when he is making
a homiletical use of the text that goes well beyond exegesis. More often
than we might realize, Paul the pastor is busy using and applying the text
in creative ways rather than simply interpreting it. In other words, he is
engaging in what has been called *pesher,* or contemporizing handling of the
text, a skill he may have learned while he was a Pharisee.

Yet there is a danger of anachronism when scholars make much of
comparisons between Paul's handling of Scripture and later techniques
found in the Mishnah, much less the Talmuds.[46] His techniques are more
appropriately compared to those used at Qumran—another eschatological
community reading scriptural texts prophetically. For instance, unlike later

---

[45]D. Cohn-Sherbok, "Paul and Rabbinic Exegesis," *Scottish Journal of Theology* 35 (1982): 132. For
the standard treatment see E. Earle Ellis, *Paul's Use of the Old Testament* (Edinburgh: Oliver &
Boyd, 1957).

[46]See Hays, *Echoes,* pp. 10-11. *Midrash* is a slippery term, being used differently by different
scholars. See A. G. Wright, "The Literary Genre *Midrash,*" *Catholic Biblical Quarterly* 28 (1966):
113-20.

rabbinic writers, Paul does not cite catenas of the views of other Jewish Scripture scholars on one text or another, though like the rabbinic writers he frequently uses composite citations of Old Testament texts.[47] Paul also uses introductory formulas with some quotations, as we find in the rabbinic corpus (see Gal 3:10, 13). Also like the rabbinic writers, Paul sometimes personifies Scriptures (see Gal 3:8). Such techniques, however, have little to do with interpretation and certainly nothing to do with midrashic interpretation. Citation formulas are not interpretations.

Echoes and Types in the Halls of Paul

In Hays's magisterial study of intertextual echoes of Hebrew Scriptures in Paul's letters, Hays has shown in detail that even when Paul is not formally quoting Scripture he is often alluding to it, relying on echoes to conjure up the larger Old Testament context.[48] If we take into account not only his formal quotations but also his allusions to the Old Testament, we quickly discover what a crucial role Scripture played in forming his thought world and symbolic universe. Of course, this mental furniture underwent some drastic rearrangement and reconception when he accepted the story of the Crucified and Risen One.

In the discussion of Philippians 4:5 we saw how Paul's allusions or echoes work.[49] Paul sees the Hebrew Scriptures as a giant repository of largely prophetic texts that have some key lessons to teach Christians. In the hands of the master applier of the Word, even seemingly unpromising texts like Deuteronomy 25:4 can be seen to teach us something about God's ways with his new covenant people (see 1 Cor 9:8-12). The principle of analogy brings the text to life again and again because Paul assumes the same God operates in the same ways in his own day as in Old Testament times. The form of the community has changed, but the character of God and God's ways with humankind have not. Yet we must be able to distinguish, as Paul himself does, between the original meaning of the text and its larger significance to the eschatological community of God's people in Christ.

As a large example of Paul's use of the principle of analogy, consider the typological use of Scripture found in 1 Corinthians 10:1-13. Paul believes

---

[47]There is, however, a certain urgency in grasping Paul's exegetical and hermeneutical approaches, for as we have already seen Paul can simply omit bits of the Abraham story which would seem to call into question his views on circumcision (e.g., there is no discussion of Genesis 17:9-14 by Paul). See the discussion in Witherington, *Grace in Galatia*, pp. 219-28.

[48]See Hays, *Echoes*.

[49]See the earlier discussion.

fervently that the things that happened to God's people in Old Testament times really happened—they are not cunningly devised fables—and that at least part of the reason these things happened and were recorded in Scripture was to provide "types" for the Christian community. Paul would claim that the Hebrew Scripture is the book of and for Jews and Gentiles united in Christ, intended especially for the instruction, edification and exhortation of that eschatological community. This is because he sees the whole as to some degree a prophetic corpus. It was of course the Scripture for those who lived before Christ as well, but Paul believes he lives in an age when the true implications and significance of these texts can more fully be seen.

The fundamental idea behind typology is that God's character never changes; thus God acts in similar ways in differing ages of history and, perhaps more important, provides persons and events that foreshadow later persons and events in salvation history. In other words, typology is not an ahistorical reading of the text but a comparison of what happened before to God's people and what is happening now. Cognizance of both stories is crucial if analogy is to be drawn. All that came before Christ was preparatory and pointed forward to what has been happening since Christ appeared.

Typology as we find it in 1 Corinthians 10 does not involve a comprehensive point-by-point comparison. For example, Paul does not believe the Corinthians have perished in the spiritual desert of the pagan world; indeed the analogy is presented so they will not do so. Yet Paul entertains the possibility that some of his converts may end up like the wilderness-wandering generation of Israelites. He wishes to use the Old Testament to show Christians how they should and should not live, in view of God's consistent judging of idolatry among his people.

Notice how 1 Corinthians 10 begins with reference to "our ancestors." The story of the Israelites is "our" story, because in Paul's view, Jew and Gentile united in Christ are the continuation and true development of the Old Testament people of God.

Paul's way of handling this text works two ways. He interprets Old Testament events in a Christian and christological manner, and he interprets contemporary events in light of Old Testament stories. In other words, he moves in two directions at once: from experience to text and from text to contemporary experience. When he says in 1 Corinthians 10:4 "and the rock was Christ," he does not say "and the rock *is* Christ," nor does he say "the rock signifies Christ." Paul finds it appropriate to read the Old Testament in light of how these texts were interpreted in Jewish sapiential literature, where Wisdom was said to be the rock that provided water for thirsty Israel in the desert (Wis 11). Paul believes Christ who is the Wisdom of God was in fact really present with Israel and provided them with benefits. This is not an interpretive or hermeneutical move so much as a theological reflection on what was actually the case during the Old Testament times.

In Paul's view, the reason this analogy works so well is that both his present audience and the one referred to in the Old Testament text received benefits from Christ. Yet those benefits didn't spare the Israelites from judgment, any more than partaking of the Christian sacraments would spare Corinthian Christians who were attending idol feasts from being judged by God. Notice how in 10:1-4 Paul stresses, using deliberately Christianized language, that *all* the Israelites partook of the so-called Mosaic sacraments. Now Paul knows very well that the Red Sea crossing was no baptismal rite (v. 2): the Israelites went across on dry ground. Nor is he really suggesting that manna had the same sacramental character as the Lord's Supper. His point is simply this: the Israelites had the same general sort of spiritual benefits (v. 3—food spiritually provided) from the same God, and it did not save them from judgment.

In what sense was the rock, or the food or the drink the Israelites had, "spiritual"? Likely the term is chosen to indicate the source of this sustenance: God, who is Spirit. Paul may also be assuming that spiritual people like himself should be able to discern the deeper spiritual lessons to be drawn from such analogies. The food was no more figurative or allegorical than were the Corinthians' sacraments. However, the spiritual significance of that reality needed to be seen.

Verse 11 is important, for it reveals something of how Paul views the Old Testament text. He says these things happened as a warning to himself and his audience, "on whom the ends of the ages have come." Paul believed that he lived in the eschatological age, when the significance and the beginning of the completion of God's designs for humankind have become apparent. The goals to which history had been pressing had begun to be realized in his day.

If one grants Paul his theological assumptions—(1) that the preexistent Christ had a hand in the affairs of the Israelites, (2) that Paul and his converts were living in the eschatological age, when all the promises and prophecies and paradigms were coming to fruition, and (3) that the Scriptures were written for God's people, and perhaps especially for the eschatological gathering of God's people—then what Paul does with this text makes very good sense. It is not a matter of exegetical legerdemain or hermeneutical hocus-pocus. It is a matter of having the right eschatological, christological and ecclesiological perspectives to see the new significance these historic texts had for Paul's audience.

The Apostle's Allegorizing and Making Sense of *Sensus Plenior*

When Paul seeks to do typology, he announces his intentions so the audience will see how he is proceeding by analogy. Likewise, when he uses another major hermeneutical technique, allegorizing a nonallegorical text, he announces his intentions. We see this in Galatians 4:21—5:1, where in the midst of the discussion Paul says, "Now this is an allegory" (4:24). *Allēgoreō* can mean either to speak or to interpret allegorically, so one must be able to distinguish among (1) a text created as an allegory, (2) an allegorizing of elements or portions of a text and (3) allegorical interpretation of a nonallegorical text. Surely Paul is well aware that he is doing a creative allegorical interpretation of a text that is not in itself an allegory, and in fact he is allegorizing only certain elements in the text. Again, this falls into the category of hermeneutics rather than exegesis—a distinction too often overlooked.

Typology is grounded in the actual characteristics of the type and antitype displayed in the narratives, and normally persons or events, not things, are set up as types or antitypes. In allegory, however, persons, places and things can all take on symbolic or secondary connotations. Likely if asked, Paul would freely admit that Hagar was not a "type" of either Mt. Sinai or the present Jerusalem. Only the concept of bondage or slavery binds them together, and allegorizing the text brings this linkage to light. Paul is not really doing exegesis here at all but presupposes a basic understanding of the story and creatively uses elements of the story for pastoral hermeneutics and application. This falls into the category of a pastoral or homiletical use of a text and should not be evaluated as a bizarre attempt at contextual exegesis.

Paul's allegorizing of the historical narrative is perhaps closest to what we find at Qumran (cf. Cairo *Damascus Document* 6.3-11, where Num 21:18 is similarly allegorized). In both cases, contemporary events outside the text (in Paul's case the presence of Judaizers in Galatia) lead to creative handlings of the text.

Hays can serve as a dialogue partner as we attempt to assess Paul's exegetical and hermeneutical techniques. Hays argues that Paul espouses the concept of *sensus plenior*, that the text has a deep, latent or even metaphorical meaning that can be liberated or ferreted out by a creative "spiritual" handling of the text.[50] But this confuses the issues of meaning

---

[50]Hays, *Echoes*, p. 154.

and significance (or application).

To a large extent, Hays reaches his conclusion on the basis of a certain reading of 2 Corinthians 3, which he takes to reveal Paul's hermeneutic: Christians are freed from bondage to a circumscribed reading of the old covenant and empowered to read it with freedom, even with reckless abandon. This conclusion comes from Hays's fundamental misreading of the contrast between letter and Spirit. Paul is not saying that one kind of interpretive move in handling the Old Testament is death-dealing while another more freewheeling kind of interpretation is life-giving. He is saying that the effect of the law, even the Ten Commandments, on fallen persons is condemnation. By contrast, the effect of the Spirit on fallen persons is to give life. In Romans and Galatians Paul says much the same thing about the effect of the law on fallen persons (e.g., Gal 3:21). Not exegesis or hermeneutics but spiritual experience is the issue.

Victor Paul Furnish sees this quite clearly: "The description Paul gives of the *new covenant* does not so much reflect his hermeneutical perspective on the law or scripture in general as it does his eschatological perspective on God's redemptive work in history."[51] Paul is offering a tale of two ministries and two covenants, not a discussion of two ways of reading or two kinds of attitudes toward the Old Testament or the law. Paul the exegete is a second-order issue relative to Paul the storyteller. He thinks these stories are coming true by the power of God, and so the primary thing is always spiritual experience, not exegesis or hermeneutics.

What about Galatians 3:8, where Paul personifies Scripture as a prophetic book? Scripture saw in advance that God would justify the Gentiles by faith and so "pre-preached" the gospel to Abraham. The point here is again not some deeper meaning in the Old Testament text. Paul actually believes that Abraham heard the essence of the gospel message— acceptability to God through faith reckoned as righteousness—and responded positively. This is not anachronism but analogy—in particular an argument, like the one in 1 Corinthians 10, based on analogous experience. Salvation-historical experience shared by Abraham and Paul's converts is the point. The only anachronism is to call the message Abraham heard and to which he responded the gospel. The gospel message is not "hidden in Old Testament Scripture"; it is in plain sight as a message once given to Abraham.[52]

In another of Hays's key texts, Romans 10:5-10, he has a stronger case.

---

[51]Victor Paul Furnish, *II Corinthians* (Garden City, N.Y.: Doubleday, 1984), p. 200.

[52]Contrast Hays, *Echoes*, p. 155.

But is Paul really arguing that there is a concealed meaning in Deuteronomy 30:11-14? To the contrary, he is arguing that there is a revealed meaning *in* the text, not behind or beneath it. Just as the word was near to the Israelites, it is all the more near to the eschatological community of faith. "The word is near you, in your mouth and in your heart" provides Paul an opportunity to talk about the word of faith that he preaches and his audience believes and confesses. Here Paul clearly is using the pesher technique of contemporizing a text. He believes the phrase had meaning in its original setting, but now he uses these scriptural words to speak about something that is true of his own preaching and the Christian's experience.

The personified "righteousness that comes from faith" (Rom 10:6) has caused no end of debate. Whoever or whatever this is, it cannot be Moses, for it is contrasted with Moses, who wrote "concerning the righteousness that comes from the law" (v. 5). This could be rendered "Moses *writes* concerning legal righteousness . . . *but* the Righteousness from faith *says* . . ." This may be a reference to Christ and the way he spoke the gospel, using Old Testament phrases, when he was on earth.[53] Alternatively, it may refer to the Christian oral tradition about righteousness from faith and the way it uses the Old Testament text to make its points. Still another possibility is that the abstract concept "righteousness from faith" has been personified (just as elsewhere Paul has personified Scripture) and is speaking the inspired word of God for today, using Old Testament phrases. This personification is in fact the personification of what Paul calls the gospel, the oral message summarized in places like Galatians 2:15-21. This last seems most likely here.

In any event, we must be able to distinguish between a contemporizing use of scriptural phrases (as here) and a theory about how Paul believed the Old Testament text had a hidden or deeper meaning. Meaning of the text is one thing; how it is used hermeneutically is another. It is hermeneutics when one sees some application for today that goes beyond a text's original meaning. This, I submit, is what Paul is doing in Romans 10. Hays is mistaken, then, to conclude from such pastoral uses of the text that "Paul's readings of Scripture are not constrained by a historical scrupulousness about the original meaning of the text. Eschatological meaning subsumes original sense."[54] I would say eschatological application extends original meaning and application, following the principle of analogy.

---

[53]See Romans 3-4, where Paul argues that God has shown forth his righteousness in a new way in Christ, the paradigmatic example of faith and faithfulness.
[54]Hays, *Echoes*, p. 156.

Yet in the end Hays is correct in noting that Paul's hermeneutic is narratively oriented, which explains the importance of typology for Paul. "Paul reads Scripture under the conviction that its story prefigures the climactic realities of his own time."[55] In other words, unlike Philo, Paul is basically not an allegorist looking for some abstract eternal truth buried in a narrative. Paul thinks in terms of historical progressions and the breaking into space and time of God's divine saving activity. The narratives in his thought world are founded and grounded in God and in history, and this of course includes the narratives about Christ and Christians. Typology is the technique of one who has a profound belief in the historical substance of what he speaks and a profound belief in the God who is sovereign over history and relates in a consistent way to his people age after age.

CONCLUSIONS

Our exploration of Paul's storytelling and exegesis has made it evident that he lives on the basis of and out of a sacred story. He constantly tries to relate his own story and world to those he finds in the Hebrew Scriptures and the Christian tradition. Like his Jewish contemporaries, but unlike many other ancients, Paul saw himself as grounded in a holy book: what Christians call the Old Testament. Yet if the Hebrew Scriptures constituted his entire range of stories, he would remained a Pharisaic Jew. His experience of the risen Lord changed everything, so that Paul felt he needed to go back and reread the Scriptures in light of Christ and the Christ experience. His former work as a Scripture scholar had not given him a true understanding of the meaning of the Word. Paul's experience of the Christ led to a very different understanding of what God had had in mind all along. In particular, it led to a major rethinking of the function of the law and the Mosaic covenant, as well as the Abrahamic covenant.

Paul's allusive handling of Scripture shows that he believed one needs to know the whole story to appreciate its parts. As an exegete and applier of the text, Paul was creative, using typology and even allegorizing to relate the Scriptures to the situations of his converts. Yet it would be a mistake to see him as an early predecessor of Augustine and others who constantly sought a *sensus plenior,* a deeper or hidden sense to Scripture. Paul, to the contrary, believed he lived in an age when the hidden had been brought to light and Scripture's meaning and truth made plain. He believed he lived in the eschatological age, when the ends and aims of all the ages were

---

[55]Ibid., p. 161.

coming to fruition through Christ and his body. Paul looked for new ways to apply the old meaning to his converts, and his hermeneutical creativity helped him find these ways.

Paul's historical and narratological consciousness dictates how he views the befores and afters of the scriptural story. He is not Philo looking for abstract Platonic ideals in the midst of the maze of historical particulars. For Paul, Scripture speaks again and again to the realms of history and experience. One needs to look into history and into the sacred story, not beyond or behind it, to find the meaning and purpose of life and the explanation for what transpires.

Paul's hermeneutic was christologically determined and focused, the Christ event being the lens through which all must be seen and understood, but it was ecclesiologically directed. It was also eschatologically generated, as Paul sees himself living in the age when the prophetic and the promissory comes to pass. The story of Christ sums up all that came before and encompasses all that is to follow. This story is the key that unlocks all the secrets and frees those who had been bound in fallenness, slavery to the powers of darkness, servitude to the law. Paul believed that the story had reached its climax and he was living in the denouement. He believed the story was being replicated in his own experience and was calling him to the imitation of Christ.

CHAPTER 8

PAUL THE ETHICIST AND THEOLOGIAN

The ethic Paul offers in his letters is community based and community directed, yet it also deals with the Christian's relationship with the world outside the church community. Paul's belief and his strategy is that change must come "in house" and that ethical demands work only in community where there can be discipline, sanctions and shared norms. Recent discussion has focused on the moral ethos of the Christian community and the sort of ethics such an ethos creates. For example, sociological studies show that the high regard for life in early Christianity (and opposition to infanticide, abortion and the like) led to greater participation of women in the church. In the Christian community, women were less likely to be marginalized than in many other communities in the Greco-Roman world. Another factor strongly affecting the ethos of early Christian communities was the viability of remaining single in such a community, as many received encouragement from Paul to do.

It is telling that as Christianity gained acceptability in the Empire and moved toward becoming the dominant religion, increasing numbers of men joined the faith, the favorable sex ratio for Christian women declined, and the roles open to them became far more limited. In other words, it was not Paul's love patriarchalism but the later patriarchal takeover of the church and its leadership structure that limited the roles of women in the body of Christ. For Paul, the role of the Spirit was too determinative in the body to allow for such an ethical move. Roles and functions in the body would be determined largely by gifts and graces, plus the social factor of who had the resources and venue to provide a safe private haven for Christian meetings.

A key to understanding Paul's ethic is to realize that he does not simply reiterate the ethics of the Old Testament, though he draws on Old Testament principles and commands from time to time. If we miss the fact that Paul is essentially a sectarian person who is drawing on his heritage for a new social situation and community, we can fall prey to fundamental misunderstandings. The absence of an exhortation to observe the sabbath or be circumcised is more telling than the presence of various Old Testament maxims and norms. This "selectivity" augurs a new situation where one is no longer under and obligated to the law, which Paul consistently sees and refers as a whole (see clearly Gal 5:3).

For Paul, Christians are under a new covenant, one whose ethical foundation is not the Mosaic law but the law of Christ, meaning both the pattern of Christ's life and the teaching Christ offered. This new set of ethical imperatives differs in some very fundamental ways from the Mosaic law. For example, Romans 12:14-21 offers an ethic of nonresistance and of truly loving and blessing one's enemy. This stands in contrast to the lex talionis *of the Mosaic covenant and shows clearly how Christians are no longer under either the moral or ritual dimensions of such a law. Paul is talking about an eschatological ethic for a new age, not merely a renewal of the old covenant.*

The believer lives between the eschatological "already" and the "not yet," being conformed to and striving to conform to the image and character of Christ. The one who gains Christ not only has gained the benefits of the story of his life and death but has also been grafted into that story, for by analogy the pattern is repeated in the believer's life. For Paul there is a very close connection between theology and ethics, between Christology and paraenesis in the life of the believer. The imperative is grounded in the indicative, but the indicative is more than past facts or a set of beliefs. It is what God is continually doing in his community, and in the individuals who are part of it, to conform them to his Son's image.

One of the great paradoxes of Paul's thought is that at the very heart of his symbolic world, his gospel and his theologizing is a contingent historical event and God's response to it: the crucifixion and resurrection of Jesus of Nazareth. Here the eternal and the temporal, the contingent facts of history and the eternal truths of theology, come together. This should caution us against too static a model of Paul's theology. Theology is not just about what God is but also about what God has done, is doing and will do in the divine-human encounter in human history through Jesus Christ. Theology, then, is not a set of eternal truths of reason or an abstract philosophical system. Christian theology always has one foot in human history.

THIS STUDY HAS ALREADY DEALT WITH VARIOUS TEXTS THAT WERE PARAENETIC OR theological in character. This chapter aims to examine Paul's moral vision and ethical strategies and to consider various ways scholars have evaluated his God-talk in search of the center or heart of his theology. The discussion should be considered with a key question in mind: What sort of person writes such heavily theological and ethical letters? What do Paul's reflections on behavior and belief tell us about the ultimate concerns of the apostle to the Gentiles?

PAUL AND THE ETHICAL IMPERATIVE

In our world there is nothing so permanent as change, especially when it comes to norms for human behavior in Western society. Perhaps this is in part why the search for Paul as an ancient ethicist has yielded so many different proposals about how to analyze the data, but there is no general satisfaction with any of them. This book's earlier discussions of Paul as chauvinist or feminist, reformer or repressor, have brought to light some of these conflicting views.[1] We may well be ready to exclaim, "Will the real Paul please stand up!" Yet lest we become either too cynical or too impatient with discussions of Paul's ethics, there are recent developments, especially in sociological analysis, that are helping us get a clearer picture of what the historical Paul had in mind when he exhorted fellow believers.

It has become a commonplace in Pauline studies to say that the imperative is built on the indicative. To put it another way, what God has done in Christ and in the believer is seen as the basis for the exhortations and the means that makes obedience possible. If all of theology can be said to be grace, then all of ethics is the response of a grateful heart.[2] But since God's saving work through Christ is eschatological in character, Paul's ethic also has an eschatological cast and framework, as believers live between the already of what has been done in Christ and the not yet of what remains to be accomplished of the divine salvific work.

Wolfgang Schrage was right to stress the close connection between Paul's theology (including his Christology and eschatology) and his ethics, but Richard B. Hays goes too far in saying, "There is no meaningful distinction between theology and ethics in Paul's thought, because Paul's theology is fundamentally an account of God's work of transforming his people into the image of Christ."[3] Surely distinctions between Pauline theology and Pauline ethics are both possible and pertinent, but at the same time—and this is in the main the burden of what Hays is saying—connections are both necessary and crucial.[4] We will return to this whole matter of transformation into Christ's image. Here it will suffice to say that when Paul says to his converts "behave," he does not simply mean "believe," and vice versa.

One of the more important insights of recent research is that Paul offers

---

[1]See the earlier discussion.

[2]See the classic discussion in Victor Paul Furnish, *Theology and Ethics in Paul* (Nashville: Abingdon, 1968). A very useful survey of recent scholarly treatments of Pauline ethics can be found in W. L. Willis, "Bibliography: Pauline Ethics, 1964-1994," in *Theology and Ethics in Paul and His Interpreters: Essays in Honor of Victor Paul Furnish*, ed. E. H. Lovering Jr. and J. L. Sumney (Nashville: Abingdon, 1996), pp. 306-18.

[3]Richard B. Hays, *The Moral Vision of the New Testament* (San Francisco: Harper & Row, 1996), p. 46. Wolfgang Schrage, *Die konkreten Einzelgebote in der paulinischen Paranese* (Gutersloh: Mohn, 1961), shows quite well how Paul's ethics are both theologically grounded and situationally specific.

[4]For a useful summary of Hays's views see his "The Role of Scripture in Paul's Ethics," in *Theology and Ethics*, ed. E. H. Lovering Jr. and J. L. Sumney (Nashville: Abingdon, 1996), pp. 30-47.

a community-based and community-directed ethic.[5] Even when Paul comments on governing officials (Rom 13), he does so not to address or exhort such officials but to exhort his fellow Christians about how they should behave in relationship to those officials. We look in vain in Paul's letters for moral discourses that Paul might offer to the pagan world. Paul's belief and strategy is that change must come "in house" and that ethical demands work only in community, where there can be discipline, sanctions and shared norms.

The social character and social basis of Paul's ethical exhortation need to be kept firmly in view. Wayne Meeks has recently urged us to ask about the moral ethos of Paul's community. Paul is well aware that he is dealing with Christians who are only partially socialized into their new moral community. As 1 Corinthians shows, many of the Corinthians were still doing the things they had always done—frequenting prostitutes, going to court to gain advantages over one another, attending meals at idol temples, following usual rules of social stratification at meals in homes, even when those meals were supposed to be Christian meals that included the Lord's Supper ceremony. In such a situation Paul's moral task is to integrate belief and behavior, showing how certain kinds of behaviors are inconsistent with Christian beliefs ("you cannot partake of the table of demons and the table of the Lord," or "you cannot be one flesh with a prostitute while being one spirit with the Lord and his body").

But did Paul simply adopt an ethical strategy based on the structure of the Greco-Roman household and then apply those notions to the body of Christ? This is in essence the argument of Gerd Theissen, who says that Paul sought to overcome social divisions in Corinth through an ethic of "love patriarchalism."[6] There are at least two major problems with this assessment. First, had this been Paul's strategy in Corinth, we might expect to see a household code, or vestiges of it, being applied to the Corinthian situation. But apart from 1 Corinthians 14:33b-35, Paul makes very little attempt to connect the household with behavior in the family of faith in these letters. Second, we have already seen that when Paul does offer Christianized versions of household codes to his churches, he reforms the codes, modifying and mitigating some of their more patriarchal features.[7]

---

[5]Besides Hays, *Moral Vision*, see also Wayne A. Meeks, *The Moral World of the First Christians* (Philadelphia: Westminster Press, 1986), and his *The Origins of Christian Morality* (New Haven, Conn.: Yale University Press, 1993).

[6]See especially Gerd Theissen, *The Social Setting of Pauline Christianity* (Philadelphia: Fortress, 1982).

[7]See the earlier discussion.

He does not simply adopt Greco-Roman codes, nor even adapt them and try to soften their harshness by exhorting everyone to love each other.

The patriarchal family was not the model for the Christian community. The Christian community, led by apostles, prophets, teachers and others, met in homes and itself led to a reformed view of family and family structure. Women were allowed to use their gifts and serve as Paul's coworkers. They, as well as men, were encouraged to remain single if they had the gift for it (1 Cor 7). The new reality in Christ was shaping both the view of the Christian community and the physical family within that community.

A bit more on the social character and moral ethos of Paul's community can be added at this point. In a revealing study, Rodney Stark has pointed out how the high regard Christians had for life, and the high ratio of participation of women to men in early Christianity compared to some other first-century religions, made for some interesting situations. Christians in general were opposed to infanticide and abortion, the former of which especially targeted females.[8] Given the church's high regard for life in general, including the lives of female infants, girls and women, along the high number of female converts, "Christian women [came to enjoy] a favorable sex ratio . . . [which] . . . resulted in Christian women's enjoying superior status in comparison to their pagan counterparts."[9] A third crucial factor affecting female status and roles in the body of Christ was Paul's argument that women need not be married (1 Cor 7). This gave them fuller opportunities to serve the Lord as some of Paul's coworkers (e.g., Rom 16; Phil 4:2-3). Stark notes tellingly that as Christianity gained wider acceptance in the Empire and moved toward becoming the dominant religion, more and more men joined the faith, the favorable sex ratio for Christian women declined, and the roles open to women became far more limited.[10] So it was not Paul's love patriarchalism but the later patriarchal takeover of the church and its leadership structure that limited the roles of women in the body of Christ.

One of the keys to understanding Paul's ethics is the distinctions he draws between the family of faith and the physical family and the distinct ways he exhorts each group without simply amalgamating the two. As Ephesians 5:21—6:9 suggests, the direction of ethical influence moved from

---

[8]Paul's instruction to avoid *pharmakeia* may refer to abortion-producing drugs—see Galatians 5:20.

[9]Rodney Stark, *The Rise of Christianity* (Princeton, N.J.: Princeton University Press, 1996), p. 101. See also Ben Witherington III, chap. 1 in *Women in the Earliest Churches* (Cambridge: Cambridge University Press, 1988).

[10]Stark, *Rise of Christianity*, p. 108.

the primary family (the family of faith) to the secondary family, with the physical family being normed and reformed within the family of faith. This process is very much in evidence in Philemon, where Paul argues that now Onesimus must be seen as a brother and so as more than a slave. His Christian status should lead to his emancipation from the traditional family role of household slave.[11]

Paul by no means simply Christianized or baptized the Greco-Roman household structure, nor did he take his cues from that structure when he exhorted the body of Christ. For Paul, the role of the Spirit was too determinative in the body to allow for such an ethical move. Roles and functions in the body would largely be determined by gifts and graces, along with the social factor of who had the resources and venue to provide a safe private haven for Christian meetings. The evidence suggests that women, along with men, took the lead in hosting churches (cf. 1 Cor 16:15, 19 to Rom 16:1-3, 12; Acts 16).

In the wake of the work of E. P. Sanders, considerable stress has been placed on the Jewish character of Paul's ethics.[12] This stress is of course not new, and it is being even more strongly reiterated by Brian S. Rosner.[13] Rosner argues that Paul stands clearly within the matrix of pre-Christian Judaism in his ethics, exegesis and understanding of covenantal community. There is a great deal of truth in this approach. Paul is far more indebted to his Jewish heritage in ethics than to the ethics of Aristotle or other influential luminaries of the Greco-Roman world. But there are at least four problems or at least inadequacies with this approach, for it does not take into account (1) Paul's approach to the Mosaic law, (2) Paul's new covenant theology, (3) the christocentric essence of Paul's ethic or (4) Victor Paul Furnish's careful survey of texts where Paul does cite Scripture in his ethical arguments. Furnish concluded, "Paul never quotes the Old Testament *in extenso* for the purpose of developing a pattern of conduct. . . . [It is] never casuistically interpreted or elaborated. . . . There is no evidence which indicates that the apostle regarded [the Old Testament] as in any sense a source book for detailed moral instruction or even a manual of ethical norms."[14]

---

[11]See the earlier discussion of Philemon.

[12]See E. P. Sanders, *Paul and Palestinian Judaism* (Philadelphia: Fortress, 1977), particularly discussions about "staying in," pp. 431-523; also his *Paul, the Law and the Jewish People* (Philadelphia: Fortress, 1983).

[13]Brian S. Rosner, *Paul, Scripture and Ethics: A Study of 1 Corinthians 5—7* (Leiden: Brill, 1994).

[14]Furnish, *Theology and Ethics*, p. 33. Not many have been convinced by the arguments of P. J. Thomson, *Paul and the Jewish Law: Halakah in the Letters of the Apostle to the Gentiles* (Minneapolis: Fortress, 1990), that Paul's ethics are deeply grounded in rabbinic traditions of Halakic scriptural interpretation.

At its heart, Paul's ethic is about the imitation of Christ, not the reiteration of Torah. As Hays puts it, "Paul seeks to commend his normative moral teachings on the basis of the gospel itself: right behavior is understood as 'the fruit of the Spirit.'"[15] I differ from Hays, however, when he concludes that for Paul moral judgment is always a matter of discerning God's will rather than obeying a law. Paul is perfectly capable of insisting on obedience to a particular norm. But when a Christian is a mature person, Paul is more apt to appeal to them to use their wise Christian judgment. Even then, though, he would not want them to forget the commandments while discerning God's will. Thus when Hays says, "Ethics would not be a matter of casuistry, not a matter of reasoning through rules and principles, but of hearing the word of God and responding in imaginative freedom to embody God's righteousness,"[16] he is speaking not of the way Paul actually addresses or deals with his converts but of how ideally Paul might like to have done so. He would have been grateful not to issue commands but to simply witness the fruit of the Spirit and a voluntary following of the Christ paradigm. If all had been positive striving, "against which there is no law," Paul perhaps would have eschewed making demands, issuing imperatives or pointing out commandments. But this was far from the case, and in view of the ongoing struggle between flesh and Spirit, ethics does necessarily entail enunciating principles and norms. The law of Christ was not just a paradigm or human model; it also involved specific commandments such as the one to love.

Paul's view of the law has been discussed elsewhere in this book.[17] Here I will simply stress that if we fail to understand that Paul is essentially a sectarian person who is drawing on his heritage for a new social situation and community, we can fall into fundamental misunderstandings. Paul's failure to exhort Christians to observe the sabbath or be circumcised is more telling than his use of various Old Testament maxims and norms. This "selectivity" augurs a new situation where believers are no longer under and obligated to the law, which Paul consistently sees and refers to as a whole (see Gal 5:3).

In Galatians 4 Paul clearly articulates a theology of multiple covenants, and as Galatians 3—4 and 2 Corinthians 3 make evident, this means that he does not see Christians as under the law or Mosaic covenant precisely

---

[15]Hays, "Role of Scripture," p. 31.

[16]Ibid., p. 47.

[17]See the earlier discussion here and the more detailed discussion in Ben Witherington III, *Grace in Galatia* (Edinburgh: T & T Clark, 1998), pp. 341-55.

because Christians are part of the new covenant community. When Paul draws ethical material from the old covenant, he uses it because he believes it is now part of the "law of Christ," meant for the new covenant community. Paul's ethics are grounded in the eschatological situation inaugurated by Christ. He uses both Jewish and pagan material (cf., e.g., the last three virtues in the list in Phil 4:8, the end of the fruit of the Spirit in Gal 5:17, and the Aristotelian epithet "against which there is no law"). The issue thus must be not the source of a given piece of ethical material but how Paul uses this material and to what end. His purpose in using any material is to give shape or contour to the new life in Christ, and he draws on all sorts of ethical material to accomplish that aim.

In short, some Old Testament material is norm because Paul considers it consistent with or an extrapolation of the life and teaching of Christ, which is the ultimate ethical litmus test. By "the law of Christ" Paul means ethical teaching that reflects the character and mandates of Christ. Even the love commandment is stressed not because it is in the Mosaic law but because Christ adopted it for his followers. The old law and commandments are simply fulfilled in Christ and in his community, the eschatological community in which the promises and mandates of the old covenant come true. The new law is applied to the eschatological community of Christ as norm and imperative.

This new law, this new set of ethical imperatives, differs in some fundamental ways from the Mosaic law. We have seen, for example, how Romans 12:14-21 offers an ethic of nonresistance and of truly loving and blessing one's enemy. This stands in contrast to the *lex talionis* of the Mosaic covenant[18] and shows clearly how Christians are no longer under such a law, whether in its ritual or even its ritual dimensions.

The new ethic comes from the character and example of Christ, which Paul regularly exhorts Christians to follow. The story of Christ, both his life and his teaching, norms the story of Christians, including Paul's own story. Also, Paul believes that the Holy Spirit is busy conforming Christians to the image of Christ, not to the image of the Old Testament saints, not even Moses. The work of God in the believer has the same aim as the believer's own work and ethical striving—conformity to the image of Christ. Walking in step with the Spirit means moving in the shadow of Christ and working out that christoform shape the Spirit is working in.

In a recent exploration of Paul's moral vision, Richard Hays rightly argues that one of the main reasons we find Paul's ethics both allusive and

---

[18]See the earlier discussion.

elusive is that he is writing to communities with whom he has already been having an ongoing discussion about ethics and other matters. Paul can presume a certain understanding of the context and content of the discussions in these communities.[19] Equally helpful is Hays's critique of the older approaches of Martin Dibelius and H. D. Betz, who see Paul simply offering general ethical maxims rather than a specifically Christian ethic grounded in theology. Were such the case, the normative status of Paul's ethics must become tenuous. "When the Christian gospel moves in time or space to a different culture, one could presumably substitute a different set of cultural norms without difficulty."[20] Paul's fundamental connection between belief and behavior is seen in the way he regularly uses his theologizing to shape the behavior of his community (e.g., Phil 2:4-11). Furthermore, theology "is for Paul never merely a speculative exercise; it is always a tool for constructing community."[21]

Certain fundamental theological convictions undergird and guide the development of Paul's ethical remarks. N. T. Wright has suggested that a few key questions will illuminate how Paul's ethics work and why they take the form they do.

What time is it?[22] Paul's answer is that the church lives in the eschatological age, the time when all ages and all biblical prophecies and promises are coming to fruition (1 Cor 10:11). They live during a time when the form of this world is passing away, and there is no point in simply living according to its ways and mandates (1 Cor 7:31). They are living in the fullness of time, when the Messiah has come, has been born under the law, and has redeemed Jewish Christians such as Paul out from under the law (Gal 4:4-5).[23] It makes no sense for a Christian to submit to the law, for the law is obsolete now that Christ and his teaching and the presence of the Spirit have come. The law was intended as a guardian for God's people in a bygone age. The benefits promised by the law are now available through faith in Christ, and the essence of what the law required is fulfilled in Christ's life and death, and in another sense and to a lesser degree in the life of Christians who love and bear one another's burdens.

Yet the Old Testament, as Scripture, is still a source in Paul's hands not just for specific norms or ethical teaching but for narratives that provide

---

[19]Hays, *Moral Vision*, p. 16.

[20]Ibid., p. 18.

[21]Ibid.

[22]Both Hays, "Role of Scripture," pp. 34-39, and the discussion here follow some suggestions of N. T. Wright. See his *Jesus and the Victory of God* (Minneapolis: Fortress, 1996).

[23]See the earlier discussion of this eschatology.

paradigms and "types"—examples of positive and negative behavior. Paul is able to make this hermeneutical move not because he believes his converts are or should be under the law covenant but because, being a sectarian person, he identifies his community of Jew and Gentile united in Christ as the continuation of Israel. It is appropriate for such a community to draw on Israel's scriptural heritage even in the new age and as part of the norms of the new covenant.[24]

Another part of Paul's answer to the question "What time is it?" is that the believer lives between the advents, between already and not yet, between the beginning and the completion of being conformed to Christ's image. There is, as Hays says, a dialectical tension in the Christian life between now and not yet, especially because the "now" has thus far only affected the believer in the spirit and mind, while believers experience the "not yet" in the still fallen condition of the body (2 Cor 4:16-18). The believer is caught in a tug-of-war: inwardly a new person experiencing renewal of mind and spirit by the Holy Spirit's internal workings, outwardly having to deal with desires and inclinations to sin, called "flesh," so that the body is the weak link in the Christian's armor.

As Hays says, the eschatological "not yet" does not lead Paul to a radical interim ethic, useless for a later age that knows Christ did not come back in the first century. Rather, possible imminence leads to the exhortation to let the Lord find one doing what one ought to be doing while keeping one eye on the horizon. Like Gideon's warriors, Christians must continue with necessary daily tasks of drinking from the well of life, but with weapon in hand and eye on the horizon (1 Thess 3:6-13; cf. Judg 7:4-8). This orientation leads to heightened ethical concern, not a neglect of ethics. Preparation for what is to come does not mean neglect of what is at hand; rather, it places current obligations in the proper eschatological perspective.

> The eschatological perspective allows Paul to counsel a high tolerance for ambiguity. Suffering and joy are present together, and the church should expect this paradoxical condition to persist until the parousia. Nonetheless, the promise of God's ultimate making right of all things allows the community to live faithfully and confidently no matter how bad things may look at present.[25]

---

[24] Hays, "Role of Scripture," p. 39. Hays is right that Paul is not a supersessionist in the sense of believing a new community simply replaces the old. Yet Paul does believe that the church is *the* legitimate development of the true Israel and therefore the locus where God's promises are being fulfilled and the place where God's words should be heard and applied.

[25] Ibid., p. 26.

Furthermore, the "church community is God's eschatological beach-head, the place where the power of God has invaded the world. All Paul's ethical judgments are worked out in this context. . . . [Thus] . . . he is sharply critical not only of the old age that is passing away but also those who claim unqualified participation already in the new age."[26] The framework for Paul's ethical remarks is eschatological.

Who or what provides the ethical paradigm? The answer to this question is not the law but Christ, and in particular Christ in his humble, loving, self-sacrificial way of life, in his death on the cross, in his resurrection. Christ's teaching is brought into the discussion chiefly to flesh out these motifs (see Rom 12). Thus Hays is right that the cross is what undergirds and shapes Paul's ethics. "For Paul, Jesus' death on the cross is an act of loving self-sacrificial obedience that becomes paradigmatic for the obedience of all who are in Christ."[27] This should not, as Hays is right to add, be taken to mean that Paul simply sees the death of Christ as an ethical example. For Paul it is a unique and unrepeatable event that provides reconciliation and redemption for humankind. The cross has both theological significance and ethical implications. Philippians 2:4-11 shows Paul offering the cross as ethical example. Just as Christ suffered obediently to the point of death, so the Philippians should stand firm in the gospel, even if it should cost them their lives (Phil 1:27-30; 2:12). "The twin themes of conformity to Christ's death and imitation of Christ are foundational elements of Paul's vision of the moral life (. . . see Rom. 6:1-14; 8:17,29-30; 15:1-7; 1 Cor. 10:23-11:1; 2 Cor. 4:7-15; 12:9-10; Gal. 2:19-20; 5:24; 6:14)."[28]

Another excellent example of how the Christ paradigm works can be seen in Romans 15:1-13. Here Paul exhorts the strong to accept the weak for the sake of building up the community, following the example of Christ. Notice how the character of Christ's work is explained by a quotation of Psalm 69:9 (Rom 15:3). Paul then adds that Christ's welcoming of Jews and Gentiles (prefigured in various Scriptures—Ps 18:49; Deut 32:43; Ps 117:1; Is 11:10) is the paradigm, and so the Roman Christians should likewise welcome one another (Rom 15:7). Christ did not please himself but sought to serve and welcome others.[29] Perhaps the most striking rhetorical move in this passage is the portrayal of Christ as the speaker in the quotations from Psalms (Rom 15:3, 9). Is this itself simply following the historical example

---

[26]Ibid., p. 27.
[27]Ibid.
[28]Ibid., p. 31.
[29]See ibid., p. 41.

of Christ, who used psalms and other Old Testament texts to exegete his own experience (e.g., Mk 14:34; 15:34)? Or should we see this as a hermeneutical move in which the (preexistent) Son of God is seen as the speaking and praying voice that originally spoke these texts?[30] In my judgment the former is more likely, but the latter cannot be ruled out, for Paul clearly believes in the preexistence of the Christ (see 1 Cor 10:4).

The centrality of the Christ paradigm for Paul is further confirmed in the phrase "the faith [faithfulness] of Christ." As Hays stresses, this phrase is a summary allusion to the story of Christ's obedience even unto death on the cross. There are a series of texts we should consider in this connection—Romans 3:22, 26; Galatians 2:16, 20; 3:16; Philippians 3:9. Romans 3:22 raises a significant question: Where is the righteousness of God chiefly manifested? Is it chiefly manifested in the obedience of Christ unto death, his faithfulness in fulfilling God's will for his life, or is it chiefly manifested in the Christian's faith? In terms of the objective means of God's manifesting his righteousness, the answer must be Christ's obedience rather than the believer's. So Paul is saying that God justifies those who live out of and trust in Christ's faithfulness even unto death, which is (as 3:22c makes clear) of course an act of faith.[31]

Philippians 3:9 is quite similar in form to Romans 3:22. It may be rendered somewhat literally as "and be found in him, not having my own righteousness based on faith, the [sort that comes] from the law, but [that which comes] through the faithfulness of Christ, the from God righteousness based on faith." Like Romans 3:22-26, this is not an either-or proposition. The text refers to both the faithfulness of Christ and the faith of the believer. Here the very last phrase refers to the believer's faith. But when Paul wishes to discuss the objective means through which righteousness is made available to human beings, he contrasts the righteousness that comes from the law and the righteousness that comes through the saving acts of Christ. As in Romans 3:22, the *dia* ("through") clause refers to something that happened in and through Jesus' life, not through believers.

The Judaizers were not enemies of subjective Christian faith; they were enemies of the notion that the cross of Christ is both the means of right standing with God and the pattern for Christian life, as opposed to the law

---

[30]On this see Richard B. Hays, "Christ Prays the Psalms: Paul's Use of an Early Christian Exegetical Convention," in *The Future of Christology: Essays in Honor of Leander E. Keck*, ed. A. J. Malherbe and Wayne A. Meeks (Minneapolis: Fortress, 1993), pp. 122-36.

[31]For a more complete exposition of these key texts see Ben Witherington III, *Paul's Narrative Thought World* (Louisville, Ky.: Westminster John Knox, 1994), pp. 268-72. I differ from Hays in some of the particulars, e.g., in regard to the translation of Romans 3:26.

(Phil 4:18). What then does it mean to "gain Christ and be found in him"? It means to be incorporated into the story of Christ and so gain the benefits of his death and resurrection.[32] Paul's life, the life of the believer, arises out of the story of Christ and the events that made the proclaiming of that gospel possible.

In Galatians 2:16-20 the issue is once more how one obtains right standing or the righteousness that comes from God: Is it by works of the law or through the faith (faithfulness) of Jesus Christ? Of course in 2:16b Paul makes clear that this benefit comes to those who believe in Christ. But 2:16a and b should not be seen as a redundancy. Paul speaks of both the objective and the subjective means of obtaining right standing—the faithfulness of Christ and the believer's receiving by faith the benefits of Christ's faithfulness.

In verse 20 Paul says he has been crucified with Christ and Christ lives in him. This means that the story of Christ is recapitulated in his own life, but there is also a sense in which he has been grafted into the story of Christ so that he gets the benefit of Christ's death and resurrection.[33] Verse 22 goes on to make clear that the Abrahamic promises are conveyable to the believer because of and through the faithfulness of Christ. One must have faith in Christ's faithful act.

Pistis, which can mean both faith and faithfulness, is a crucial term for Paul—the term by which he links the story of Christ and the story of Christians. Christ is a paradigm of faithful living. Because of his faithful act of dying for sin, believers can die to sin; because he was raised, believers can arise and live in newness of life. Christ's faithfulness unto death can also be emulated by Christians under pressure and persecution. Those who have gained Christ have gained not only the benefits of the story of his life and death; they have been grafted into that story, so that by analogy the pattern is repeated in their lives. Christ's death as both experience and pattern norms the life of Christians and guides them along to the path to greater Christlikeness. These texts show the very close connection between theology and ethics, between Christology and paraenesis, in the life of the believer.

How then should believers live? This third question is as important as the

---

[32]The narrative framework that provides the final warrant for Paul's ethical guidance is larger than Christ's story. It involves scriptural stories that predate Christ's incarnation. In Paul's view, the story of Christ brings one to the turning point of the entire drama. See Hays, "Role of Scripture," pp. 34-35.

[33]Again I would differ from Hays's view that both halves of Galatians 2:20 refer to the faithfulness of Christ. See Witherington, *Grace in Galatia,* pp. 190-93.

previous two. Its answer has several dimensions: (1) imitate Christ, follow and fulfill the normative pattern of Christ and his teaching; (2) walk in the Spirit and do not fulfill the works of the flesh; (3) live as a community in unity. The Christian life has theological, cognitive, experiential and social dimensions.

Significantly, all these dimensions include elements of both experience and behavior. By the internal work of the Holy Spirit, the believer is being conformed to the image of Christ at the same time he or she is seeking to imitate Christ. The internal work of the Holy Spirit produces fruit, which the believer is called upon to manifest actively in behavior and relationships. By the internal work of the Spirit the believer has also been joined to the body of Christ; but he or she must act and behave in such a way that that body is served not severed, unified not divided.

Hays notes three "warrants" for obedience that are inherent parts of Paul's gospel. (1) Through union with Christ, we undergo transformation that should cause us to "walk in newness of life." (2) Because God has liberated us from sin's power, we should transfer our allegiance to the One who liberated us. (3) Because the Spirit is at work in the community of faith, the fruit of the Spirit should be exhibited in the community's life.[34] Notice the trinitarian character of these warrants. Pauline ethics is grounded in God, or better said in the divine saving activity that is part of the divine-human encounter. This produces new creatures with a new inward source of life, power and character formation—the Holy Spirit. The theological grounding of Paul's ethics also makes quite clear that his ethics are not simply ad hoc. Though Paul tailors his rhetoric to address the particular ethical situation of his converts, the substance of his ethical material comes from a deep preexisting well.

The flip side of the positive warrants is of course negative sanctions, and the major form of sanction is exclusion from final fellowship with God in Christ in the kingdom. Note that Paul offers such warnings *to those he considers Christians.*

Sometimes the sanction involves Christians' being saved but enduring judgment of their earthly works (cf. 1 Cor 3:10-15; Gal 6:7-9). It appears to be seen as fortunate that the judge of Christians will be Christ, to whom they must give an account of their behavior. Notice the progression in 2 Corinthians 5:9-10: "We make it our aim to please [God.] For all of us must appear before the judgment seat of Christ, so that each may receive recompense for what has been done in the body."

---

[34]Hays, "Role of Scripture," p. 39.

At times, though, Paul trots out the ultimate sanction—the danger of exclusion from the kingdom of God, apparently for major and habitual sin that is neither ceased nor repented of (1 Cor 6:9-11; Gal 5:19-21). Since the warning is addressed to Christians, it appears certain that Paul believes in the possibility of apostasy, either theological or ethical in character. One is not eternally secure until one is securely in eternity.[35] Yet Paul is not talking about "losing" one's salvation. He is talking about deliberately, through acts of rebellion, throwing it away. This possibility, however unlikely in any particular instance, has the effect of inculcating moral earnestness. While it may be said that good works cannot get a person into the kingdom, it appears that habitual bad works could in the end keep out someone who began as a Christian.

Much of Paul's ethical teaching has a significant social dimension. Its aim is not just to enhance personal virtue or one's relationship with Christ. Indeed, as is especially clear from Paul's discussion of the gifts of the Spirit in 1 Corinthians 14, personal benefit is only a byproduct of building up the community, edifying others and glorifying God. Each person is given such gifts for the common good.

Notice how we tend to misread a text like Philippians 2:12-13. Modern Western individualists have tended to see this as an exhortation to individuals to get on with earnest moral striving—but this overlooks the fact that Paul's *you* here is plural. Paul is saying, "Together, as a community, work out your [plural] own salvation with fear and trembling." The community, not the closet, is the place where salvation is worked out, expressed, manifested in deeds of piety and charity. The image of the race, with its disciplined effort of striving toward a goal, suggests that Paul believes that progress, even moral progress, is possible in the Christian life (Phil 3:12-14). Paul is not an early advocate of *simul justus et peccator,* if by the second half of that equation one means that progressive sanctification, victory over sin, growth and positive development in the Christian life are not possible.

As we have seen already, it is a mistake to think that Paul presents Romans 7:14-25 as the story of the Christian life.[36] The tension in the Christian life is not between old person and new person but between flesh and the Holy Spirit. Walk in the Spirit, says Paul, and you will not indulge the works of the flesh. Such statements do not make him an optimist or idealist in regard to human nature; they simply prove he really believes in the transforming power of God's grace operating in the believer by means

---

[35]See the earlier discussion.
[36]See the earlier discussion.

of the Holy Spirit.

The quest for the historical Paul as ethicist leads us, then, to discover that Paul does his ethics as a member of a community and directs his remarks to that community. Even his ethic of moral athleticism presupposes flexing one's muscles with not only "moral" support from the sidelines but actual team play to reach the goal line.

Paul believes that persons become what they admire, and so he holds up examples and paradigms for his converts to follow, chiefly that of Christ. It is this paradigm, and the fleshing out of it in Christ's teaching, that Paul calls the law of Christ. Paul was certainly not unwilling to command, but he preferred to persuade. He was not averse to urging good works, working out the community's shared salvation by means of piety and charity.

In his Christian manifesto of freedom, Galatians, he is not chiefly concerned with legalism versus libertinism or alien righteousness versus works righteousness. Rather, his concern is of a salvation-historical nature. Now that Christ has inaugurated a new covenant, Christ's followers ought not to impose or demand obedience to an obsolescent covenant.

Believers need to remember what time it is—that they stand between the already and not yet, between the beginning of the new age and its consummation. Believers wrestle with the tension between flesh and Spirit.

Paul's ethic of freedom does allow a place for patterns, models, norms and even commands when necessary. It allows for the law of Christ to replace the Mosaic law. It allows for the exhortation that habitual serious sin may keep someone who is presently a Christian from entering the final kingdom of God.

So ethics for Paul are community based and oriented, christoform in character and trajectory, involving both models and norms, both warrants and sanctions, and grounded from start to finish in Paul's narrative thought world, especially the story of Christ and God's people. There is no time, nor any need, to retrace steps to Sinai, since a path has been blazed by the pioneer, the Risen One, a path with clear boundaries and one that leads into the final Dominion of God. Believers must simply follow his lead and in his footsteps, remembering his instructions, and all will be well.

PAUL AND THE THEOLOGICAL INDICATIVE

The reader interested in Pauline theology may be forgiven for saying "Finally!" upon arriving at this last section of our study. Certainly, ever since the Reformation, Pauline theology has always been on the front burner of scholarly discussion, often to the neglect of Paul's ethics and a host of other Pauline topics. It has been kept on the front burner of late by the Society of Biblical Literature's Pauline Theology Group, which led to four major collections of articles on the subject and an important festschrift for Victor Paul Furnish. Here, once more, we are concerned with what Pauline theology tells us about Paul himself and the kind of person he was.

The nature of Paul's storied world was considered in the previous chapter.[37] As this study comes to a close, however, we need to reflect on some major elements of recent discussion about the character and center of Paul's theology. Several cautionary remarks are in order first.

The Starting Point

No letter by Paul, not even Romans, could be called a theological compendium or primer. Some letters have more theological substance (e.g., Romans), some have less (e.g., Philemon), but none are altogether devoid of theological substance. For a representative sampling of Paul's theological discourse, then, we must cast our net widely. If we were to make the mistake of taking Romans as a theological compendium, we might conclude that neither the Lord's Supper nor the resurrection was particularly important to Paul. Paul's letters are all occasional and situation-specific, and Romans is no exception.

J. D. G. Dunn has taken Romans—because he sees it as the Pauline letter least concerned with situation-specific concerns and a letter written to a church Paul didn't found—as the key clue to how Paul would do a theology, how he would set out and defend his mature understanding of the gospel.[38] But there are several problems with this approach. (1) As just noted, major components of Paul's gospel are missing from Romans (e.g., any substantive treatment of the resurrection). (2) Paul also wrote Colossians to a church he did not found, but that does not make that letter not situation-specific. (3) Getting to Romans 9—11, one strongly suspects that Paul really was all along driving toward these remarks for Gentile Christians in Rome who had doubts about a gospel that was for the Jew first, or even still for the Jew. In other words, Romans is not Paul's generic telling of the gospel, but a letter to a largely Gentile church that did not understand the place of Jews and Israel in the plan of God, the relationship of Jews and Gentiles in that plan, and the nature and goal of the redemption wrought in Christ: to create one people of God, Jew and Gentile united in Christ.

---

[37]See the earlier discussion.
[38]J. D. G. Dunn, *The Theology of Paul the Apostle* (Grand Rapids, Mich.: Eerdmans, 1997), p. 25.

Sometimes scholars have prematurely narrowed the field of Pauline theology by eliminating certain letters as *necessarily* un-Pauline because their authenticity is under debate. It would be better first to see whether a letter adds anything to the discussion and evaluate the consistency of its substance with the undisputed Paulines. Then one could make appropriate critical judgments. Furthermore, it is a mistake to dismiss the possibility that we might learn anything about Paul's theology from examining the speeches attributed to him in Acts. This is especially a mistake if indeed Luke was a sometime companion of Paul, particularly if he heard the famous Miletus speech (Acts 20:17-38). Still, our primary source for discerning Paul's theology must be the Pauline letters themselves, and especially the capital or undisputed Paulines which have more theological substance than the Pastoral Epistles.

Paul's theology is embedded within rhetorical arguments, which in turn are found in an epistolary framework.[39] Theology cannot just be read off the surface of the letters; often the meaning of a text will be missed if one does not recognize the rhetorical function of a given piece of material. In each letter Paul has an overall argumentative focus, purpose and strategy, and the parts and individual arguments need to be seen in relationship to the whole. Careful attention to the *propositio* (the purpose statement) or the *peroratio* (the summary of major arguments) of these letters will provide definite clues as to Paul's rhetorical aims and main concerns and how he may use theological material to address those aims. For example, Galatians 2:15-21 as a *propositio* shows that justification is a very important matter for Paul, even though it appears prominently only in Galatians and Romans.

Beyond this, there is the question of the sources and development of Paul's theology—a matter that has already been addressed in a couple of places in this study. I have suggested that the major developments in Paul's thought happened before any of the letters were written, and that his conversion was the pivot that produced a Copernican revolution in his thinking. This is not to deny that there is some evidence of development from the earlier to later letters—for example, in the matter of cosmic Christology (Christ as Lord over the universe)—but on the whole all of Paul's letters reflect the mature thinker. C. K. Barrett puts it this way: it is not

> possible (except at one or two points) to trace lines of development in his thinking. This has been tried (notably by C. H. Dodd) but without success. The attempt, for example, to trace development in his eschatological thinking from

[39]See H. D. Betz, "Paul," in *Anchor Bible Dictionary*, ed. D. N. Freedman (New York: Doubleday, 1992), 5:192.

a strictly futuristic view in the earliest letters to one in which he saw eschatological conditions as already realized in the present, founders on the recur-
rence in what is probably the latest of his letters of the old futuristic view:
Philippians 3:20, 21 . . . (cf. 1 Cor. 15:23; 1 Thess. 4.15-17).[40]

H. D. Betz summarizes the sorts of questions scholars have raised about
these matters:

> Did he work with a fixed theological "system" in the back of his mind? Or did
> he develop his arguments *ad hoc*, based only on a limited set of assumptions?
> Did Paul have a consistent theology throughout his apostolic career, or did his
> theology gradually evolve in the context of mission and controversy in which
> he was constantly involved? If he worked with a fixed theological system, was
> that system pre-Christian (Pharisaic, rabbinic, or apocalyptic) with his
> Christian convictions simply overlaid or appended? Or was his theology
> something altogether new that grew out of his vision of Christ and his
> commission to take the gospel to the gentiles? In short, how creative and
> dynamic a theologian was the apostle Paul?[41]

There are several problems even with the way these questions are
framed. In the first place, few if any scholars would want to suggest that
Paul was operating with a "fixed theological system" that he simply
brought over into his Christian life. This way of putting matters is anachronistic, to say the least. Furthermore, the either/ors in some of these
questions could just as well be both/ands. For example, Paul could have
had a rather consistent theology throughout his Christian life, yet this
theology could have undergone some development as he pursued some
lines of thought that needed fleshing out. In fact, I suggest that this is
basically the way we should view Pauline theology, even though today it is
all too common to simply accuse Paul of blatant contradictions from one
letter to the next.

Paul's view of the law especially comes in for this sort of criticism.[42] I
have responded to such criticism of Paul's view of the law elsewhere.[43]
Dunn properly warns us to use "contradiction" as a hermeneutic only as a
last resort:

---

[40]On the attempt and failure to find development in Paul's eschatological thinking see C. K.
Barrett, *Paul: An Introduction to His Thought* (Louisville, Ky.: Westminster John Knox, 1994),
pp. 55-57. Barrett thinks it probable that the major development in Paul's thought came before
the writing of all the letters.

[41]Betz, "Paul," p. 192.

[42]See, e.g., Hans Hübner, *Law in Paul's Thought* (Edinburgh: T & T Clark, 1984), although he is
arguing for a conscious change of mind. On contradictions see especially H. Räisänen, *Paul
and the Law* (Tübingen: Mohr, 1983).

[43]See Witherington, *Grace in Galatia*, pp. 341-55.

Basic to good exegesis is respect for the integrity of the text, and in the case of someone like Paul, respect for his intellectual calibre and theological competence. Such a respect includes a constant bearing in mind the possibility or indeed likelihood that the situations confronting Paul were more complex than we can now be aware of, or include important aspects which are now invisible to us.[44]

This judicious remark also reminds us that there are various *aporia*, or gaps, in our knowledge of Pauline theology. A "systematic" or reasonably comprehensive analysis of his thought is quite impossible. Paul does not comment on a host of important topics, so we have no idea what his views were on them (e.g., the virginal conception of Jesus); he touches on other subjects only briefly or allusively (e.g., a proper theology of baptism).[45] Yet the fact that Paul addresses particular situations does not mean he was not a coherent and even systematic thinker. As Barrett argues, beyond "the occasionalism of Paul's theology there is a real unity; he reacts to circumstances spontaneously but he does not react at random; he reacts in accordance with principles, seldom stated as such but detectable."[46]

Again, Betz's either/ors can be taken as both/ands. For instance, did Paul bring a good deal of theology into Christianity from Judaism, or was he theologically dynamic and creative? Clearly both can be the case. There is much to be said about Paul's indebtedness to his Jewish heritage; nevertheless, he often transforms what he takes over, especially in light of the Christ event and its implications. For example, in 1 Corinthians 8:6 Paul cites the Shema ("Hear, oh Israel . . ." [Deut 6:5]), but he bifurcates the references such that *God* refers to the Father and *Lord* refers to Jesus Christ. Similarly, Paul takes over the Pharisaic notion of resurrection at the eschaton, but he introduces the first and latter fruit concept in order to account for Jesus' resurrection as an isolated event prior to the general resurrection

---

[44]J. D. G. Dunn, "Works of the Law and the Curse of the Law (Galatians 3:10-14)," *New Testament Studies* 31 (1985): 523. See also J. P. Sampley, "From Text to Thought World," in *Pauline Theology*, vol. 1, *Thessalonians, Philippians, Galatians, Philemon*, ed. J. M. Bassler (Philadelphia: Fortress, 1991), p. 4.

[45]Some think we have a reasonably clear idea about Paul's theology of baptism. However, Paul does not seem to equate water baptism with Spirit baptism as it is discussed in, for example, 1 Corinthians 12:13. This text would appear to read "by one Spirit we have all been baptized into one body." This must be compared to Paul's thankfulness that he had not water-baptized more of his converts (1 Cor 1:14-17) and his statement that God did not send him to perform a water rite. In short, Paul is quite capable of distinguishing between conversion and initiation, with the former being critical and happening in response to the preached word (cf. Rom 10), and the latter clearly being less critical. On this matter see J. D. G. Dunn, *Baptism in the Holy Spirit* (London: SCM Press, 1970).

[46]Barrett, *Paul*, p. 56.

of the righteous (1 Cor 15).

Assessing continuity versus discontinuity with Judaism in Paul's thinking is critical. As a sectarian person, Paul over and over again takes up and uses his Jewish heritage but modifies it in light of his understanding of the Christ event. This modification is profound, not trivial, affecting the way he views the nature of God, the function and purpose of the law, who the true people of God are, the criteria for being in that people, and the coming fulfillment of all things will be brought about.

A recent discussion about how we get at Paul's theology, in volume four of the Society for Biblical Literature's *Pauline Theology,* makes some helpful and telling distinctions. For example, should we identify Paul's theology with his symbolic world—that fount of images, ideas and stories he draws on in expressing his theology? Or should his theology be identified with the activity of theologizing in response to particular situations (an activity reflected in the letters)? Or is Paul's theology the final product that is the result of theologizing, such that *we* order and synthesize the pieces we find and call this Paul's theology?

Furnish appropriately presses for a distinction between Paul's gospel, his bedrock convictions and beliefs about the death and resurrection of the crucified Jesus, and Paul's theology and theologizing, which is done on the basis of those core convictions.[47] In fact, one can go further and say that what we have in Paul's letters is the second-order additions, further explanations and corrections that Paul offers those who have already heard his gospel and now need more information. When we talk about Paul's gospel from this perspective, we mean not just his convictions but also his proclamation that led to his having converts in the first place. Clearly Paul's letters are addressed to those who are already Christians, much like modern preaching in the church, and this will not be identical with what he would have said to unbelievers, though of course there must have been overlap in content between the two kinds of communication.

Moreover, Paul's theology should not be identified simply with his storied world, because to a large extent he shared that storied world with other early Christians. It is what Paul *does* with the articulation and application of that storied world that constitutes his theologizing.

Finally, Paul W. Meyer's plea and proposal is apt: "Instead of assuming most of the time that Paul's 'theology' or 'convictions' are the resource or starting-point from which he addresses the issues placed before him, may

---

[47]Victor Paul Furnish, "Where Is 'the Truth' of the Gospel," in *Pauline Theology,* vol. 4, *Looking Back, Pressing On,* ed. E. E. Johnson and D. M. Hay (Atlanta: Scholars Press, 1997), pp. 161-77.

one rather . . . think of them more consistently as the end product and result, the *outcome to* which he arrives in the process of his argument, his 'hermeneutic' or his 'theologizing'?"[48] This statement stands in danger of confusing Paul's theologizing with his theology, but Meyer clarifies it by saying that Paul's theology is not the father but the child of his theologizing.

Thus we are led to at least a threefold or fourfold equation, as follows.

First, there are Paul's bedrock beliefs—his symbolic universe or storied world. This is not his theology but the convictions out of which he does his preaching and theologizing.

Second, there is Paul's gospel, the initial articulation of those beliefs for a non-Christian audience. Paul's gospel is not entirely a Pauline creation (as if we could also talk about Peter's gospel or Apollo's gospel) but something he mostly shared with his fellow early Christians—though clearly Paul added something, namely the gospel's implications for and applications to Gentiles. The unique revelation of Christ he received on the Damascus Road led him to couch the gospel as a grace-filled and law-free message to Gentiles.

Third, there is theologizing, which we see in progress in Paul's letters. Paul's theologizing is done on the basis of his convictions, his storied world and his earlier proclamation of the Gospel.

Finally, there is theology, the results of Paul's theologizing. We do not have a compendium of this anywhere. We must deduce it from a careful analysis of his theologizing, which was always a contingent exercise, of expressing his thinking in a particular way for a particular audience at a particular time.

It is one of the great paradoxes of Paul's thought (and early Christian thought in general) that the very heart of his symbolic world, his gospel and his theologizing is a contingent historical event and God's response to it: the crucifixion and resurrection of Jesus of Nazareth. Here the eternal and the temporal, the contingent facts of history and the eternal truths of theology come together. This should warn us against too static a model of Paul's theology. Theology is not just about who God is but also about what God has done, is doing and will do in the divine-human encounter in history through Jesus Christ.

Theology, then, is not some set of eternal truths of reason or an abstract philosophical system. Christian theology always has one foot in history, and the Christian theologian must always say, "Now we see through a

---

[48]P. W. Meyer, "Pauline Theology: A Proposal for a Pause in Its Pursuit," in *Pauline Theology* 4:150.

glass darkly, but then face to face; now we know in part, then we shall know as we are known." Paul's theology looks different to various scholars largely because they assemble the pieces of his theologizing differently; some are more prone to abstract the pieces from their original historical contexts, and some do this less.

How we get at the heart or center of Paul's theology is a complex issue. As J. P. Sampley says,

> Paul holds fundamental matters in his thought world together in a delicate equilibrium: the faithfulness and the freedom of God, for example, or what is already and what is not yet available to the believer. . . . It is not a case of either/or, but both/and—and not only of both/and, but both/and in equilibrium. . . . Precisely because Paul's thought is cast in balances and not in isolated ideas, the nuclear model with its single "center" is not adequate.[49]

Sampley offers up an electromagnetic model, with no single charge sufficient to set up a field. While this is not a "static" model, the model of narrative with major themes, climax and denouement makes better sense of Paul's theology. For example, justification by grace through faith is certainly a key idea for Paul, but it has to do with how one gets into the body of Christ. Positionally, the heart of the story of Christians for Paul has to do not just with Christ but with being in Christ, not just about getting into Christ's body but about growing in Christ. Yet the heart of the story of Christians is not the generative center of Paul's theology. The heart in that sense is the death and resurrection of Jesus. This is gospel proper for Paul.[50]

Justification has to do with the entrance way, the door or, in narrative terms, the opening or catalyst that sets the story in motion. The objective work of Christ and its initial subjective benefits to those who respond in faith form the essence of Paul's initial teaching and preaching. Since all of his letters are written to those who are already Christians, it is not surprising that he does not spend lots of time on how one gets in. It is only when, as with the Galatians, a sort of amnesia has set in that Paul must go back and review the "first things" and what believers gained upon their entrance. Then he can speak to them directly about "going on" in Christ and not making the mistake of submitting to the Mosaic law.

Still, Sampley is quite right that in almost all of his letters Paul is responding to imbalance and lack of understanding:

---

[49]Sampley, "From Text to Thought World," p. 6.
[50]For a useful classical statement of Paul's theology with some critique of Sanders's "covenantal nomism" approach to Judaism and Paul's view of the law see Barrett, *Paul*, pp. 55-142.

When Paul sees one of these delicate balances twisted askew by his churches or by his opponents, he usually responds not by reaffirming the balance but by stressing the neglected pole. . . . Thus, for example, he responds to the Corinthians' individualistic enthusiasm by stressing their communal claims and responsibilities. So the *nature* and *degree* of Paul's polemical or apologetical intent and his rhetorical strategy must be discerned if our interpretation is to recover what Paul would have seen as the proper balance.[51]

To understand Paul's theology, then, we must understand his method of argumentation, which is to say we must understand his use of rhetoric.[52] Neglect of this factor has caused all sorts of distorted analyses of Paul's thought world, his intent and the content of his thought.

This leads to a list of desideratum for those who wish to prepare to understand Paul's thought world, his gospel and his theologizing:
- a thorough knowledge of the Hebrew Scriptures and the Septuagint
- a thorough knowledge of early Judaism
- a thorough knowledge of early Christianity
- a thorough knowledge of the ancient art of persuasion
- a thorough knowledge of the social matrix of the Greco-Roman world in which Paul's converts lived, including ancient social networks, social structures, core Greco-Roman values, theories of ancient personality and anthropology

Armed with this knowledge, one will be in a position to assess where both the author and the audience stand in the dialogue and what influences, ideas and stories are being exchanged, debated and discussed. Paul's letters are indeed conversations set in contexts. The more one knows about the contexts—literary, rhetorical, historical, theological, social—the less likely one is to misread the content of the letters and so misread Paul's thought.

Inductive or Deductive

The recent series of books on Pauline theology deriving from participants in the Pauline Theology Seminar of the SBL have raised again the question whether an understanding of Pauline theology can be built up, brick by brick, or whether one needs to have a blueprint in hand to see the structure of things.[53] I suggest that both inductive and deductive procedures are

[51]Sampley, "From Text to Thought World," p. 7.
[52]Ibid., p. 8.
[53]See also D. M. Hay, ed., *Pauline Theology*, vol. 2, *1 and 2 Corinthians* (Minneapolis: Fortress, 1993); D. M. Hay and E. E. Johnson, eds., *Pauline Theology*, vol. 3, *Romans* (Minneapolis: Fortress, 1995).

needed. One must look at the letters separately but realize they are only part of a larger discussion and express only part of Paul's thoughts, and that the expression is articulated to address the situation at hand. One must also look at the letters together, and I agree with Sampley that looking at the letters together will yield more data than will original investigations of individual letters. Dunn is quite right to plead for a theology of *Paul* rather than just a theology or theologies of his individual letters.[54] For example, the principle enunciated in 1 Corinthians 10:23-24 about not seeking one's own way is reiterated in Philippians 2:4. This shows this is an established principle in Paul's thought world, one he is prepared to reiterate in different situations.[55] Paul's letters are by no means entirely ad hoc, though his thought is expressed or articulated in ways that make it a word on target for a specific audience.

Letters do not have theologies, people do. It is therefore a methodological mistake to look for the "theology" of a particular Pauline letter, as if these letters were discrete units with self-contained semantic fields and thought worlds. They are not. The letters express a portion of the mind of Paul about various subjects. That mind did not cease working after he had written a particular letter, nor did it fully express itself in any one letter. Nor is any one topic fully discussed in any one letter. Paul's thought must not be abstracted from what we can learn about Paul as an ancient person. A history-of-ideas approach to Paul's letters will always lack the "personal" touch necessary to grasp what Paul is up to and what he means. More will be said on this point in the conclusion of this chapter.

Sampley has set up a series of tests that can be applied to the letters to help us get at what theological and ethical matters Paul thinks are really important:

1. Look for a positive repeated pattern, such as the example cited above from Philippians 2:4 and 1 Corinthians 1:9, cf. 2 Corinthians 1:18.

2. What does Paul say that is evident, clear or plain? For example, it is clear that no one is justified by the law (Gal 3:11; cf. 1 Cor 15:27).

3. When does Paul simply dismiss or write off an idea, attitude or action (2 Cor 10:12)?

4. What matters are treated as among the "indifferent things" (*adiaphora;* Rom 14:5-9; 1 Cor 7:19; Gal 6:15)?

---

[54]Dunn, *Theology of Paul,* p. 17: "In enquiring about the theology of Paul it is simply not realistic to attempt to confine ourselves to the theologies of Paul's individual letters. At best that would give us the theology of Paul's controversies rather than the theology of Paul."

[55]Sampley, "From Text to Thought World," p. 10.

5. What does Paul expect from all his churches (1 Cor 11:16; 14:33b) or all believers (Phil 4:4)?

6. What does Paul say one is never to do (Rom 12:11, 16, 19)?

Actually most of these dicta are more focused on what ethical or practical matters Paul deems important, except 1 and 2.

Sampley, however, offers a few more useful tests. For example, he asks, what can the structures of Paul's arguments tell us about primary assumptions within Paul's thought world? For example, when Paul offers rhetorical questions, or questions where the answer is assumed to be already known, he is probably getting at something rather fundamental (cf. 1 Cor 10:22; Gal 3:21). Similarly, the "if" part of an "if . . . then" statement shows what Paul takes as a given, and such a statement also reveals something of the connections entailed in Paul's logic (Gal 4:7). Finally, consider some of Paul's theological maxims that are simply asserted, not argued for (e.g., "God is not a God of confusion"—1 Cor 14:33). There is much to commend in Sampley's analysis. He moves us some way toward getting at Paul's theology without ignoring Paul the person or the contexts of his thought world.

Contingency or Coherency

The work of J. C. Beker has sparked what is often called the contingency-coherency debate. Beker has made his case in various venues, but his contribution to the Pauline Theology Seminar of the SBL appears to be his most nuanced piece.[56] He begins with an assumption that is largely uncontroversial—that Paul was not a systematic theologian or even a pastoral counselor but an interpreter of both the Old Testament and Christian traditions, which he reformulates in distinctive and creative ways. Paul then is seen as more of a reformulator than a creator.

There is a large measure of truth to this assessment, yet Paul's gospel includes some distinctive notes that he claims came to him as part of—or as a result of reflecting on—his initial vision of Christ (Gal 1). These elements did not come to him from either Judaism or early Jewish Christianity. The law-free gospel for the Gentiles, focusing on justification by grace through faith followed by walking in the Spirit according to the law or pattern of Christ, probably did not come to Paul from his oral and written sources.

By "coherence" Beker means those stable or constant elements that

---

[56]See J. Christiaan Beker, "Recasting Pauline Theology: The Coherence-Contingency Scheme as Interpretive Model," in *Pauline Theology* 1:15-24.

express the "truth of the gospel," the "convictional basis of Paul's proclamation."[57] To defect from the truth of the gospel is in Paul's view tantamount to apostasy. This is Paul's *sine qua non* of Christian belief and faith.
By "contingency" Beker means the variable element, "that is, the variety
and particularity of sociological, economic, and psychological situations
which Paul faces in his churches."[58] This definition of contingency differs
from what Beker seemed to be saying in his major work *Paul the Apostle: The
Triumph of God in Life and Thought.* There it appeared he was talking about
the contingency of some of Paul's thought or teaching, but the more recent
definition refers to the varied contingent situations Paul faces and must
address, which affect how he must express himself to offer a word on
target. If Beker is simply suggesting that Paul distills certain key teachings
into a form to address a particular situation, this conclusion is uncontroversial.[59] But the language of "core," "center," "stable" or "constant"
elements suggests that peripheral, unstable or infrequent elements exist in
Paul's thought as well. This way of putting things does not suggest merely
contingent situations or particular ways of expressing core truths.

Beker believes, moreover, that "Jewish apocalyptic is the substratum and
master symbolism of Paul's thought because it constituted the linguistic
world of Paul the Pharisee and therefore the indispensable filter, context,
and grammar by which he appropriated and interpreted the Christ-event."
Thus he sees the interaction between the coherent and contingent as "the
conjunction of the apocalyptic substratum with contingent contexts."[60] But
it is Paul's thought that addresses these contexts, not the apocalyptic
substratum, however indebted Paul may be to such Jewish material. Beker
believes that apocalyptic motifs dominate Paul's thought and that Paul
modifies these motifs to communicate his gospel. He goes on to say,
though, that it is the apocalyptic *interpretation* of the death and resurrection
of Jesus Christ that constitutes the coherence of Paul's gospel.

Beker refers first to apocalyptic substratum, then to apocalyptic motifs,
then to apocalyptic interpretation. But these are by no means all one and
the same. And if the death and resurrection of Jesus is at the heart of Paul's
gospel, at least the crucified Christ part of that message is certainly not
indebted to Jewish apocalyptic. Nor is the notion of a crucified and risen
messiah indebted to that source. Furthermore, the notion of resurrection is
not exclusively found in apocalyptic literature or formulations. One of the

---

[57]Ibid., p. 15.
[58]Ibid.
[59]See J. Christiaan Beker, *Paul the Apostle* (Philadelphia: Fortress, 1980), p. 351.
[60]Beker, "Recasting," p. 17.

problems with Beker is that he does not adequately distinguish between eschatological and apocalyptic motifs, and usually what he means by "apocalyptic" is the expectation of an imminent end—something that is by no means characteristic of all apocalyptic literature.[61] Beker's argument is thus marred by both terminological and conceptual confusion.

Hermeneutical flexibility is not the same as exegetical or theological fluidity. Yet Beker is correct in saying that Paul "formulated more clearly than other early Christian theologians the coherent structure of the gospel, that is the abiding truth of the gospel, and so bequeathed to Christianity the beginnings of a doctrinal 'orthodox' structure."[62] Beker also notes accurately that Paul was a pragmatic hermeneutician. This still does not resolve the issue of what would constitute noncore ideas, noncentral concepts, nonessential or at least peripheral theology for Paul.

It becomes clear that Beker offers the coherence-contingency model as an alternative to certain developmental models of Paul's thought. I agree with him that we may apply a hermeneutic of suspicion to hypothetical chronologies of Paul's life that are now being used to generate a new reading of the order of Paul's letters and so of the development of his thought.[63] Beker is also right to ask whether development could not simply be along the same trajectories as before or whether we must see the old coherent core being replaced by new ideas.

Beker is rightly suspicious of this latter understanding of development, given the lack of hard evidence to support it. In an important essay Eduard Lohse has argued at some length that while Paul changed his modes of expression, he did not change his fundamental theological thought. His theology is better described not as linear and developing but as complex and dialectical.[64] I would prefer to say that his *theologizing* is complex and dialectical.

Beker sees the coherence-contingency model as a hedge against the notion that there was no enduring core to Paul's thought. He also sees it as

---

[61]See the nuanced discussions by J. J. Collins, *The Apocalyptic Imagination* (New York: Crossroad, 1984).

[62]Beker, "Recasting," p. 19.

[63]See the later discussion of Pauline chronology.

[64]Eduard Lohse, "Change of Thought in Pauline Theology? Some Reflections on Paul's Ethical Teaching in the Context of His Theology," in *Theology and Ethics in Paul and His Interpreters*, ed. E. H. Lovering Jr. and J. L. Sumney, p. 160. Lohse is basically following Furnish's seminal essay and its conclusion. See Victor Paul Furnish, "Development in Paul's Thought," *Journal of the American Academy of Religion* 38 (1970): 289-303. I like Lohse's suggestion that we think of an unfolding and articulation of Paul's thought in response to situations, and I agree that the fundamental change in his thought came at the beginning of his Christian life.

a *via media* between the extremes of pure contingency (pure sociological analysis of Paul's thought) and a dogmatic imposition of a specific center on Paul's thought. He rests in the belief of a dialectical back-and-forth between the truth of the gospel and its becoming a word on target for people's particular lives.[65]

In his critique of both Sampley and Beker, Paul J. Achtemeier rightly notes some of the "incoherencies" and "incongruities" especially in Beker's analysis.[66] Achtemeier, like Beker, is doubtful about attempts to see development in Paul's thought based on a certain ordering of his letters, since such an ordering is always to some extent hypothetical. He also agrees with Beker against those who would see Paul as inept and his letters replete with contradictions. Rather, "Paul was a coherent thinker—and often far more skilled in rhetoric than his critics want to believe. Careful attention to language, rhetorical structure, and context will often show supposed contradictions to rest more with careless exegesis than with Paul."[67]

Achtemeier faults Beker for lack of clarity of method. How does one discern what Paul regarded as peripheral and what he saw as core? Where in particular do we find expressions of this core? If there is a reciprocal and circular interaction of coherency and contingency as Beker suggests, does this not mean that in fact there is no bedrock, no real lasting core? Again, is contingency a matter of the means or mode of expression in view of the contingent situation, and/or a matter of elements on the outskirts of Paul's thought world? Beker seems to mean the latter, though sometimes he expresses himself in terms of the former.

Achtemeier agrees with Beker that the apocalyptic framework constitutes a noncontingent element in Paul's gospel and was part of the ongoing solution that Paul offered to his churches. Yet Achtemeier is far less shy about delineating that central core of essential beliefs. It has to do with the crucified and risen Christ, with the resurrection said to be an absolute sine qua non in 1 Corinthians 15. Achtemeier believes that the autobiographical Philippians 3:4-14 reveals a good deal of what Paul now sees as peripheral or able to be counted as loss, as well as what is crucial—righteousness,

---

[65]Beker, "Recasting," p. 24. Note that Beker also is not satisfied with E. P. Sanders's distinction between Paul's basic convictions and their varied expressions (cf. Sanders, *Paul, the Law and the Jewish People,* pp. 147-48). The problem with this distinction is that one divorces one's convictions from their linguistic expression, and thus what is behind the text becomes crucial or central but exists only in the mind of Paul. I agree with Beker that we cannot arrive at a psychological "middle" or center of Paul's thought apart from Paul's self-expression in his letters.

[66]Paul J. Achtemeier, "Finding the Way to Paul's Theology," in *Pauline Theology* 1:25-36.

[67]Ibid., p. 27.

faith, suffering, resurrection.[68] If Achtemeier is right, Dunn's proposal to use Romans as the essential expression of Paul's gospel is significantly compromised.

Achtemeier's discussion of Sampley's views leads to an interesting insight: If we are trying to determine and understand *Paul's* theology, it really does not matter whether Paul understands the problems he is addressing correctly. It does not really matter whether he understands his opponents' real views. Whether or not he has read the situation right, "Paul will draw in his arguments from the same gospel and will apply what he draws in the same way whether his perception of the situation corresponds to the perception of others or not."[69]

In other words, we cannot know for sure whether Paul's word is a word on target, whether it really has been fine-tuned in just the right way to address the contingent situation, as we have no independent witness to the situation or to the views of Paul's interlocutors. For the purposes of determining Paul's *own* theology, the audience and their views and situation do not much matter. This is all the more the case if contingency is not a matter of content but of how Paul's theology is articulated and what part of it is expressed on what occasion. Further, if contingency, qua Beker's definition (see above), has to do with the situation addressed, it has even less to do with figuring out Paul's theology.

Mirror-Reading in the Dark

Mirror-reading of Paul's letters to figure out what views he opposes is a difficult art that leads to far from certain results.[70] This is not to say that such a practice should be avoided at all costs;[71] it is simply to say that Paul's theology should be evaluated primarily on its expression and what lies in the background of such expression (both in his life and in his larger thought and social world), not what lies in the foreground. Of efforts to construct Paul's theology on the basis of what he is assumed to be reacting to, one can only say, "That way lies madness." When one enters the halls of mirror-reading, one almost always ends up seeing one's own reflection or whatever else one projects into the mirror. And if the mirror used is not perfectly made, there will be distortion, however clever and careful a

---

[68]Ibid., pp. 30-31.

[69]Ibid., p. 32.

[70]See the earlier description of mirror-reading.

[71]I would say mirror-reading to some extent enables the reader to understand Paul's audience and their situation. Whether it is necessary for understanding Paul's theology is another question.

reader-between-the-lines one may be.

Achtemeier echoes Sampley's concern for the finely balanced nature of Paul's thought, for the dynamic way he can express the same idea in a variety of formulas instead of merely trotting out fixed maxims (though quotation is also part of his modus operandi) and for the insistence that Paul's rhetoric and rhetorical purposes is a key to the form and function of his thought, especially since his thought comes to us in the form of rhetorical arguments.[72]

In the end, Achtemeier suggests that Paul must be seen as a coherent and logical thinker. In particular he argues that when Paul's view of Jesus Christ changed, he was forced to systematically reevaluate such things as the resurrection, the law, the character of God's people, the nature of salvation, the proper manner in which God's people should live, and the like.[73] In Paul's case "a generative conviction begets a further network of coherent beliefs (e.g. how one enters and maintains a relationship with God, the nature of the new religious community, the relationship of the Christian to the secular culture), . . . [and] . . . the identification of such generative convictions allows one to reconstruct certain coherences within the contingent expressions of Paul's gospel."[74]

Yet Achtemeier had not spoken his last on this subject when he offered the above suggestions. A fuller discussion in the festschrift for Furnish merits close scrutiny.[75] Achtemeier is well aware that we may need to distinguish between the distinctive elements in Paul's theology (e.g., a law-free gospel to the Gentiles) and the central elements that in most cases Paul shared with his fellow Christians leaders (e.g., the saving character of the death and resurrection of Jesus).

The Catalyst of Confession

Thus Achtemeier sets out on a quest for the catalyst or generative center of Paul's theology. Rather than justification, the center is contended to be that God raised Jesus from the dead.[76] This belief leads to the other beliefs that Paul articulates. In support of his contention, Achtemeier can point to 1 Corinthians 15, where Paul identifies the resurrection of Jesus as the one event of absolute foundational importance to Christian faith. Without this

---

[72]Achtemeir, "Finding the Way," pp. 33-34.

[73]Ibid., pp. 35-36.

[74]Ibid., p. 36.

[75]Paul J. Achtemeier, "The Continuing Quest for Coherence in St. Paul: An Experiment in Thought," in *Theology and Ethics*, ed. E. H. Lovering Jr. and J. L. Sumney (Nashville: Abingdon, 1996), pp. 132-45.

[76]Ibid., p. 138.

event, the Christian faith is meaningless and vain. Yet it is not just the resurrection of Jesus but the fact that it was *God* who raised and thus vindicated Jesus that makes this event so special in Paul's mind. It is no accident, says Achtemeier, that when Paul alludes to the experience that changed his life, he speaks of how he saw the risen Lord (1 Cor 9:1), of how God "revealed his [risen] Son in me" (Gal 1:15-16); and when Paul expresses his personal goal, it is to know Christ and the power of his resurrection (Phil 3:10). Theology and autobiography overlap and provide clues to the generative center of Paul's thought.

But what were the implications of God's raising Jesus? First, that the eschatological age had already begun. Second, that there must have been something true about Jesus that was not true about the Maccabean martyrs. God must have had a reason for vindicating Jesus in particular—because he was special, because he had a unique relationship with God. Since he experienced resurrection first, Jesus must be the One anointed by God to begin the new age.[77]

Yet if God raised Jesus, he must have disagreed with the assessment and verdict of those who put him to death. Those who executed Jesus must have been wrong and indeed must have been opposing God's own evaluation of Jesus.

Achtemeier thinks the cross should not be seen as the generative center of Paul's thought, in part because Paul expresses his *theologia crucis* in a variety of ways.[78] At this point I disagree. It seems closer to the mark to say the death and resurrection of Jesus are *both* at the heart of Paul's theology, and that second-order questions include the means by which one gets the benefit of these salvific events (justification) and the way one should live as a result of these events (walk in the Spirit). Notice that both the death and the resurrection of Jesus provide the pattern for the Christian life, in terms of both experience and behavior. Not just the resurrection but also the cross are at the heart of Christian life because they at the heart of Paul's Christology, which is to say his theology.

In spite of this caveat, Achtemeier's method of beginning with the generative heart or center of Paul's theology and then seeing how that center accounts for Paul's other views indeed allows us to begin to see the coherence of his thought.[79]

The work of Dunn reminds us of the importance of the stories that are

---

[77]Ibid., pp. 140-41.
[78]Ibid., p. 142.
[79]See ibid., pp. 144-45.

foundational to Paul's thought world. He quotes approvingly Hays's conclusion that the framework of Paul's thought is constituted neither by a system of doctrines nor by his personal religious experience but by a sacred story.[80] But if this is true, shouldn't we be looking for the climaxes in Paul's storied world, rather than the center of his thought? Would it not be better to take the various stories as our guide or doorway into his thought, rather than the rhetorical and orderly presentation of some of those thoughts in any particular letter, even Romans? I submit that it is better to approach Paul's thought in this way if the goal is to understand Paul himself and not just Paul the talking head. For it is the stories one tells over and over again, not one's occasional or ad hoc arguments, that most reveal one's character and personality. Yet to counterbalance this point, Dunn has rightly stressed that Paul's letters are by and large made up of arguments, not the stories that are the basis of those arguments, though the stories occasionally surface (e.g., in the Christ hymn in Phil 2).

What the stories tell us is that Paul was a man of great passion and zeal—passion for Christ, Christ's story, Christ's people. He was a profoundly devout individual who could not stop talking and thinking about matters theological and ethical, human relationships with God and with other human beings. These stories tell us that Paul was enthralled by the gospel, energized by his relationship with the Risen One, embedded in Christ's people but evangelizing the world. He was no lone ranger for God, no isolated individual, though like his Master he was certainly a pioneer and a trailblazer. His was a world-transforming, not world-negating, message, yet Paul set about changing the world by constructing an alternate community, a subculture within his society.[81] But this is the way a nonviolent sectarian person would necessarily have to set about changing the world. His aim was a city set on a hill, his philosophy "If God builds it, they will come." Paul saw his communities as God's option in Corinth, Philippi, Thessalonica and elsewhere. They were to be Christ-bearing and Christ-sharing communities.

He himself, as the agent of God to these communities, was prepared to go to any lengths, endure any suffering, write any number of letters that they might become the true body of Christ figuring forth the Crucified and Risen One. Paul was in the end not just their apostle but also their servant, and the sacrifices he made to bring Christ to these people and help them

---

[80]Dunn, *Theology of Paul*, p. 18.

[81]See Richard Horsley, "1 Corinthians: A Case Study of Paul's Assembly as an Alternative Society," in *Paul and Empire: Religion and Power in Roman Imperial Society*, ed. R. Horsley (Harrisburg, Penn.: Trinity Press, 1997), pp. 242-52.

grow in Christ show what kind of person he was—perhaps the most grace-ful and grace-filled person, save One, to have lived in that era.

His gospel was not just talk but power, not just a flame but the crucible through which lives could be changed and lasting relationships between God and humankind, and between humans, could be formed. It is a collec-tivist person who has these sorts of life goals. It is a collectivist person who talks as Paul talks in all these letters. Indeed it is a collectivist person, not a radical modern individual, who takes the time, energy and passion to write the number and sorts of letters he wrote, for they were surrogates for face-to-face dialogue.

For us, the letters are episodic transcripts of the story of Paul and his converts. If we had only documents like the homily we call James from Paul's hand, we might never have gotten a true glimpse at the person behind the words. We may be thankful, then, that this apostle believed that the pen which wrote passionate and loving letters to build up communities and relationships was mightier than the sword which divided communities and destroyed lives. We have yet to fully grasp how Paul the ancient person could write both timely and timeless letters and fill them with stories, and allusions to stories, that still bear analysis and retelling.

CONCLUSIONS

The story of Christ, especially its earthly conclusion, is at the heart of Paul's theologizing. Unfortunately, almost none of the proposals discussed in the latter half of this chapter so much as mention Paul's narrative thought world and its storied character; Dunn, though he does mention them, does not make the stories the basis of his exposition of Paul's theology. I suggest this is a mistake, caused by a failure to think as ancient persons like Paul did. Not a linear development of nodal ideas as we post-Enlightenment folk are used to analyzing, but events within a drama that make up a plot are at the heart of Paul's thought and theology.

The story of Christ is the hinge on which hang all the stories that come before and after; it is also the key to interpreting all those stories. From the perspective of ethics, it is proper to say that Christ's history is the believer's destiny, and Christ's life pattern is the model of Christian behavior. Paul's focus on Christ is well reflected in the words of Frederick Buechner:

> What is the ultimate purpose of God in his creation? To make worlds, to make [humans], to make life in all its wildness and beauty? "The whole creation groaneth and travaileth in pain together until now," he says, until [humankind] . . . is transformed "unto a perfect man, unto the measure of the

stature of the fullness of Christ." In other words, the ultimate purpose of God in his creation is to make Christs of us, Paul says.

So once again, for the last time or the first time, we face that face. . . . Take it or leave it, if nothing else it is at least a face we would know anywhere—a face that belongs to us somehow, our age, our culture; a face we somehow belong to. Like the faces of the people we love, it has become so familiar that unless we take pains we hardly see it at all. Take pains. See it for what it is and see it whole, see it too for what it is just possible that it will become: the face of Jesus as the face of our own secret and innermost destiny: The face of Jesus as our face.[82]

The Paul who offered letters full of theologizing and ethics had himself been transformed and was being transformed into the image of Christ. Christ was his "best thought by day or by night." It was his one supreme passion to know Christ more, to love him more, to praise him better, to convey the gospel about him more adequately. Paul had been enraptured by a spiritual beauty, and he could not stop talking about it. He saw the glory of God in the face of Christ on the Damascus Road, and he was never the same person thereafter.

Paul's sense of identity was so bound up with Christ not just because like most ancients he manifested a dyadic personality and would naturally adhere to his leader, but because Christ had impinged on his life, changed his loyalties, redirected his passions.

No armchair theologian or ethicist, Paul was a pastor and advocate, a seeker and pilgrim, a man of the Spirit and a spirited man. He had experienced his theology before he ever expressed it, had striven to live out his ethics before he ever exhorted others to go and do likewise.

Paul would have been seen as a deviant not only by his former Jewish friends but also by some of his Jewish Christian contemporaries who looked askance at the one "untimely born." Yet he did not worry about this. He had long since given up seeking the approval of his contemporaries or worrying about how other people viewed his honor ratings. His only goal was to please and glorify Christ and to serve and honor his people. His new communities of converts, the body of Christ, gave him a context in which he could be embedded and do theology and ethics. He knew very well who he was, because he knew whose he was, and to whom he was called to preach and teach and nurture. His world was Christ and his body, and his thought as expressed in his letters makes regular journeys between these two poles.

---

[82]Frederick Buechner, *The Life of Jesus* (New York: Weathervane Books, 1974), p. 14.

Yet we must not forget Paul the evangelist and his public face as he confronted the world for Christ. By and large we see this Paul primarily in Acts, not in his letters, yet it is a side of the man we neglect to our peril, for here we learn about Paul's gospel. Another entire study needs to be done on Luke's presentation of Paul in Acts, how it may be integrated with and how it may illuminate the Paul of the epistles. Elsewhere I have begun to address this task.[83]

No one study can encompass all the facets of a complex person like Saul of Tarsus. May the readers of this book be challenged to embark on their own long and diligent "Paul quest"—and to join the apostle to the Gentiles in his quest "to know Christ and the power of his resurrection and the sharing of his sufferings by becoming like him."

---

[83]See Ben Witherington III, *The Acts of the Apostles* (Grand Rapids, Mich.: Eerdmans, 1997).

CONCLUSION

A PORTRAIT OF PAUL

WE CAN NO LONGER TREAT PAUL AS A LATE WESTERN INDIVIDUAL JUST LIKE ourselves. Cultural and anthropological studies of the first-century milieu make quite clear that the social component that shapes human personality will not allow any such facile comparisons of persons now and then. It can even be asserted that Paul was not an "individual" in the modern sense at all. He believed, and it was largely true, that his identity was established by whose he was, not who he was, by who he was related to, not how he stood out from the crowd. He reflected the collectivist mentality of first-century culture. Yet those who were not in his communities, and especially those who opposed his ministry, viewed him as not merely a sectarian person (although that was certainly true) but a deviant person, an outcast, an abortion of an apostle.

A SECTARIAN CAUSE CÉLÈBRE

As a sectarian person, Paul helped lead a group of people, including many Jews and some Gentiles, to define themselves as the people of God and take over for themselves the terminology and concepts that previously had been applied almost exclusively to non-Christian Jews. This social agenda, along with Paul's zealous mode of pursuing it, is what produced such strong and even at times violent reactions to him and his ministry. One either loved or hated him. There was hardly any middle ground.

We must take seriously the litany of opposition and rejection that Paul lays out in 2 Corinthians 11:23-27. Though he was loved by many, he was not popular at all in many circles both within and without the boundaries of the early Christian churches. Controverted and controversial, he would have won no popularity contests. But then such has generally been the lot of the boat rockers, radical reformers, prophetic figures and charismatic leaders of the world.

Yet when Paul set about his mission to change the world, his choice of weapon was rhetoric, the ancient art of persuasion, first through oral proclamation and then in his letters, which served as surrogates for his presence in the communities he had started. The leaven of the gospel was, apart from the initial acts of evangelism, mainly placed into the lump of society indirectly, by working for social change within the communities he had founded. Paul's discourse in his letters is community based and community directed. Like most prophets of the Old Testament, Paul directed his words of praise and censure, prediction and confirmation to those who were already a part of God's people.

Paul was no ordinary wordsmith, no backwoods preacher, despite his rhetoric about proclaiming to the Corinthians nothing but Christ and him crucified. He partook fully of a rhetorically saturated oral culture and used this great love of rhetoric to his advantage in numerous ways, yet without compromising the integrity of his gospel. It is a measure of his success as a rhetor that he was able to convince people of socially disconcerting notions about servanthood, self-sacrifice, equality of personhood, love of enemies and grace rather than reciprocity, using the formal conventions of his day to his advantage. Indeed, nothing short of grace itself could have convinced the Greco-Roman world about these sorts of values.

To moderns Paul's boasting seems offputting, but to ancients what would have been striking was not his boasting (a normal feature of a honor and shame culture) nor merely that he knew the rhetorical rules for inoffensive self-praise, but what he chose to boast about—a crucified Savior, power in weakness, reversal of roles between the haves and have-nots, and the like.

It would be wrong to underestimate the social level of Paul. His education was considerable, his Roman citizenship important, and his deliberate agenda of stepping down the social ladder impressive, a clear parable of grace to the less fortunate of society. We must not be misled by his choice to occasionally make or mend tents. While Paul was not among the tiny minority of the Greco-Roman aristocracy, he was part of an elite echelon that came just below the patricians, and not just because of his education.

Pauline Paradoxes

Oddly, few recent analyses of Paul have taken note of what a paradoxical person he was.

• On the one hand he was a Jew who continued to affirm various aspects of his Jewish heritage. This made him part of a group that many Greeks and Romans looked down on as a despised minority. And his faith in Christ made him part of an even smaller and less known (or liked?) minority. Yet Paul was also a Roman citizen, which gave him considerable status.

• On the one hand Paul was a prophet, which gave him considerable status in the Greco-Roman world, but on the other hand he chose to work with his hands, which would not have endeared him to the elite.

• On the one hand Paul advocated submitting to the governing authorities, but on the other hand he set about to deconstruct many of the major social values of Greco-Roman culture which the authorities spent no little time and money to support.

• On the one hand, on a superficial analysis of Paul's household codes he would seem to support the patriarchal status quo, with its harsher aspects mitigated by love. Yet when one looks closer one discovers that Paul is trying to give women more options (by advocating singleness), give slaves more hope and sense of self-worth by advocating their personhood in Christ, give children a chance to avoid abuse, and rein in the power and authority of the head of the family by tying him to following Christ's model of servanthood and love.

Given such paradoxes, it is not surprising that moderns have a hard time deciding which anachronistic pigeonhole, chauvinist or feminist, to place Paul in. But this square peg will fit in neither of those modern round holes.

Recent discussions of Paul's thought world and theology have made some progress in getting beyond treating his utterances in a Western history-of-ideas fashion, but not much. Those who advocate careful attention to Paul's storied world are still in a distinct minority. Yet without due attention to this factor, the debate about Paul's view of the law will likely never make much progress, for the key to Paul's view is where he places the law in the timetable of the story of God's people relative to where he sees God's people now, as a result of Christ's coming.

A Telling Story

The discussion of contingency and coherency in Paul's thought and the search for the heart of Paul's theology also fails to recognize that in an oral culture dominated by defining narratives, one needs to be looking for the climax to a story, not the center of a body of thought. It also fails to recognize that Paul's theology is not a static system. Rather it is the result of his thinking and theologizing into the various situations of his converts. Yet those situations do not dictate what Paul says; they are only the occasions for particular articulations of his gospel and narrative thought world. Paul's letters theologize on the basis of a symbolic universe and the stories within that universe, particularly the story of Christ, the gospel. It still is too little recognized that to speak of "Paul's theology" is to speak of a modern creation, a modern putting together of the pieces of Paul's theologizing. To an extent, to assemble Paul's theology out of his theologizing is artificial, and it certainly involves various debatable interpretive judgments. Nevertheless, this task is necessary if we are to have a full-orbed picture of Paul.

The same problem arises with Paul's ethics, not only because these are words on target but also because they are grounded in Paul's theologizing and narrative thought world. The story of Christ in particular plays a crucial role, not only as the basis of theologizing but also as the paradigm for Christian living.

Paul the exegete draws on the substance of Old Testament stories and commandments to address his converts, but he reconfigures them in the light of Christ and in light of the eschatological situation he sees Christians living, caught between already and not yet, between flesh and Spirit. Paul's exegetical strategies bear some resemblance to those of the Qumranites because of a similar eschatological perspective, but attempts to see Paul as being like later rabbinic exegetes is less than convincing. He is basically not an allegorist, although he is not loath to allegorize and so contemporize a story he knows is not inherently an allegory. Paul's historical and narrative sensibilities are such that he prefers typology to allegory as a hermeneutical move. None of this is clear without a firm grasp of the way Paul's narrative thought world conditions how he thinks.

The Paul who emerges from the explorations of the new quest for the apostle appears to have been a remarkably flexible person in a very inflexible world. It is very odd language for an early Jew to speak of living in such a way as to be a Jew to the Jew and a Gentile to the Gentile in order by all means to win some. This is not to say that Paul does not have fixed and unalterable commitments to the gospel and its theological and ethical ramifications; but the way Paul theologizes and thinks ethically out of these commitments is remarkably adaptable to his audience's situation. It is both coherent (with his thought world) and contingent in its expression and application. The old distinction between eternal principles and culturally relative practices is in some ways still a helpful one, but only if one recognizes that the middle term between these two is the theologizing and ethicizing Paul does in order to relate the former to the latter.

We must keep steadily in mind that Paul was a pastor, not an armchair theorist. He did not intend for his letters to become fodder for systematicians or fertile fields for doctoral theses—yet both things have happened, and not without profit.

The definitive biography of the man is yet to be written and may never be written. But were the apostle to have written an autobiography, without doubt he would have stressed the cruciform and christocentric pattern of his life. He stood in the shadow of the Galilean and not infrequently reflected the character of the One he served. No higher compliment can be paid to a Christian than to say he lived out of and strove to emulate the story of Christ. No wonder so many have loved this passionate and paradoxical man and have striven to imitate him. We become what we admire.

Finally, I suspect that were Paul to visit us today, he would still be a social outcast and deviant, still be seen as a fanatic, even in many conservative religious circles. Prophetic figures tend to be heroes only long after they are dead, when their ground-shaking presence, power and pungency are no longer directly felt.

Yet if Paul had not been the person he was, the Christian movement might never have become the Gentile-dominated entity it has been for almost all of the last two thousand years. There might never have been a Lutheran reformation, a Wesleyan revival or a Geneva awakening. If the measure of a person's stature is the degree of impact the person's life and work have had on subsequent generations, then the historical Paul is clearly the most important figure in Christian history and the history of the West after Jesus. We will do well to continue to search for ever-clearer portraits of the man.

APPENDIX

TIMELY REMARKS
ON THE LIFE
OF PAUL

ANY HUMAN LIFE IS TO A SIGNIFICANT DEGREE A FUNCTION OF TIME, IN PARTICULAR the time and times in which one lives. If we are to understand as complex a figure as Saul of Tarsus, placing him in his appropriate chronological setting is a crucial part of examining him in his historical context.

THE FIRST HALF

Saul: The Early Years

There are very few firm points of chronological reference by which we can place Paul in his historical setting. Certainly it is clear enough that Paul lived in the first two-thirds of the first century A.D., and it is equally clear that any interaction between him and the followers of Jesus, whether before or after his conversion, took place after the death of Jesus. The New Testament tells us precious little about the life of Saul of Tarsus prior to his encounter with Christians in Jerusalem shortly after Jesus' death. It follows that if we can determine the date of Jesus' death, we have a reasonably good chance of determining when Saul became a figure of importance for earliest Christianity.

Though the dating of the life and times of Jesus of Nazareth involves a variety of problems, it is universally agreed that Jesus died during the time Pontius Pilate was procurator in Judea. Not only the canonical Gospels but also Roman historiography is clear on this point (Tacitus *Annals* 15.44). This means that Jesus died sometime between A.D. 26 and 36.[1]

Several factors allow us to narrow down the time further: the relationship between the ministry of Jesus and that of John the Baptist; our knowledge of the years when Passover fell on a Friday; and finally the date of the death of Herod Philip. It appears reasonably clear that Herod Philip was dead no later than A.D. 34. If Luke 3:1-2 contains historically valuable information on the relationship between the time of Jesus' ministry and the reign of Herod Philip, as most scholars would accept, then Jesus' ministry was likely over before Herod Philip's death.[2] This means that Jesus died no later than about A.D. 33.

The dating of Passover on a Friday in this general time period gives us two primary choices: A.D. 30 and 33. Choosing the latter creates a problem in regard to the length of Jesus' ministry and its relationship to that of John the Baptist. We have no evidence that suggests Jesus' ministry was any longer than three years. Furthermore, we know that John the Baptist was executed by Herod Antipas and that he was active while Pontius Pilate ruled in Judea. This means that the Baptist's ministry was taking place during and after A.D. 26, when Pilate came to Judea, and most would put his execution somewhere around A.D. 27 or 28.[3] This in turn places the beginning of Jesus' ministry about A.D. 28. On this showing, A.D. 33 is probably too late to be the date of Jesus' death. Thus it makes sense to conclude that Jesus died on Nisan 14 (April 7) in A.D. 30.[4]

It follows from these considerations that Paul could not have been converted to Christianity before A.D. 30. Indeed, in view of the evidence in both Galatians 1 and Acts 7—9 that Saul of Tarsus was a persecutor of Jerusalem Christians for some time before his conversion, it must have been later than that date. I suggest that the earliest likely date for his conversion, allowing for persecution of Christians in Jerusalem and, once

---

[1]On this time frame for the rule of Pontius Pilate see J. Blinzler, *Der Prozess Jesu*, 4th ed. (Regensburg: Pustet, 1969), pp. 271-75.

[2]See the discussion in John P. Meier, *A Marginal Jew: Rethinking the Historical Jesus* (New York: Doubleday, 1991), pp. 372-84.

[3]See ibid., pp. 374-76.

[4]These conclusions hinge in part on whether we follow John's chronology of Passion events or the Synoptic one. I agree with both John P. Meier and Raymond E. Brown that John's chronology makes better sense of all the data. This in turn may mean that Jesus was executed on Passover Eve or the day when the lambs were slaughtered for Passover. The figuring of Jewish days went from sunset to sunset, not from midnight to midnight. Therefore, if Jesus died at or about 3 p.m. he died before the onset of Passover, which began on Friday evening. This means that the Passover meal Jesus shared with his disciples was nonetheless not eaten on Passover. It probably is not necessary to resort to the conjecture that Galileans calculated Passover differently from Judean Jews.

he had accomplished that task, a trip to Damascus to continue the work, is A.D. 32 or 33, though it is perhaps best to leave a little more leeway and suggest that Paul was converted about A.D. 34.[5] This means that Paul likely persecuted Christians between about 31 and 34.

It is at the beginning of this period of persecution that we first hear of Saul of Tarsus in Acts 7:58 as a "young man" who was present at the stoning of Stephen. What does the word *neanios* mean in this text? The usual range of age given for this term is between twenty-four and forty, but it was most often used for unmarried men, and Jewish men usually married no later than their twenties or thirties. Luke's audience would likely have assumed the term referred to the lower part of the age range. It is likely, then, that Luke has in mind a man thirty or younger.[6] This means that Saul was probably born after the turn of the era.[7]

The only firm data we have about the life of Saul of Tarsus prior to his persecutions of Jerusalem Christians is found in passing remarks in Acts 22:3 and 26:4. The meaning of these verses has been sometimes disputed, as has also the historical worth of these remarks, but such skepticism is probably unwarranted, especially if Acts was written by a sometime companion of Paul. These verses suggest that while Saul was born in Tarsus, his formative years—when he was receiving his education—were spent in Jerusalem. There is no real counterevidence in the Pauline epistles themselves to suggest that Saul spent his youth in Tarsus.[8] W. C. Van

---

[5]Throughout this study I assume that Luke-Acts was written by a sometime companion of Paul and presents us with material of considerable historical substance, though there are certainly some historical problems that arise from Luke's writings. I have argued for this conclusion in Ben Witherington III, *The Acts of the Apostles* (Grand Rapids, Mich.: Eerdmans, 1997).

[6]See ibid.

[7]This conclusion has some repurcussions for the terminus of Paul's life as well. In Philemon 9 Paul refers to himself as an "old man" *(presbytēs)*. If as Jerome Murphy-O'Connor *(Paul: A Critical Life* [Oxford: Oxford University Press, 1996], p. 4) suggests we follow the Jewish understanding of this term to refer to a man of about sixty years of age (see *m. 'Abot* 5.21), this letter in all likelihood was not written before about A.D. 60 or a little later. This creates some problems for those who wish to connect that letter to an Ephesian imprisonment earlier in the life of Paul, an imprisonment not recorded in Acts and not clearly suggested in the undisputed Pauline letters either.

[8]Against Murphy-O'Connor, *Paul: A Critical Life,* pp. 8-15, who takes a pick-and-choose approach to the data in Acts, often without historical justification or rationale. There is no good reason to accept Luke's statement that Paul was born in Tarsus and then reject the conclusion that he was raised in Jerusalem when both these facts are mentioned in the same text in the same breath. Nothing in Paul's letters suggests we should reject this data. When Paul says in Galatians 1:22 that he was still unknown by sight to the churches of Judea, it must be born in mind that (1) Acts does *not* tell us Paul persecuted Christians outside of Jerusalem but in Judea; (2) Judea here likely has its provincial sense, which would include Samaria and Galilee; (3) Paul admits various Christians in Jerusalem knew him and the fact of his conver-

Unnik's conclusions regarding the meaning of Acts 22:3—that it claims that Paul was raised and received his education in Jerusalem—have been accepted by the majority of Acts specialists, and this evidence should not be dismissed without proper counterevidence.[9]

Careful scrutiny of these data leads to the following reconstruction of phase one of Saul's life:

A.D. 5 (give or take three or four years): Saul is born in Tarsus in Cilicia of conservative Jewish parents who have Roman citizenship.

A.D. 10 (or a little earlier): Saul's family moves to Jerusalem, while Saul is still quite young.

A.D. 15-20: Saul begins his studies in Jerusalem with Rabbi Gamaliel, grandson of Rabbi Gamaliel the Elder.

A.D. 30: Jesus is crucified by Pontius Pilate.

A.D. 31-33 (or 34): Saul persecutes the church in Jerusalem.

A.D. 34 (or 35): Saul is converted on the road to Damascus and travels on to Damascus.[10]

Saul of Arabia

Although Acts makes no mention of it, Galatians 1:17 informs us that immediately after his conversion (and his initial time in Damascus) Paul went away into Arabia, later returning to Damascus. This intriguing passing remark has led to no end of speculation. For example, N. T. Wright has suggested on the basis of Galatians 4:25, and relying on the argument that Paul saw himself as a prophet like Elijah, that he actually made a trip to Mt. Sinai.[11] The problem with this thesis is at least fourfold.

1. When Paul speaks of his call/conversion, he uses language reminiscent of the prophetic call of Jeremiah and perhaps the Isaianic servant of God (see Gal 1:15-16), not in terms of the call of Elijah (although his zeal may have led him to see people like Phineas and Elijah as prototypes).

2. More important, this theory leaves 2 Corinthians 11:32-33 totally unexplained. Why would the ethnarch of King Aretas of Nabatea be after

---

son quite well, and they were able to relate to the churches in Judea the fact that he had indeed been converted. See Ben Witherington III, *Grace in Galatia* (Edinburgh: T & T Clark, 1998), ad loc.

[9]See W. C. Van Unnik, *Tarsus or Jerusalem: The City of Paul's Youth,* trans. G. Ogg (London: Epworth, 1962).

[10]See the discussion in J. Becker, *Paul: Apostle to the Gentiles* (Louisville, Ky.: Westminster John Knox, 1993), pp. 17-31.

[11]See Wright, "Paul, Arabia and Elijah," *Journal of Biblical Literature* 115 (1996): 683-92.

Paul if he had visited Mt. Sinai in the Sinai peninsula? It makes far better sense to link Galatians 1:17 to what is said in 2 Corinthians 11:32-33 than to a hypothetical connection between Paul and Elijah.[12]

3. The Arabia Paul would have known as a dweller in Jerusalem is the same Arabia that Josephus says can be seen from Jerusalem on a clear day—Petran Arabia, not Mt. Sinai (see *Jewish Wars* 5.159-60; cf. *Antiquities of the Jews* 5.82). Furthermore, the Arabia that Paul's audience would have known would have been the Nabatean kingdom that had contacts with Asia Minor through trade by way of Damascus.

4. Though Paul refers to Mt. Sinai in Arabia in Galatians 4, it is not necessary to deduce that Mt. Sinai is the part of Arabia Paul had in mind in Galatians 1 as well. Paul surely knew very well that the general designation such as we find in Galatians 4 would connote to his audience the area in and around Petra, the famous capital and major population center of Arabia. When he wants to be more specific and refer to a location not near Petra, Paul must explain to his audience in Galatians 4 that Mt. Sinai was also in the southern part of Arabia.[13]

Again, the Arabia Paul's audience woud have likely been familiar with, and more important, the Arabia Paul himself would have known and been able to see from the tower of Psephinus in Jerusalem (as Josephus says: *Jewish Wars* 5.159-60), lay on the desert side of the Decapolis and east-southeast of the Herodian fortress called Machaerus. This region was called Arabia Petrea (Josephus *Antiquities of the Jews* 18.109), meaning "the Arabia that belongs to Petra," because the latter was its capital.

The more crucial question is *why* Paul went immediately away into Arabia, and here we are helped by Jerome Murphy-O'Connor. He has argued convincingly that Paul was seeking a venue to begin to share the gospel message with non-Jews.[14] There was a long history of bad blood

---

[12]See the definitive discussion by Martin Hengel and Anne-Maria Schwemer, *Paul Between Damascus and Antioch* (Louisville, Ky.: Westminster John Knox, 1997), pp. 106-20. Aretas III had claims on southern Syria well before the time of the debacle with Aretas IV in Damascus. It would not be surprising if Aretas IV also had designs, indeed claims, on Damascus. Certainly there was also a strong presence of Jews in Damascus at the time.

[13]It is interesting that Jews of Paul's day apparently often located Mt. Sinai east of the Dead Sea in the southern part of the Nabatean kingdom near Hegra (see Hengel and Schwemer, *Paul Between Damascus and Antioch,* pp. 113-14). This would distinguish it from where Mt. Sinai is said today to be located, at Jebel Musa. The connection between the name Hegra and Hagar is also pointed out in Hengel's discussion, which may suggest that Paul has a location near Hegra in mind in Galatians 4:24-25. It is even possible that in Galatians 4:25 Paul means "But the Hagar of Mt. Sinai is in Arabia in line *[systoichei]* with the present Jerusalem." This would mean that Arabia is opposite Jerusalem or even within sight of Jerusalem.

[14]Murphy-O'Connor, *Paul: A Critical Life,* pp. 81-85.

between Jews and Nabateans, including various struggles for land between the Aretas family and the neighboring Herodians and other Jewish rulers. The idea of a Jew coming and proselytizing in his capital would have surely raised the ire of King Aretas IV against Paul.

But when would King Aretas IV have ruled in Petra, and more to the point, when would he have had some influence or representatives or even control in Damascus? First of all, we know that the rule of Aretas IV ended in A.D. 40. The incident in Damascus could not have taken place that late. It is possible that at the beginning of the reign of Caligula, Aretas had regained control of Damascus, making it part of the Nabatean kingdom. It is most unlikely that this happened before the end of Tiberius's reign. In other words, it could not have happened before about A.D. 37, and correspondingly neither could Paul's escape in a basket from Damascus have taken place before then (cf. Acts 9:24-25). We are told neither how long Paul was in Arabia nor how long he spent in Damascus. All we know from Galatians 1:17-18 is that the sum total of this period in Damascus and Arabia lasted about three years. This suggests we are definitely on the right track in dating Paul's conversion as late as A.D. 34 or 35.

We must conclude, then, that Paul was in Arabia a portion of the period A.D. 34-37, perhaps the majority of that period, for he had to have been proselytizing long enough to draw the attention of the ruler of the kingdom. Paul returned to Damascus, but he still had not escaped the reach of Aretas until he left that city in 37. Only at that point, some three years after his conversion, did Paul finally visit Jerusalem for the first time as a Christian. So the following dates can now be added to the timeline.

A.D. 34-37: Paul in Arabia and Damascus.

A.D. 37: Paul's first visit as a Christian to Jerusalem.

Paul Goes Home

Home for Paul could be said to be Jerusalem or Tarsus in Cilicia. It appears that at this point Paul had occasion to visit both—first Jerusalem and then Cilicia, apparently including Tarsus. In Galatians Paul emphasizes that he visited with only two of the Jerusalem leaders or apostles, Peter and James, to make clear that he did not get the distinctives of his gospel or his apostolic commission from the Jerusalem leaders. He says in Galatians 1:18 that he spent fifteen days with Peter, but he does not say that this is the total time he spent in Jerusalem or that he saw no other Christians in Jerusalem other than Peter and James. It is thus possible that Acts 9:26-29 summarizes these activities plus the other things Paul did on this visit to Jerusalem in

A.D. 37, things that fell outside of the scope of what Paul needed and wanted to say in Galatians. In any event, the two accounts agree that Paul went off to Cilicia (Acts 9:30; Gal 1:21). Luke tells us he visited Tarsus in particular, which seems altogether believable. We would be surprised if Paul had not visited this great metropolis where he was born, knowing what we know about his urban strategy of missionary work.[15]

About Paul's time in Cilicia we know nothing, or next to nothing. We may surmise that he continued his missionary work, but none of his extant letters give us hints that he was any more successful in Cilicia than in Arabia—that is, we have no evidence he was successful at all in these locales.[16] In fact Paul passes over in almost complete silence the next ten-plus years while he was in Syria and Cilicia. We know only that at some point during these many years, in either 41 or 42, he had a visionary experience that he recounts in 2 Corinthians 12:1-10. Acts adds very little: that Paul spent about a year in Antioch teaching prior to his second visit to Jerusalem (Acts 11:25-26). It is likely that some of the travails listed in 2 Corinthians 11:23-29 transpired during this hidden period.

Clearly there are not enough data to construct a full life of Paul. We are in the dark about large portions of his curriculum vitae. These hidden years make up the next portion of our timetable.

A.D. 37-46: Paul preaches in his home region. Results unknown, but possibly a time of great persecutions (see 2 Cor 11:23-29).
A.D. 41-42: Paul's visionary experience and thorn in the flesh (2 Cor 12:1-10).
A.D. 47 (approx.): Barnabas finds Paul in Tarsus and brings him to Antioch.

One issue having to do with events in the early forties, during the early part of the reign of Claudius, has a significant bearing on how we understand both the Pauline corpus and the progress of Paul's life. It has become fashionable to argue that the synchronizing of Acts 18:2 with events recorded in Roman histories for the end of the 40s, in particular A.D. 48 or 49, is an error.[17] In particular, it is argued that Luke and various scholars

---

[15]See the later discussion.
[16]See, however, Hengel and Schwemer, *Paul Between Damascus and Antioch.*
[17]See the discussions in Murphy-O'Connor, *Paul: A Critical Life,* pp. 8-15; also Gerd Luedemann, *Paul, Apostle to the Gentiles: Studies in Chronology* (Minneapolis: Fortress, 1984), pp. 164-70, and his "Dase Judenedikt des Claudius (Apg 18, 2)," in *Der Treue Gottes Trauen: Beitrage zum Werk des Lukas-Festschrift fur Gerhard Schneider,* ed. C. Bussmann and W. Radl (Freiburg: Herder, 1991), pp. 289-98. Note that as critical a scholar as Becker (*Paul,* pp. 29-31) argues against the earlier dating of Luedemann.

following him have gotten confused about the timing of the expulsion or censuring of Jews in Rome, and that in fact this event must be dated to the beginning of the 40s, not the end. Gerd Luedemann uses this conclusion as a springboard to argue that Paul did missionary work in Asia Minor and even west of Asia Minor in the early to mid-40s; Murphy-O'Connor argues for Paul's presence in Galatia in 46-48, and even in Macedonia during 48-50.

In both cases these conclusions are drawn at the expense of Luke's account and involve other assumptions. Murphy-O'Connor, for example, assumes that Paul's first major missionary journey took him from Galatia in Asia Minor on to Macedonia, founding churches, and that Acts is wrong in suggesting that Paul spent only a few weeks in Philippi and Thessalonica when he first visited. Luedemann even assumes that Paul undertook his mission in Philippi and Thessalonica in the late 30s, was in Corinth in A.D. 41 and wrote 1 Thessalonians then from that location![18]

Such speculations have no substantiation in Acts and often involve a radical rearranging of the usual ordering and understanding of Paul's writing of his letters. These views do not represent the consensus among critical New Testament scholars, and older critical surveys of Pauline chronology are quite innocent of such tenuous speculations,[19] as are some of the recent critical studies of the book of Acts.[20] Ancient historians are also loath to place the expulsion of Christians from Rome under Claudius before A.D. 49.[21]

What *does* the evidence tell us? First, Acts 18:2 and the expulsion from Rome must be placed in the larger setting of the treatment of Jews by Roman emperors in the first century, beginning with Augustus. Careful investigation of relevant classical sources shows that there were regular censures as well as other actions taken against Jews during the early Empire. More particularly, it is clear that Claudius took such actions on

---

[18]Luedemann, *Paul*, pp. 262-63.

[19]Cf. Robert Jewett, *A Chronology of Paul's Life* (Philadelphia: Fortress, 1979), and G. Ogg, *The Chronology of the Life of Paul* (London: Epworth, 1968). For a much sounder approach by a critical scholar see L. C. A. Alexander, "Chronology of Paul," in *Dictionary of Paul and His Letters*, ed. Gerald F. Hawthorne, Ralph P. Martin and Daniel G. Reid (Downers Grove, Ill.: InterVarsity Press, 1993), pp. 115-23.

[20]See the detailed treatment of some of these issues in C. Hemer, *The Book of Acts in the Setting of Hellenistic History* (Winona Lake, Ind.: Eisenbrauns, 1989), pp. 244-54; see also C. K. Barrett, *The Acts of the Apostles* (Edinburgh: T & T Clark, 1994), 1:608-11, on the viable Antiochene traditions about Paul's first missionary journey to Cyprus and then to south Galatia, but leaving out Macedonia. For a careful critique of some of Luedemann's theories see F. F. Bruce, "Chronological Questions in the Acts of the Apostles," *Bulletin of the John Rylands University Library of Manchester* 68 (1986): 273-95, especially pp. 280-82.

[21]See A. N. Wilson, *Paul: The Mind of the Apostle* (New York: Norton, 1997), p. 103.

various occasions.[22] There is then no a priori reason to collapse actions undertaken in 41 and 49 into one event, on the theory that Claudius could not have censured Jews on more than one occasion.[23] In fact, classical sources make clear that he took multiple actions against Jews in different parts of the Empire during his reign, particularly during the 40s.

When we examine the classical evidence closely, the following points come to light.

1. Suetonius is quite clear that during the reign of Claudius, Jews were expelled from Rome for "constantly making disturbances at the instigation of Chrestus" (*Claudius* 25.4).

2. Equally clear is the later fifth-century Christian writer Paul Orosius, who refers to an otherwise unknown text from Josephus which says that Claudius expelled Jews from Rome in his ninth year—that is, between January 49 and January 50 (*Historiae adversus paganos* 7.6.15-16).

3. Dio Cassius's *History* (60.6.6) makes reference not to Jews' being driven out of Rome but their being ordered not to hold meetings. Given Dio's annalistic arrangement of material, this latter episode transpired in 41.

Were Luke, Suetonius and Orosius simply confused about what actually happened, and perhaps also about the timing of the event? At this juncture Murphy-O'Connor helpfully brings to light the similarity between Dio Cassius and Philo's *Legatio ad Gaium* 156-57. Philo remarks in A.D. 41 that Augustus at least had never removed Jews from Rome, nor did he deprive them of their rights as Roman citizens, nor did he forbid their assembling in synagogues.[24] Being in Rome at the time, Philo may well have heard of such actions taken or contemplated against the Jews and sought to head them off or correct them by appealing to Claudius's great model, Augustus.

This text from Philo, however, hardly provides clear evidence of exactly what Claudius *did* in 41. It is meant to show what he ought not to do or to have done based on the example of Augustus, with the worst possible outcome (expulsion of Jews) mentioned first.

We may take it that Philo knows something about Claudius's possible or real actions, but we may no more conclude from this that Philo knows Claudius expelled Jews in 41 than that he knows some Jews were stripped

---

[22]See the detailed discussion in Witherington, *Acts of the Apostles,* at Acts 18:2.

[23]Nor is Tacitus's silence about an expulsion of Jews from Rome in A.D. 49 a good reason to collapse the various accounts into one. Tacitus's account is selective and focuses on matters other than Judaism.

[24]Murphy-O'Connor, *Paul: A Critical Life,* pp. 12-13.

of their rights as Roman citizens at this point. Philo probably knew that Tiberius had previously expelled Jews from Rome (see below), and he feared such an action by Claudius in 41. In any case, all these actions are the things Philo feared and sought to prevent.

Murphy-O'Connor deems the account by Dio Cassius implausible in that it refers to the emperor's rule forbidding Jews to assemble in synagogues in Rome. This action is perfectly plausible, however, in view of the way Rome had regularly dealt with cults or sects that were believed to have a deleterious effect on Roman piety. For example, it is well known that meetings of the Isis cult were forbidden within the city earlier in the first century. In fact, not until A.D. 38 was this popular cult officially allowed within the city walls of Rome.[25] Furthermore, Tacitus records legislation attempting to eliminate certain Egyptian and Jewish rites within the city of Rome (*Annals* 2.85). So there is nothing at all implausible about Dio Cassius's account. Such actions were precedented and not uncommon.

Furthermore, H. Dixon Slingerland's careful examination of Dio Cassius has pointed out that we do not know whether Dio Cassius knew of Suetonius's account, but Cassius writes of the event in A.D. 41 after having narrated what Tiberius had done: he had expelled various Jews from Rome (57.18.5). We can learn nothing from Suetonius about the expulsion event's timing, because Suetonius arranged events topically rather than chrono- logically. Thus we are left with the material in Dio Cassius to date this material. This evidence supports an action taken against Roman Jews in A.D. 41, an action with more than sufficient historical precedent.[26]

Slingerland's summary shows the misguided nature of attempts to harmonize or identify the accounts in Dio and in Suetonius. In spite of elements common to both accounts, their actual details do not correspond. Among differences, Suetonius states that there were Jewish tumults, Dio that there existed only the potential for such; Suetonius that Claudius resorted to expulsion, Dio that he did not; Suetonius that Claudius acted against Jews, Dio that he acted against Jewish institutions.[27]

There is no good reason to assume that Dio is correcting Suetonius or even that he knows Suetonius's account. Furthermore, if one still insists that these two accounts are of one event and that we must prefer one

---

[25]See Ben Witherington III, *Women in the Earliest Churches* (Cambridge: Cambridge University Press, 1988), pp. 21-28 and notes.

[26]See H. Dixon Slingerland, "Suetonius *Claudius* 25.4 and the Account in Cassius Dio," *Jewish Quarterly Review* 79 (1989): 305-22, and also "Acts 18:1-7 and Gerd Luedemann's Pauline Chronology," *Journal of Biblical Literature* 109 (1990): 686-90.

[27]Slingerland, "Acts 18:1-7," p. 688.

account over another, surely the honor must go to the second-century account of Suetonius, not the third-century account of Dio. Suetonius's account comports with that in Acts 18:2, and the Acts account is surely earlier than that of Suetonius and almost two centuries earlier than that of Dio Cassius.

Should we then dismiss the evidence from Orosius that the expulsion took place in 49—a fact he says he got from a now-lost text of the first-century Jewish historian Josephus? His date comports extremely well with the account in Acts, which goes on to tell us that Paul was in Corinth during the proconsulship of Gallio. This last event (see below) is one of the few fixed stars in the Pauline chronological constellation that almost all scholars accept, and it places Paul in Corinth A.D. 50-51.

On the prima facie evidence of Acts 18, it is perfectly logical to conclude that the expulsion from Rome must have taken place not long before the arrival of Priscilla and Aquila in Corinth, which happened not long before Paul's arrival there. In other words, A.D. 49 suits this expulsion event quite well, and it does not appear that Orosius is basing his conclusions simply on a knowledge of the book of Acts. So at this point novel reconstructions of the Pauline chronology, based on doubts about Acts and dubious readings of the classical sources, should not prevail against long-standing majority opinions about these matters.

Antioch, Jerusalem and Beyond

Apart from a few remarks in Galatians, all that we know about what happened to Paul during the years of his joint ministry with Barnabas come to us from Acts, especially chapters 13—14. For our purposes, most significant is that Paul's letters give no evidence to suggest that the "first missionary journey" was not as described in Acts 13—14.

It is often assumed that a correspondence between Acts 11:29-30 and 12:24 and Galatians 2:1-10 is unlikely. Many scholars, perhaps a slight majority in fact, have wished to argue that Galatians 2:1-10 records the Pauline version of the apostolic council recorded in Acts 15, and that either Luke has bifurcated one visit to Jerusalem into two (found in Acts 11 and 15) or that Acts 11 records an otherwise unknown visit of Paul to Jerusalem, a visit that Paul does not bother to mention in Galatians 1 or 2.

No view of these issues is without problems. I have endeavored to deal in detail with these historical difficulties in two separate places,[28] and here

---

[28]See the discussion on Acts 11 and 15 in Witherington, *Acts,* and on Galatians 1—2 in *Grace in Galatia,* ad loc.

I will simply summarize my conclusions. The view that causes the least number of difficulties all around is that (1) Acts 11 = Galatians 2 and (2) Galatians is likely the first extant letter we have from Paul's hand.

Since most scholars view Paul as the primary source on these matters, I will begin with the Pauline evidence, though the rhetorical and tendentious character of Paul's account must be considered. Paul is not writing as a historian but as an apostle and an advocate. Luke, on the other hand, does appear to have some desire to write as a good Hellenistic historian. Thus Luke's account may be as valuable to us as Paul's, especially because Luke is writing with the benefit of hindsight and with an apparent knowledge of how things turned out in the long run. He is not writing in the heat of the moment as Paul is.

First of all, Galatians contains definite clues of close proximity between the time when Paul visited Galatia and when he wrote this letter. It is also quite clear that the issue of whether his converts should be circumcised and observe the Mosaic law is being hotly debated at the time he writes Galatians. The brief time since he visited is evident, for example, in 1:6, where Paul says he is amazed that the Galatians are so quickly departing from what he preached to them. Equally telling is Galatians 2's suggestion that the incident at Antioch between Paul and Peter is in the recent past. Furthermore, there is no hint that any local leadership has had time to develop in the Galatian congregations. The people are susceptible to the influence of the circumcision party precisely for this reason. There is also the fact that at this point in his ministry Paul has no well-known or highly experienced coworkers to call on to support his cause or to send to Galatia to deal with the problem. No time in Paul's ministerial career so well suits these facts as the period at or near the beginning of his Antioch-based ministry.

One cannot escape the feeling that Paul is paddling hard upstream when he writes Galatians, and if he had been able to appeal to a decree of James to the effect that circumcision was not required of Gentile converts, he surely would have played this trump card. Equally, if there had already been an apostolic council anything like what we find in Acts 15, how could the circumcision party have made such an impression in Galatia or have (apparently) claimed to have the backing of Jerusalem? Peter's actions in Antioch are inexplicable as well if Acts 15, and a decision about Gentiles and Jewish food laws, has already happened. In other words, Paul's circumstances, those of the circumcision party and those of Peter bespeak a time when circumcision and food questions have not been formally or publicly settled, even in the Jerusalem church, let alone in the churches elsewhere.

There is another reason for thinking Galatians was written before, though only shortly before, the apostolic council. The letter includes absolutely no appeal to the Galatians to contribute to the collection for the saints in Jerusalem. Indeed, there is only a hint in Galatians 2:10 that this need has begun to be dealt with. When Paul writes "which was actually what I was eager to do," he is likely alluding retrospectively to what he had already done, as recorded in Acts 11:29-30.

Furthermore, in 1 Corinthians 16:1 Paul speaks retrospectively of instructions given to the churches in Galatia about the collection. The way 1 Corinthians 16:1 is worded, these instructions seem to have been given sometime prior to the writing of 1 Corinthians, but they are not found in our Galatians. This means that Paul is likely referring to oral instructions given to the Galatians, not on a first trip through Galatia, of which our Galatians gives not a hint nor a word of reinforcement, but on some subsequent trip through the region. It would have to have been a trip before 1 Corinthians was written, though. If we date 1 Corinthians to about A.D. 53 or 54, then we must date a second trip through Galatia prior to that time. Yet we know that Paul was in Corinth in 50-51; he was apparently there for a year and a half (see Acts 18:11). This means that the most plausible time for a first trip through Galatia must be prior to 50-51, and a second trip must have been made through Galatia sometime between Paul's leaving Corinth in 51 and his writing of 1 Corinthians in 53.[29]

As for the relationship between Acts 11 and Galatians 2, several considerations are important. According to Acts, Paul made three visits to Jerusalem by the time of the apostolic council. A straightforward reading of Galatians 2:1 suggests Paul is referring to his second visit to Jerusalem. In view of the importance for Paul's argument that he account for all his time in Jerusalem, it is highly unlikely that he deliberately omitted reference to a visit. One could of course fault the Acts account and claim that Luke has divided one visit into two parts, but it is surely less drastic to suggest simply that Galatians was written prior to Paul's third visit to Jerusalem as a Christian.[30]

The Sources and Development

Beyond all this, there are some serious problems with the prevalent identi-

---

[29]For far more detailed arguments in support of this line of reasoning see Witherington, *Grace in Galatia*, pp. 13-20.

[30]In private conversation C. K. Barrett has suggested that the actual council may have transpired at the time Acts 21 mentions the issue and that Luke may have retrojected the issue to Acts 15, making it central to the narrative. This is a real possibility and would allow for Galatians to be written before the Acts council, though still in the 50s.

fication of Galatians 2 with Acts 15. In Galatians it appears that the circumcision issue is raised after Paul arrives in Jerusalem, whereas in Acts 15 it
has been a live issue before Paul's arrival. In Galatians Paul says he went
up to Jerusalem "by" or in response to a revelation, but in Acts 15 he is
clearly sent up as an emissary of a church. In Galatians Paul is quite clear
that he met privately with the pillar apostles, even though some intruders
invaded this private meeting. Acts 15 portrays a public or large congregational meeting. As has been noted, Paul does not mention the decree at all
in Galatians, and it would have been most advantageous for him to do so
if he knew of it. In Galatians 2 Paul evidently plays a major role in the
Jerusalem discussions, whereas in Acts 15 he plays a minor role and is allot-
ted only one verse! In view of Luke's admiration for Paul, this would be
strange if Luke knew Paul played a significant role at the council.
Furthermore, Galatians 2:11-14 depicts a defensive Paul and a vacillating
Peter, a situation more likely prior to the apostolic council than after it. The
incident at Antioch would likely have arisen only at a time when guidelines
for Jewish and Gentile table fellowship were unclear. The topic of discussion for the meeting recorded in Galatians 2 was Paul's gospel and the
legitimacy of his mission to the Gentiles, not food rules that would facili-
tate fellowship between those already Christians.

Finally, several considerations strongly favor the Acts 11 = Galatians 2
equation. Both narratives speak of going to Jerusalem in response to a
revelation. Paul does not say that he had personally received the revelation,
and in Acts the "revelation" leads to a prophecy of severe famine. This
equation also solves the problem of whether there were two or three visits,
if Galatians was written before the decree. Notice too that Acts 11:30/12:25
is about famine relief for the poor, something Paul alludes to in Galatians
2:10. We know that such a famine struck the region in the late 40s, and thus
the timing of this visit in about A.D. 48 fits this fact.[31] The upshot of all the
above is as follows.

A.D. 48: Paul makes his second visit to Jerusalem (Acts 11 = Gal 2), the
famine visit with Barnabas (and Titus). There is a private agreement
between Paul and the "pillars" of the Jerusalem church that he and
Barnabas will go to the Gentiles while Peter and others go to the Jews.
Circumcision is not imposed on Titus, and issues of food and fellowship are
apparently not resolved at this meeting.

A.D. 48: Paul's first missionary journey with Barnabas follows his second

---

[31]See Witherington, *Acts*, pp. 77-96.

visit to Jerusalem (Acts 13—14), including a visit to south Galatia.

A.D. 49: Paul and Barnabas return to Antioch. The "men who came from James" visit the church there, and the Antioch incident transpires (Gal 2:11-14).

A.D. 49: Later the same year, Paul discovers that the circumcision party has visited his congregations in Asia Minor and has bewitched some of his converts there. Paul writes Galatians in response to this crisis shortly before going up to Jerusalem for the third time.

A.D. 49 or 50: The apostolic council is held in Jerusalem (Acts 15). Public agreement is reached that Gentile converts do not need to be circumcised, but they do need to avoid basic actions that offend Jews: idolatry and immorality, in particular the sort that transpired in pagan temples. They are not to attend idol feasts in idol temples.

A.D. 50-52: The second missionary journey takes Paul and Silas not only to Asia Minor but also to Macedonia and Greece. This period of Paul's life is recorded in Acts 15:40—18:23. During this time Paul picks up Timothy in Lystra (Acts 16:1) and Luke in Troas (16:10-13).

This leads to the discussion of the next, and in some ways most crucial, chronological point in the middle of Paul's Christian life: Paul's encounter with the proconsul of Achaia, Gallio.

Paul in Corinth

According to Acts 18, Paul spent a year and a half in Corinth. This crucial crossroads of the Mediterranean certainly warranted this degree of evangelistic attention from the apostle. The length of his stay reminds us that it is something of a misnomer to speak of Paul's missionary "journeys," as if he were always racing breathlessly around the Mediterranean Crescent leaving half-converted Christians in his wake.[32] To the contrary, we have evidence that after his first missionary journey Paul set up shop in several major cities for a considerable periods of time—a year and a half in Corinth, three years in Ephesus, two years at least in Rome.

Our concern at this point is with the first of these three lengthy periods, A.D. 50-52, when Paul was in Corinth. During this stay it appears a variety of notable things happened, not least being that Paul, with his coworker Silas, corresponded with his new converts in Thessalonica, writing 1 and 2

---

[32]See the discussion in Ben Witherington III, *Conflict and Community in Corinth* (Grand Rapids, Mich.: Eerdmans, 1994), pp. 19-23.

Thessalonians. It was also about halfway through this period that Paul endured the "Gallio incident."

We are able to be rather confident in dating L. Junius Gallio's proconsulship in Corinth, due to an inscription at Delphi that can be dated to the time of the twenty-sixth acclamation of Claudius as emperor, which must have transpired before August 1, 52, for the twenty-seventh acclamation was made sometime between April and July 52 (see Frontius *Aqueducts* 1.13).[33] It appears that the twenty-sixth acclamation took place between April and November 51.

According to Dio Cassius (*History* 57.14.5), Claudius sent a letter in either April or May 52 mentioning that Gallio had drawn the emperor's attention to depopulation problems in Delphi and that the emperor was now responding. This must mean that Gallio was proconsul prior to that date. We know from Gallio's brother Seneca (*Epistulae Morales* 104.1) that Gallio served only a portion of his term in Corinth due to illness. This means he served only a part of either 50-51 or perhaps 51-52. Murphy-O'Connor is probably right that the encounter between Paul and Gallio transpired between July and September 51, for after the latter date it appears that Gallio sailed back to Rome.

This places Paul in Corinth during A.D. 51. The impression left by Acts 18 (cf. v. 11 and v. 18) is that he stayed a good while after the encounter with the proconsul. Perhaps Paul left Corinth in the spring of 52 and returned to Antioch, which was something of a home base for him, after making a report to Jerusalem about the progress of the gospel (18:22). The chronology of the middle of Paul's Christian life then looks like this.

A.D. 49: Claudius expels Jews from Rome, leading to the arrival of Priscilla and Aquila in Corinth.
A.D. 50-52: Paul stays in Corinth. He writes 1 and 2 Thessalonians.
A.D. 51: The Gallio incident transpires (Acts 18:12-18).
A.D. 52: Paul returns to Antioch after a brief visit to Jerusalem (Acts 18:22).

BEYOND THE EARLY HORIZON: PAUL'S LATER YEARS

In some ways we know both more and less about Paul's later years than about his earlier years. We know more because on any showing the bulk of the extant Pauline corpus was likely written after A.D. 52, and because Acts becomes progressively more detailed and expansive in the "we" sections

---

[33]See Murphy-O'Connor, *Paul: A Critical Life,* p. 16.

(Acts 16:10-17; 20:5-15; 21:1-18; 27:1—28:16), especially the "we" passages that begin at Acts 20:5. We know less because Paul's letters only allude or occasionally refer to his own travels, activities and whereabouts. His letters are far more concerned with instructions for his converts and what is happening with them. We also know less because for this period of time there are far fewer possible synchronisms between either Acts and secular literature or Paul's letters and secular events. Only the reigns of Felix and Festus in Judea help us get a reasonably clear fix on when Paul was incarcerated in Caesarea. Furthermore, the Pastoral Epistles, if they were written by Paul (which is highly debated), do not fit into any period described in the book of Acts. Thus we lose Acts, our second major source, for chronologically locating material. After A.D. 62, the last year in which any of the events in Acts could have transpired, we either are in the dark about Paul or must rely solely on the Pastoral Epistles.

The Ephesus Connection
According to Acts 18:23—21:26, Paul's so-called third missionary journey involved a very extended period in Ephesus, possibly for close to three years (cf. Acts 19:8-10). There was also an additional three months in Greece (Acts 20:3). These accounts in Acts neither say nor suggest that Paul was under arrest during this period, in particular during his time in Ephesus. Luke was not at all reluctant to record such incarcerations, as the accounts in Acts 16:16-40, 21:27-40 and 28:16 make quite clear. But since it has become a popular argument from silence to suggest that Paul wrote his captivity epistles while incarcerated in Ephesus during this part of his life, we need to address this theory.

The theory of Ephesian imprisonment is not new.[34] Indeed it may go back to the second-century apocryphal *Acts of Paul,* which speak of his being imprisoned in Ephesus and being condemned to fight wild beasts (cf. 3.20-22; 7.1-4), a speculation based on a probably overly literal reading of 1 Corinthians 15:32. This theory has had a revival of popularity of late. It is based on certain references in Philemon, Colossians, Philippians, and to a lesser degree Ephesians and even 1 Corinthians 15:32. It is also based on the assumptions that (1) Rome was too far for Onesimus to travel from the Lycus Valley and too far for Paul to write to Philemon inquiring about a room; (2) Paul was in fact incarcerated and not merely under some sort of

---

[34]See, e.g., G. S. Duncan, *St. Paul's Ephesian Ministry: A Reconstruction with Special Reference to the Ephesian Origin of the Imprisonment Epistles* (London: Hodder & Stoughton, 1929). For the most recent exposition of this view see Murphy-O'Connor, *Paul: A Critical Life,* pp. 175-80.

house arrest; (3) Paul either was not a Roman citizen or could not extricate himself from Roman imprisonment in Ephesus very readily, as shown by the writing of several letters while in this condition; (4) the number of trips to and fro between Philippi and where Paul is imprisoned, as chronicled in Philippians, is too great to support Rome as the point of origin for these letters. It must be said that there are flaws in all of these assumptions.

Do any of these letters in fact tell us that Paul was in prison? Here we are helped immensely by a very detailed study by Brian Rapske.[35] Unlike the case in the West today, imprisonment was not generally a Roman form of punishment. It was a means of detaining a person until trial, or until punishment was carried out, or until one was declared innocent and free to go. Second, the phrase *en . . . desmois* literally means "in chains." While it can have the more extended sense of "in prison," normally the phrase was meant literally, especially in reference to Roman custody. Though occasionally a high-status prisoner was left unfettered, normal Roman practice was to chain prisoners, whether while holding them in custody or while taking them to Rome to plead their case (cf., e.g., Livy 29.19.5; Suetonius *Nero* 6.36.2).[36]

Furthermore, it is likely that Paul, as the narrative in Acts 22—28 suggests, was in military custody both during his journey to Rome and during his two years there under house arrest. Military custody in a private house, as described in Acts 28, was a fairly common form of custody for foreign prisoners awaiting trial in Rome,[37] and in such circumstances it is perfectly plausible that Paul might refer to the praetorian guard as his custodians. A close scrutiny of Philippians 1:13 in its immediate context—especially when also comparing it to Tacitus's *History* 1.20 and 2.11 and Suetonius's *Nero* 9—shows that it is far more likely that Paul is using *praetorium* to refer to a group of persons rather than to a place. It is to the praetorian guard and all the others that Paul's chains are evident. Furthermore, we lack evidence for the use of the term *praetorium* for the headquarters of a proconsul in a senatorial province such as Asia.[38]

When we couple this fact with the mention of Caesar's household in

---

[35]Brian Rapske, *The Book of Acts in Its First-Century Settings,* vol. 3, *Paul in Roman Custody* (Grand Rapids, Mich.: Eerdmans, 1994).

[36]See the discussion in ibid., pp. 25-29.

[37]See ibid., pp. 28-30.

[38]On these matters see the discussion in Ben Witherington III, *Friendship and Finances in Philippi* (Valley Forge, Penn.: Trinity Press International, 1994), p. 45; J. B. Lightfoot, *St. Paul's Epistle to the Philippians* (London: Macmillan, 1894), pp. 101-4. For a similar case of a Jewish prisoner under house arrest in Rome, in the care of a Praetorian guard, see Josephus *Antiquities* 18.6.5-7.

Philippians 4:22, which is most naturally taken as a reference to some of the emperor's extended family, or more likely slaves, the case for Philippians being written from Ephesus is quite weak indeed. Of some six hundred inscriptions that mention Caesar's household, all but a few refer to the "familia Caesaris" in Rome.[39] Moreover, the personal greetings and the evidence of traffic back and forth between where Paul is and Philippi are not at all improbable if Paul is in Rome. There was heavy traffic, business and otherwise, on the Via Egnatia, which went straight through Macedonia and on to Dyrrhachium, from whence one could readily sail to Puteoli in Italy. The traffic was heavy not least because Philippi was an important Roman colony.

Is the case any stronger for references to an Ephesian imprisonment in Philemon and Colossians? The argument that an Ephesian location would put Paul in close proximity to the Lycus Valley has only limited usefulness. Indeed, it can be turned on its head. Why would a sensible slave only run to the nearest large city when trying to escape his condition? Is not this precisely the sort of place to which Onesimus's master Philemon would expect his slave to flee, to try to blend in with the crowd? Would it not be far more sensible to get much farther away—perhaps to a city such as Rome, where close to a majority of the residents were slaves and one could readily disappear forever with no fear that a master in Asia Minor might find one? There is also a good positive reason Onesimus might flee to Rome: to find Paul and have him plead his case. Peter Lampe has rightly pointed to a provision in Roman law that allowed a slave in danger of punishment to seek out a friend of his owner to serve as a mediator in order to reestablish good relationships.[40] Very likely this is exactly what Onesimus sought to do. He did not simply happen upon Paul in Rome. He sought him out, just as we find another slave doing with a master's friend in Pliny's *Letter* 9.21-24.

It is not necessary to argue that Paul's reference to preparing a guest room in Asia Minor is unlikely if he was incarcerated in Rome (see Philemon 22). Many ancients, including Paul, were highly mobile. For example, from this very region of the Lycus Valley (in this case Hierapolis) we find the inscribed tomb of Flavius Zeugsis, which mentions no fewer than seventy-two voyages from Asia Minor to Rome over the course of his

---

[39]There is to my knowledge only one inscription from Ephesus or its environs that refers to imperial slaves in these sorts of terms. See Witherington, *Friendship and Finances*, pp. 136-37 and notes.

[40]Peter Lampe, "Keine 'Sklavenflucht' des Onesimus," *Zeitschrift für die neutestamentliche Wissenschaft* 76 (1985): 135-37.

business career of some thirty years![41] There is nothing at all improbable about Paul's request if he was in earnest about returning to Asia Minor when released and if he anticipated that release soon. It must be remembered that it would have likely taken many weeks for this letter to reach Philemon. If Paul was released shortly after the letter was sent, he might well have arrived at Philemon's door not long after the arrival of the letter, even though it might take him eight or nine weeks to make the trip.

Finally, there is nothing in Colossians that really points to an Ephesian locale for Paul, much less an Ephesian imprisonment. The many greetings and considerable interaction between Paul and other Christians recorded in Colossians 4:7-17 suggest a situation of open custody, so that Paul is able to carry out a good deal of Christian ministry through his coworkers and friends who have ready access to him. This does not suggest imprisonment in any particular location. It does suggest that Paul is in chains, as Colossians 4:18 strongly implies.[42]

I conclude from all this that the traditional view, held by the earliest commentators on Paul's letters, should stand: Paul wrote these letters during house arrest in Rome.[43] This means that these letters do not help us much, if at all, in reconstructing the middle phase of Paul's career. We must turn to Acts and the earlier capital Paulines, 1 and 2 Corinthians and Romans, for such reconstruction.

Paul's Roman citizenship has been addressed earlier in this book.[44] Most of those who argue for an Ephesian imprisonment accept the probability that Paul was a Roman citizen. If this was indeed the case, then barring a gross miscarriage of justice, Paul was in no real danger of execution or death if he was imprisoned in Ephesus. As a Roman citizen, he could always appeal to the justice of the emperor. Yet in Philippians especially, Paul does reckon with the possibility of death by execution. The only place we may reasonably suppose a Roman citizen might really fear execution at the hands of the Roman authorities is in Rome itself.[45] There was no high court to appeal to beyond the emperor.

---

[41]This was discussed by J. Walter, "The Apostle Paul's Travels in Light of the Traveler's Tomb of Flavius Zeugsis from Hierapolis" (Philadelphia, SBL national meeting, 1995). His conclusion is that Paul traveled no more than many professional travelers in the ancient world.

[42]I do not take into consideration Ephesians, which really adds nothing one way or another to this discussion, especially in light of the doubt about its audience or audiences. Many would argue against its being by Paul as well.

[43]See the discussion in J. Curran, "Tradition and the Roman Origin of the Captivity Epistles," *Theological Studies* 5 (1945): 163-205.

[44]See the discussion in chapter two.

[45]See Rapske, *Paul in Custody,* pp. 83-90.

The last missionary period for Paul as a free man likely began in A.D. 53, when he set out from Antioch to cross Asia Minor for the last time prior to his imprisonment in Rome. He journeyed on to Ephesus, which he would use as his base at least until 55, and perhaps until sometime in 56. There Paul wrote his first (currently extant) letter to the Corinthians in about 53 or 54. Unfortunately this letter did not succeed in its intended purpose, as 2 Corinthians makes very evident. Paul received news of real trouble in Corinth from one of his coworkers, and this precipitated the so-called painful visit to Corinth from Ephesus early in 55—a visit mentioned only in 2 Corinthians 2:1. This visit was a disaster, and it was followed by a stinging letter of rebuke, sometimes identified wrongly with 2 Corinthians 10—13.[46] Titus was the bearer of this stinging letter, and Paul became fearful that he had overdone it. After some missionary work in Troas, he crossed over into Macedonia, hoping to meet Titus and hear how his letter had been received. This journey is referred to in both 2 Corinthians 2:12-13 and Acts 20:1-16.

In the fall of 55 (or possibly 56), a relieved Paul wrote 2 Corinthians, probably from Philippi or somewhere in Macedonia. Afterward he visited Corinth for three months and then returned to Philippi in time for Passover. Sometime in either late 56 or early 57 Paul was again in Corinth, where he wrote Romans (see Rom 16:1) in preparation for his planned trip to Rome after a visit to Jerusalem (Rom 15:25).

In A.D. 57 Paul, traveling by boat, set out for what would be his last trip to Jerusalem. He sailed from Philippi to Troas (see Acts 20:7-12) and then on to Miletus. He hurried on in order to be in Jerusalem in time for Pentecost in May 57. Landing at Tyre, he strengthened Christians there and was warned not to go on to Jerusalem. Nonetheless, he continued south, stopping in Caesarea Maritima for a visit with Philip the evangelist and his prophesying daughters (Acts 21:8-9). After arriving in Jerusalem and briefly visiting with the Christians there, Paul was taken into Roman custody after something of a riot in the temple precincts.

Between 57 and 59 Paul was in custody in Caesarea Maritima, awaiting the resolution of his case.

Felix, Festus and an Appealing Situation

I have a coin minted during the governorship of Felix (on whom see Acts 23:23—24:23), which I bought when I was last in Jerusalem.[47] Part of the

---

[46]See the discussion in Witherington, *Conflict and Community,* pp. 327-30.

[47]The coin has distinctive markings that characterized those minted by Felix.

inscription clearly reads "KLAY.KAIC," the abbreviation for Claudius Caesar, which makes rather clear that Felix was already governor before Nero took the throne in about A.D. 54.[48] In addition, we know there was a change in Judean provincial coinage in Nero's fifth year, or 58-59. It is most unlikely that this would have been done by an outgoing procurator, especially since Felix had already minted a huge number of coins with his name on them. It is far more likely that the incoming governor would have undertaken this task. Thus we should likely place the departure of Felix to Rome in 58 and the coming of his successor Festus in 59. In all likelihood this transition happened in the summer, following the pattern of traveling east only after the good spring winds had made the Mediterranean Sea safe for sailing.

What all this means for Pauline chronology is that we may be reasonably sure that Paul was incarcerated in Caesarea during 58 and 59. This helps us by giving us a fixed point for both earlier and later Pauline chronology.

An attentive reader of the exciting and interesting account of Paul's sea voyage to Rome will observe that he was sailing at least a portion of the way on a grain freighter during the risky time of year, after the turning of the winds in October. Probably Festus dealt summarily with the Paul issue near the beginning of his time in Judea and Paul was sent packing in the fall of that year. This means that Paul likely arrived in Rome at least by February 60 (cf. Acts 27—28).

If Acts 28 is to be believed, Paul was under house arrest in Rome for some two years before his case was resolved. During this period he would have had both time and opportunity, probably toward the end of his incarceration, to write Colossians, Philemon and Philippians, and if it is Pauline, possibly Ephesians as well. While in custody Paul would not, according to Roman law, have been allowed to practice his trade and so would need support (see Phil 4). But he would have had opportunity to practice his religion; the Romans would not normally interfere so long as it was not seen as seditious or dangerous.

What we know about justice during Nero's reign suggests that it was a slow, cumbersome but careful process. Even in A.D. 62 we are still dealing with what have usually been called the "good" or "enlightened" years of Nero's reign, prior to the death of the close and wise associates who kept his bad tendencies in check. This is well before the Roman fire in 64, after which Nero began to look for scapegoats to take the heat, so to speak.[49]

---

[48]Nero succeeded Claudius as emperor in A.D. 54.

[49]See Rapske, *Paul in Custody,* pp. 182-89.

If indeed Paul was a Roman citizen (and of course he would not have been in Rome on appeal if that were not the case), and if indeed his accusers did not follow him to Rome, it is entirely plausible that he may have been released in 62. Acts 28 shows that Luke knows Paul's house arrest lasted only two years, and according to his account, at no point during the judicial process has Paul been convicted of any crime by Roman justice (cf. especially Acts 24—26). It is not very plausible that Luke would end his work on such a positive note if in fact he knew that Paul was executed after the two years of house arrest. What would have been the point of an often favorable portrait of Roman justice throughout Acts if that were the case?

All discussions of Pauline chronology beyond this point become quite conjectural, since Acts ends with Paul under house arrest in Rome. Even if the Pastoral Epistles are by Paul, they do not tell us much about his movements, other than to indicate that he definitely went back east after his release from house arrest.[50] The Pastorals suggest at least a summer in Asia Minor and perhaps a summer and winter in Crete and Greece. Clement of Rome (5.5-7; cf. *Muratorian Fragment* 38-39) tells us that Paul went west to Spain, a view that is developed by Murphy-O'Connor.[51] He may well have had time to travel both to the east and then west to Spain, but we cannot be sure.[52]

In any event, these last missionary endeavors would have been followed by another arrest, likely after the burning of Rome in 64, when Nero launched a limited persecution of Christians, blaming them for the fire. This time Paul's arrest was followed by trial and execution. The execution may have transpired anywhere between 65 and 68. According to tradition as well as normal Roman practice, Paul as a Roman citizen was not crucified but beheaded.[53]

So the last phase of Pauline chronology is considerably fuzzier than the earlier parts, but a reasonable conjecture produces the following.

---

[50]Murphy-O'Connor, *Paul: A Critical Life*, pp. 356-65, has made at least a reasonable case for 2 Timothy being by Paul. While I agree in principle that each of the Pastorals should be judged separately on the authenticity question, these three documents are so similar in style, vocabulary and basic concepts that they appear to be all from the same hand, and at the same time they differ in various respects on these fronts from the undisputed Paulines. This is why I would suggest that someone like Luke wrote the Pastorals, either at the behest of Paul because he is now in a real prison and is incapacitated (perhaps in the Mamertine in Rome) or perhaps shortly after the death of Paul on the basis of notes taken from Paul's last days, publishing them as a sort of last will and testament. On the similarities in style and vocabulary of the Pastorals to Luke's writings see S. Wilson, *Luke and the Pastoral Epistles* (London: SPCK, 1979).

[51]Murphy-O'Connor, *Paul: A Critical Life*, pp. 361-65.

[52] Adolf Deissmann (*Paul: A Study of Social and Religious History* [New York: Harper & Brothers, 1957], p. 248) thinks it probable that Paul was released and went to Spain.

[53]See the discussion in Bruce, *Paul*, pp. 444-55.

A.D. 57-59: Incarceration in Caesarea.

A.D. 59 (fall): Journey to Rome.

A.D. 60 (spring): Arrival in Rome.

A.D. 60-62: House arrest in Rome. Production of the captivity epistles.

A.D. 62: Release from house arrest.[54]

A.D. 62-64: Further missionary travels east, and possibly also west.

A.D. 64-65: Re-arrest during the Neronian crackdown after the fire in July 64.

A.D. 65-68?: Imprisonment in Mamertine Prison. Production of the Pastoral Epistles, shortly before or after Paul's execution.

A.D. 66-68?: Paul's execution in Rome by beheading.[55]

It should be noted that a great deal of speculation is required to produce a Pauline chronology, especially for his later years. Only a few synchronisms—such as the date of Jesus' death, that of Aretas IV, Gallio's rule in Corinth, and the rule of Felix and Festus in Judea—are available to help us get our bearings. Most scholarly argument is about how one should read the internal evidence in Paul's letters and how much historical value one should place on the accounts in Acts. If Acts indeed constitutes material of considerable historical worth, the conclusions drawn in this appendix are plausible. A summary table shows why there is good reason to take seriously the synchronisms between Paul's letters and Acts, especially if we arrange the letters in the order suggested in this chapter.

Chronological Comparison: Paul's Letters and Acts[56]

Letters		Acts
	Saul the persecutor	
Galatians 1:13-14		Acts 7:58; 8:1-3
	Paul's call; conversion near Damascus	
Galatians 1:15-17		Acts 9:1-22 (etc.)
	To Arabia	
2 Corinthians 12:1-10; Galatians 1:17b		

---

[54]Though it is also possible that Paul was executed at this juncture, in which case he could not have written the Pastoral Epistles since they deal with a time subsequent to the end of Acts.

[55]See chronological remarks and chart by Hengel and Schwemer, *Paul*, pp. xi-xiv; and Becker, *Paul*, pp. 29-31. We learn from *1 Clement* 5 that Paul was beheaded during the reign of Nero.

[56]This chart represents my response to and adaptation of some of the elements in the charts found in T. H. Campbell, "Paul's Missionary Journeys As Reflected in His Letters," *Journal of Biblical Literature* 74 (1955): 80-87, and J. A. Fitzmyer, "The Pauline Letters and the Lucan Account of Paul's Missionary Journeys," in *SBL 1988 Seminar Papers*, ed. D. J. Lull (Atlanta: Scholars Press, 1988), pp. 82-89. My basic disagreement has to do with the placement, dating and audience of Galatians.

Return to Damascus

Galatians 1:17c (3 years)

Flight from Damascus

2 Corinthians 11:32-33   Acts 9:23-25

First visit to Jerusalem as a Christian

Galatians 1:18-20   Acts 9:26-29

To the regions of Syria and Cilicia

Galatians 1:21-22   Acts 9:30 (Tarsus from Caesarea)

To Antioch

see Galatians 2:11-14   Acts 11:25-56

Second visit to Jerusalem/Antioch famine fund

Galatians 2:1-10   Acts 11:29-30/12:25

First missionary journey

Galatians 4:13-15   Acts 13—14

Return to Antioch

see Galatians 2:11-14   Acts 14:26-28

Judaizers to Antioch/Antioch incident

Galatians 2:11-14   Acts 15:1-2

Judaizers to Galatia

Cf. Galatians 1:6-9; 3:1; 4:17—5:12; 6:12-13

Galatians written from Antioch

Third visit to Jerusalem (Paul and Barnabas)

Acts 15:2-29

Return to Antioch/reading of decree

Acts 15:30-35

Second missionary journey with Silas, Timothy

Acts 15:36—18:18

*Return to South Galatia (picking up Timothy),
passing through Galactic, Phrygia,
Mysia, Troas (picking up Luke)*

1 Thessalonians 2:2   Acts 16:1-10

Philippi (Luke left here)

Philippians 4:15-16   Acts 16:11-40

Amphipolis, Apollonia, Thessalonica

Acts 17:1-9

Berea

Acts 17:10-14

Athens

1 Thessalonians 2:17—3:1   Acts 17:15-34

Paul in Corinth for eighteen months

Acts 18:1-18

Paul arrives in Corinth,
probably with Silas

1 Thessalonians 3:6; see 1 Thessalonians 1:1   Acts 18:5

Paul, Timothy, Silas evangelize Corinth at length

2 Corinthians 1:19

1 & 2 Thessalonians written from Corinth by Paul and Silas

Paul leaves from Cenchreae

Acts 18:18b

Paul leaves Priscilla and Aquila in Ephesus

Acts 18:19-21

Apollos sent to Achaia by Ephesian
church and Priscilla and Aquila

Acts 18:17

Paul to Caesarea Maritima
(and to Jerusalem?)

Acts 18:22

Return to Antioch by way of Jerusalem

Acts 18:22-23a

Third missionary journey

Galatians instructed about collection

1 Corinthians 16:1

Travels through Galatia and Phrygia

Acts 18:23

Paul in Ephesus

1 Corinthians 16:2-8

Paul in Ephesus for two to three years

Acts 19:1—20:1, 31

Apollos also in Ephesus, urged to go to Corinth

1 Corinthians 16:12

Visit of Chloe, Stephanas et al. to Paul
in Ephesus, bringing a letter

1 Corinthians 1:11; 7:1; 16:17

1 Corinthians written from Ephesus
Timothy sent to Corinth
1 Corinthians 4:17; 16:10-11
*Paul in debacle in Ephesus, dragged
into theater by rioting mob*
1 Corinthians 15:32; 2 Corinthians 1:8-11   Acts 19:21-41
Paul plans to visit Macedonia, Achaia, Jerusalem
1 Corinthians 16:3-8 (cf. 2 Corinthians 1:15-16)   Acts 19:21
Paul's second painful visit to Corinth
2 Corinthians 13:2
Titus sent to Corinth with Paul's tearful letter
2 Corinthians 2:13
Ministry in Troas
2 Corinthians 2:12
Ministry in Macedonia
2 Corinthians 2:13; 7:5; 9:2-4   Acts 20:1b
Arrival of Titus in Macedonia
2 Corinthians 7:6

2 Corinthians written from Macedonia
Titus sent ahead to Corinth with 2 Corinthians
2 Corinthians 7:16-17
Paul in Illyricum?
Romans 15:19
Paul in Achaia three months (third *visit to Corinth*)
Romans 15:26; 16:1   Acts 20:2-3

Romans written from Corinth (plans to visit Rome and Spain)
Paul begins return to Syria via Macedonia, Troas
                                                                   Acts 20:3-12
Miletus
                                                                   Acts 20:15-38
Tyre, Ptolemais, Caesarea
                                                                    Acts 21:7-14
Jerusalem
                                                                  Acts 21:15—23:30
Two years imprisoned in Caesarea
                                                                  Acts 23:31—26:32
Journey to Rome
                                                                  Acts 27:1—28:14

Rome

Acts 28:15-31

It is probably not a coincidence that the earliest events in the chart are spoken of in Galatians almost without exception, and the next earliest in 1 Thessalonians. Paul's letters are topical and tend to refer to events of the recent past. All other things being equal, this points rather strongly to the early date of Galatians as well as of 1 Thessalonians.

This chart provides solid evidence that this analysis of Pauline chronology is likely on the right track.

Bibliography

Commentaries

Barth, Markus. *Ephesians 4—6*. Garden City, N.Y.: Doubleday, 1974.

Betz, Hans Dieter. *Galatians: A Commentary on Paul's Letter to the Churches in Galatia*. Philadelphia: Fortress, 1979.

Bruce, F. F. *Commentary on Galatians*. Grand Rapids, Mich.: Eerdmans, 1982.

———. *1 and 2 Thessalonians*. Waco, Tex.: Word, 1982.

Dunn, James D. G. *The Epistles to the Colossians and Philemon*. Grand Rapids, Mich.: Eerdmans, 1996.

———. *Romans 9—16*. Waco, Tex.: Word, 1988.

Fitzmyer, Joseph. *Romans*. Garden City, N.Y.: Doubleday, 1993.

Furnish, Victor Paul. *II Corinthians*. Garden City, N.Y.: Doubleday, 1984.

Lincoln, Andrew T. *Ephesians*. Waco, Tex.: Word, 1990.

Longenecker, Richard N. *Galatians*. Waco, Tex.: Word, 1990.

Martin, Ralph P. *2 Corinthians*. Waco, Tex.: Word, 1986.

Moule, C. F. D. *The Epistle of Paul the Apostle to the Colossians and to Philemon*. Cambridge: Cambridge University Press, 1957.

O'Brien, Peter T. *Colossians, Philemon*. Waco, Tex.: Word, 1982.

Wall, Robert W. *Colossians and Philemon*. IVP New Testament Commentary. Downers Grove, Ill.: InterVarsity Press, 1993.

Witherington, Ben, III. *Acts of the Apostles*. Grand Rapids, Mich.: Eerdmans, 1997.

———. *Conflict and Community in Corinth*. Grand Rapids, Mich.: Eerdmans, 1995.

———. *Friendship and Finances in Philippi*. The New Testament in Context. Valley Forge, Penn.: Trinity Press International, 1995.

———. *Grace in Galatia*. Edinburgh: T & T Clark, 1998.

Zeisler, J. *Paul's Letter to the Romans*. Philadelphia: Trinity Press International, 1989.

Monographs, Studies and Collections of Essays

Atkins, Robert A. *Egalitarian Community: Ethnography and Exegesis*. Tuscaloosa: University of Alabama Press, 1991.

Aune, David E. *Prophecy in Early Christianity*. Grand Rapids, Mich.: Eerdmans, 1983.

Barrett, C. K. *From First Adam to Last*. London: A & C Black, 1962.

———. *The New Testament Background: Selected Documents*. Rev. ed. San Francisco: Harper & Row, 1987.

———. *Paul: An Introduction to His Thought*. Louisville, Ky.: Westminster John Knox, 1994.

———. *The Signs of an Apostle*. Philadelphia: Fortress, 1972.

Bartchy, S. Scott. *"Mallon Chresai": First Century Slavery and the Interpretation of 1 Cor. 7.21*. Missoula, Mont.: Scholars Press, 1973.

Bassler, Jouette, ed. *Pauline Theology*. Vol. 1, *Thessalonians, Philippians, Galatians, Philemon*. Minneapolis: Fortress, 1991.

Becker, Jürgen. *Paul: Apostle to the Gentiles*. Translated by O. C. Dean Jr. Louisville, Ky.: Westminster John Knox, 1993.

Beker, Johann Christiaan. *Heirs of Paul*. Minneapolis: Fortress, 1991.

———. *Paul the Apostle: The Triumph of God in Life and Thought*. Philadelphia: Fortress, 1980.

———. *Paul's Apocalyptic Gospel: The Coming Triumph of God*. Philadelphia: Fortress, 1982.

Blasi, Anthony J. *Making Charisma: The Social Construction of Paul's Public Image*. New Brunswick, N.J.: Transaction, 1991.

Bonner, Stanley F. *Education in Ancient Rome*. Berkeley: University of California Press, 1977.

Boyarin, Daniel. *Paul and the Politics of Identity*. Berkeley: University of California Press, 1994.

———. *A Radical Jew: Paul and the Politics of Identity*. Berkeley: University of California Press, 1994.

Brockhaus, Ulrich. *Charisma und Amt: Die paulinische Charismenlehre auf dem Hintergrund der frühchristlichen Gemeindefunktionen*. Wuppertal, Germany: R. Brockhaus, 1972.

Bruce, F. F. *Paul: Apostle of the Heart Set Free*. Grand Rapids, Mich.: Eerdmans, 1977.

Buechner, Frederick. *The Life of Jesus*. New York: Weathervane, 1974.

Bultmann, Rudolf. *Theology of the New Testament*. Vol. 1. New York: Scribner's, 1951.

Burridge, Richard A. *What Are the Gospels? A Comparison with Graeco-Roman Biography*. Society for New Testament Studies Monograph Series 70. Cambridge: Cambridge University Press, 1992.

Caird, G. B. *New Testament Theology*. Completed and edited by Lincoln D. Hurst. Oxford: Oxford University Press, 1994.

Cannon, George E. *The Use of Traditional Materials in Colossians*. Macon, Ga.: Mercer University Press, 1983.

Chow, John K. *Patronage and Power: A Study of Social Networks in Corinth. Journal for the Study of the New Testament* Supplement Series 75. Sheffield, U.K.: JSOT Press, 1992.

Clapp, Rodney. *Families at the Crossroads: Beyond Traditional and Modern Options*. Downers Grove, Ill.: InterVarsity Press, 1993.

Clarke, Martin L. *Higher Education in the Ancient World*. Albuquerque: University of New Mexico Press, 1971.

Collins, John J. *The Apocalyptic Imagination*. New York: Crossroad, 1984.

Crouch, James E. *The Origin and Intention of the Colossian Haustafeln*. Göttingen, Germany: Vandenhoeck & Ruprecht, 1972.

Deissmann, Adolf. *Light from the Ancient East*. Grand Rapids, Mich.: Baker, 1978.

———. *Paul: A Study of Social and Religious History*. New York: Harper & Brothers, 1957.

Dodds, Eric Robertson. *Pagan and Christian in an Age of Anxiety*. Cambridge: Cambridge University Press, 1965.

Donaldson, Terence L. *Paul and the Gentiles: Remapping the Apostle's Convictional World*. Minneapolis: Fortress, 1997.

Douglas, Mary. *Purity and Danger: An Analysis of the Concepts of Pollution and Taboo*. Baltimore: Pelican, 1970.

Dunn, James D. G. *Baptism in the Holy Spirit*. London: SCM Press, 1970.

———. *The Theology of Paul the Apostle*. Grand Rapids, Mich.: Eerdmans, 1997.

———. *The Theology of Paul's Letter to the Galatians*. Cambridge: Cambridge University Press, 1993.

Elliott, Neil. *Liberating Paul: The Justice of God and the Politics of the Apostle*. Maryknoll, N.Y.: Orbis, 1994.

Ellis, Earle E. *Paul's Use of the Old Testament*. Edinburgh: Oliver and Boyd, 1957.

———. *Prophecy and Hermeneutic in Early Christianity*. Grand Rapids, Mich.: Eerdmans, 1978.

Fowl, Stephen E. *The Story of Christ in the Ethics of Paul*. Sheffield, U.K.: JSOT Press, 1990.

Furnish, Victor Paul. *The Love Commandment in the New Testament*. Nashville: Abingdon, 1972.

———. *Theology and Ethics in Paul*. Nashville: Abingdon, 1968.

Gamble, Harry Y. *Books and Readers in the Early Church*. New Haven, Conn.: Yale University Press, 1995.

Georgi, Dieter. *The Opponents of Paul in Second Corinthians*. Philadelphia: Fortress, 1986.

Grudem, Wayne. *The Gift of Prophecy in 1 Corinthians*. Lanham, Md.: University Press of America, 1982.

Gulzow, Henneke L. *Christentum und Sklaverei in den ersten drei Jahrhunderten*. Bonn: Habelt, 1969.

Gundry, Robert H. *"Sōma" in Biblical Theology: With Special Emphasis on Pauline Anthropology.* Cambridge: Cambridge University Press, 1976.

Harris, William V. *Ancient Literacy.* Cambridge, Mass.: Harvard University Press, 1989.

Hay, David M. *An Investigation of the Narrative Substructure of Galatians 3:1-4:11.* Chico, Calif.: Scholars Press, 1983.

Hay, David M., ed. *Pauline Theology.* Vol. 2, *1 & 2 Corinthians.* Minneapolis: Fortress, 1993.

Hay, David M., and E. Elizabeth Johnson, eds. *Pauline Theology.* Vol. 3, *Romans.* Minneapolis: Fortress, 1995.

Hays, Richard B. *Echoes of Scripture in the Letters of Paul.* New Haven, Conn.: Yale University Press, 1989.

———. *The Faith of Jesus Christ: The Narrative Substructure of Galatians 3:1—4:11.* Society for Biblical Literature Dissertation Series 56. Chico, Calif.: Scholars Press, 1983.

———. *The Moral Vision of the New Testament.* San Francisco: HarperCollins, 1996.

Hengel, Martin. *The Hellenization of Judaea in the First Century After Christ.* Philadelphia: Trinity Press International, 1989.

———. *The Pre-Christian Paul.* Valley Forge, Penn.: Trinity Press International, 1991.

Hengel, Martin, and Anna Maria Schwemer. *Paul Between Damascus and Antioch: The Unknown Years.* Louisville, Ky.: Westminster John Knox, 1997.

Hock, Ronald. *The Social Context of Paul's Ministry: Tentmaking and Apostleship.* Philadelphia: Fortress, 1980.

Holmberg, Bengt. *Sociology and the New Testament.* Minneapolis: Fortress, 1990.

Hooker, Morna D., and Stephen G. Wilson, eds. *Paul and Paulinism: Essays in Honour of C. K. Barrett.* London: SPCK, 1982.

Horrell, David G. *The Social Ethos of the Corinthians Correspondence: Interests and Ideology from 1 Corinthians to 1 Clement.* Edinburgh: T & T Clark, 1996.

Hübner, Hans. *Law in Paul's Thought.* Edinburgh: T & T Clark, 1984.

Jewett, Robert. *Paul's Anthropological Terms.* Leiden: E. J. Brill, 1971.

Johnson, E. Elizabeth, and David M. Hay, eds. *Pauline Theology.* Vol. 4, *Looking Back, Pressing On.* Atlanta: Scholars Press, 1997.

Judge, E. A. *Rank and Status in the World of the Caesars and of St. Paul.* Christchurch, New Zealand: University of Canterbury, 1982.

———. *The Social Pattern of the Christian Groups in the First Century.* London: Tyndale Press, 1960.

Kennedy, George A. *New Testament Interpretation Through Rhetorical Criticism.* Chapel Hill: University of North Carolina Press, 1984.

Klausner, Joseph. *From Jesus to Paul.* New York: Macmillan, 1943.

Knight, George W. *The New Testament Teaching on the Role Relationship of Men and Women.* Grand Rapids, Mich.: Baker, 1977.

Kopf, D. A. *Die Schrift als Zeuge des Evangeliums: Untersuchungen zur Verwendung und zum Verstandnis der Schrift bei Paulus.* Tübingen, Germany: J. C. B. Mohr, 1986.

Kroeger, Richard C., and Catherine Clark Kroeger. *I Suffer Not a Woman: Rethinking 1 Timothy 2.11-15 in Light of Ancient Evidence.* Grand Rapids, Mich.: Baker, 1992.

Leisgang, H. *Die vorchirstlichen Anschauungen und lehren vom pneuma under der mystisch-intuitiven Erekenntnis.* Leipzig: Hinrichs, 1919.

Litfin, Duane A. *St. Paul's Theology of Proclamation: 1 Corinthians 1—4 and Greco-Roman Rhetoric.* Cambridge: Cambridge University Press, 1994.

Longman, Tremper, III, and Daniel G. Reid. *God Is a Warrior.* Grand Rapids, Mich.: Zondervan, 1995.

Lovering, Eugene H., Jr., and Jerry L. Sumney, eds. *Theology and Ethics in Paul and His Interpreters: Essays in Honor of Victor Paul Furnish.* Nashville: Abingdon, 1996.

Lyons, George. *Pauline Autobiography: Toward a New Understanding.* Atlanta: Scholars Press, 1985.

MacMullen, Ramsey. *Roman Social Relations 50 B.C. to A.D. 284.* New Haven, Conn.: Yale University Press, 1974.

Malina, Bruce J. *The New Testament World: Insights from Cultural Anthropology.* Rev. ed. Louisville, Ky.: Westminster John Knox, 1993.

Malina, Bruce J., and Jerome H. Neyrey. *Portraits of Paul: An Archaeology of Ancient Personality.* Louisville, Ky.: Westminster John Knox, 1996.

Marrou, Henri I. *A History of Education in Antiquity.* New York: Sheed & Ward, 1956.

Marshall, Peter. *Enmity in Corinth: Social Conventions in Paul's Relations with the Corinthians.* Tübingen, Germany: J. C. B. Mohr, 1987.

Martin, Dale B. *The Corinthian Body.* New Haven, Conn.: Yale University Press, 1995.

———. *Slavery as Salvation: The Metaphor of Slavery in Pauline Christianity.* New Haven, Conn.: Yale University Press, 1990.

Meade, David G. *Pseudonymity and Canon.* Grand Rapids, Mich.: Eerdmans, 1986.

Meeks, Wayne A. *The First Urban Christians.* New Haven, Conn.: Yale University Press, 1983.

———. *The Moral World of the First Christians.* Philadelphia: Westminster Press, 1986.

———. *The Origins of Christian Morality.* New Haven, Conn.: Yale University Press, 1993.

Metzger, Bruce M. *A Textual Commentary on the Greek New Testament.* London: United Bible Society, 1971.

Mitchell, Margaret M. *Paul and the Rhetoric of Reconciliation.* Tübingen, Germany: J. C. B. Mohr, 1991.

Montefiore, Claude G. *Judaism and St. Paul.* London: Max Goshen, 1914.

Moore, George Foot. *Judaism in the First Centuries of the Christian Era.* 2 vols. Cambridge, Mass.: Harvard University Press, 1927.

Morris, Colin M. *Epistles to the Apostle: Tarsus Please Forward.* Nashville: Abingdon, 1974.

Murphy-O'Connor, Jerome. *Paul: A Critical Life.* Oxford: Clarendon, 1996.

———. *St. Paul the Letter-Writer: His World, His Options, His Skill.* Collegeville, Minn.: Liturgical, 1995.

Murray, Gilbert. *Five Stages of Greek Religion.* New York: Putnam, 1912.

Neusner, Jacob, William S. Green and Ernest Frerichs, eds. *Judaisms and Their Messiahs at the Turn of the Christian Era.* Cambridge: Cambridge University Press, 1987.

———. *Rabbinic Traditions About Pharisees Before 70.* Leiden: E. J. Brill, 1971.

Neyrey, Jerome H. *Paul in Other Words: A Cultural Reading of His Letters.* Louisville, Ky.: Westminister John Knox, 1990.

———. *Portraits of Paul.* Louisville, Ky.: Westminster John Knox, 1996.

Nock, Arthur Darby. *St. Paul.* New York: Harper, 1938.

Patte, Daniel. *Paul's Faith and the Power of the Gospel.* Philadelphia: Fortress, 1983.

Patterson, Orlando. *Slavery and Social Death: A Comparative Study.* Cambridge, Mass.: Harvard University Press, 1982.

Petersen, Norman. *Rediscovering Paul: Philemon and the Sociology of Paul's Narrative World.* Philadelphia: Fortress, 1985.

Pilch, John J., and Bruce J. Malina, eds. *Biblical Social Values and Their Meaning.* Peabody, Mass.: Hendrickson, 1993.

Pogoloff, Stephen M. *Logos and Sophia: The Rhetorical Situation of 1 Corinthians.* Atlanta: Scholars Press, 1992.

Potter, David Stone. *Prophets and Emperors: Human and Divine Authority from Augustus to Theodosius.* Cambridge, Mass.: Harvard University Press, 1994.

Räisänen, Heikki. *Paul and the Law.* Tübingen, Germany: J. C. B. Mohr, 1983.

Reitzenstein, Richard. *Die hellenistichen Mysterienreligionen: Ihr Grundgedanken und Wirkungen.* Leipzig: Teubner, 1927.

Richards, E. Randolph. *The Secretary in the Letters of Paul.* Tübingen, Germany: J. C. B. Mohr, 1991.

Roetzel, Calvin. *The Letters of Paul: Conversations in Context.* 3rd ed. Louisville, Ky.: Wesminster John Knox, 1991.

Rosner, Brian S. *Paul, Scripture and Ethics: A Study of 1 Corinthians 5—7.* Leiden: E. J. Brill, 1994.

Saller, Richard P. *Personal Patronage Under the Empire.* Cambridge: Cambridge University Press, 1982.

Sanders, E. P. *Paul and Palestinian Judaism.* Philadelphia: Fortress, 1977.

———. *Paul, the Law and the Jewish People.* Philadelphia: Fortress, 1983.

Sandnes, Karl Olav. *Paul: One of the Prophets?* Tübingen, Germany: J. C. B. Mohr, 1991.

Schneemelcher, Wilhelm. *New Testament Apocrypha.* Vol. 2. Translated by R. Mcl. Wilson. Louisville, Ky.: Westminster John Knox, 1992.

Schoeps, Hans Joachim. *Paul: The Theology of the Apostle in the Light of Jewish Religious History.* Philadelphia: Westminster Press, 1961.

Schrage, Wolfgang. *Die konkreten Einzelgebote in der paulinischen Paranese.* Gütersloh, Germany: Mohn, 1961.

Schüssler Fiorenza, Elisabeth. *In Memory of Her.* New York: Crossroad, 1984.

Schweitzer, Albert. *The Mysticism of Paul the Apostle.* Translated by W. Montgomery. New York: Holt, 1931.

Segal, Alan F. *Paul the Convert: The Apostolate and Apostasy of Saul the Pharisee.* New Haven, Conn.: Yale University Press, 1990.

Sevenster, Jan Nicolaas. *Do You Know Greek? How Much Greek Could the First Jewish Christians Have Known?* Leiden: E. J. Brill, 1968.

Stark, Rodney. *The Rise of Christianity.* Princeton, N.J.: Princeton University Press, 1996.

Stendahl, Krister. *Paul Among Jews and Gentiles.* Philadelphia: Fortress, 1976.

Stowers, Stanley K. *Letter Writing in Greco-Roman Antiquity.* Philadelphia: Westminster Press, 1986.

Sumney, Jerry L. *Identifying Paul's Opponents: The Question of Method in 2 Corinthians.* Sheffield, U.K.: JSOT, 1990.

Theissen, Gerd. *Psychological Aspects of Pauline Theology.* Philadelphia: Fortress, 1987.

———. *The Social Setting of Pauline Christianity.* Philadelphia: Fortress, 1982.

Tomson, Peter J. *Paul and the Jewish Law: Halakha in the Letters of the Apostle to the Gentiles.* Minneapolis: Fortress, 1990.

Van Unnik, W. C. *Tarsus or Jerusalem, the City of Paul's Youth. Sparsa Collecta I.* Leiden: E. J. Brill, 1973.

Vos, Gerhardus. *The Pauline Eschatology.* Grand Rapids, Mich.: Eerdmans, 1972.

Wacholder, Ben Zion. *Nicolaus of Damascus.* Berkeley: University of California Press, 1962.

Westerholm, Stephen. *Preface to the Study of Paul.* Grand Rapids, Mich.: Eerdmans, 1997.

Westermann, Claus. *Prophetic Oracles of Salvation in the Old Testament.* Louisville, Ky.: Westminster John Knox, 1991.

White, L. Michael, ed. *Social Networks in the Early Christian Environment: Issues and Methods for Social History.* Atlanta: Scholars Press, 1992.

Wiedemann, Thomas. *Greek and Roman Slavery.* Baltimore: Johns Hopkins University Press, 1981.

Wilson, Stephen G. *Luke and the Pastoral Epistles.* London: SPCK, 1979.

Wimbush, Vincent L. *Paul the Worldly Ascetic: Response to the World and Self-Understanding According to 1 Corinthians 7.* Macon, Ga.: Mercer University Press, 1987.

Wink, Walter. *Naming the Powers.* Philadelphia: Fortress, 1984.

Winter, Bruce. *Are Paul and Philo Among the Sophists?* Cambridge: Cambridge University Press, 1996.

Wire, Antoinette Clark. *The Corinthian Women Prophets: A Reconstruction Through Paul's Rhetoric.* Minneapolis: Fortress, 1990.

Witherington, Ben, III. *Jesus, Paul and the End of the World.* Downers Grove, Ill.: InterVarsity Press, 1992.

———. *Jesus the Sage: The Pilgrimage of Wisdom.* Minneapolis: Fortress, 1994.

———. *Paul's Narrative Thought World.* Louisville, Ky.: Westminster John Knox, 1994.

———. *Women in the Earliest Churches.* Cambridge: Cambridge University Press, 1988.

———. *Women in the Ministry of Jesus.* Cambridge: Cambridge University Press, 1984.

Wright, N. T. *Jesus and the Victory of God.* Minneapolis: Fortress, 1996.

———. *The New Testament and the People of God.* Minneapolis: Fortress, 1992.

———. *What Saint Paul Really Said.* Grand Rapids, Mich.: Eerdmans, 1997.

Yoder, John Howard. *The Politics of Jesus.* Grand Rapids, Mich.: Eerdmans, 1972.

Articles and Essays

Achtemeier, Paul J. "The Continuing Quest for Coherence in St. Paul: An Experiment in Thought." In *Theology and Ethics in Paul and His Interpreters: Essays in Honor of Victor Paul Furnish*, pp. 132-45. Edited by Eugene H. Lovering Jr. and Jerry L. Sumney. Nashville: Abingdon, 1996.

————. "Finding the Way to Paul's Theology." In *Pauline Theology*. Vol. 1, *Thessalonians, Philippians, Galatians, Philemon*, pp. 25-36. Edited by Jouette M. Bassler. Minneapolis: Fortress, 1991.

Baird, W. "Pauline Eschatology in Hermeneutic Perspective." *New Testament Studies* 17 (1970-1971): 314-27.

Barnett, Paul W. "Apostle." In *Dictionary of Paul and His Letters*, pp. 45-51. Edited by Gerald F. Hawthorne, Ralph P. Martin and Daniel G. Reid. Downers Grove, Ill.: InterVarsity Press, 1993.

Beker, Johann Christiaan. "Recasting Pauline Theology: The Coherency-Contingency Scheme as Interpretive Model." In *Pauline Theology*. Vol. 1, *Thessalonians, Philippians, Galatians, Philemon*, pp. 15-24. Edited by Jouette M. Bassler. Minneapolis: Fortress, 1991.

Betz, Hans Dieter. "Apostle." In *The Anchor Bible Dictionary*, 1:309-11. Edited by David Noel Freedman. 6 vols. New York: Doubleday, 1992.

————. "Paul." In *The Anchor Bible Dictionary*, 5:186-201. Edited by David Noel Freedman. 6 vols. New York: Doubleday, 1992.

Booth, A. D. "Elementary and Secondary Education in the Roman Empire." *Florilegium* 1 (1979): 1-14.

Boring, Eugene. "Prophecy, Early Christian." In *The Anchor Bible Dictionary*, 5:495-502. Edited by David Noel Freedman. 6 vols. New York: Doubleday, 1992.

Church, F. F. "Rhetorical Structure and Design in Paul's Letter to Philemon." *Harvard Theological Review* 71 (1978): 17-33.

Cohn-Sherbok, Daniel. "Paul and Rabbinic Exegesis." *Scottish Journal of Theology* 35 (1982): 132.

Dodd, C. H. "The Mind of Paul," pts. 1-2. In *New Testament Studies*, pp. 67-82, 83-128. Manchester: University of Manchester Press, 1952.

Dunn, James D. G. "Works of the Law and the Curse of the Law (Galatians 3.10-14)." *New Testament Studies* 31 (1985).

Elliott, J. H. "Patronage and Clientism in Early Christian Society." *Forum* 3 (1987): 39-48.

Ellis, E. Earle. "Pastoral Letters." In *Dictionary of Paul and His Letters*, pp. 658-66. Edited by Gerald F. Hawthorne, Ralph P. Martin and Daniel G. Reid. Downers Grove, Ill.: InterVarsity Press, 1993.

Evans, Craig A. "Prophet, Paul as." In *Dictionary of Paul and His Letters*, pp. 762-65. Edited by Gerald F. Hawthorne, Ralph P. Martin and Daniel G. Reid. Downers Grove, Ill.: InterVarsity Press, 1993.

Friedrich, J. W., and Peter Stuhlmacher. "Zur historischen Situation und Intention von Rom. 13.1-7." *Zeitschrift für Theologie und Kirche* 73 (1976): 131-66.

Furnish, Victor Paul. "Development in Paul's Thought." *Journal of the American Academy of Religion* 38 (1970): 289-303.

————. "Where Is 'the Truth' of the Gospel?" In *Pauline Theology*. Vol. 4, *Looking Back, Pressing On*, pp. 161-77. Edited by E. Elizabeth Johnson and David M. Hay. Atlanta: Scholars Press, 1997.

Hays, Richard B. "Christ Prays the Psalms: Paul's Use of an Early Christian Exegetical Convention." In *The Future of Christology: Essays in Honor of Leander E. Keck*, pp. 122-36. Edited by Abraham J. Malherbe and Wayne A. Meeks. Minneapolis: Fortress, 1993.

————. "The Role of Scripture in Paul's Ethics." In *Theology and Ethics in Paul and His Interpreters: Essays in Honor of Victor Paul Furnish*, pp. 30-47. Edited by Eugene H. Lovering Jr. and Jerry L. Sumney. Nashville: Abingdon, 1996.

Hendrix, H. "Benefactor/Patron Networks in the Urban Environment: Evidence from Thessalonica." In *Social Networks in the Early Christian Environment: Issues and Methods for Social History*, pp. 39-58. Edited by L. Michael White. Atlanta: Scholars Press, 1992.

Hester, J. D. "The Rhetorical Structure of Galatians 1.11-14." *Journal of Biblical Literature* 103 (1984): 223-33.

Holladay, Carl A. "1 Corinthians 13: Paul as Apostolic Paradigm." In *Greeks, Romans and Christians: Essays in Honor of Abraham J. Malherbe,* pp. 80-98. Edited by David L. Balch, Everett Ferguson and Wayne A. Meeks. Minneapolis: Fortress, 1990.

Horsley, Richard. "1 Corinthians: A Case Study of Paul's Assembly as an Alternative Society." In *Paul and Empire: Religion and Power in Roman Imperial Society,* pp. 242-52. Edited by Richard Horsley. Harrisburg, Penn.: Trinity Press, 1997.

Lohse, Eduard. "Change of Thought in Pauline Theology? Some Reflections on Paul's Ethical Teaching in the Context of his Theology." In *Theology and Ethics in Paul and His Interpreters: Essays in Honor of Victor Paul Furnish,* pp. 146-60. Edited by Eugene H. Lovering Jr. and Jerry L. Sumney. Nashville: Abingdon, 1996.

Malherbe, Abraham. "A Physical Description of Paul." *Harvard Theological Review* 79 (1986): 170-75.

Marshall, I. Howard. "Incarnational Christology in the New Testament." In *Christ the Lord: Studies in Christology Presented to Donald Guthrie,* pp. 1-16. Edited by Harold H. Rowdon. Downers Grove, Ill.: InterVarsity Press, 1982.

Meeks, Wayne A. "The Image of the Androgyne: Some Uses of a Symbol in Earliest Christianity." *History of Religions* 13 (1974): 165-208.

Meyer, Paul W. "Pauline Theology: A Proposal for a Pause in Its Pursuit." In *Pauline Theology.* Vol. 4, *Looking Back, Pressing On,* pp. 140-60. Edited by E. Elizabeth Johnson and David M. Hay. Atlanta: Scholars Press, 1997.

Moxnes, Halvor. "Honor, Shame and the Outside World in Paul's Letter to the Romans." In *The Social World of Formative Christianity and Judaism,* pp. 207-18. Edited by Jacob Neusner et al. Philadelphia: Fortress, 1988.

Murphy-O'Connor, Jerome. "1 Corinthians 11:2-16 Once Again." *Catholic Biblical Quarterly* 50 (1988): 265-74.

Padgett, Alan G. "The Pauline Rationale for Submission: Biblical Feminism and the *Hina* Clauses of Titus 2:1-10." *Evangelical Quarterly* 59 (1987): 39-52.

Ramsay, William M. "The Manifest God." *Expository Times* 10 (1899): 208.

Rengstorf, Karl H. "ἀπόστολος" In *Theological Dictionary of the New Testament,* 1:407-45. Edited by Gerhard Kittel and Gerhard Friedrich. 10 vols. Grand Rapids, Mich.: Eerdmans, 1964-1976.

Sampley, J. Paul. "From Text to Thought World: The Route to Paul's Ways." In *Pauline Theology.* Vol. 1, *Thessalonians, Philipppians, Galatians, Philemon,* pp. 3-14. Edited by Jouette M. Bassler. Minneapolis: Fortress, 1991.

Schrage, Wolfgang. "Zur Ethik der neutestamentlichen Haustafeln." *New Testament Studies* 21 (1974-75): 1-22.

Schroeder, D. *Die Haustafeln des Neuen Testaments (ihre Herkunft und Theologischer Sinn).* Ph.D. diss. Hamburg: Mikrocopie, 1959.

Schüssler Fiorenza, Elisabeth. "Women in the Pre-Pauline and Pauline Churches." *Union Seminary Quarterly Review* 33 (1978): 153-66.

Stulhmacher, Peter. "Jesustradition im Romerbrief." *Theologische Beiträge* 14 (1983): 240-50.

———. "Paul's Understanding of the Law in the Letter to the Romans." *Svensk Exegetisk Årbosk* 50 (1985): 87-104.

Wagner, Ross. " 'Not Beyond the Things Which Are Written': A Call to Boast Only in the Lord (1 Cor. 4:6)." *New Testament Studies* (forthcoming).

Walker, Peter. "The Burden of Proof in Identifying Pauline Letters as Interpolations." *New Testament Studies* 33 (1987): 610-18.

Watson, Duane F. "A Rhetorical Analysis of Philippians and Its Implications for the Unity Question." *Novum Testamentum* 39 (1988): 57-87.

Wedderburn, A. J. M. "The Problem of the Denial of the Resurrection in 1 Corinthians XV."

Novum Testamentum 23 (1981): 229-41.

Witherington, Ben, III. "Christ." In *Dictionary of Paul and His Letters,* pp. 95-100. Edited by Gerald F. Hawthorne, Ralph P. Martin and Daniel G. Reid. Downers Grove, Ill.: InterVarsity Press, 1993.

———. "Christology." In *Dictionary of Paul and His Letters,* pp. 100-115. Edited by Gerald F. Hawthorne, Ralph P. Martin and Daniel G. Reid. Downers Grove, Ill.: InterVarsity Press, 1993.

———. "Rite and Rights for Women—Gal. 3.28." *New Testament Studies* 27 (1981): 593-604.

Wright, A. G. "The Literary Genre Midrash." *Catholic Biblical Quarterly* 28 (1966): 113-20.

Youtie, H. C. "*Agrammatos:* An Aspect of Greek Society in Egypt." *Harvard Studies in Classical Philology* 75 (1971): 161-76.

———. "*Upographeus:* The Social Impact of Illiteracy in Graeco-Roman Egypt." *Zeitschrift für Papyrologie und Epigraphik* 17 (1975): 201-21.

Ziesel, W. "Does *Kephalē* Mean 'Source' or 'Authority Over' in Greek Literature? A Survey of 2,336 Examples." *Trinity Journal* n.s. 6 (1985): 38-59.

———. "*Univira:* An Example of Continuity and Change in Roman Society." *Church History* 46 (1977): 19-32.

Index of Authors

Achtemeier, Paul J., 291-94
Alexander, Loveday C. A., 311
Atkins, Robert A., 22, 163
Aune, David E., 133, 135, 151, 152
Baird, W., 144
Barnett, Paul, 156, 157
Barrett, C. K., 15, 70, 104, 157, 161, 237, 280-82, 285, 311, 316
Bartchy, S. Scott, 190, 196
Bassler, Jouette M., 234, 282
Becker, Jürgen, 16, 307, 310, 327
Beker, J. Christiaan, 111, 142, 147, 234, 288-91
Betz, Hans Dieter, 119, 157, 271, 280, 281
Blasi, Anthony J., 162
Blinzler, J., 305
Bonner, Stanley F., 116
Booth, A. D., 91
Boring, Eugene, 13, 133
Boyarin, Daniel, 21, 53-55, 67, 159, 253
Brockhaus, Ulrich, 160
Bruce, F. F., 15, 22, 28, 42, 44, 53, 103, 144, 208, 215, 311, 326
Buechner, Frederick, 296, 297
Bultmann, Rudolf, 88, 207-9, 212
Burridge, Richard A., 23
Caird, G. B., 137-39
Campbell, T. H., 327
Cannon, George E., 187
Carson, D. A., 63
Castelli, E., 86
Chamblin, J. Knox, 208
Chow, John K., 48
Church, F. F., 166
Clapp, Rodney, 24
Clarke, M. L., 91
Collins, John J., 55, 142, 290
Craddock, Fred, 62
Crouch, James E., 187, 189
Curran, J., 323
Daube, David, 59
Deissmann, Adolf, 13-14, 16, 93, 98, 127, 128, 146, 160, 169, 201

Dodd, C. H., 21, 280
Dodds, Eric Robertson, 21
Donaldson, Terence L., 59, 234
Douglas, Mary, 22
Duncan, G. S., 320
Dunn, J. D. G., 65, 66, 69, 82, 85, 181, 182, 183, 186, 187, 209-11, 213, 222, 234, 235, 279, 281, 282, 287, 294-96
Elliott, Neil, 10, 11, 48, 176, 177
Ellis, E. Earle, 111, 113, 133, 254
Evans, Craig A., 133, 134
Fee, Gordon D., 79, 82
Fishbane, Michael, 136
Fitzmyer, Joseph, 140, 177, 327
Fowl, Stephen E., 236, 242, 243, 246
Friedrich, G., 157, 178
Furnish, Victor Paul, 189, 212, 259, 265, 268, 279, 283, 290, 293
Gamble, Harry, 92, 100, 104
Grudem, Wayne, 133-35, 224
Gundry, Robert H., 208, 212
Guzlow, H., 194
Harrer, G. A., 72
Harris, William V., 91, 92
Hay, David M., 283, 286
Hays, Richard B., 65, 225, 235-37, 243, 245, 254, 255, 258-61, 265, 266, 269, 270-76
Hemer, Colin J., 72, 311
Hendrix, Holland, 168
Hengel, Martin, 16, 59, 71, 79, 82, 94-98, 127, 129, 133, 134, 170, 233, 249, 308, 310, 327
Hester, J. D., 119
Hock, Ronald, 128
Holladay, Carl A., 81, 123, 132
Hooker, Morna, 5
Horrell, David G., 227, 228
Horsley, Richard, 70, 295
Jewett, Robert, 208, 209, 311
Johnson, E. Elizabeth, 283, 286
Johnson, Luke Timothy, 112
Judge, Edwin A., 22, 70, 128
Kanter, R., 77
Keck, Leander E., 9, 11, 274
Kennedy, George A., 119, 120

Kim, Seyoon, 78
Klausner, J., 53
Knight, George W., 112, 224
Kopf, D. A., 96
Kroeger, Catherine Clark, 224
Kroeger, Richard C., 224
Lampe, Peter, 322
Leary, T. J., 72
Leisgang, H., 133
Lentz, J. C., 70
Lincoln, Andrew T., 80, 201
Litfin, Duane A., 118
Lohse, Eduard, 290
Longenecker, Richard N., 78, 119, 250
Longman, Tremper III, 144
Lovering, Eugene H. Jr., 265, 290
Luedemann, Gerd, 16, 310
Lyons, George, 56
MacMullen, Ramsey, 128
Malherbe, Abraham J., 43, 70, 274
Malina, Bruce J., 22, 29-31, 35, 40, 41, 43, 44,
    47, 75, 208
Marrou, H. I., 91, 95
Marshall, I. Howard, 10, 111, 246
Marshall, Peter, 49
Martin, Dale B., 23, 35, 36, 197, 206, 210, 216
Martin, Ralph P., 133, 146, 208, 311
Meade, David G., 111
Meeks, Wayne A., 21, 22, 70, 123, 132, 221,
    266, 274
Meier, John P., 305
Metzger, Bruce M., 192
Meyer, Paul W., 284
Mitchell, Margaret M., 5, 123
Montefiore, C. G., 53
Morris, Colin, 108
Moule, C. F. D., 198
Moxnes, Halvor, 45
Murray, Gilbert, 103
Neusner, Jacob, 45, 54, 55, 96
Neyrey, Jerome, 22, 28, 31, 35, 40, 41, 43, 47,
    75, 208, 209, 214
Nock, Arthur Darby, 14, 15, 17, 76, 98
Ogg, G., 311
Padgett, Alan G., 224
Patte, Daniel, 234
Patterson, Orlando, 194

Petersen, Norman R., 198, 233, 235
Pilch, John J., 44
Pogoloff, Stephen, 123
Potter, David Stone, 152
Ramsay, William M., 146
Rapske, Brian, 70, 71, 320, 321, 323, 325
Reid, Daniel G., 133, 144, 208, 311
Reitzenstein, Richard, 133
Rengstorf, Karl, 157
Richards, E. Randolph, 100, 101, 104
Roetzel, Calvin, 105
Rosner, Brian S., 268
Saldarini, Anthony J., 59
Saller, Richard P., 49
Sampley, J. Paul, 282, 285, 287, 288, 291
Sanders, E. P., 11, 55, 65, 66, 69, 268, 291
Sandnes, Karl Olav, 133
Schneemelcher, E., 42
Schoeps, Hans Joachim, 53
Schrage, Wolfgang, 188, 265
Schroeder, David, 187
Schüssler Fiorenza, Elisabeth, 224
Schweitzer, Albert, 137, 142
Schwemer, Anna Maria, 16, 17, 59, 71, 79, 82,
    88, 98, 127, 129, 134, 170, 233, 308, 310, 327
Segal, Alan F., 21, 53-55, 57-58, 64, 76, 159
Sevenster, J. N., 91
Slingerland, H. Dixon, 313
Stark, Rodney, 22, 93, 108, 267
Stendahl, Krister, 21, 58, 62, 63, 77, 78, 177,
    207
Stowers, Stanley K., 100, 105
Stulhmacher, Peter, 183
Sumney, Jerry L., 162, 265, 290
Theissen, Gerd, 21, 22, 208, 228, 266
Thielman, Frank, 65, 66, 68
Van Unnik, W. C., 95, 307
Vos, Gerhardus, 148
Wacholder, Ben Zion, 98
Wagner, Ross, 236, 237
Walker, Peter, 224
Wall, Robert W., 124, 165
Walter, J., 323
Watson, Duane F., 122
Wedderburn, A. J. M., 148
Westerholm, Stephen, 19, 65
Westermann, Claus, 152

White, L. M., 167
Wiedemann, Thomas, 194, 197
Wilson, A. N., 17, 229, 311
Wilson, Stephen G., 10, 112, 326
Wimbush, Vincent L., 214
Wink, Walter, 179
Winter, Bruce, 22
Wire, Antoinette Clark, 223, 224
Witherington, Ben, III, 1, 4, 10, 29, 30, 32, 41, 44, 48, 49, 55-57, 65, 67, 69, 71, 76, 79, 82-87, 94, 98, 117, 121-24, 132, 137, 140, 143, 149-53, 157, 158, 160, 161, 169, 170, 177, 187, 193, 196, 202, 207, 214, 217, 219, 225, 226, 232, 241, 244, 246, 251, 253, 255, 267, 269, 274, 275, 281, 298, 307, 312-14, 316-18, 321, 322, 324
Wright, A. G., 254
Wright, N. T., 17, 58, 59, 137-39, 235, 243, 248, 253, 271, 306, 307
Yoder, John H., 178
Youtie, H. C., 91
Zeisler, John, 184
Ziesel, W., 46

Index of Subjects

advocate, 7, 12, 52, 114, 175, 204, 205, 207, 218, 219, 222, 226, 229, 277, 297, 301, 314

allegory, 54, 97, 121, 257, 258, 302

ancient personality, 7, 18, 20, 22, 23, 286

androcentricism, 24, 51

anthropologist, 12, 204, 206-18

anthropology, 21-23, 31, 50, 66, 86, 204, 206-9, 211, 215, 286, 299

Antioch, 16, 17, 34, 59, 71, 79, 82, 88, 98, 115, 121, 127, 129, 134, 157, 161, 170, 195, 233, 308-10, 313, 314, 316-18, 323, 327, 328

apocalyptic, 64, 75, 132, 142, 143, 147, 151, 154, 281, 289-91

apostle, apostleship, 7, 10-13, 15-17, 19, 21, 27, 39, 42, 43, 53, 57, 74, 79, 81, 84, 88, 90, 91, 95, 103, 108, 109, 112, 114, 125, 126, 128-31, 133, 134, 137, 144, 147, 153, 155-65, 168-72, 176, 177, 188, 198, 205, 208, 210, 229, 232, 234, 238, 250, 251, 264, 268, 279, 281, 289, 295, 296, 298, 299, 302, 303, 307, 310, 311, 314, 317, 323

Arabia, 34, 58, 77, 306-9, 326

aural culture, 89, 93, 100

boasting, 18, 52, 55, 61, 62, 70, 72, 79-81, 110, 124, 144, 146, 170, 236, 300

body, 18, 22, 23, 28, 33-44, 50, 51, 80, 83, 84, 86, 93, 105-7, 114, 130, 146, 148, 150, 154, 155, 163, 164, 170, 175, 178, 204-6, 208-21, 223, 226-29, 231, 242, 251, 262, 263, 266-68, 272, 276, 282, 285, 295, 297, 301

Caesarea, 319, 323, 324, 326-28, 330

charisma, 160, 162

chronology, 12, 16, 20, 79, 127, 233, 242, 290, 303, 305, 310, 311, 313, 317, 318, 324-27, 330

citizen, citizenship, 12, 14, 23, 50-53, 69-73, 87-89, 94, 115, 116, 174, 176, 181, 197, 300, 301, 306, 320, 322, 325

coherence and contingency, 234, 282, 288-93, 301, 302

Colossae, 186

conversion, 18, 20, 21, 33-35, 52-55, 57-60, 62-64, 66, 73-78, 80, 86, 90, 96, 108, 115, 118, 120, 126, 133, 135, 140, 156-59, 163, 167, 169, 176, 195, 196, 198, 212, 220, 239, 249-51, 280, 282, 303, 304-8, 317, 326

Corinth, 44, 48, 49, 73, 94, 115, 125, 127-29, 136, 143, 149, 158, 161, 162, 167, 168, 177, 195, 196, 217, 223, 224, 229, 266, 295, 310, 313, 315, 317, 318, 323, 326-28, 330

Cynics, 24, 39, 129

Day of the Lord, 108, 137, 140, 141, 143, 146, 147, 206, 216

diaspora, 14, 53, 59-61, 76, 95, 97, 116

diatribe, 206

dyadic personality, 18, 31, 34, 35, 50, 77, 88, 297

echoes of Scripture, 65, 140, 222, 235-37, 245, 249, 254, 255, 258-60, 293

education, 4, 17, 24, 26, 31, 59, 60, 70, 89-92, 94, 95, 97, 98, 104, 114-16, 119, 126, 129, 195, 300, 305, 306

Ephesus, 94, 115, 128, 168, 317, 319-23, 328

epideictic rhetoric, 11, 111, 116, 117, 119, 123

epistles, epistolary style/features, 10, 85, 89, 90, 92, 98, 101, 103-8, 110-12, 114, 119, 121, 122, 124, 125, 187, 198, 222, 234, 280, 298, 305, 319, 320, 321, 323, 325, 326, 327

eschatological prophet, 132, 154

ethics, Paul as ethicist, 7, 12, 46, 113, 123, 140, 148, 232, 233, 236, 243, 253, 263-65, 267-73, 275, 276, 278, 279, 290, 293, 296, 297, 302

exhortation, 83, 84, 87, 88, 106, 120, 126, 139, 178, 183, 187-93, 199, 200, 201, 256, 263, 265, 266, 272, 277, 278

family, 18, 24-32, 34, 35, 42, 46, 47, 51, 58, 71, 72, 77, 88, 98, 102, 108, 109, 127, 164, 167, 175, 185-94, 198, 202, 205, 266-68, 301, 306, 308, 321

feminism, 204-6, 224, 265, 301

forensic rhetoric, 117, 120, 124

Galatia, 19, 34, 55-57, 65, 67, 69, 85, 119-21, 127, 158, 161, 193, 214, 221, 244, 251, 255, 258, 269, 275, 281, 307, 310, 311, 314-17, 327, 328

gender, 18, 26, 28, 31-33, 41, 42, 46, 51, 169, 194, 205, 206, 226, 228 generation, 18, 26, 28, 31, 33, 41, 42, 46, 51, 122, 139, 256

geography, 18, 28, 31-33, 41, 42, 46, 51, 56

glossolalia, 82

historical Paul, 9-13, 19, 50, 54, 55, 88, 91, 104, 114, 158, 179, 181, 209, 224, 252, 265, 278, 303

honor, 10, 18, 22, 27, 32, 42, 44-51, 55, 56, 62, 111, 156, 158, 164-66, 170, 181, 189, 192, 193, 248, 265, 274, 297, 300, 313

honor and shame codes, 44, 46, 47

honor challenge, 47, 56, 158, 164, 166, 248

household codes, 177, 185-90, 191, 194, 201, 202, 266, 301

husbands, 25, 30, 46, 103, 167, 175, 186-94, 223, 241

imitation, 37, 86-88, 113, 120, 145, 170, 236, 246, 247, 250, 262, 269, 273, 276, 303

initiation, 76, 77, 220, 282

introspection, 21, 34, 62, 207

Jerusalem, 13, 20, 32, 34, 57-59, 60, 77, 89, 94, 95, 97, 98, 116, 121, 137, 138, 146, 157, 158, 160, 180, 219, 258, 303-9, 313-18, 323, 327, 328, 330

Jewish heritage, 52, 55, 56, 59, 71, 126, 268, 282, 283, 301

kinship, 25-31, 35, 57, 192

law, 11, 14, 19, 31, 47, 48, 52, 53, 55-60, 62-69, 74, 76, 78, 86, 95, 97, 116, 120-22, 158, 159, 164, 177, 183, 196, 198, 210, 215, 225, 231, 240, 241, 244, 245, 253, 254, 259-64, 268-75, 278, 281-85, 287, 288, 291, 293, 301, 314, 321, 324

leadership, 10, 92, 93, 112, 131, 160, 162, 165, 167, 169-72, 197, 205, 223, 228, 263, 267, 297, 314

letter writing, 89, 90, 94, 98-100, 101, 103-5, 113, 114, 127, 153

letters, 9-13, 16, 19, 22, 33, 41, 42, 53, 56, 58, 63, 65, 69-73, 82, 84-90, 92, 93, 98, 100-115, 118, 119, 122-26, 129, 133, 135, 136, 142, 144, 151-53, 155, 162, 171, 176, 186, 196, 208, 211, 214, 218, 220, 223, 224, 230, 232-38, 253, 254, 255, 263, 264, 266, 268, 279-81, 283-87, 290-92, 295-98, 300, 302, 303, 306, 309, 310, 311, 313, 319, 320, 322, 326, 327, 330

literacy, 24, 89-92, 94, 95, 97, 109, 114, 232

manumission of slaves, 165, 169, 194-98, 223, 229

mirror-reading, 18, 23, 162, 170, 239, 292

Mosaic covenant/law, 19, 52, 55-57, 60, 62, 64-69, 78, 120, 158, 231, 244, 245, 254, 261, 264, 268, 269, 270, 278, 285, 314

narrative, 9, 11, 63, 66, 69, 83, 86, 119, 121, 198, 207, 226, 230, 232, 233-37, 241, 244, 246, 248, 252, 253, 258, 261, 262, 274, 275, 278, 285, 296, 302, 316, 320

narrative thought world, 11, 66, 69, 83, 207, 230, 232, 235, 236, 241, 244, 246, 253, 274, 278, 296, 302

nonviolence, 60, 174, 176, 181, 295

orality, oral culture, 89, 90, 93, 100, 108, 115, 119, 230, 232, 237, 260, 288, 300, 301, 315

orator, oratory, 89, 98, 116, 118, 129

parousia, 140, 142-45, 216, 272

Pastoral Epistles, 10, 92, 110-12, 114, 280, 319, 326-27

patriarchy, 186

patrons, patronage, 47-51, 60, 70, 115, 116, 128, 129, 161, 165, 166, 168, 169

Paul the exegete, 7, 12, 14, 229-32, 236, 253-61, 274, 302

Paul the Jew, 23, 53, 55

personality, 7, 13, 15, 18-23, 26, 31, 33-36, 39-41, 44, 48, 50-52, 75, 77, 86, 89, 100, 114, 131, 204, 206, 208-12, 226, 243, 286, 295, 297, 299

Pharisee, Pharisaism, 18, 19, 31, 52, 54, 59, 60, 62-64, 78, 94, 96-98, 114, 116, 130, 138, 147, 154, 159, 174, 176, 181, 231, 242, 254, 261, 289

Philippi, 73, 83, 94, 115, 122, 127, 140, 196, 223, 295, 310, 320, 321, 323, 327

power, 36, 45, 47-49, 68, 81, 83, 86, 130-32, 148, 150, 152, 154-56, 158, 162, 168-70, 172, 174, 178, 189, 193, 200, 202, 215, 216, 219, 234, 247, 248, 259, 273, 276, 277, 294-96, 298, 300, 301, 303

powers, 15, 115, 116, 132, 163, 168, 174, 177-79, 193, 202, 219, 222, 229, 238, 262

prison, 112, 172, 212, 320, 326

prisoner, prisoners, 164, 172, 194, 320, 321

prophecy, prophecies, 33, 79, 82, 131-33, 135-37, 142, 143, 147, 149, 151-56, 163, 173, 224, 225, 257, 271, 316 prophet, prophets, 7, 12, 14, 27, 58, 74, 81, 115, 129-37, 142, 143, 147, 151-56, 171, 172, 223, 225, 267, 300, 301, 306

pseudepigraphy, 101, 113

psychology, 15, 17, 21, 36, 37, 62, 207-9, 289, 291

quest for Paul, 55, 127

reading and writing, 92, 95, 96

realist, 7, 12, 174-84, 202

realized eschatology, 111, 142, 149

reciprocity, 18, 47-49, 51, 60, 164, 166, 201, 291, 300

resurrection, 13, 38, 39, 59, 64, 65, 83, 84, 87, 130, 138, 139, 140, 143, 144, 147-51, 154, 157, 204, 213, 222, 228, 236, 247, 248, 250-52, 264, 273, 275, 279, 282-85, 289, 291-94, 298

revelation, 14, 15, 62, 74, 75, 78-81, 130, 132, 142, 143, 147, 151, 153, 155, 156, 284, 316

revolutionary, 149, 174-76, 181

rhetoric, 10-12, 14, 16, 51, 56, 59, 61, 70, 73, 78, 89, 90, 91, 93, 97, 98, 100, 101, 104, 111, 115, 117-19, 122-27, 129, 131, 149, 158, 162, 163, 166, 167, 198, 223, 230, 234, 273, 276, 280, 286, 288, 291, 293, 295, 300, 306, 314

rhetors, 7, 12, 70, 88-90, 98, 114, 115, 117, 118, 127, 162, 166, 300

Roman citizenship, 12, 23, 50-52, 53, 69-73, 87, 89, 94, 115, 116, 174, 176, 181, 300, 301, 306, 320, 322, 325

Rome, 15, 32, 73, 88, 106, 113, 116, 140, 161, 171, 174, 177, 178, 180-82, 184, 194, 195, 223, 279, 310-13, 317-26, 330

secretaries, 91, 100-102, 109-11, 113

sectarianism, 57, 69, 77, 88, 181, 182, 205, 216, 217, 263, 269, 272, 283, 295, 299

sensus plenior, 231, 258, 261

servant, servanthood, 18, 86, 87, 114, 131, 135, 156, 169-72, 179, 188-90, 194, 197, 231, 236, 245, 246, 248-50, 295, 300, 301, 306

shame, 22, 40, 44-47, 49, 51, 61, 300

slave, slavery, 28, 45, 46, 66, 67, 72, 74, 87, 94, 101, 105, 128, 163-65, 169, 170, 175, 176, 181, 185, 187, 190, 193-202, 205, 211, 219, 221-23, 226, 228, 229, 241, 242, 248, 258, 262, 268, 301, 321, 322

story, storytelling, 7, 12, 25, 27, 32-34, 41, 42, 66, 79, 80, 132, 157, 158, 229-53, 255, 256, 258, 259, 261, 262, 264, 270, 274, 275, 277, 278, 285, 295, 296, 301-3

tentmaking, 31, 90, 115, 128

theologian, 7, 12, 232, 253, 263, 278-98

theology, 11, 21, 53, 66, 68, 88, 113, 142, 212, 234, 235, 237, 264, 265, 268, 269, 271, 275, 278-88, 290, 292-94, 296, 297, 301, 302

types, typology, 23, 41, 100, 231, 255, 256, 258, 261, 272, 302

visions, 24, 49, 51, 75, 79, 80, 127, 131, 132, 135, 136, 142, 143, 150, 151, 154, 158, 169, 175, 203, 205, 219, 220, 222, 225-28, 252, 264-66, 270, 271, 273, 281, 288

wives, 30, 46, 58, 103, 108, 109, 167, 186-94, 205, 223

women, 25, 26, 28-30, 41, 42, 45-47, 131, 169, 176, 177, 185-87, 188, 200, 203, 205, 216-19, 221-27, 229, 239, 263, 267, 268, 301, 313

zeal, 52, 58-60, 98, 115, 295, 306